UG and External Systems

Linguistik Aktuell/Linguistics Today

Linguistik Aktuell/Linguistics Today (LA) provides a platform for original monograph studies into synchronic and diachronic linguistics. Studies in LA confront empirical and theoretical problems as these are currently discussed in syntax, semantics, morphology, phonology, and systematic pragmatics with the aim to establish robust empirical generalizations within a universalistic perspective.

Volume 75

UG and External Systems: Language, brain and computation
Edited by Anna Maria Di Sciullo

UG and External Systems

Language, brain and computation

Edited by

Anna Maria Di Sciullo

John Benjamins Publishing Company

Amsterdam / Philadelphia

™ The paper used in this publication meets the minimum requirements
of American National Standard for Information Sciences – Permanence
of Paper for Printed Library Materials, ANSI z39.48-1984.

Library of Congress Cataloging-in-Publication Data

UG and external systems : language, brain and computation / edited by Anna
    Maria Di Sciullo.
        p. cm. (Linguistik Aktuell/Linguistics Today, ISSN 0166–0829 ; v. 75)
    Includes bibliographical references and index.
        1. Grammar--Comparative and general. 2. Psycholinguistics. 3.
    Computational linguistics. I. Di Sciullo, Anne-Marie, 1951-. II. Series.

    P201.U36 2005
    415--dc22   2005041002
    ISBN 90 272 2799 3 (Eur.) / 1 58811 623 9 (US) (Hb; alk. paper)

John Benjamins Publishing Co. · P.O. Box 36224 · 1020 ME Amsterdam · The Netherlands
John Benjamins North America · P.O. Box 27519 · Philadelphia PA 19118-0519 · USA

Table of contents

UG and external systems

Anna Maria Di Sciullo

Introduction

This collection of papers aims at contributing to our knowledge of Universal Grammar (UG) and the external systems, conceptual-intentional and sensori-motor, in the sense of Chomsky (1995, 2000, 2001).

In linguistic theory, the expressions generated by the grammar must be legible by the external systems and the connection between these systems can be accessed through the analyses of the syntax-semantic and phonology-phonetic interfaces. Recent proposals in generative grammar point in the same direction: UG can be defined in terms of properties of relations, which play a central role in the explanation of linguistic phenomena. Properties of relations such as symmetry and asymmetry have been proposed to be part of the definitions of the operations of the grammar, as in Chomsky's (2001) Set-Merge and Pair-Merge. According to Kayne (1994), asymmetric c-command maps onto precedence relations at the phonetic interface (PF). According to Moro (2000), movement is triggered by the requirement to eliminate points of symmetry generated in syntactic derivations. Asymmetric c-command is determinant at the semantic interface (LF), as scope and argument structure relations are assumed to be legible under asymmetric c-command relations (cf. Fox 2000; Hale & Keyser 2002). Moreover, the asymmetry is a characteristic property of morphological relations, given the strict linear order and the scope relations between affixes and roots (cf. Di Sciullo 2005). These hypotheses point to the same direction: asymmetry is a basic property of the relations generated by the Grammar. It might be the case that this property of relations ensures the optimal legibility/interpretation of linguistic expressions at the interfaces with the external systems.

In psycholinguistic, questions related to human learnability and comprehension of language are at stake. What makes humans capable of acquiring the language to which they are exposed? Why are there typical differences in the comprehension of certain sorts of linguistic structures and not others? Experimental results from Tsapkini, Jarema, & Di Sciullo (2004) indicate that configurational asymmetry plays a role in human processing of morphological structures. It might be the case that the basic properties of Grammar, including asymmetry, are part of a restrictive set and are actualized in all the components. If UG did not consist of a restricted set of properties, it would be difficult to explain why language acquisition follows the same stages independently of the language or the ethnic group (e.g., production of substantial categories, then functional categories; production of components including minimal asymmetries, then extended asymmetries). It might be the case that the basic asymmetric property of relations contributes to explain why the language development in humans, like his anatomical and biological evolution, results from genetic determinism that limits the possible choices of developments.

In computational linguistics, parsing theories are of central interest in the study of the interaction of Grammar and the external (computational) systems. In this area, questions arise with respect to the relative autonomy of the grammar and the parser, the choice of optimal parsing strategies, and parsing efficiency. The parser includes the axiomatization of linguistic knowledge and control strategies determining how this knowledge is used. Different strategies are available (left to right, ascending or descending, deterministic or non-deterministic, sequential or parallel) to associate one or more structures to a linguistic expression taken as input. The research in this area aims at reducing the possible analyses that can be generated by the parser to the one or the very few that correspond to the actual structure of the linguistic expressions under analysis, reducing possible choice points. The importance of configurational relations in computational linguistics has already been established, given the role played by asymmetric c-command in principle-based parsing (generate-and-filter type) based on GB Theory (Chomsky 1981), and in the check-and-generate parsing incorporating Minimalist grammars (Chomsky 1995, 2001). The current problem in computational linguistics is to formulate a model that can process linguistic expressions efficiently and quickly.

Notwithstanding the progress achieved, questions still remain with respect to the nature of the properties of UG and their role in the legibility of linguistic expressions by the external systems. In the perspective of raising some of these questions and providing possible answers, this volume assembles contributions in three related areas of research: language, brain, and computation.

The *Language* section brings to the fore the role of configurational asymmetry in the expressions generated by the grammar and interpreted at the interfaces with the external systems. Daniela Isac considers the LF properties of subject-oriented and object-oriented depictives and proposes to express the differences in terms of the position of the modifier within the verbal projection. Stanca Somesfalean attributes the PF variation in the order of clitics to minimal differences in features specifications in functional projections along the lines of Asymmetry Theory.

Edit Jakab makes a similar point with different data: the lack of agreement in Russian imperatives is reduced to minimal differences in the projection and checking of functional features. Nicola Munaro discusses the relation between the syntactic expressions and their illocutionary force, and develops an analysis of conditional clause preposing structures on the basis of a hierarchical clausal typing. Manuela Ambar also considers the properties of constituents moving at the left periphery and proposes an analysis of clefts in terms of tense asymmetries. Mellander shows that configurational asymmetries are also crucial in the relation between rhythm and constituency in metrical domains.

The papers in the *Brain* section deal with questions related to learnability and human comprehension of natural language. Tom Roeper and William Snyder suggest that the learning of compounds, notwithstanding linguistic variation, is triggered by the recursive operations that apply in their derivations. Sharon Armon-Lotem and Idit Avram consider the acquisition of the Hebrew definite article taking into consideration syntax and pragmatics. Helen Goodluck analyzes the subject/object asymmetry in the comprehension of D(discourse)-Linked vs. non-D-Linked questions in children and aphasics considering the role of lexical information and perceptual factors. Ronnie Wilbur shows that syntactic asymmetries are also observed in American Sign Language. Ning Pan and William Snyder propose two binary parameters in the framework of Government Phonology to account for the acquisition of syllable types. Matt Bauer presents experimental results related to the question of whether stress shift helps the parser to determine phrase ending.

The papers in the *Computation* section present different perspectives on how the properties of UG can be implemented in a parser, and how the parser is capable of recovering them. Several grammatical relations have been already indirectly embedded in the parser. This is the case, for example, in the treatment of subjacency in Marcus's (1980) deterministic parser, in the treatment of c-command in Berwick & Weinberg's (1984) parser, and in the satisfaction of feature-based constraints in Stabler (1997). Anna Maria Di Sciullo and Sandiway Fong describe a morphological parser based on Di Sciullo's (1996) configurational selection theory. Sourabh Niyogi and Robert Berwick report the properties of a parser implementing Hale & Keyser's (1993, 1998) incorporation theory. Henk Harkema describes a recognizer implementing the features of Chomsky's (1995) Minimalist Program. Sandiway Fong presents the main features of a parser implementing Chomsky's (2001) Probe and Goal model. Furthermore, Rodolfo Delmonte describes the properties of a hybrid parser for the handling of large corpora. Philippe Blache presents a general framework and a quantitative method to account for variability in natural language processing.

The papers are summarized in detail in the following paragraphs.

Language

In 'Depictives. Syntactic and interpretive asymmetries', Daniela Isac argues that subject-oriented depictives differ from object-oriented ones both syntactically and semantically. She proposes that both subject depictives and object depictives are part of a conjunction relation, but subject-oriented depictives attach to a verbal projection and are like circumstantial adverbs, while object-oriented ones attach to a nominal projection. Semantically, subject depictives are e-predicates. The x-predicate reading of subject depictives can be derived by virtue of the fact that both the depictive and the vP have an x-variable which is simultaneously saturated by one and the same individual. Object depictives, on the other hand, are x-predicates. Their e-predication reading follows from the fact that the head of the PredP that includes the object and the depictive is anaphorically bound by the Tense of the main clause. Daniela Isac also argues that what is relevant for the classification of depictives into two classes is not the syntactic function of the depicted nominal, but the structural position of all the copies of the depicted nominal: depictives can be directly predicated about nominals for which all copies are inside the VP, but not about nominals that have at least one copy outside the VP. This analysis sheds new light on the properties of the edge of a phase. Given that vPs are phases according to Chomsky (2001), the edge of the vP phase differs from the non-edge within the vP not only for Move and Agree operations (Chomsky's Phase Impenetrability Condition 2001), but also for predication, or modification relations. A nominal within the non-edge of the vP phase can be depicted directly by a secondary predicate, while a nominal at the edge of the vP phase can only be 'depicted' indirectly.

In her paper 'On two issues related to the clitic clusters in Romance languages', Stanca Somesfalean points out the fact that even though they are highly rigid constructions, clitic clusters manifest a certain degree of variation in Romance languages. This paper concentrates on the behaviour of argumental clitic clusters in Romanian, Italian, and French, more specifically, on two issues related to these constructions: the order within the cluster and the impenetrability of the elements entering the cluster, along the lines of Di Sciullo (2005). Previous analyses are mainly based on a template that will account for the clitic order in a given language. Here, the aim is an analysis that involves more than one module of grammar. The postulation of a template is avoided in the syntactic analysis where the order of the clitics within the cluster reflects the order of the argument XPs.

In her paper, 'On the question of (non)-agreement in the use of Russian imperatives', Edit Jakab analyzes conditional-type imperative and contrastive imperative constructions which represent instances in which the Russian imperative shows no agreement with its clause-mate "subject". In contrast with regular imperatives, these non-canonical imperatives have no TP (cf. Platzack & Rosengren 1998), and hence no AgrSP, which accounts for the lack of agreement between the subject and the imperative. It is proposed that while the subject of canonical imperatives has case, which is checked in Spec-AgrSP, the subject of non-canonical imperatives is caseless or receives default case-marking (which is not subject to case-feature checking) since the potential nominative case checking positions, Spec-TP and Spec-AgrSP, are missing. It is also shown that since the φ-features of the subject are interpretable, they do not need to be checked. Moreover, case is checked under AGREE; since this relation is absent, there can be no case assignment to the subject (cf. Chomsky 2000). This prediction is borne out in the light of these Russian data.

Nicola Munaro's paper, 'Computational puzzles of conditional clause preposing', aims at providing an account of the fact that conditional clauses containing an inversion between the subject and the inflected verb generally precede the main clause. On the basis of data from standard Italian and some North-Eastern Italian dialects, it is argued that clausal typing can be achieved inside a conditional clause by verb raising to an appropriate head of the CP field; this results in activating the head of the TopicP, thereby determining the topical status of the clause, which in turn triggers raising of the clausal adjunct to the relevant specifier of the matrix CP field in order to enter a local relation with a Force node. The movement operation affecting conditionals targets the specifier of two functional projections located in the upper portion of the CP area, ConcessiveP for alternative concessive conditionals and HypotheticalP for counterfactual and optative conditionals; by encoding specific instances of clausal typing, these projections also codify interclausal relations. Relying on previous work on the structural articulation of the left periphery, it is proposed that the projections devoted to clausal typing are hierarchically organized in a sequence which reflects a right-to-left increasing degree of assertive force. In line with some recent proposals on the internal shape of clausal adjuncts, it is also suggested that conditional clauses have a structurally deficient CP layer in that they lack both a node encoding informational structure and a node responsible for internal focalization of phrasal constituents.

In her paper *Clefts and Tense Asymmetries* Manuela Ambar discusses the literature on clefts. She presents data on these constructions not considered in the literature and she proposes an analysis able to account for the new extended empirical domain and, consequently, for variation across languages concerning these structures. She presents evidence, drawn from the behaviour of tense in these constructions, against the idea that clefts derive from relatives and that the cleft element is the predicate of a small clause, selected by *be*, whose subject is the relative clause – subject and predicate being in a symmetric relation. Tense asymmetries will become a diagnostics for distinguishing clefts from relatives. Edit Jakab comes back to an analysis of clefts much in the spirit of Chomsky (1977) and Emonds (1976), reinterpreted in minimalist terms. This analysis provides an explanation for the contexts described in clefts, for the tense identity requirement between the copula and the lexical verb, existing in Portuguese, though not in French or English, for the absence vs. presence of constructions such as Infl-less clefts and that-less clefts across languages, and for the contrasts existing in each type of structure. At the same time her analysis provides empirical evidence for Di Sciullo's (2005) Asymmetry Theory, including the hypothesis that asymmetry is a core property of the Language Faculty.

In his paper, 'Generating configurational asymmetries in prosodic phonology', Evan Mellander examines a number of asymmetries in the types of internal configurations permitted in syllables and feet cross-linguistically, including consonantal and diphthongal moraicity and the *iambic/trochaic law*. It is demonstrated that when these restrictions are analyzed in terms of rhythmic constituency, striking parallels emerge with respect to the position of strong beats within the relevant metrical domain. A unified analysis for the attested patterns is proposed in the framework of Optimality Theory (Prince & Smolensky 1993), exploiting an asymmetric set of rhythmic well-formedness constraints (Levelt & Van de Vijver 1998). The strong cross-linguistic preference for initial prominence in binary domains is explained through a conspiracy effect in constraint interaction, whereby different rankings converge on a single output (McCarthy & Prince 1986).

Brain

In their paper 'Language learnability and the forms of recursion', Thomas Roeper and William B. Snyder assume that recursion is the central characteristic of human language. What is its role in language acquisition? This paper argues that the precise set of recursive operations varies across languages, and that the child's central task as language-learner is to determine which are available. Endocentric root compounding is examined as a case study, with reference to French, Swedish, and English. The differences across these languages are characterized in terms of the Abstract Clitic Hypothesis of Roeper & Keyser (1992). Evidence that an operation has applied recursively, for example to create a compound inside another compound, is proposed as the critical form of triggering experience for the child.

In their paper, 'The autonomous contribution of syntax and pragmatics to the acquisition of the Hebrew definite article', Sharon Armon-Lotem and Idit Avram discuss the acquisition of definiteness, in light of the typological differences between Hebrew and English, looking at acquisition of syntactic and pragmatic aspects of the definite system. This is discussed from a wider perspective to see if the pragmatic aspects of definiteness can be linked to the Theory of Mind. Forty Hebrew-speaking children aged 2–5 were tested for their use of the definite article in definite discourse-related and non-discourse-related contexts and in indefinite referential and non-referential contexts. Children of all ages groups used the definite article. A few additions of the definite article were found in referential contexts but never in the non-referential contexts, and were limited to the two-year-olds. This suggests that the Hebrew-speaking children have acquired the concept of non-shared knowledge, as is evidenced from the absence of overgeneralizations of the definite article beyond the age of three. There were also some omissions of the definite article in the non-discourse-related definite context, a context which requires world knowledge, rather than unique syntactic knowledge. This suggests that while Hebrew-speaking children clearly differentiate the speaker's knowledge from the hearer's knowledge before the age of three, they do not know by the age of four which beliefs can be attributed to the hearer based on shared knowledge, that is, they are lacking the pragmatic concept of shared knowledge.

In her paper, 'D(iscourse)-Linking and question formation: Comprehension effects in children and aphasics', Helen Goodluck points out that recent studies of the comprehension of d(iscourse)-linked questions by children and aphasics show a subject-object asymmetry: d-linked object questions are harder than d-linked subject questions. A similar asymmetry is not found for non-d-linked questions. This study provides evidence that this asymmetry may be linked to the lexical content of the d-linked question. This calls into question one previous account of the subject-object asymmetry and suggests that part of the difficulty with d-linked questions may derive from perceptual factors in the set-up of the experiment.

In her paper, 'Evidence from ASL and ÖGS for Asymmetries in UG', Ronnie Wilbur provides arguments from two signed languages for the hypothesis that configurational asymmetry is part of UG. Because the arguments for asymmetry and UG in general have been based on spoken languages, the inclusion of sign language arguments represents a significant source of additional support for the traditional hypothesis. Three types of syntactic asymmetries are discussed. First, argument asymmetries in ASL include the behaviour with respect to different verb categories; negation and distributivity; genericity; and stage versus individual level predicates. Second, structural asymmetries related to the peripheries and headedness for ASL and ÖGS are shown by the following properties: differential treatment of presupposed information to a left-CP slot and focused information to the right edge of CP; left dislocation but no right dislocation; wh-phrases on the left but only wh-words on the right; head-final C in ASL and head-initial C in ÖGS; and head-initial V and I in ASL but head-final in ÖGS. Finally, domain asymmetries in the scope of non manual markers in ASL are shown by the differential spreading of brow raise (limited to the restriction clause of [-wh]-operators) and brow furrow (c-command domain). This paper demonstrates that asymmetry in syntax is not limited to spoken languages, but is rather a more general phenomenon that deserves a place as part of UG.

Levelt, Schiller & Levelt (2000) propose that Dutch-learning children acquire the earliest four-syllable types in a consistent sequence, one after another: (1) CV,

(2) CVC, (3) V, and (4) VC. In Ning Pan and William Snyder's paper, 'Acquisition of phonological empty categories: A case study of early child Dutch', the same data (available through CHILDES: Fikkert 1994; Levelt 1994; MacWhinney & Snow 1990) are re-examined using frequency-based modified sign tests. The results are that CV can be acquired genuinely earlier than CVC/V/VC, but the latter three-syllable types are actually acquired as a group. This pattern is analyzed within a parametric model of phonology – Government Phonology (Kaye, Lowenstamm & Vergnaud 1990). Two parameters are proposed to account for the early stages of syllable acquisition: [+/– empty onset] and [+/– empty nucleus]. These two parameters are shown to make accurate predictions for the syllable type inventories of adult languages, and to account for the acquisitional evidence from Dutch.

In his paper, 'Prosodic cues during online processing of speech: Evidence from stress shift in American English', Matt Bauer presents two experiments designed to test whether speakers of American English use cues from stress shift to facilitate parsing decisions. Stress shift is a prosodic phenomenon that alters the rhythm of two adjacent, clashing stress peaks (Selkirk 1982). It is triggered when a word with final stress is followed by a word with initial stress. The predictability of when stress shift applies might help the parser determine phrase endings. So, if stress shift is a useful cue and applies inappropriately, speakers might make the wrong parsing decision. Results from the experiments were unable to confirm that the parser uses stress shift to mark intonation boundaries. Possibly, a confound was introduced by the designs of the experiments. Alternatively, the findings might suggest that cues from stress shift, though acoustically perceptible, are unavailable to the parsing mechanism or just not used.

Computation

In 'Morpho-syntactic parsing', Anna Maria Di Sciullo and Sandiway Fong describe an implemented bottom-up parser for a theory of morphological selection defined in (Di Sciullo 1996). Core lexical properties of derivational affixes, generally encoded in terms of subcategorization frames, are articulated in terms of asymmetrical relations. The selection of affixes is encoded in a uniform specifier-head-complement configuration, and predictions can be made with respect to composition and linking relation. Thus, the so-called lexical gaps fall out from the theory. They consider the computational implications of three different implementations. In particular, they examine the effect on bottom-up parsing of varying the specifier-head-complement order. Furthermore, computational motivation for the logical separation of overt and covert affixation is provided.

Traditional accounts of verb subcategorization, from the classic work of Fillmore on, require either a considerable number of syntactic rules to account for diverse sentence constructions, including cross-language variation, or else complex linking rules mapping the thematic roles of semantic event templates with possible syntactic forms. In their paper, 'A Minimalist implementation of Hale-Keyser incorporation theory', Sourabh Niyogi and Robert C. Berwick exhibit a third approach: they implement, via an explicit parser and lexicon, Hale & Keyser's (2002) incorporation theory to systematically cover most patterns in English Verb Classes and Alternations (Levin 1993), typically using only 1 or 2 lexical entries per verb. This subsumes a large number of syntactic constructions and also most information typically contained in semantic event templates, and, further, replaces the notion of thematic roles with precise structural configurations. The implemented parser uses the merge and move operations formalized by Stabler (1997) in the minimalist framework of Chomsky (2001). As a side benefit, they extend Harkema's (2000) minimalist recognizer to a full parsing implementation.

Henk Harkema describes a top-down recognition method for languages generated by Minimalist Grammars in 'Parsing minimalist languages'. Minimalist Grammars are simple, formal grammars modeling some important aspects of the kind of grammars developed in the framework of Chomsky's Minimalist Program. A Minimalist Grammar is defined by a set of lexical items, which varies from language to language, and two universal structure building functions, which are defined on trees: Merge and Move. The recognition method presented in this paper is based on reducing trees to simple expressions that encode the trees' behavior with regard to the functions Merge and Move. The recognizer has the correct prefix property: for an ungrammatical sentence, it will halt at the first word of the sentence that does not fit into a grammatical structure.

In 'Computation with probes and goals: A parsing perspective', Sandiway Fong presents a parsing architecture for a left-to-right implementation of the probe-goal Case agreement model, within the Minimalist Program. Parsing imposes special constraints on theory. For example, in left-to-right parsing, the assembly of phrase structure must proceed through elementary tree composition, rather than through the operations Merge and Move directly. On-line processing also poses challenges for the incremental computation of probe/goal relations. The paper describes an implemented parser that computes these relations and assembles phrase structure, while respecting the incremental and left-to-right nature of parsing.

In his paper, 'Deep & shallow linguistically based parsing: Parameterizing ambiguity in a hybrid parser', Rodolfo Delmonte criticizes current statistical approaches for being inherently ill-founded and derived from a false presupposition. People working in the empirical framework have tried to credit the point of view that what happened to the speech research paradigm was also applicable to the NLP paradigm as a whole. In other words, the independence hypothesis which is at the heart of the use of Markov models imported from the speech community into the empirical statistical approaches to NLP does not seem to be well suited to the task at hand simply because the linguistic unit under consideration – the word, the single tag or both – are insufficient to assure enough contextual information, given language model building techniques based on word-tags with tagsets containing only lexical and part-of-speech information. The paper purports the view that the implementation of sound parsing algorithm must go hand in hand with sound grammar construction.

In his paper, 'Towards a quantitative theory of variability', Philippe Blache presents a general framework making it possible to describe and explain relations between different components of linguistic analysis (e.g. prosody, syntax, semantics, etc.). He proposes more specifically a stability principle specified for a given object by means of weights defined for each component plus an equilibrium threshold to be reached. The basic mechanism consists in summing up the different weights, the result being the quantity to be compared with the threshold. Such an approach explains some variability phenomena: the possibility of choosing between different realizations for an object at a given domain depends on whether the stability threshold is reached by means of the weights of other domains. This kind of information, on top of its linguistic interest, constitutes a first element of answer for an account of variability in some natural language processing applications.

The papers assembled in this collection came out from the Second Conference of the Federation on Natural Language Processing, held at the Università di Venezia in October 2002 and from the First Conference of the Federation on Natural Language Processing, held at the Université du Québec à Montréal in October 2001. Many thanks to the members of the Natural Language Processing project and to the members of the Asymmetry Project for their help in the organization of these conferences. Their names are listed in the project homepage www.interfaceasymmetry.uqam.ca and www.asymmetryproject.uqam.ca. I am grateful to the Social Sciences and Humanities Research Council of Canada and to Valorisation-Recherche Québec for the financial support, throught which these conferences took place. Finally, I would like to thank Rodolfo Delmonte for the local organization of the Conference held in Venezia in October 2002.

References

Berwick, R. & Weinberg, A. (1984). *The Grammatical Basis of Linguistic Performance*. Cambridge, Mass.: The MIT Press.

Chomsky, N. (1977) On wh-movement. In P. Culicover et al. (Eds.), *Formal Syntax* (pp. 69–132). Academic Press: New York.

Chomsky, N. (1981). *Lectures on Government and Binding*. Dordrecht: Foris.

Chomsky, N. (1995). *The Minimalist Program*. Cambridge, Mass.: The MIT Press.

Chomsky, N. (2000). Minimalist inquiries: The framework, In R. Martin, D. Michaels, & J. Uriagereka (Eds.), *Step by Step: Essays on Minimalist Syntax in Honor of Howard Lasnik* (pp. 89–155). Cambridge, Mass.: MIT Press.

Chomsky, N. (2001). Derivation by phase. In M. Kenstowicz (Ed.), *Ken Hale: A Life in Language* (pp. 1–52). Cambridge, Mass: The MIT Press.

Di Sciullo, A. M. (1996). X-bar selection. In J. Roorick & L. Zaring (Eds.), *Phrase Structure and the Lexicon* (pp. 77–108). Dordrecht: Kluwer.

Di Sciullo, A. M. (2005). *Asymmetry in Morphology*. In press. Cambridge, Mass.: The MIT Press.

Emonds, J. (1976). *A Transformational Approach to English Syntax: Root, Structure-Preserving, and Local Transformations*. New York: Academic Press.

Fikkert, P. (1994). *On the Acquisition of Prosodic Structure*. Ph.D. Dissertation. Leiden University, The Netherlands.

Fox, D. (2000). *Economy and Semantic Interpretation*. Cambridge, Mass.: MIT Press.

Hale, K. & Keyser, J. (1993). On argument structure and the lexical expression of syntactic relations. In K. Hale & S. J. Keyser (Eds.), *The View from Building 20* (pp. 53–109). Cambridge, Mass.: MIT Press.

Hale, K. & Keyser, S. J. (1998). The basic elements of argument structure. In H. Harley (Ed.), *MIT Working Papers in Linguistics* 32 (pp. 73–118). MITWPL, Department of Linguistics and Philosophy, MIT, Cambridge, Mass.

Hale, K. & Keyser, J. (2002). *Prolegomena to a Theory of Argument Structure*. Cambridge, Mass.: The MIT Press

Harkema, H. (2000). A recognizer for minimalist grammars. In *Proceedings of the 6th International Workshop on Parsing Technologies* (pp. 111–122). Trento, Italy.

Kaye, L., Lowenstamm, J. & Vergnaud, J.-R. (1990). Constituent structure and government in phonology. *Phonology, 7* (2), 193–231.

Kayne, R. (1994). *The Antisymmetry of Syntax*. Cambridge, Mass.: The MIT Press.

Levelt, C. (1994). *On the Acquisition of Place*. The Hague: Holland Academic Graphics.

Levelt, C., Schiller, N. O., & Levelt, W. J. (2000). The acquisition of syllable types. *Language Acquisition, 8*, 237–264.

Levelt, C. & Van de Vijver, R. (1998). Syllable types in cross-linguistic and developmental grammar. Paper presented at the *Third Biennal Utrecht Phonology Workshop*. Utrecht, The Netherlands.

Levin, B. (1993). *English Verb Classes and Alternations: A Preliminary Investigation*. Chicago, Illinois: University of Chicago Press.

MacWhinney, B. & Snow, C. (1990). The child language data exchange system: An update. *Journal of Child Language, 17*, 457–472.

Marcus, M. (1980). *A Theory of Syntactic Recognition for Natural Language*. Cambridge, Mass.: The MIT Press.

McCarthy, J. & Prince, A. (1986). Prosodic Morphology. *RUCCS Technical Report* 32. Piscataway. NJ.

Moro, A. (2000). *Dynamic Antisymmetry*. Cambridge, Mass.: MIT Press.

Platzack, C. & Rosengren, I. (1998). On the subject of imperatives: A minimalist account of imperative clauses. *The Journal of Comparative Germanic Linguistics, 1*, 177–224.

Prince, A. & Smolensky, P. (1993). Optimality Theory: Constraint interaction in generative grammar. *Technical Reports of Rutgers Center for Cognitive Science 2*. Piscataway. NJ.

Roeper, T. & Keyser, J. (1992). The abstract clitic hypothesis. *Linguistic Inquiry, 23*, 89–125.

Selkirk, E. (1982). *The Syntax of Word*. Cambridge, Mass.: The MIT Press.

Stabler, E. P. (1997). Derivational Minimalism. In P. de Groote, G. F. Morill, & C. Retoré, (Eds.), *Lectures Notes in Artificial Intelligence* 2099, *Logical Aspects of Computational Linguistics* (pp. 68–95). Berlin, Germany: Springler.

Tsapkini, K., Jarema, G. & Di Sciullo, A. M. (2004). The role of configurational asymmetry in the lexical access of prefixed verbs: Evidence from French. *Brain and Language, 90*, 143–150.

Language

Depictives

Syntactic and interpretive asymmetries*

Daniela Isac
Université du Québec à Montréal

This paper proposes that subject and object depictives correspond to two different configurations and hence to two different ways in which function composition applies at LF. The syntactic differences are not only related to the hierarchical level at which the depictive is merged, but also to the type of phrase that the depictive predicates something about. We propose that object-oriented depictives attach to object DPs and are interpreted as individual level predicates, whereas subject-oriented depictives apply to VPs and are interpreted as event predicates. In that, subject depictives are analyzed as 'circumstantial' adverbs, while object depictives are analyzed as predicative adjectives.

1. Introduction

This paper develops an account of the syntax semantics interface of a particular type of non-primary predicates, i.e. the so-called depictives (Rothstein 1983).

(1) a. John ate *the supper* cold.   (object oriented depictive)
     b. *John* ate the supper naked.   (subject oriented depictive)

Depictive secondary predicates express a state or an event pertaining to one participant of the main predicate, and in that, they resemble attributive modifiers. In (1a), the depictive *cold* predicates something about one of the participants in the main predicate *eat*, namely *the supper*. In (1b) a similar predication relation obtains between *naked* and *John*. However, depictives are different from attributive modifiers in that the property expressed by the depictive is also related to the event expressed by the verbal predicate. More specifically, the property expressed by the depictive holds true specifically at the time that the event described by the main predicate takes place.

(2) John ate the supper naked.
     -attributive, x-predicate reading (predicate of an individual): he was naked
     -e-predicate reading (predicate of an event): he ate the supper while he was naked.

Depending on the syntactic function of the nominal that is targeted by the depictive, depictive secondary predicates have been divided into two subgroups: subject oriented and object oriented depictives.

Depictives therefore pose an interesting problem for LF legibility: if a depictive has a 'choice' between being oriented towards the object or towards the subject, how does LF 'know' which nominal the depictive refers to? Also, what determines the interpretation of depictives as attributive modifiers and as adverbial modifiers at the same time?

It has been argued (see Hoshi 2000 for discussion) that performance systems can invade CHL (the computational system of human language) and that syntactic operations such as Move could be triggered by the external systems.

Basic syntactic structure building operations, such as Merge, on the other hand, are assumed not to be affected by performance systems at all. However, there is some sense in which the legitimacy of a phrase requires that the meaning of that phrase be compatible with the meaning associated with that position (e.g. telicity in object position, Kratzer 2004; Ramchand 1997; Kiparsky 1998). In this paper we argue that the interpretation of secondary predicates, such as depictives, is a direct mapping of the structural position of the depictive. We argue that the two types of depictives correspond to two different configurations and hence to two different ways in which function composition applies at LF. More specifically, we argue that the differences in configuration are not only related to the hierarchical level at which the depictive is merged, but also to the type of phrase that acts as the 'subject' for the depictive secondary predicate.

We propose that object oriented depictives attach to the object DP and are interpreted as individual level predicates, whereas subject oriented depictives apply to VPs and are interpreted as event predicates. In that, subject depictives are analyzed on a par with 'circumstantial' adverbs of time, manner, place, etc., while object depictives are analyzed as predicative adjectives.

(3) He ate [$_{DP}$the supper [$_{AP}$ cold]]
     He [[$_{VP}$ ate the supper] [$_{AP}$ naked]]

Since we argue against an adjunction analysis of depictives, our view enables a restrictive theory of phrase structure, in compliance with the Strict Asymmetry Hypothesis (Di Sciullo 1999, 2000).

(4)   Grammatical relations are asymmetrical

Given this hypothesis, all structural relations, at any point in the derivation must be asymmetrical. Since our proposal is that depictives are merged as complements of some functional head, and that a predication relation holds between the phrase in the Specifier of this functional projection and its complement, the condition in (4) is met.

This analysis sheds new light on the properties of an edge of a phase. It is well known that the the edge of a phase contrasts with the edge of a non-phase, regarding the availability of Move and Agree operations (Chomsky 2001, the Phase Impenetrability Condition). In particular, the edge of the *v*P phase contrasts with the edge of a non-phase, as far as the availability of extraction operations goes (see Di Sciullo, Paul, & Somesfalean 2003, for an extended discussion). What our analyis shows is that the edge of the *v*P phase also differs from the non edge for secondary predication relations. A nominal within the non-edge of the *v*P phase can be depicted directly by a secondary predicate, while a nominal at the edge of the *v*P phase can only be 'depicted' indirectly.

The paper is organised as follows: in Section 2, we show that one can distinguish between two classes of depictives, based on a set of tests; in Section 3 we overview several proposals that have been suggested for the analysis of depictives and we show that they cannot account for the differences mentioned in Section 2; in Section 4 we formulate a proposal which is able to account for these differences and we discuss its details; in Section 5, we show that what is responsible for the different properties of the two types of depictives is whether the depicted nominal is inside or outside the VP domain, and not its syntactic function (subject vs object or complement vs non-complement); in Section 6, we present the conclusions.

2.   Two classes of depictives

In this section we present several tests that can be used in order to classify depictives into two groups. The two classes have been called subject depictives and object depictives, according to the syntactic function of the depicted nominal with respect to the main verbal predicate. For convenience, we will adopt this terminology for the time being, but we will revise it later on in the paper, when we show that what is relevant for the distinction between the two classes of depictives is not necessarily the syntactic function of the depicted nominal.

Below is a sum up of a number of differences between two types of depictives, some of which have been previously mentioned in the literature.

First, when more than one depictive occurs in a sentence, they seem to be ordered in a rigid way. In particular, when both an object oriented depictive and a subject oriented one occur at the end of a clause, the object related one must precede the subject related one (Dechaine 1993).

(5)   John ate the salad undressed naked as a jailbird.   (Dechaine 1993)
      *John ate the salad naked as a jailbird undressed.
      John ate the meat raw tired.
      *John ate the meat tired raw.

Second, subject oriented depictives survive ellipsis, but object related ones do not. (Dechaine 1993)

(6)   John$_i$ read the letter outraged$_i$ and Bill$_j$ did upset$_j$.   (Dechaine 1993)
      *John submitted his text$_i$ finished$_i$ and Bill did unfinished$_j$.

Similarly, *do-so* substitution shows that in object depictives the verb and the object do not form a constituent, while in subject depictives they do.

(7)   Subject depictives:
      Jason wiped the table tired and Mat did so$_{[wiped\ the\ table]}$ wide awake.
                                                          (Levin & Rappaport 1995)

(8)   Object depictives
      *Fred ate the meat raw, but I did so$_{[ate\ the\ meat]}$ cooked.   (Simpson 1983)
      *John saw the apartment dirty and Mary did so$_{[saw\ the\ apartment]}$ unpainted.

Clefting also points to a different constituency of the constructions involving subject depictives versus the ones involving object depictives.

(9)   What he ate was [the meat raw].
      *Who ate the soup was [him naked].

Last, but not least, subject depictives behave as if they were scopeless elements. They can appear in various orders in the syntax without a substantial difference in meaning.

(10)   John ate his supper [in the garden] [naked].
       John ate his supper [naked] [in the garden].

In contrast, object depictives have a fixed scope with respect to other modifiers.

(11)   John ate his supper [cold] [in the garden].
       *John ate his supper [in the garden] [cold].

Any analysis of depictives should account for these differences. In the next section, we will review some of the analyses of depictives previously proposed in the literature, and we will show to which extent each of these analyses accounts for the differences identified above.

3.   Previous analyses

3.1 The Small Clause / control analysis (Williams 1980; Chomsky 1981;
Stowell 1983; Hoekstra 1988; Rothstein 1983; Roberts 1988; Dechaine
1993; Winkler 1997)

Under this approach, the depictive is assumed to be a predicate inside a Small
Clause, as in (12). The 'subject' of the Small Clause is a PRO which is controlled by
a nominal in the main clause.

(12)   a.   John [$_{VP}$[$_{VP}$ ate the supper$_i$] [$_{SC}$ PRO$_i$ cold]]   (object depictives)
       b.   John$_i$ [$_{VP}$[$_{VP}$ ate the supper] [$_{SC}$ PRO$_i$ naked]].   (subject depictives)

The 'adjective-like' property of depictives follows from the relation of predication
that obtains between the depictive adjective and PRO. Since PRO is controlled
by a nominal inside the main clause, and therefore coindexed with it, the depictive adjective indirectly establishes a predication relation with the controller. The
'adverb-like' property of depictives follows from the fact that the Small Clause is
adjoined to the VP.

The way in which such an analysis can distinguish between subject depictives
and object depictives is through the syntactic function of the nominal that controlls
the reference of PRO: if the controller is the object, then the depictive is object
oriented, as in (12a), if it is the subject, the depictive is subject oriented, as in (12b).

However, this analysis only accounts for the semantic differences between the
two types of depictives (whether the depictive is a predicate about the subject
or about the object), but none of the structural differences mentioned in Section 2 above can be predicted, because structurally, both subject depictives and
object depictives are similar under this approach. More specifically, the depictive
establishes a direct predication relation with PRO, and only indirectly with the
controller. Since PRO is structurally in the same position, whether it is controlled
by the subject or by the object, the Small Clause analysis offers no way of integrating the structural differences between subjects and objects into an account of
the properties that distinguish between subject and object depictives, as listed in
Section 2 above.

3.2 The complex predicate analysis (Cormack & Smith 1999; Geuder 2000)

An alternative to the control analysis briefly sketched above is to assume that the
depictive phrase does not stand in a predication relation with a nominal constituent, but that instead it combines directly with the verb. The 'verbal modification' property is immediately derived by virtue of the direct function composition
between the two predicates – the verbal one and the depictive, as in (13a). A suit-

able paraphrase for (13a) will thus be (13b). The 'nominal modification' property obtains in (13) because the complex predicate made up of the verb and the depictive applies to the nominal expressed by the subject. A predication relation is thus simultaneously established between the verb and the subject, on the one hand, and between the depictive and the subject, on the other hand.

(13) a. We [[had eaten] [tired]].
      b. We had eaten and we were tired at the time.
      c. $\exists t \{t < t_0$ & λx [$\exists e$ (eat(e)(x) & $\exists s$ [$e_0 s$ & tired(s)(x)]]) &
          =AFTER(e)](we)
               there is an event of x eating and a state of x being
               tired and the event and state temporally overlap.

The problem with this analysis is that it is meant to cover both subject and object depictives. However, even though it offers a satisfactory account of subject depictives, it is not so clear how it could be extended to object depictives. In particular, it is difficult to see how the 'nominal modification' relation obtains between the depictive and the object in (14).

(14) a. John left the room messy.
      b. John [left messy] the room.

The depictive first composes with the verb in order to form a complex predicate, as in (14b). The object is related to the verb by virtue of the latter's selectional properties. However, it is not so clear what forces any predication relation between the depictive and the object. The difficulty is related to the fact that the two predicates which are part of the complex predicate in (14b) entertain a different type of relation with the object. The relation between the verb and the object is one of selection, whereas the relation between the depictive and the object is one of predication. If both the verb and the depictive are part of the same complex predicate, such an asymmetry is unexpected.

It is clear that an approach under which both subject and object depictives have the same adjunction site (assumed to be some VP projection) cannot account for these different properties. Let us therefore focus on previous approaches that advocate a different adjunction site for the object vs. subject depictives.

3.3 Analyses arguing for disjoint adjunction sites

Let us mention first that we will disregard analyses such as Hornstein and Lightfoot's (1987), who assume that object oriented depictives are adjoined to V', while subject oriented ones are adjoined to VP. Although technically, such analyses argue for different adjunction sites for object and subject depictives, in fact, given the small vP hypothesis, and given the fact that the subject always moves out of the VP, this analysis amounts to saying that subject and object depictives have similar adjunction sites. The analyses that we are going to consider include the ones proposed by Rothstein (1983), Nakajima (1990), Dechaine (1993), Gueron & Hoekstra (1995), Pylkkänen (2002). Under all of these approaches, object depictives attach to the VP level, while subject depictives attach to some higher functional projection which is part of the extended projection of the verb (the AgrS projection with Dechaine (1993) and Gueron & Hoekstra (1995), the IP projection with Rothstein (1983) and Nakajima (1990), and the VoiceP projection wih Pylkkänen (2002)). All of these approaches, however, face the following problems identified by Roberts (1988), which indicate that subject depictives cannot be attached at a higher level than VP.

First, standard VP tests like VP fronting, tough movement, and pseudoclefts show that depictives cannot be stranded by these processes that affect VP. We illustrate below with pseudoclefts.

(15) Pseudoclefts:
      What John did was leave the room happy.
      ??What John did happy was leave the room.

Second, negation invariably has scope over depictives, as illustrated in (16) below.

(16) Bill didn't leave angry at John.

(16) cannot mean that Bill, angry at John, didn't leave. If adjunction at the IP level were possible, or even obligatory, this would not be expected. In this respect, depictives differ from certain other right adjoined elements. Thus, the examples in (17) are ambiguous in that the adjuncts can be interpreted inside or outside the scope of negation.

(17) John didn't kiss his wife [because he loves her].
      John didn't kiss his wife (,) deliberately.

To sum up so far, we have shown that previous analyses of depictives, even those that acknowledge a different adjunction site for subject and object depictives, cannot account for the different properties that these two types of depictives have. Basically, the two types of depictives show different enough properties to point to a structural difference (a different adjunction site), but the difference is not exclusively a hiararchical one. In other words, the different properties of the two types of depictives cannot exclusively be attributed to a difference in the exact level within the extended V projection at which the respective depictive attaches. Although it looks like the hierarchical syntactic level of adjunction does play a role, something else seems to be going on.

4. Our proposal

We propose that subject depictives differ from object depictives not only in the hierarchical level of the projection to which they attach, but also in the nature of this projection. The proposal is that object oriented depictives attach to the object DP and are interpreted as individual level predicates, whereas subject oriented depictives apply to VPs and are interpreted as event predicates. In that, subject depictives are analyzed on a par with 'circumstantial' adverbs of time, manner, place, etc., while object depictives are analyzed as predicative adjectives.

4.1 Subject depictives

In Cinque's (1999) view, there are two types of adverbs: adverbs that are licensed in the Specifier of some functional projection in the extended projection of the verb (AdvP 'proper'), and circumstantial adverbs of place, time, manner, which differ from the former in the following ways:

a. circumstantial adverbs follow the verb's complement;

  (18)   Mary ate her lunch in the bus.
         *Mary ate in the bus her lunch.

b. circumstantial adverbs cannot appear in any of the pre-verbal positions open to AdvP proper;

  (19)   She often visits Mary.
         *She yesterday visited Mary.
         She visited Mary yesterday.

c. circumstantials behave as if they were scopeless elements. They can appear in various orders in the syntax without a substantial difference in meaning

  (20)   Tom kissed Sandy [passionately] [on the porch].
         Tom kissed Sandy [on the porch] [passionately].

Interestingly, subject depictives exhibit the same properties; they follow the verb's complement, as illustrated in (21), they cannot appear in a pre-verbal position, as shown in (22), and they behave as if they were scopeless elements, as shown in (23).

  (21)   John left the room happy.
         *John left happy the room.

  (22)   *John happy left the room.

  (23)   John ate his supper [in the garden] [naked].
         John ate his supper [naked] [in the garden].

By virtue of these similarities, let us assume that subject depictives have the same syntactic and semantic properties as circumstantial adverbs.

4.1.1   *Syntax of subject depictives*

In order to account for the diffferences between circumstantial adverbs and adverbs 'proper', Cinque (1999) (quoting Øystein Nilsen, p.c.) proposes to analyze circumstantial adverbs on a par with predicative adjectives. The underlying assumption is that there is a parallelism between the structure of clauses and that of DPs. Just as DPs have, in addition to attributive adjectives (in pre-NP position), predicative adjectives as their most deeply embedded constituents within the NP (Cinque 1994; Kayne 1994), so do clauses have "attributive" adverbials (in pre-VP position) and "predicative" adverbials as their most deeply embedded constituents within VP. Taking this parallelism strictly implies that the circumstantial adverbials are actually predicates predicated of the VP.

(24)

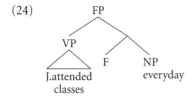

By virtue of the analogy proposed above, subject depictives can be assumed to have a similar syntax, i.e. we will assume that they are in a predication relation with the VP.

(25)

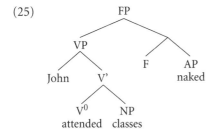

We propose that the relevant FP for depictive constructions is actually a Conjunction Phrase, as defined in Munn (1992), Johannessen (1998) and Kayne (1994), and that the way to integrate this CoP in the hierarchy of functional projections is as in (26) below.

(26)

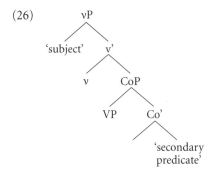

(27)   a.   John left the room angry.
       b.   John $[_{CoP} [_{vP}$ [left the room] [Co [angry]]].
            cf. [John left the room] and [John was angry at the time].

As pointed out by Rubin (1996), the Conjunction head may be overt in some environments in English (in quasi-serials) and in other languages, for instance Tagalog, it may be overt in noun modification.

Notice that in (26) above, two predication relations are involved: first, the secondary predicate (the depictive, or the circumstantial adverb) enters a predication relation with the VP, and second, the resulting predicate (CoP) enters a predication relation with the subject. This double predication relation directly maps into semantic composition rules, as it will become clear below, in Section 4.1.2.

One problem related to the structure in (26) above is that it introduces a split within the class of secondary predicates: some of them are Merged in Specifiers of functional projections, whereas others are merged as in (26) above. The question is whether there is any way to predict where exactly a given secondary predicate will be Merged, in the Specifier of a functional projection that is higher than vP, or in the complement of CoP. We propose that the two classes of secondary predicates can be distinguished both syntactically and semantically. Semantically, secondary predicates that are Merged in the complement position of CoP in (26) above are predicative (as opposed to attributive). Syntactically, the distinction between the two classes of secondary predicates is parrallel to the distinction between weak and strong pronouns proposed in Cardinaletti & Starke (1999), which in fact they explicitly extend to adverbs. What we propose is that this distinction should be matched with a difference in the syntactic position that adverbs occupy: pre-vP modifiers are weak, whereas final-vP modifiers are strong. This correlates with Cinque's (1999) observation that adverbs that occur in final vP position must be able to bear stress, and that they are most natural when reinforced by a Specifier. Some have even a morphologically heavier variant which is the one preferentially chosen in the vP final position (*di gia, neancora*[1])

(28) a. *Gianni non legge l''alfabeto (NE)ANCORA.*   (Italian; Cinque 1999)
          Gianni does not read the alphabet yet.
      b. *Gianni non vince le partite mica PIU o casi PIU.*
          Gianni does not win his matches not any longer/ any longer or almost
          any longer.

Also, as pointed out by Cardinaletti & Starke (1999), there is a subset of Greek adverbs that exhibit a transparent morphological difference between the weak variant
and the strong one. Crucially, this difference correlates with a distributional difference: the weak form *sigo* occurs in a pre-vP position, while the strong form has no
such restriction and preferentially appears in final-vP position.

(29) a. *To (*sigá) évrasa (sigá).*   (Greek, Cardinaletti & Starke 1999)
      b. *To (sigo) – évrasa (sigo).*
          It slowly I-boiled slowly.

Similarly, in certain languages, there is a class of adverbs which necessarily occur in
a pre-vP position, and never in a final-vP position.

(30) a. We even invited them over (*even).
          We are still trying (*still).
      b. *O mai caut (*mai).*   (Romanian)
          Her/it more look-for-I.
          'I am still looking for it/ her'.

Even if there are some problems related to the fact that only weak adverbs are con-
fined to a fixed syntactic position (the pre-vP position), while strong adverbs seem
to have a choice between the pre-vP or final-vP position, these problems go beyond
the scope of this paper. What is of interest for us is that depictives are not flexible
in this sense, and that they are always in final-vP position Depictives meet both
conditions mentioned above: they are 'complex XPs' since potentially the depictive
could be realized as a head followed by a complement, or as a head modified by a
Specifier, and they are interpreted predicatively.

(31) a. John delivered the speech [dressed [in pyjamas]].
      b. John delivered the speech [partly [undressed]].

4.1.2 *Semantics of subject depictives*

The interpretation of subject depictives can be derived from the same assumption
that the latter are parallel to circumstantial adverbs. Semantically, circumstantial
adverbials can be seen (following Davidson 1967) as predicates over an underlying
event variable (Parsons 1990).

(32)   John [[kissed Sandy(e, x)] [passionately (e)]].

Similarly, we will assume that subject depictives are predicated of the event variable introduced by the *v*P. This assumption can straightforwardly account for the temporal simultaneity relation between the event expressed by the VP and the state/event expressed by the adjective: the Tense operator which binds the event variable of the predicate resulting after function application of the depictive to the verbal predicate will simultaneously bind the *e* variable introduced by the VP and the one introduced by the AP.

(33)   He read the book drunk.
       He read the book while/ when he was drunk.

This analysis poses a challenge related to the way in which one could derive the predicate over individuals interpretation of subject depictives.

Let us first notice, with Geuder (2000), that circumstantials can be used both as event-predicates (*e*-predicates) and as individual-predicates (*x*-predicates), as illustrated in (34). This contrasts with preverbal adverbs, which can only be used as operators (functions mapping propositions to propositions, or predicates to predicates), as illustrated in (35).

(34)   Tom kissed Sandy passionately.   (e-predicate)
       The kissing was passionate.   (x-predicate)

(35)   Tom often kissed Sandy.   (e-operator)
       *The kissing was often.

Given the analogy proposed above between circumstantials and subject depictives, there should be an x-reading available for depictives, as well. We propose that the x-predicate reading of subject depictives is derived via application of the function resulting from combining the depictive adjective with the VP to the individual expressed by the subject. Whatever nominal will satisfy the variable of this complex function will simultaneously saturate both the VP function and the AP function.

The picture that emerges includes two instances of function application in the case of subject depictives: (i) function application of the depictive adjective to the Davidsonian argument *e* introduced by the VP; and (ii) application of the resulting function to the individual *x* expressed by the subject. This algorithm straightforwardly matches the syntactic structure proposed in (26) above, where the depictive is first the complement of a projection (CoP) whose Specifier position is filled by the VP, and then the whole resulting phrase (the CoP) is the complement of a projection whose Specifier position is occupied by the subject DP.

At this point, it is possible to spell out the differences between circumstantials and subject depictives. So far, we have drawn on the similarities between the two.

However, the question arises whether there is any difference between (36a) below, which contains a circumstantial, and (36b), which contains a subject depictive.

(36) a.   John wrote the letter   angrily.
      b.   John wrote the letter   angry.

The interpretation of (36a) differs from that of (36b). (36b) is non-committal with regard to the way in which John wrote the letter (perhaps his anger was obvious from the way he wrote the letter, perhaps it wasn't). In (36a), on the other hand, the main focus is on the manner of writing, John behaved in an angry fashion, but he may, or he may not, be angry (see Simpson 1983; Aarts 1992). As noted by Schultze-Berndt & Himmelmann 2003, this semantic difference is also illustrated by the fact that for some types of adjuncts only a depictive reading makes sense, but not an adverbial reading in which the modifier is taken to designate a quality of the process expressed by the main predicate (compare *She drinks her coffee black* with *??She drinks her coffee blackly*). Furthermore, in some languages, such as English, the semantic difference between depictives and adverbials has clear morpho-syntactic correlates. Thus, (at least some) English adverbials are marked by the suffix *-ly*, in contrast with depictives, which never exhibit this affix.

In our view, this difference follows from the type of variables modified by adverbials and by depictives, respectively. Crucially, circumstantials introduce only an event variable, to the exclusion of an individual variable. When the circumstantial, which, as proposed above, acts as a predicate on events, applies to the event introduced by the VP, the result is a function that has an individual variable position x, which is actually introduced by the verb, and is not shared by the circumstantial.

(37) a.   John [[wrote-the-letter (e, x)][angrily(e)]].
      b.   John [angrily (wrote-the-letter (x))].
      c.   [angrily (wrote-the-letter (John))].

In contrast, subject depictives introduce both an event variable and an individual variable (i.e. they are predicates on events and predicates on individuals at the same time). The result of applying the depictive to the VP is a function that contains an individual variable which is shared by both the verb and the depictive.

(38) a.   John [[wrote-the-letter (e, x)] [drunk(e, x)]].
      b.   John [drunk (wrote-the-letter (x), x)].
      c.   [drunk (wrote-the-letter (John), John)].

4.1.3   *'Big' VP or 'little' vP?*

Notice that in (26) above, the first conjunct is a big VP and not a little *v*P. There are two reasons why we chose VP over *v*P. First, in a Conjunction Phrase, the two conjuncts should have the same semantic category. Little *v*P is propositional, whereas big VP is an open function. Since the second conjunct (the depictive) is an open function, rather than a proposition, a conjunction analysis 'enforces' a VP rather than *v*P, as the first conjunct. A second reason for proposing that the first conjunct is VP, rather than *v*P is related to cross linguistic considerations. Under the assumption that the first conjunct is a big VP, one can easily derive the predication relation between the depictive and the subject, which is placed in Spec,*v*P, and thus outside the whole CoP in (26) above. Under the assumption that the first conjunct in (26) is the little *v*P, one can still derive the predication relation between the subject and the depictive for languages in which the subject moves out of the *v*P, to a higher position. However, for languages in which the subject can stay in situ, no predication relation could obtain between the depictive and the subject, and therefore the prediction would be that for these languages subject depictives are not possible, or if they are, they would have to have different properties than the English type subject depictives.

An investigation of the properties of subject depictives in VSO languages shows, however, that they have exactly the same properties as subject depictives in SVO languages. This is illustrated below, with Romanian examples.

Romanian subjects can occur either in situ, post verbally,[2] as in (39a) or in a topicalized or focused preverbal position, as in (39b).

(39) a. *A plecat Maria supărată.*   (Romanian)
          has left   Maria upset.
      b. *Maria a plecat supărată.*
          Maria has left   upset.

The following examples show that Romanian subject depictives have the same properties as English subject depictives, and that these properties show no sensitivity to the preverbal postverbal position of the subject.

First, when both an object oriented depictive and a subject oriented one occur at the end of a clause, the object related one must precede the subject related one. This ordering restriction operates the same with preverbal subjects and with postverbal ones.

(40) a. *Bea*   *pisica*   *laptele*   *fiert*   *însetată.*   (Romanian)
          drink-3.s.   cat-the-3.s.f.   milk-the   boiled   thirsty-3.s.f.

(41) a. **Bea*   *pisica*   *laptele*   *însetată*   *fiert.*
          drink-3.s.   cat-the-3.s.f.   milk-the   thirsty-3.s.f   boiled
      b. **Pisica*   *bea*   *laptele*   *însetată*   *fiert.*
          cat-the-3.s.f.   drink-3.s.   milk-the   thirsty-3.s.f.   boiled

Second, subject oriented depictives survive ellipsis, irespective of whether the subject is pre-verbal or post-verbal.

(42) a. *A plecat Maria supărată si   Ioana enervată*   (Romanian)
          has left Maria upset   and Ioana outraged.
      b. *Maria a plecat supărată si   Ioana enervată.*
          Maria has left upset   and Ioana outraged.

Movement operations, such as topicalization also point to the fact that the subject and the depictive do not make up a constituent, in spite of the apparent adjacency of postverbal subjects and the depictive.

(43) a. *A plecat Maria supărată de acasă.*   (Romanian)
          has left Maria upset from home.
      b. *[Maria supărată] a plecat de acasă.*
          Maria upset   has left from home.

Finally, subject depictives show no ordering restricctions when they occur with circumstantial adverbs, irrespective of whether they are pre-verbal or post-verbal.

(44) a. *A plecat Maria [supărată] [de acasă]*   (Romanian)
          has left Maria upset   from home.
      b. *A plecat Maria [de acasă] [supărată].*
          has left Maria from home upset.

(45) a. *Maria a plecat [supărată] [de acasă].*
          Maria has left upset   from home.
      b. *Maria a plecat [de acasă] [supărată].*
          Maria has left from home upset.

Given these properties, which show that subject depictives with the subject in situ are similar to subject depictives with the subject in a preverbal position, we conclude that the subject position must be outside the first conjunct in (26) for both types of subject depictives, and thus that the first conjunct in (26) is a VP, and not a *v*P.

4.2 Object depictives

As illustrated above, in Section 2, object depictives have different properties than subject depictives. We propose that these differences stem from a difference in the syntax of these two types of depictives.

4.2.1   *Syntax of object depictives*

What we propose for the analysis of object depictives is that they attach to the object DP, rather than to a verbal projection. We propose that the predication relation between the depictive and the object is mediated by a functional head, that can be assimilated to Bowers' (1993) Predication Phrase, as in (46).

(46)
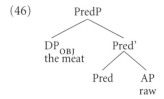

Just as in the case of subject depictives, we will assume that the structure in (46) above gets integrated into the hierarchy of functional projections through a Conjunction Phrase, as in (47) below. In (47), the PredP is the complement of the Co head, and the whole CoP is the complement of the verbal head.

(47)
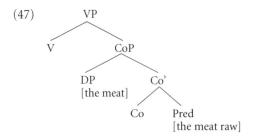

There are important differences between the structure in (47) above and the structure in (26) proposed for subject depictives. The CoP in (47) above is the complement of the verbal head, whereas in the case of subject depictives the verb is the head of one of the conjuncts. In the case of subject depictives, the depictive predicate conjoins to the verbal predicate, and then the resulting predicate applies to the subject DP. In the case of object depictives, the order is reversed: first, the depictive applies to the object DP, and then, the resulting projection is conjoined to the DP object. This difference has consequences for the way in which the two types of depictives are interpreted, to which we return below, under Section 4.2.2.

If a coordination analysis for object depictives is on the right track, we expect the two conjuncts to enjoy a certain amount of freedom. Typically, we expect that identical substrings inside the two coordinates should be possibly targeted by Conjunction Reduction, which deletes substrings which are shared by both conjuncts (Hankamer 1979; Neijt 1979; Postal 1974; Ross 1970; Sag 1976). We propose that this is precisely what happens in (47) above: one of the two instances of *the meat* is 'deleted'. There are two possible Conjunction Reduction operations – Gapping, which operates in the second or non-initial conjunct, and Right Node Raising, which operates in the first conjunct. Since Gapping targets the main predicate in the non-initial conjunct, and since *the meat*, in the second conjunct in (47) above is not the main predicate within this second conjunct, Gapping cannot apply. We will assume instead, that it is the other possible Conjunction Reduction operation that applies in this case, i.e. Right Node Raising, as shown in (48) below.

(48)

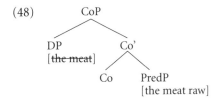

(48) is thus similar to a typical instance of Right Node Raising (RNR), such as (49).

(49)   She organizes ~~her life~~ and actually runs her life.

4.2.2   *Semantics of object depictives*

The proposal in (47) for object depictives can easily account for the *x*-predication interpretation of object depictives. In (47) above, the depictive adjective is in a predication relation with the individual *x* denoted by the object DP.

It is less obvious, though, how one could derive the event predication reading of object depictives. In other words, if object depictives are in a direct syntactic relation with the DP object, but not with the VP, how can the temporal simultaneity effect illustrated in (50) be derived?

(50)   a.   John read the newspaper folded.
       b.   John read the newspaper and the newspaper was folded at the time
           of reading. (the event of reading and the state of being folded tempo-
           rally overlap)

We propose that this temporal dependency of the state expressed by the object depictive on the event expressed by the verb is due to a binding relation between the Tense head and the Pred head in (47) above. The secondary predicate 'raw' does not describe an event, and as such, it does not introduce its own event (e) variable position. Instead, 'raw' is part of the event described by the VP 'eat the meat raw', which introduces a unique event variable. This unique variable is bound by the Tense operator that c-commands the VP. One way of capturing this intuition is to say that the Pred head is an anaphor that needs to be bound by Tense in a local domain.

4.3 Back to the differences between the two classes of depictives

The proposal above can easily account for the differences between subject depictives and object depictives identified in Section 2.

The ordering restrictions (the object depictive precedes the subject depictive) follow from our proposal that object depictives are attached to the object DP, while subject depictives are 'attached' to the VP.

(51)

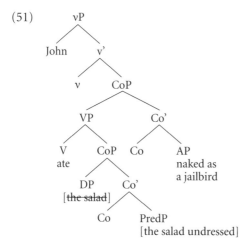

The structure above is also able to account for why subject depictives can appear in various orders in the syntax without a substantial difference in meaning, in contrast to object depictives, which have a fixed scope (narrow) with respect to other modifiers.

The ellipsis facts also follow from our analysis. Assuming that ellipsis applies to VPs, it is to be expected that this operation can apply in (26) above, but not in (47). In (26), VP ellipsis affects the first conjunct of the CoP. In contrast, in (47), VP ellipsis cannot apply and leave the object depictive unaffected, since the object depictive is part of the VP.

The constituency facts can also be accounted for by our assumptions. Clefting can apply to objects modified by depictives, but not subjects modified by depictives. This is because the subject and the depictive do not make up a constituent, i.e. they are not exclusively dominated by any node in (26) above. In contrast, the object and the depictive do make up a constituent – PredP in (47) above. Similarly, *do-so* substitution works with subject depictives but not with object depictives because in subject depictives the verb and the object form a constituent, while in object depictives they do not.

5.   Direct and indirect secondary predication

The analysis proposed above shows that the different properties exhibited by the two types of depictives follow from the structural position of the nominal to which the depictive is related. What seems to be crucial is whether the respective nominal is placed inside or outside the big VP. The generalization seems to be that a nominal inside the VP can be modified directly by a depictive, as in (47), while a nominal outside the VP can be modified by a depictive only indirectly, in a structure like (26). Moreover, it seems that a direct predication relation correlates with object depictives, while an indirect predication relation correlates with subject depictives. In this section we show that this generalization cannot be stated in terms of subjects and objects and that it should be refined in the sense that all the copies of the depicted nominal must be taken into account. A nominal can be directly modified by a depictive if the nominal is within the VP and if no copy of that nomial is outside the VP. Conversely, if there is at least one copy of a nominal outside the VP, a depictive cannot be applied directly to that VP, and must be applied indirectly, as in (26).

In order to show this, we consider cases in which an object nominal is outside the VP, i.e. the object of unaccusatives and topicalized objects.

5.1 Depictives and unaccusatives

The unique argument of unaccusatives starts off within the VP, as an object, so according to our generalization the prediction would be that the nominal involved in unaccusatives can be modified directly by depictives, in a manner similar to (47) above.

However, the following properties of depictive constructions applied to unaccusatives show that they pattern with subject depictives, rather than with object depictives.

Just like subject depictives, unaccusative depictive constructions survive ellipsis, in contrast to object related depictives.

(52)   John$_i$ read the letter outraged$_i$ and Bill$_j$ did upset$_j$.
     *John submitted his text$_i$ finished$_i$ and Bill did unfinished$_j$.
     John fell down the stairs drunk and Bill did sober.

Second, the nominal and the depictive in an unaccusative construction do not make up a constituent, just like subject depictives, and in contrast to object depictives. This is shown in (53) below by using the clefting test.

(53)   What he ate was the meat raw.
       *Who ate the soup was him naked.
       *Who fell down the stairs was him drunk.

Third, just as subject depictives, and unlike object depictives, unaccusative depictives behave as if they were scopeless elements, and they can appear in various orders in the syntax without a substantial difference in meaning.

(54)   John fell down the stairs naked.
       John fell naked down the stairs.

The problem raised by unaccusatives is thus that even though they have a VP internal nominal, the depictive does not apply directly to that nominal, as predicted by our generalization, but indirectly, in a manner similar to subject depictives. These properties of unaccusative depictives can obviously be related to the fact that the object of unaccusatives moves out of its VP internal position. The solution then is to slightly modify our generalization, and to take into account all copies of the relevant nominal. In other words, a nominal can be directly modified by a depictive if the nominal is within the VP and if no copy of that nomial is outside the VP. Conversely, if there is at least one copy of a nominal outside the VP, a depictive cannot be applied directly to that VP, and must be applied indirectly, as in (26).

5.2 Topicalized objects

The same conclusion is supported by objects of transitive verbs that move out of the VP. This is the case of objects that are topicalized and thus moved to the preverbal field to a Topic position. Depicted topicalized objects pattern with subject depictives, rather than with object depictives.

First, a depictive modifying a topicalized object does not seem to show any ordering constraints with respect to a depictive modifying a subject, or with respect to a circumstantial, and thus has the distribution of a typical subject depictive.

(55)   *Maria a băut   ceaiul   cald   înghetată.*   (Romanian)
       Maria has drunk tea-the.M hot-F frozen.F.
       **Maria a băut   ceaiul   înghetată cald.*
       Maria has drunk tea-the.M frozen.F hot-M.

(56)   *Ceaiul*$_{TOP}$ *Maria l-a băut cald   înghetată.*   (Romanian)
       Tea-the.M Maria it-has drunk hot-M frozen.F.
       Ceaiul$_{TOP}$ *Maria l-a băut   înghetată cald.*
       Tea-the.M Maria it-has drunk frozen.F hot-M.

Second, depicted topicalized objects behave like subject oriented depictives in that they survive ellipsis. This contrasts with non-topicalized, in-situ objects, which do not survive ellipsis.

(57)   *Ceaiul   Maria l-a băut cald   si Petre rece.*   (Romanian)
       Tea-the.M Maria it-has drunk hot-M   and Petre cold-M.
       **Maria a băut   ceaiul cald   si Petre rece.*
       Maria has drunk tea-the.M. hot.M and Petre cold.M.

To sum up, the analysis proposed above shows that the different properties exhibited by the two types of depictives follow from the structural position of (all the copies of) the nominal to which the depictive is related. Even though this position is directly correlated to the syntactic function of a nominal, the generalization cannot be stated in terms of subjects and objects, because all the copies of the respective nominal have to be taken into account. A nominal can be directly modified by a depictive if the nominal is within the VP and if no copy of that nominal is outside the VP. Conversely, if there is at least one copy of a nominal outside the VP, a depictive cannot be applied directly to that VP, and must be applied indirectly, as in (26).

6.   Conclusions

In this paper we have argued that what is relevant for the classification of depictives into two classes is not the syntactic function of the depicted nominal, but the structural position of all the copies of the depicted nominal: depictives can be directly predicated about nominals for which all copies are inside the VP, but not about nominals that have at least one copy outside the VP.

Our analysis proposes that the interpretation of depictives is a direct mapping of a particular type of configuration. We argued that the two types of depictives correspond to two different configurations and hence to two different ways in which function composition applies at LF.

Semantically, subject depictives are e-predicates. The x-predicate reading of subject depictives can be derived by virtue of the fact that both the depictive and the vP have an x-variable which is simultaneously saturated by one and the same individual.

Object depictives, on the other hand, are x-predicates. Their e-predication reading follows from the fact that the head of the PredP that includes the object and the depictive is anaphorically bound by the Tense of the main clause.

We also argued against an adjunction analysis of depictives, and implicitly for a restrictive theory of phrase structure, in compliance with the Strict Asymmetry Hypothesis (Di Sciullo 1999, 2000, see (4) above).

Last, but not least, this analysis sheds new light on the properties of an edge of a phase. What our analyis shows is that the edge of the vP phase differs from its non edge not only for the availability of Move and Agree operations, but also for secondary predication relations. A nominal within the non-edge of the vP phase can be depicted directly by a secondary predicate, while a nominal at the edge of the vP phase can only be 'depicted' indirectly.

Notes

* This research has been partly supported by the Social Sciences and Humanities Research Council of Canada (grant # 412-97-0016), for the project entitled "Asymmetries in Natural Languages and their Treatment by the Performance Systems", awarded to professor Anna Maria Di Sciullo, in the Department of Linguistics at the Université du Québec à Montréal (UQAM).

1. As indicated by Cinque, 1999, the latter is possible in Northern varieties

2. Romanian verbs overtly raise out of the vP.

References

Aarts, B. (1992). *Small Clauses in English: The Nonverbal Types.* Berlin: Mouton de Gruyter

Bowers, J. (1993). The syntax of predication. *Linguistic Inquiry, 24,* 591–656.

Cardinaletti, A. & Starke, M. (1999). The typology of structural deficiency: A case study of the three classes of pronouns. In H. van Riemsdijk (Ed.), *Clitics in the Languages of Europe* (pp. 145–234). Berlin, New York: Mouton de Gruyter.

Chomsky, N. (1981). *Lectures on Government and Binding.* Dordrecht: Foris.

Chomsky, N. (2001). Derivation by phase. In M. Kenstowicz (Ed.), *Ken Hale: A Life in Language* (pp. 1–52). Cambridge, Mass: The MIT Press.

Cinque, G. (1994). A null theory of phrase and compound stress. *Linguistic Inquiry, 24,* 239–298.

Cinque, G. (1999). *Adverbs and Functional Heads. A Cross-Linguistic Perspective.* Oxford University Press.

Cormack, A. & Smith, N. (1999). Why are depictives different from resultatives. *Phonetics and Linguistics, 11,* 251–284. University College London.

Davidson, D. (1967). The logical form of action sentences. In N. Rescher (Ed.), *The Logic of Decision and Action* (pp. 81–120). Pittsburg: University of Pittsburg Press.

Dechaine, R-M. (1993). Predicates across categories. Ph.D. Dissertation. University of Massachusetts, Amherst.

Di Sciullo, A-M. (1999). The local asymmetry connection. In L. Pylkkänen, A. van Hout, & H. Harley (Eds.), *Papers from the UPenn/MIT Roundtable on the Lexicon. MIT Working Papers in Linguistics* (pp. 26–45). Cambridge, Mass.

Di Sciullo, A-M. (2000). Paths in Words. In *ESSLLI. (European Summer School in Logic Language and Information)* (pp. 78–94). Birmingham, United Kingdom.

Di Sciullo, A-M., Paul, I., & Somesfalean, S. (2003). The clause structure of extraction asymmetries. In A. M. Di Sciullo (Ed.), *Asymmetry in Grammar, Vol. 1: Syntax and Semantics* (pp. 279–301). Amsterdam: John Benjamins.

Geuder, W. (2000). Oriented adverbs. Issues in the lexical semantics of event adverbs. Ph.D. Dissertation.

Gueron, J. & Hoekstra, T. (1995). The temporal interpretation of predication. In A. Cardinalletti & T.Guasti (Eds.), *Syntax and Semantics* 28 (pp. 77–108). San Diego: Academic Press.

Hankamer, J. (1979). *Deletion in Coordinate Structures.* New York: Garland.

Hoekstra, T. (1988). Small clause results. *Lingua, 74,* 101–139.

Hornstein, N. & Lightfoot, D. (1987). Predication and PRO. *Language, 63,* 23–52.

Hoshi, H. (2000). After spell-out. A theory of computation in PF. In *University of California Working Papers in Linguistics, 6,* 17–39.

Johannessen, J. B. (1998). *Coordination.* New York: Oxford University Press.

Kayne, R. (1994). *The Antisymmetry of Syntax.* Cambridge, Mass.: MIT Press.

Kiparsky, P. (1998). Partitive case and aspect. In M. Butt & W. Geuder (Eds.), *The Projection of Arguments* (pp. 265–307). Stanford: CSLI Publications.

Kratzer, A. (1995). Stage level and individual level predicates. In G. N. Carlson & F. J. Pelletier (Eds.), *The Generic Book* (pp. 125–175). Chicago: The University of Chicago Press.

Kratzer, A. (2004). Telicity and the meaning of objective case. In J. Guéron & J. Lecarme (Eds.), *The Syntax of Tense.* Cambridge, Mass.: MIT Press.

Levin, B. & Rappaport, M. (1995). *Unaccusativity.* Cambridge. Mass.: MIT Press.

Munn, A. B. (1992). A null operator analysis of ATB gaps. *The Linguistic Review, 9,* 1–26.

Nakajima, H. (1990). Secondary predication. *The Linguistic Review, 7* (3), 275–309.

Neijt, A. (1979). *Gapping: A Contribution to Sentence Grammar.* Dordrecht: Foris.

Parsons, T. (1990). *Events in the Semantics of English.* Cambridge Mass.: MIT Press.

Postal, P. (1974). *On Raising.* Cambridge, Mass.: MIT Press.

Pylkkänen, L. (2002). Distributing depictives. Talk delivered at NELS 33. MIT. 2002.

Ramchand, G. C. (1997). *Aspect and Predication. The Semantics of Argument Structure.* Oxford: Clarendon Press.

Roberts, I. (1988). Predicative APs. *Linguistic Inquiry, 19,* 703–710.

Ross, J-R. (1970). Gapping and the order of constituents. In Bierwisch & Heidolph (Eds.), *Progress in Linguistics* (pp. 249–259). The Hague: Mouton & Co.

Rothstein, S. (1983). The syntactic forms of predication. Ph.D. dissertation. MIT.

Rubin, E. J. (1996). The transparent syntax and semantics of modifiers. In *WCCFL, 15,* 429–439.

Sag, I. (1976). Deletion and logical form. Ph.D. dissertation, MIT. Cambridge, Mass.

Schultze-Berndt, E. & Himmelmann, N. P. (2003). Depictive secondary predicates in cross-linguistic perspective. *Linguistic Typology, 8,* 59–131.

Simpson, J. (1983). Resultatives. In B. Levin, M. Rappaport & A Zaenen (Eds.), *Papers in Lexical Functional Grammar* (pp. 143–157). Bloomington: IULC.

Stowell, T. (1983). Subjects across categories. *The Linguistic Review, 2,* 285–312.

Williams, E. (1980). Predication. *Linguistic Inquiry, 11,* 208–238.

Winkler, S. (1997). *Focus and Secondary Predication.* Berlin: Mouton de Greuter.

On two issues related to the clitic clusters in Romance languages*

Stanca Somesfalean
Université du Québec à Montréal

Even though they are highly rigid constructions, clitic clusters manifest a certain degree of variation in Romance languages. This paper concentrates on the behaviour of argumental clitic clusters in Romanian, Italian and French, more specifically, on two issues related to these constructions: the order within the cluster and the impenetrability of the elements entering the cluster. The typical analysis is mainly based on a template that will account for the clitic order in a given language. Here, we aim for an analysis that involves more than one module of grammar. The postulation of a template will be avoided by proposing an analysis where the order of the clitics within the cluster reflects the order of the argument XPs. We will see that language variation can be restricted to the constructions involving the 3rd person Dative clitics and the imperative constructions. Thus, 3rd person features are a locus of variation in grammar. Furthermore, we will eliminate the apparent problem posed by the imperative constructions, showing that they are not true clitic clusters, hence not subject to the same restrictions.

1.   Goal

The goal of this paper is to shed some light on the clitic cluster constructions in some Romance languages, particularly in Romanian, French and Italian. Clitics are elements whose particular status (contested between morphology, phonology and syntax, and having restricted semantics) allows for an analysis where the interaction between UG and the external systems becomes visible, as different modules of the grammar are at play. At the PF interface, they are manifestations of phi-features, while at the LF interface, they have a restricted reference. Specifically, we concentrate on two issues related to these constructions, i.e. the order within the cluster and the impenetrability of the elements forming the cluster. We show that what is often assumed to be a difference between these three languages with respect to the order of clitics reduces to two particular situations, i.e. the combinations including the 3rd person Dative clitic and the imperative constructions. We avoid the postulation of a template responsible for the order of the two argumental clitics within the cluster by proposing a syntactic analysis where the order of the clitics reflects the order of the argument XPs. Furthermore, we eliminate the apparent problem posed by the imperatives by showing that they do not involve true clitic clusters, but rather a simple sequence of a verb and an argumental clitic, followed by another pronominal argument.

2.   Clitic clusters

2.1 The particular status of clitics

Clitics have been approached within different frameworks in the literature, as belonging either to the morphological, the syntactic or the phonetic component of the grammar. The fact that they cannot stand alone, that they need to attach to some host, that they have a rigid order, etc. make them comparable to affixes. On the other hand, the fact that they do have a certain independence suggests that pronominal clitics are syntactic units that originate in argument or adjunct positions. For example, there are elements like negation or certain adverbs that may intervene between the clitic and the verbal element (assumed to be its host):

(1) *Îl*   *mai* văd şi   *mâine*   *dimineaţă.*
    3rd-ACC again see and tomorrow morning
    'I see him tomorrow morning as well.'

The accounts put forth by Zwicky (1977), Klavans (1985), Bonet (1991), Sportiche (1992, 1999), Anderson (1992), among many others, illustrate the fact that the very nature of clitics makes them susceptible of being considered at times independent elements with syntactic import, affixes that only play a role in morphology, or phonetic entities dealt with at PF.

   In this paper, we are particularly interested in the clitic cluster constructions, which, given their characteristics, are likely to reveal interesting facts about the nature of the clitics involved in such constructions and about the general properties of the syntax of the languages in question. These constructions have been approached in a number of studies, few of which have been of a syntactic nature. The majority of such studies rely on morphology to explain the strict ordering constraints that characterise them and propose some kind of template which accounts for the specific order of elements and which differs from one language to another. The approach we consider here is essentially of syntactic nature. However, a purely syntactic account is not sufficient, since by definition clitics are elements that are at the boundary of different modules of the grammar. Hence, different modules may interact while accounting for their behaviour.[1]

The clitic cluster constructions involve a sequence of pronominal argumental clitics and other clitics, such as partitives, locatives, auxiliaries, negation, etc.[2]

(2) să   nu   o   mai   fi   văzut
     SUBJ not 3rd-ACC again be seen
     'that (I) should not have seen her again'

For the purposes of this paper, we will limit the investigation to the argumental clitic clusters, of the type presented in (3), but further investigations are intended in order to have a clear view of the clitic phenomena as a whole.

(3) Je   te   le   donne.
     1st-NOM 2nd-DAT 3rd-ACC give
     'I give it to you.'

2.2 Distribution

The data presented in (4)–(6) has often been used to illustrate the fact that there are differences within the Romance languages with respect to the pronominal argumental clitic order within the clitic cluster.

(4) I   l-   am   trimis ieri.
     3rd-DAT 3rd-ACC have sent   yesterday.
     'I have sent it to him/her yesterday.'

(5) Glielo   spedito ieri.
     3rd-DAT 3rd-ACC sent   yesterday.
     'I have sent it to him/her yesterday.'

(6) Je le   lui   ai   envoyé hier.
     I 3rd-ACC 3rd-DAT have sent   yesterday.
     'I have sent it to him/her yesterday.'

The examples in (4)–(6) show that in Romanian and Italian, for example, the order of the two object clitics is Dat>Acc, see (4) and (5), but in French it is Acc>Dat, see (6).[3]

However, a closer look at these types of constructions indicates that the clitic order is not always different in the languages in question. In the following paradigms, the order of the clitics in Romanian, Italian and French is Dat>Acc, with the exception of the French combination involving a 3rd person Dative and Accusative, as in (7c) and (7f):

(7)   French:

a. *Il me le donne.*
    He 1st-DAT 3rd-ACC gives
    'He gives it to me.'

b. *Il te le donne.*
    He 2nd-DAT 3rd-ACC gives.
    'He gives it to you.'

c. *Il le lui donne. / *Il lui le donne.*
    He 3rd-ACC 3rd-DAT gives /
    *3rd-DAT 3rd-ACC
    'He gives it to him/her.'

d. *Il nous le donne.*
    He 1st-DAT 3rd-ACC gives
    'He gives it to us.'

e. *Il vous le donne.*
    He 2nd-DAT 3rd-ACC gives
    'He gives it to you.'

f. *Il le leur donne / *Il leur le donne.*
    He 3rd-ACC 3rd-DAT gives /
    *3rd dat 3rd-ACC
    'He gives it to them.'

(8)   Italian:

a. *Lui me lo darà.*
    He 1st-DAT 3rd-ACC give,FUT.
    'He will give it to me.'

b. *Lui te lo darà.*
    He 2nd-DAT 3rd-ACC give,FUT.
    'He will give it to you.'

c. *Lui glielo darà.*
    He 3rd-DAT 3rd-ACC give,FUT.
    'He will give it to him/her.'

d. *Lui ce lo darà.*
    He 1st-DAT 3rd-ACC give,FUT.
    'He will give it to us.'

e. *Lui ve lo darà.*
    He 2nd-DAT 3rd-ACC give,FUT.
    'He will give it to you.'

f. *Lui glielo darà.*
    He 3rd-DAT 3rd-ACC give,fut
    'He will give it to them.'

(9)   Romanian:

a. *El mi-l dā.*
    He 1st-DAT 3rd-ACC give.
    'He gives it to me.'

b. *El ţi-l dā.*
    He 2nd-DAT 3rd-ACC give.
    'He gives it to you.'

c. *El i-l dā.*
    He 3rd-DAT 3rd-ACC give.
    'He gives it to him/her.'

d. *El ni-l dă.*
    He 1st-DAT 3rd-ACC gives
    'He gives it to us.'

e. *El vi-l dă.*
    He 2nd-DAT 3rd-DAT gives
    'He gives it to you.'

f. *El li-l dă.*
    He 3rd-DAT 3rd-ACC gives
    'He gives it to them.'

However, yet another type of data comes to show that in imperatives, for example, we find again a difference between French, on one hand, and Romanian and Italian, on the other.

(10) French:

a. *Donne-le-moi!*
Give 3rd-ACC 1st-DAT
'Give it to me!'

b. *Donne-le-toi!*
give 3rd-ACC 2nd-DAT
'Give it to you!'

c. *Donne-le-lui!*
give 3rd-ACC 3rd-DAT
'Give it to him/her!'

d. *Donne-le-nous!*
give 3rd-ACC 1st-DAT
'Give it to us!'

e. *Donne-le-vous!*
give 3rd-ACC 2nd-DAT
'Give it to you!'

f. *Donne-le-leur!*
give 3rd-ACC 3rd-DAT
'Give it to them!'

(11) Italian:

a. *Spediscimelo!*
send 3rd-DAT 3rd-ACC
'Send it to me!'

b. *Spediscitelo!*
send 2nd-DAT 3rd-ACC
'Send it to you!'

c. *Spedisciglielo!*
send 3rd-DAT 3rd-ACC
'Send it to him/her!'

d. *Spediscicelo!*
send 1st-DAT 3rd-ACC
'Send it to us!'

e. *Spediscivelo!*
send 2nd-DAT 3rd-ACC
'Send it to you!'

f. *Spedisciglielo!*
send 3rd-DAT 3rd-ACC
'Send it to them!'

(12) Romanian:

a. *Dă-mi-l!*
give 1st-DAT 3rd-ACC
'Give it to me!'

b. *Dă-ți-l!*
give 2nd-DAT 3rd-ACC
'Give it to you!'

c. *Dă-i-l!*
give 3rd-DAT 3rd-ACC
'Give it to him/her!'

d. *Dă-ni-l!*
give 1st-DAT 3rd-ACC
'Give it to us!'

e. *Dă-vi-l!*
give 2nd-DAT 3rd-ACC
'Give it to you!'

f. *Dă-li-l!*
give 3rd-DAT 3rd-ACC
'Give it to them!'

The examination of the data presented in (1)–(9) above shows that Romanian, Italian and French realise the order Dat>Acc within the clitic cluster, with the exception of the 3rd person singular and plural Dative paradigms. Furthermore, these languages behave differently in the imperative constructions, as we have seen in (10)–(12), allowing the grouping of the Romanian, Italian, on the one side, as realising the Dat>Acc order, and Standard French on the other hand, realising the Acc>Dat order. In fact, Morin (1979) notes that Romance languages have preserved clitic sequences so that the order of proclisis and enclisis is identical,

Standard French being the only noticeable exception. Furthermore, according to him, Romance languages have been generally submitted to a process of transformation of the original Acc>Dat object clitic order, to the Dat>Acc order observed today, starting in the Middle French period. This change affected different French dialects, and independently, Catalan, Provençal, Southern Italian and some Northern Italian dialects, where the change affected both the enclisis and the proclisis. Standard French is exceptional in the sense that it is the only language that has suffered only a partial change, i.e. the change affected only proclisis and only the sequences containing 1st and 2nd person Datives and reflexive Datives, but did not affect the 3rd person Dative clitics.

(13) Old French → Modern French:
      il me le donne → donne-le-moi
      il le lui donne → donne-le-lui

Note that while in some of the dialects that have changed the order of Acc>Dat to Dat>Acc, the 3rd person Dative still constitutes an exception (in Québec French, e.g., (14)), in other dialects of French the 3rd person Dative precedes the Accusative in imperatives, see (15), i.e. the order of enclitics and proclitics is the same. Furthermore, note that there is no change in the form of the 3rd person Dative.

(14) Québec French (QF):
      Donne-moi-le!
      *Donne-le-lui! / *Donne-lui-le!*

(15) a. Lorrain
          il me le donne ; donne-me-le   DAT>ACC
          there is no sequence 'le lui' or 'lui le' in this dialect
      b. Vendéen:
          il me le donne; donne-me-le   DAT>ACC
          il lui le donne ; donne-lui-le   DAT>ACC
      c. Walloon
          il me le donne ; donne-me-le   DAT>ACC
      d. Normand
          il me le donne; donne-moi-le (moi and *me* are not clearly distinct, since
          they are both pronounced [me]) DAT>ACC
          il lui-le-donne; donne-lui-le   DAT>ACC
      e. Gallo
          il me le donne; donne-moi-le   DAT>ACC
          il lui le donne; donne-lui-le   DAT>ACC

                                                        (Morin 1979: 307)

3. Issues and ways to deal with them

3.1 Impenetrability

3.1.1 *Empirical evidence*
One of the most important properties of pronominal clitic clusters is the fact that no element whatsoever can intervene between the two argumental clitics.

The Romanian data shows that no element can intervene between the two clitics involved in a cluster, see (16) and (17). More specifically, there may be certain types of adverbs that intervene between the pronominal clitics and the verb,[4] as in (18)–(19), but there may be no argumental elements between the two clitics of the same type, i.e. between the two pronominal argumental clitics:

(16) a. *ţi   l-   am   dat   pe douā zile*
         2nd-DAT 3rd-ACC have given for two days
         'I have given it to you for two days.'
    b. **ţi am îl dat pe douā zile*

(17) a. *mi   -l   va   aduce mâine*
         1st-DAT 3rd-ACC will bring tomorrow
         '(He/she) will bring it to me tomorrow.'
    b. **îmi va îl aduce mâine*

(18) a. *nu ţi   -l   mai dau pentru cā...*
         not 2nd-DAT 3rd-ACC again give because...
         'I do not give it to you any more because...'
    b. **nu ţi mai îl dau pentru cā...*

(19) a. *nu ţi   l-   aş   mai fi dat   niciodatā...*
         not 2nd-DAT 3rd-ACC would again be given never
         'I would have never given it to you any more.'
    b. **nu ţi aş mai îl fi dat niciodatā...*

Negation can never intervene inside the argumental cluster either:

(20) a. *Nu mi   -l   mai dā.*
         not 1st-DAT 3rd-ACC again give
         'He/she does not give it to me any more.'
    b. **Mi nu îl mai dā.*[5]

The judgements hold for Italian and French as well. Particularly for these languages, that do not only have pronominal argumental clitics, but also locatives and partitives, note that nothing may intervene between the two clitic objects:

(21) a. *Paul me l'y donnera.*
          Paul 1st-DAT 3rd-ACC there give-FUT.
          'Paul will give it to me there.'
      b. **Paul m'y le donnera.*

(22) a. *Paolo non me lo ci darà.*
          Paolo not 1st-DAT 3rd-ACC there give-FUT.
          'Paolo will not give it to me.'
      b. **Paolo me non ci lo darà.*

3.1.2   Structure: Analysis

The facts above would indicate that the clitics are part of the same projection. But considering a theory where clitics are adjoined to some functional projection, having them adjoin to the same one implies multiple adjunction; and if Kayne's (1994) LCA holds true, multiple adjunction is excluded. Another possibility would be to partially adopt a solution in line with Sportiche (1992) and consider that clitics are heads of a projection of their own in the functional domain (a Clitic Voice, in Sportiche's terms). This projection would be situated at the periphery of the projection hosting the verb, since clitics are phonologically weak elements in need of a host. Thus, there would be a PF-active condition such that the verb would act as a phonetic host for the clitics.[6]

In Romanian, clitics cannot be adjoined directly to the head hosting the verb, because as we have seen in the examples (18)–(19) above, certain types of clitics may intervene between the pronominal clitics (argumental) and the verb. Hence, the clitic projection would have to be situated between the projection hosting the verb (i.e. MP for Romanian, as proposed by Cornilescu 1999 and others) and the negation, which is higher (see (20)). However, in other Romance languages, this may not necessarily be the case. In French, no adverb may intervene between the clitic cluster and the verb:[7]

(23) *Il ne me l'a jamais offert.*
      He not 1st-DAT 3rd-ACC have never offered
      'He has never offered it to me.'
      *Il ne me le jamais a offert.

(24) *Il me l'envoie toujours par courriel.*
      He 1st-DAT 3rd-ACC send always by e-mail
      'He always sends it to me by e-mail.'
      *Il me le toujours envoie par courriel.

On the other hand, Italian seems to allow some material between the verb and the clitic cluster:

(25) *Non glielo mai chiesto se voleva andare.*
not 3rd-DAT 3rd-ACC never ask if wanted go
'I have never asked him/her if he/she wanted to go.'

(26) *Non glielo mai più spedito.*
not 3rd-DAT 3rd-ACC never again send
'I haven't sent it to him/her ever again.'

A third possibility for the clitic placement would be in terms of adjunction to a functional head, as a result of strong features of specificity and referentiality, as in Uriagereka (1995), or an adjunction to a simple place holder functional projection, as in Terzi (1999).[8]

There are several possibilities with respect to the configurational formation hosting the two argumental clitics in our cluster:

a. the projection F is a type of Clitic Voice where the clitic is the head or is at least adjoined to a functional head; in line with Sportiche (1992), Terzi (1999), Uriagereka (1995), as in (27) below;

b. the projection is a Shell type proposed in Di Sciullo (2005) where the clitic is in fact found in the Specifier position of a functional projection, and is linked to an argument projection within the VP, thus preserving uniformity of chains, as in (28) below:

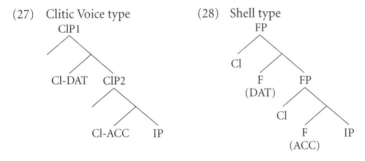

(27) Clitic Voice type

(28) Shell type

c. a projection where clitics adjoin to one another and then to the head of a functional projection, as proposed by Terzi (1999), as in (29):

(29)

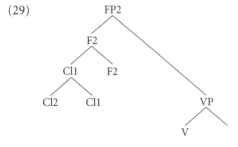

d. a structure where the two argumental clitics would belong to the same projection (say, a Complex Clitic Projection), where the Accusative clitic would occupy the head position, and the Dative clitic would occupy the specifier position, as in (30) below:

(30)

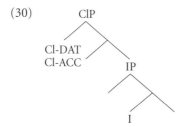

Further refinements are needed in any of the solutions above.

In the first case, i.e. (27), we need an additional requirement that the Specifier of the lower ClP be always empty, in order to capture the strict adjacency condition on the two clitics. On the other hand, a structure such as (29) relies on multiple adjunction and hence should be excluded.[9] The solution in (28) allows for conformity with the Uniformity principle, i.e. chains (of clitics) are always uniform: since clitics are arguments, they are XPs. Furthermore, the relation between a Comp position and a Spec position is independently motivated (take, for example, the object movement to (Spec, V) within an extended v projection). On the other hand, (28) goes against the assumed idea that clitics differ from XPs, since they cannot bear stress, cannot be coordinated, etc. Still, it is able to account for languages having the same order within the clitic clusters, be they in a preverbal or a postverbal position, and for the cases of the clitic climbing such as the ones in (31), where the order of the clitics is also preserved:

(31) a. *voglio offrirtelo*
          want offer-3rd-DAT-3rd-ACC
          'I want to offer it to you.'
      b. *te lo voglio offrire*
      c. **lo voglio offrirti*
      d. **ti voglio offrirlo*

The solution in (30) would capture the intuition that the two clitics (Accusative and Dative) are different grammatical objects, i.e. there are different properties associated to each one of them: the DO is argumental whilst the IO is less, in the sense that it is more of a locative argument (in an abstract sense of location).[10] It is almost always preceded by a preposition, it is more flexible than the direct object (allows for Dative shift), etc. Also, the IO clitic is involved in doubling in a much more unrestricted manner then the DO clitic. The solution in (30) would also render the impenetrability condition easily accountable for, without further stipulations: there is nothing that may intervene between the specifier and the head of a projection. Keeping in mind that the intuition we need to capture here is that these elements form an impenetrable unit, we can view them almost as a morphological unit,[11] and thus a structure of a complex clitic projection (say of the type (30)) is not to be excluded, but it can be improved with the added refinement that the two clitics in the cluster are not adjoined in a simple manner, but they actually form a layered structure (à la Di Sciullo 2000). The fact of considering these sequences a single morphological word could be confirmed by the Québec French data, where the whole cluster '*le lui*' may be replaced by the clitic '*y*':[12]

(32) *Je le lui donne.*   ≈   *J'y donne.*
      I 3rd-ACC 3rd-DAT give
      'I give it to him.'

In fact, the characteristics of these constructions: the rigidity of order, the impenetrability, impossibility of extraction, impossibility of bearing stress, etc. allow a certain analogy with morphological words with a complex internal structure, as the ones previously examined by Di Sciullo (2000), such as the wh-words, th-words, affixed words, for which a layered Shell structure was proposed, that was capturing their internal properties. The generally observed order (Dat>Acc) is also reminiscent of the External prefix > Internal prefix fixed order also examined in Di Sciullo's works. In this line of thinking, the Dative would be reminiscent of the External prefix, since it is the one argument that is almost always prepositional, and more similar to an adjunct. On the other hand, the accusative would resemble the argument / Internal prefix.

3.2 Rigidity of order

3.2.1 *Previous analyses*

We have seen above that in the constructions involving clitic clusters, a rigid order has to be respected. We have also seen that in general, for the languages examined here, the order of the two pronominal clitics is Dat>Acc.

As to why would that be so, there are different proposals in the literature, proposals that rely mainly on the postulation of some kind of template responsible for the ordering within the cluster. This template may vary in nature from one author to the other: for example, it is mainly based on morphological features in Bonet (1995), but it is based on aspectual features in Manzini and Savoia (1999). In either case, the template essentially imposes an order of the clitics, and differs parametrically from one language to the other.

3.2.2 *Analysis*

As remarked at the beginning of this paper, the analysis we aim for here is mainly of a syntactic nature, so we will look at the properties of objects in the languages in question and see what we can say about clitic positioning in a cluster.

There are different proposals in the literature with respect to the datives being merged in a higher position than the accusatives: Demonte (1995), Pylkkänen (2000), Cuervo (2002).

Larson (1988) proposed tests that showed that in terms of argument structure, the recipient role ranges over the theme role. In these terms, the hierarchy of argument structure would be actor/agent>goal/recipient>patient/theme.[13] Cuervo (2001) proposes an analysis of the Spanish ditransitive (Dative) constructions where the surface word order DAT<ACC is determined by the DP goal being merged higher than the DP theme. She bases her analysis on the difference that Pylkkänen (2000) makes between "low applicatives" – that are merged below the lexical verb – and "high applicatives" – that are merged above the verb. According to this view, Datives would be low applicatives, as the low applicative heads have prepositional meaning, relating an individual to the direct object (the interpretation is that of directional possessive relations or benefactives).[14]

The tests used in Cuervo (2001) for determining the position of the object within the VP include binding asymmetries and weak cross-over constructions. The judgements she proposes for Spanish hold for Romanian as well. We illustrate here with weak cross-over constructions, parallel to the ones in Cuervo (2001: 14).

(33) a. *Ce_i i-a înapoiat stăpînului său$_i$ t_i Lilus?
          what 3rd-DAT has returned owner-DAT 3rd-POSS Lilus
          'What did Lilus return to its owner?'
      b. Cui_i i-a înapoiat t_i caietul său$_i$ Lilus?
          who-DAT 3rd-DAT has returned notebook-ACC 3rd-POSS Lilus
          'Who did Lilus return his notebook?'

In (33) above, questioning the low direct object causes ungrammaticality, whilst questioning the high indirect object is allowed, confirming the Dat>Acc order.

In the same line of thought, Bruening (2001) discusses the fact that in English double-object constructions, the direct object cannot have scope over the indirect object. This, according to him, would be due to the Minimal Link Condition, hence it implies assuming that the dative is structurally higher than the accusative.

The scope predictions hold for Romanian as well:

(34) *Maria i-a trimis fiecare carte unui copil.*
      Maria 3rd-DAT has sent each book a-DAT child
      'Maria has sent each book to a child.'
          *fiecare > unui

(35) *Maria i-a dat o prăjitură fiecărui copil.*
Maria 3rd-DAT has given a cake each-DAT child
'Maria has given a cake to each child.'
      fiecărui > o

In (34) above, the meaning associated with the quantifier cannot be a distributive one, meaning that the Accusative cannot have scope over the Dative. In (35) on the other hand, the meaning is distributive, since the Dative has scope over the Accusative. This confirms the findings of Cuervo (2001), Bruening (2001) among others, we will thus assume a structure of the Romanian *v*P where the Dative is generated higher than the Accusative.

The equivalent Italian examples in (36)–(37) also confirm this structure, since the indirect object has scope over the direct object:

(36) *Maria a spedito ogni libro a un bambino.*
'Maria has sent each book to a child.'

      *ogni > un

(37) *Maria a offerto un dolce a ogni bambino.*
'Maria has sent a cake to each child.'

      ogni > un

As for French, it seems that in this language the same scope constraints apply as in the other languages investigated.[15]

(38) *Marie a envoyé chaque livre à un enfant.*
'Marie has sent each book to a child.'

      *chaque>un

(39) *Marie a donné un gâteau à chaque enfant.*
'Marie has given a cake to each child.'

      chaque>un

On the basis of the scope evidence from the languages under consideration, we can assume that the underlying order of the XP arguments within the verbal projection is Dat>Acc.

We hold that the order of the pronominal clitics within the clitic cluster corresponds to the order of the argument XPs within the verb, hence the generalised Dat>Acc underlying order. Thus, we avoid the postulation of a language-dependent template in order to account for the order of the argumental clitics within the cluster.

4.   Language variation

As we have seen in the previous section, there is unanimity of order within the cluster in Romanian, Italian and French. The generalisation is that they all realise the order Dat>Acc.

However, the combination involving a 3rd person Dative in French no longer respects the Dat>Acc order, as we can see in (40):

(40)   a.   *Je lui le donne.*
        I 3rd-DAT 3rd-ACC give
        'I give it to him.'
   b.   *Je le lui donne.*
        I 3rd-ACC 3rd-DAT give
        'I give it to him.'

Also, we have seen in (10) above that the imperative forms of French reflect a different order within the cluster: Acc>Dat.

(41)   *Donne-le-moi!*
     give 3rd-ACC 1st-DAT
     'Give it to me!'

Note again that in Québec French the inverse order is possible:

(42)   *Donne-moi-le!*
     give 1st-DAT 3rd-ACC
     'Give it to me!'

In the following sections we will take a look at these two issues.

4.1   The 3rd person

It has been observed that in a number of languages, certain person/number combinations are impossible.

For example, the combination of a 1st person singular/plural Accusative and a 3rd person singular/plural Dative renders illicit constructions:

(43)   a.   *Mă   îi   prezintă.*
        1st-ACC 3rd-DAT introduces
        'He/she introduces me to him/her.'
   b.   *îi   mă   prezintă*
        3rd-DAT 1st-ACC introduces
        'He/she introduces me to him/her.'

The same happens when combining a 1st person singular/plural Accusative and a 2nd person singular/plural Dative:

(44) *Paul mā   le-   a prezentat.
     Paul 1st-ACC 3rd-pl-DAT has introduced.
     'Paul has introduced me to them.'

(45) *mā   vā   prezint
     1st-ACC 2nd-pl-ACC introduce
     'I introduce you to me.'

(46) *mi   vā   prezint
     1st-DAT 2nd-pl-ACC introduce
     'I introduce myself to you.'

This holds in general for French and Italian as well. Examples are given below for Italian :

(47) a. *Emanuela presenta me a te.*
         'Emanuela introduces me to you.'
     b. *Emanuela me ti presenta.*
     c. *Emanuela te mi presenta.*

                              (Gerlach & Grijzenhout 2000:11)

(48) a. *Emanuela presenta me a lui.*
         'Emanuela introduces me to him.'
     b. *Emanuela gli mi presenta.*

                              (Gerlach & Grijzenhout 2000:11)

However, these constructions are also subject to much debate as to their acceptability. Wanner (1987), Giusti (p.c.) affirm that there are dialects of Italian where these types of combinations are licit.

(49) a. I>II; REFL>X; ACC>DAT
         Non mi vi voglio raccomandare con questi propositi.
         'I don't want to recommend myself to you with these arguments.'
     b. I>II; X>REFL; DAT>ACC
         Non mi vi volete raccomandare con questi propositi.
         'You don't want to recommend me to you with these arguments.'

                              (Wanner 1987:32)

Roberge & Vinet (1989) give examples of "gévaudanais", where these combinations are also possible:

(50)   *Me le presento.*
       1st-ACC 3rd-DAT presents
       'S/he presents me to him.'

(51)   *Soumete li te.*
       submit 3rd-DAT 2nd-ACC
       'Submit you to him.'

(Roberge & Vinet 1989:51)

It is important to note that there is a generalised agreement among the various authors that these controversial examples are rendered acceptable when the Dative clitic is replaced with its strong pronoun correspondent, for example:

(52)   *Non ti puoi raccomandare a noi con questi propositi.*
       not 2nd-ACC can recommend to us with these arguments
       'You cannot recommend yourself to us with these arguments.'

(Wanner 1987:32)

Kayne (1975) also notes that a construction with an Accusative clitic other than the 3rd person is possible, but then the Dative has to be a strong pronoun:

(53)   *Paul me présentera à lui.*
       Paul 1st-ACC introduce to 3rd-DAT
       'Paul will introduce me to him.'

Interestingly though, the construction cannot be rescued if the Dative remains a clitic and the Accusative is strong:

(54)   **Paul lui présentera moi.*
       Paul 3rd-DAT introduce 1st-ACC
       'Paul will introduce me to him.'

Furthermore, one issue which is not controversial is the fact that under the inverse order (i.e. Dat>Acc) these examples are completely unacceptable.

But leaving aside controversial examples as the ones involving a combination of 1st and 2nd person clitics, we can safely say that descriptively, in a legitimate sequence of argumental clitics, there must be one 3rd person.

Different authors have proposed a way of dealing with these constructions and their restrictiveness.

Perlmutter (1970) observes that Spanish clitics are ordered by person, while French clitics are ordered by Case.[16]

Bonet (1991) proposes the Person-Case constraint, see (55), according to which if there is a dative clitic related to some argument, the clitic related to the direct object has to be 3rd person. She notes that the combination of 1st and

2nd person argument-related clitics is impossible for many speakers of Romance languages.

(55) *Me lui /I-II Constraint:
- a. STRONG VERSION: the direct object has to be third person.
- b. WEAK VERSION: if there is a third person it has to be the direct object.

(Bonet 1991:182)

This constraint, according to her, affects clitic combinations, agreement markers combinations and weak pronoun combinations. Languages have repair strategies in order to escape the constraint, such as the "Spell-out elsewhere" strategy, which essentially allows the pronominal argument to be spelled-out either in the clitics (Infl-adjoined) position, or in the argument (VP-internal) position.[17]

Farkas & Kazazis (1980) also propose two topicality hierarchies in order to explain these types of restrictions: Ethical > Goal > Theme; 1st pers. > 2nd pers. > 3rd pers.

These constraints restate the empirical observation that in the majority of the dialects of the Romance languages[18] it is impossible to combine two argument-related clitics in 1st and 2nd persons among each other or with a 3rd person Dative clitic. Hence, when two clitics are involved (one Accusative and one Dative), the Accusative is always 3rd person.

Recall that the problematic constructions in the French paradigm presented in (7), repeated here as (56), involve both clitics in the 3rd person:

(56)   French:

a. *Il me le donne.*
   He 1st-DAT 3rd-ACC gives
   'He gives it to me.'

b. *Il te le donne.*
   He 2nd-DAT 3rd-ACC gives.
   'He gives it to you.'

c. *Il le lui donne. / *Il lui le donne.*
   He 3rd-ACC 3rd-DAT gives/
   *3rd-DAT 3rd-ACC
   'He gives it to him/her.'

d. *Il nous le donne.*
   He 1st-DAT 3rd-ACC gives
   'He gives it to us.'

e. *Il vous le donne.*
   He 2nd-DAT 3rd-ACC gives
   'He gives it to you.'

f. *Il le leur donne / *Il leur le donne.*
   He 3rd-ACC 3rd-DAT gives /
   *3rd-DAT 3rd-ACC
   'He gives it to them.'

The behaviour noted for French reflects the fact that the third person has different properties than the 1st and 2nd persons, and this seems to be universally valid. In fact, the 3rd person constructions may be submitted to more variation than their equivalents in the 1st or 2nd person. Uriagereka (1995) holds that the 1st and 2nd person clitics have different properties than the 3rd person clitics. Based on the distinction made by Cardinaletti & Starke (1999) between different classes of pronouns, he considers the 1st and 2nd person clitics as strong and the 3rd person clitics as weak. Also, according to him, strong clitics usually precede weak ones and two strong clitics may not co-occur, while two weak clitics may. In terms of Optimality Theory, for example, Gerlach (1998) postulates that the restriction on the combination of 1st and 2nd person clitics is given by the non-existence of a difference in markedness between these elements.

On independent evidence, the existence of a morpho-syntactic split between the 1st and 2nd persons, on one hand, and the 3rd person, on the other hand, has been attested in different languages. For example, Aissen (2000) discusses data from different languages (Dyirbal, Nocte, Lummi) where the 3rd person behaves differently than the 1st and 2nd with respect to the interaction between voice and thematic role. Roberts (2000) mentions this while referring to K'ichee', where agreement is triggered by the 1st or 2nd person argument when one of these competes with a 3rd person argument (Hale & Storto 1996), and to Basque, where the 1st and 2nd persons show nominative/accusative agreement on the verb, whilst the 3rd person arguments show ergative agreement (Fernandez 1999). Other works that emphasise the role of person features include Silverstein (1976), Sharma (2001), Grimshaw (1999).

From a semantic point of view, this split is equally justified: the 1st and 2nd are the persons of the speaker and the hearer, the only participants in the speech act to have "true grammatical person features", according to Speas & Tenny (2002), while the 3rd person referent is not a discourse participant. In fact, Speas & Tenny (2002) propose a system where the roles of speaker and hearer (basically manifestations of the 1st and 2nd persons) are configurationally organised. If this holds true and the syntax is sensible to these notions previously seen in post-syntactic components, it looks like only the 1st and 2nd person have a representation in syntax, whilst the 3rd person gives rise to variation.

Given this and the abundance of empirical evidence from different languages, we can generalise the fact that the 3rd person features are a locus of variation within languages.

For the case at hand, it may be the case that, given the fact that two 3rd person clitics are involved, and since the 3rd person is the unmarked value for person (as in Benveniste 1966; Silverstein 1976; Bonet 1991), the data we have seen in (56) for French is due to a parametric choice of that language for a prominence of the theme (Accusative) in the discourse. This would be consistent with the theory of Alexiadou & Anagnostopoulou (2002), who propose that in languages like Romanian and Spanish, the relevant split is not as much concerning the person, but the animacy features. Thus, when both clitics are in the 3rd person, the animacy features prevail, determining the precedence of the direct object (as a theme, not animate) over the indirect object (as a beneficiary, animate).

4.2 Imperatives

The imperatives seem to pose yet another problem to the clitic ordering issues, since it looks like in these constructions the expected order Dat>Acc is inverted. A closer examination of these constructions would allow us to show that we are in the presence of an apparent problem, because in fact we are dealing with two completely different types of structures and we are not in the presence of a cluster at all.

(57) *Donne-le-moi!*
       give 3rd-ACC 1st-DAT
       'Give it to me!'

Note that in the imperatives, examples (10) and (57) here, the Dative – Accusative combination is no longer the same as in the affirmatives. The Dative form of the pronoun is not the clitic '*me*' (me, DAT), but the stronger form '*moi*' (me, DAT), fact that is particular for French, but not for Romanian or Italian. Leaving aside the 3rd person constructions, it seems that in the French instances where the Accusative precedes the Dative, the Dative is no longer a clitic, but a different grammatical object: as we can see in (58)–(59) the distribution is not the same:

(58) a. **Je toi le donne.*
              I 1st-DAT 3rd-ACC give.
              'I give it to you.'
       b. *Je te le donne.*

(59) a. **Il moi voit.*
              He 1st-DAT see
              'He sees me.'
       b. *Il me voit.*

According to Cardinaletti & Starke (1999), following Kayne (1975), there are structural differences between clitics, weak pronouns and strong pronouns. Thus, strong and weak pronouns are XPs and occupy Specifier positions, while the clitics are X^0s (heads) and have a deficient structure. Assuming for the moment that this distinction holds true, the fact that the Standard French imperatives combine no longer two clitics but rather a clitic and a strong pronoun, would be an indicator that in this particular case we are then no longer in the presence of a true clitic cluster, but this is a simple combination of a clitic-verb construction and the indirect object clitic, a strong pronoun. This strong pronoun indirect object would not raise out of the lower lexical field, since we have seen in the examples above that its presence in the preverbal field is not licit.[19] The object clitic, on the other hand, would be high in the functional field. When the verb raises higher than the clitic for imperative force feature checking, the desired order is derived: VB>ACC>DAT.

There seem to be two problems with this analysis:

1) In a footnote (ft.32) in their paper, Cardinaletti & Starke (1999) assume the French 'lui' to be a weak pronoun, as opposed to 'à lui', its strong counterpart. This would not be visible in the Accusative paradigm, but in the Dative. According to them, "the relevant difference between "proclisis" and "enclisis" must be that imperatives, for some reason to be determined, render the clitic form impossible, and therefore the choice principle forces the next stronger form, weak pronoun"(p. 221).[20]

The tests they propose for distinguishing the two classes (clitics and weak pronouns cannot coordinate, but strong pronouns can) hold for the case at hand. If 'lui" in (60a) were a strong pronoun, its coordination would be possible and the data in (60b–e) would be acceptable:

(60)   a.   *Donne-le-lui!*
       b.   **Donne-le-lui et à eux!*
            give 3rd-ACC 3rd-DAT and to 3rd-DAT(strong) 'Give it to them and to them.'
       c.   **Donne-le-leur et à eux.*
       d.   **Donne-le-lui et à Pierre!*
       e.   **Donne-le-moi et toi!*

The distinction made between 'lui' and 'à lui' seems to be confirmed by the fact that the examples in (61) are rendered grammatical if both pronouns are «strong»:

(61)   a.   *Donne-le à lui et à nous!*
            give 3rd-ACC to 3rd-DAT and to 1st-DAT
            'Give it to him and to us.'
       b.   *Donne-le à lui et à Pierre!*
       c.   *Donne-le à moi et à eux.*
       d.   *Donne-le à eux et à eux.*

Furthermore, Cardinaletti & Starke (1999) assume that the weak pronoun would have to move out of the lexical field in order to check its deficient structure, so we could not maintain our analysis in terms of the indirect object remaining low in the structure and hence following the verb+accusative clitic combination, resulting in the verb-Acc-Dat order.

One way out of this problem is to assume, with other authors, that there are reasons to believe that the empirical basis of the theory proposed in Cardinaletti and Starke does not hold across the board (Dobrovie-Sorin 1999; Bouchard 2002, etc.). The differences they see between the classes of clitics are not always clear cut.[21] The reason for the impossibility of coordination in (65b–e) can be simply due to the fact that two different objects are involved (an X^0 and an XP).[22] The label of the element involved is, for the issue at hand, irrelevant. Furthermore, their argument is based on the element '*lui*', which is indeed a clitic in French, so its presence in the preverbal field is licit (*Je lui donne mon livre.*). On the other hand, the issue here is the change in form with respect to the 1st and 2nd person: '*moi*' and '*toi*' cannot be clitic elements and can never raise in the preverbal field, as we have seen in (58) and (59) above. Once established the fact that these elements cannot occupy a pre-verbal position, our intuition is maintained, such that indeed we are no longer dealing with a true clitic cluster, but with a construction formed by the verb and the direct object clitic – in the preverbal field – and the indirect object – in the post-verbal field.

2) However, an analysis on these lines would still face some problems given that, as mentioned before, in Québec French (and in other French dialects, as noted by Morin 1979), even though the form of the pronoun changes in the imperatives in the same way as it does in Standard French, the order is preserved (i.e. Dat>Acc), see (62). Hence, this language behaves like Romanian and Italian in preserving the order of the clitic sequence whether preceding or following the verb.

(62)   *Donne-moi-le!*   (63)   **Donne-me-le!*
       give 1st-DAT 3rd-ACC
       'Give it to me.'

One way to account for this is to assume that in one language (SF) the form of the pronominal argument is a strong pronoun, while in the other (QF) the same form is a clitic. If doubling constructions would implicate the 'moi' type forms in QF, then we could assume that they are indeed clitics in this language.[23] That would allow us to make the distinction between the SF and the QF and keep our analysis as such.

Note however that the examples we have seen in (15) from dialects of French, where the form of the clitic does not change, do not pose a problem. These are cases where the order (and the form) remains identical in enclisis and proclisis. Also, they are the same cases where the order is invariably Dat > Acc. In such cases, the clitic cluster is maintained and the order is identical pre- and post-verbally, as expected.

In conclusion, in this section we have shown that the imperatives involve a different structure than the true clitic clusters for the majority of languages under examination. However, the diversity of data found in the different languages and in their dialects make a unified account difficult to obtain. For the time being, the languages that maintain the same order of clitics follow the pattern of Romanian and Italian and are predicted by the previous analysis, but the data from SF and QF are subject to further research.

5.   Conclusion

In this paper we have approached the subject of clitic clusters in Romance, dealing particularly with the issue of ordering within the cluster and with the impenetrability of such constructions. The generalised order of the two argumental clitics across the languages we considered here is Dat>Acc. We have shown that this corresponds to the order of the arguments XP in the verbal domain of the languages under consideration, rather than relying on a pre-imposed language-specific template. We have dealt with language variation in terms of features (the 3rd person features seem to be a locus of variation among a great number of languages). We have equally attempted to eliminate the apparent problem posed by the Standard French imperatives, by showing that they have in fact a different structure and that they do not involve clusters at all.

Finally, the pronominal argument clusters seem to be structures that are best analysed as complex projections of the Shell-type (proposed in Di Sciullo 2000, 2005) that remain invariable: this predicts that whatever the order of the clitics within the cluster is in a given language, it should always be the same whether pre- or post-verbal, as is expected in the Asymmetry Theory. As for the finer-grained articulation of this complex projection hosting the clitics, it is subject to further research.

Clitics are best accounted for in an approach that relies on UG principles, while taking in consideration the conditions at the interfaces and handling language variation. Thus, morpho-syntactic predictions (the order of verbal arguments) combine with discourse-related and referentiality issues (the 3rd person features interpretation) as well as PF restrictions, accounting for the behaviour of clitics as elements whose varying form is the result of interface conditions.

Notes

* This research has been partly supported by the Social Sciences and Humanities Research Council of Canada (grant # 412-97-0016), for the project entitled "Asymmetries in Natural Languages and their Treatment by the Performance Systems", awarded to professor Anna Maria Di Sciullo, in the Department of Linguistics at the Université du Québec à Montréal (UQAM). We wish to thank Anna Maria Di Sciullo for her valuable suggestions and discussions.

1. Several works (Perlmutter 1971; Bonet 1991, 1995, among others) have also emphasised the fact that a purely syntactic account of the clitic ordering is untenable. There are morpho-phonological processes that also affect the Spell-out of the clitic sequences that need to be taken into account.

2. Note however that Romanian does not have partitive and locative clitics (as the French *en* and *y*).

3. Roberge & Vinet (1989) study also other Romance dialects where the order of the object clitics is Dat>Acc.

4. Dobrovie-Sorin (1994) considers these adverbs clitic elements, along with the negation particle and the auxiliary verbs.

5. Note that even if a strong pronoun were to be used here, i.e. 'mie' instead of 'mi', that still doesn't rescue the construction, since a clitic doubling will be required, giving rise to a cluster:

(i)   *Mie   nu mi - l   mai   dă.*
      1st-DAT not 1st-DAT 3rd-ACC again give
      'He/she does not give it to me any more.'

6. However, the verb is not the only possible phonetic host of the clitic, as there are cases where a stronger clitic (a «weak pronoun» in the typology of Cardinaletti & Starke 1999) can act as a host for another clitic (a «clitic» in the same typology). Example:

(i)   *Ti - am   spus sā   mi - l   dai.*
      2nd-DAT have told SUBJ 1st-DAT 3rd-ACC give
      'I told you to give it to me.'

7. However, Tellier (1997) gives examples of Old French, where it was possible to have an element intervening between the clitic (cluster) and the verb:

(i)   *Le bien lire vaudrait la peine.*
      Ý'It would be worthy to read it well.'

(ii) *Ne le pas lire serait dommage.*
      'It would be a pity not to read it.'   (Tellier 1997:175)

8. The main difference between Uriagereka (1995) and Terzi (1999) is that while the first considers that clitics always adjoin to the same functional projection, the second fundamentally uses two projections (F and T), according to the context (finite vs. non-finite).

9. According to Kayne's LCA, in a configuration of multiple adjunction there is no way of ordering the elements at Spell-out.

10. The double object constructions are similar to the locative constructions of the type:

(i)   *J'ai envoyé une lettre à Marie.*
      'I have sent a letter to Mary.'

(ii) *J'ai envoyé une lettre à Londres.*
      'I have sent a letter to London.'

Still, there are tests that determine the fact that these two types of constructions are submitted to different properties, but the fact remains that the indirect object can be considered a different grammatical object than the direct object.

11. Harris (1995) and Spencer (2000) refer to the clitic cluster as a «morphological unit».

12. Of course, a purely phonological explanation of this phenomenon is not excluded.

13. Parodi 1998:90

14. Cuervo assumes that when the Acc>Dat object order is realised in Spanish, the further movement of the direct object across the indirect one is motivated by the EPP features on *v*(which do not target the closer Dative DP because this already has inherent Case).

15. Kayne (1975) discusses data involving the quantifier "tous" (all):

(i) *?Je les leur ai tous toutes montrés.*
      I 3rd-pl-ACC 3rd-pl-DAT have all, MASC. all, FEM. shown, MASC.

The interpretation of the construction above is that "leur" is associated with "toutes" and "les" with "tous", hence the dative quantifier has to precede the accusative.

16. However, Bonet (1991) rejects the implication of case in the interaction of clitics within the cluster, on the basis of examples such as the following:

(i) **Cette nouvelle nous lui a fait téléphoner.*
      this news 1st-pl-DAT 3rd-DAT has made telephone
      'This news made us phone him/her.'   (Kayne 1975:297)

In this example, the ungrammaticality is not due to Case, since both arguments here are Dative.

17. However, even the author acknowledges that examples such as the ones given by Kayne (1975), here in (i), pose problems for this strategy:

(i) **Paul lui présentera moi.*
      Paul 3rd-DAT will introduce 1st-ACC
      'Paul will introduce me to him.'

18. However, an exhaustive examination of all dialects has not been done.

19. Except, of course, the dislocation constructions.

20. This remark is due to Cardinaletti (p.c.).

21. For example, Cardinaletti and Starke sustain that «clitic-doubling, left-dislocation and right-dislocation are allowed with clitic pronouns, but not with weak pronouns» (p. 281). This is not all that straightforward in Romanian, as we can see in the following examples:

(i) *Îl voi vedea pe Mihai mâine dimineată.*
      3rd-ACC will see pe Mihai tomorrow morning
      'I will see Mihai tomorrow morning.'

(ii) *Îi dădusem voie copilului să plece.*
      3rd-DAT give permission child, the SUBJ. leave
      'I have given permission to the child to leave'.

Here, the doubling takes place even with so-called "weak pronouns", which, in principle, should not participate in clitic doubling constructions. Thus, in Romanian, the clitics and the weak pronouns of Cardinaletti & Starke (1999) seem to behave syntactically similar, hence the difference is irrelevant.

22. As noted by Isac (1999).

23. Data such as (i) seems not that bad to QF natives:

(i) *Je te le donne à toi.*
     I 2nd-DAT 3rd-DAT give to you
     'I give it to you.'

References

Aissen, J. (2000). Differential object marking: iconicity vs. economy. Ms. University of California, Santa Cruz.

Alexiadou, A. & Anagnostopoulou, E. (2002). Person and animacy splits: Form hierarchies to features. Paper presented at the *25th GLOW Colloquium*, Amsterdam.

Anderson, S. (1992). *A-Morphous Morphology*. 434 p. Cambridge: Cambridge University Press.

Benveniste, E. (1966). *Problèmes de linguistique générale*. Paris: Gallimard.

Bonet, E. (1991). Morphology after syntax: Pronominal clitics in Romance. Ph.D. Dissertation, MIT.

Bonet, E. (1995). The where and how of clitic order. *Revue québecoise de linguistique, 24*, 61–81.

Bouchard, D. (2002). *Adjectives, Number and Interfaces. Why Languages Vary*. Amsterdam: Elsevier.

Bruening, B. (2001). QR obeys superiority: Frozen scope and ACD. *Linguistic Inquiry, 32*, 233–273.

Cardinaletti, A. & Starke, M. (1999). The typology of structural deficiency: A case study of the three classes of pronouns. In H. van Riemsdijk (Ed.), *Clitics in the Languages of Europe* (pp. 145–235). Berlin/New York: Mouton de Gruyter.

Cornilescu, A. (1999). The double subject construction in Romanian. Notes on the syntax of the subject. Ms. University of Bucharest.

Cuervo, M. C. (2001). The dative alternation. Talk presented at ApplFest, MIT.

Cuervo, M. C. (2002). Structural asymmetries but the same word order: The dative alternation in Spanish. In A. M. Di Sciullo (Ed.), *Asymmetry in Grammar, Vol. 1: Syntax and Semantics* (pp. 117–145). Amsterdam/Philadelphia: John Benjamins.

Demonte, V. (1995). Dative alternation in Spanish. *Probus, 7*, 5–30.

Di Sciullo, A. M. (2000). Paths in words. In *ESSLLI (European Summer School in Logic, Language and Information)* (pp. 78–94). Birmingham, UK.

Di Sciullo, A. M. (2005). *Asymmetry in Morphology*. In press. Cambridge, Mass.: MIT Press.

Dobrovie-Sorin, C. (1994). *The Syntax of Romanian: Comparative Studies in Romance*. Berlin/New York: Mouton de Gruyter.

Dobrovie-Sorin, C. (1999). Clitics across categories: The case of Romanian. In H. van Riemsdijk (Ed.), *Clitics in the Languages of Europe* (pp. 515–543). Berlin/New York: Mouton de Gruyter.

Farkas, D. & Kazazis, K. (1980). Clitic pronouns and topicality in Romanian. In *Papers from the Regional Meeting of the Chicago Linguistic Society* (pp. 88–97). Chicago: University of Chicago Press.

Fernandez, B. (1999). On split ergativity: Evidence from Basque. *MIT Working Papers in linguistics, 34,* 177–190.

Gerlach, B. (1998). Optimale Klitikesequenzen. *Arbeiten des Sonderforsxhungsbereichs* 282 "*Théorie des Lexi-kons*" No. 103, Universitat Dusseldorf. – cited in Parodi (1998).

Gerlach, B. & Grijzenhout, J. (2000). Clitics from different perspectives. In B. Gerlach & J. Grijzenhout (Eds.), *Clitics in Phonology, Morphology and Syntax* (pp. 1–31). Amsterdam/Philadelphia: John Benjamins.

Grimshaw, J. (1999). Optimal clitic positions and the lexicon in Romance clitic systems. Ms. Rutgers University.

Hale, K. & Storto, L. (1996). Agreement and spurious antipassives. Ms. MIT.

Harris, J. (1995). The morphology of Spanish clitics. In H. Campos (Ed.), *Evolution and Revolution in Linguistic Theory* (pp. 168–197). Washington, D.C.: Georgetown University Press.

Isac, D. (1999). Clitics as operators. Ms. UQAM

Kayne, R. (1994). *The Antisymmetry of Syntax.* Cambridge, Mass.: MIT Press.

Kayne, R. (1975). *French Syntax. The Transformational Cycle.* Cambridge, Mass.: MIT Press.

Klavans, J. (1985). The independence of syntax and phonology and cliticization. *Language, 61,* 95–120.

Larson, R. (1988). On the double object construction. *Linguistic Inquiry, 19,* 335–391.

Manzini, M. R. & Savoia, L. M. (1999). The syntax of middle-reflexive and object clitics: A case of parametrization in arberesh dialects. In M. Mandalà (Ed.), *Studi in onore di Luigi Marlekaj* (pp. 283–328). Bari: Adriatica.

Morin, Y-C. (1979). More remarks on French clitic order. *Linguistic Analysis, 5,* 293–312.

Parodi, T. (1998). Aspects of clitic doubling and clitic clusters in Spanish In R. Fabri, A. Ortmann & T. Parodi (Eds.), *Models of Inflection* (pp. 85–102). Tübingen: Niemeyer.

Pylkkänen, L. (2000). What applicative heads apply to. In M. Minnick, A. Williams & E. Kaiser (Eds.), *Proceedings of the 24th Annual Penn Linguistics Colloquium, Upenn Working Papers in Linguistics,* Vol. 7.1.

Perlmutter. D. (1970). Surface structure constraints in syntax. *Linguistic Inquiry, 1,* 187–255.

Perlmutter, D. (1971). *Deep and Surface Structure Constraints in Syntax.* New York: Holt, Reinhart and Winston.

Roberts, T. (2000). Clitics and agreement. Ph.D. Dissertation. MIT.

Roberge, Y. & Vinet, M.-T. (1989). *La variation dialectale en grammaire universelle.* Montréal: Les presses de l'Université de Montréal.

Sharma, D. (2001). Kashmiri case clitics and person hierarchy effects. In P. Sells (Ed.), *Formal and Empirical Issues in Optimality Theoretic Syntax* (pp. 225–256). CSLI Publications.

Silverstein, M. (1976). Hierarchy of features and ergativity. In R. M. W. Dixon (Ed.), *Grammatical Categories in Australian Languages* (pp. 112–172). New Jersey: Humanities Press.

Speas, P. & Tenny, C. (2002). Configurational properties of point of view roles. In A. M. Di Sciullo (Ed.), *Asymmetry in Grammar, Vol. 1: Syntax and Semantics* (pp. 315–345). Amsterdam/Philadelphia: John Benjamins.

Spencer, A. (2000). Verbal clitics in Bulgarian: A paradigm function approach. In B. Gerlach & J. Grijzenhout (Eds.), *Clitics in Phonology, Morphology and Syntax* (pp. 355–387). Amsterdam/Philadelphia: John Benjamins.

Sportiche, D. (1992). Clitic constructions. Ms. UCLA

Sportiche, D. (1999). *Partitions and Atoms of Clause Structure.* London/New York: Routledge.

Tellier, C. (1997). *Éléments de syntaxe du français. Méthodes d'analyse en grammaire générative.* Montréal: Les presses de l'Université de Montréal.

Terzi, A. (1999). Clitic combination, their hosts and their ordering. *Natural Language and Linguistic Theory, 17,* 85–121.

Uriagereka, J. (1995). Aspects of the syntax of clitic placement in Western Romance. *Linguistic Inquiry, 26,* 79–123.

Wanner, D. (1987). *The Development of Romance Clitic Pronouns. From Latin to Old Romance.* Berlin/New York/Amsterdam: Mouton de Gruyter.

Zwicky, A. (1977). *On Clitics.* Bloomington: Indiana University Linguistics Club.

On the question of (non)-agreement in the uses of Russian imperatives*

Edit Jakab
Université du Québec à Montréal

This study provides a possible explanation for agreement or lack thereof in the various uses of Russian imperatives: ordinary imperatives and imperatives functioning as conditionals as well as imperatives in contrastive constructions. The difference will be traced back to configurational asymmetries. The case of the subject of such imperatives will be examined as well. Since case is checked under AGREE, and because this relation is missing between the subject and the imperative in the conditional and contrastive constructions, the case of the subject is predicted to be default; this prediction will be shown to be realized.

1. Introduction

1.1 The goals

The central aim of this paper is to account for the distinct agreement features found in the uses of imperatives in Russian: (1) ordinary imperatives, (2) counterfactual conditional-type imperatives and (3) contrastive imperatives. (3) can be divided into two subtypes: one subtype expresses obligation, as in (3a), and the other a sudden, unexpected action with respect to the state described in its conjoined clause, as in (3b).

Regular imperative:

(1) a. *Zakroj   okno!*   b. *Zakroj-te   okno!*
        close-IMP2SG window-ACC   close-IMP2PL window-ACC
        'Close the window.' [familiar]   'Close the window.' [formal]

Conditional-type imperative:

(2) *Znaj   ja   ego xarakter,   ja by   ne   pytalsja*
    know-IMP2SG I-NOM his character-ACC I   MOD NEG tried
    emu   vozražat'.
    he-DAT object-INF
    'Had I known his character, I would not have tried to object to him.'
                                                    (Barnetová et al. 1979:197)

Contrastive imperative:

(3) a. *On vsje vremja igrajet v karty s   druz'jami, a   ja*
       he all time   plays in cards with friends   but I-NOM
       rabotaju   na kuxne.
       work-IMP2SG on kitchen
       'He plays cards all the time with his friends, and I have to work in the
       kitchen.'   (Townsend 1970:257)
    b. *Prožili oni god duša v dušu, a   na drugoj-to god ona*
       lived   they year soul in soul but on second   year she-NOM
       voz'mi   da i   pomri.
       take-IMP2SG PRT and die-IMP2SG
       'They lived for a year in full happiness, and then, in the second year,
       she takes it into her head and dies.'

The salient difference between the imperative in (1) and in (2)–(3) is that in (1)
there is agreement between the verb and its clause-mate subject, whereas in (2)–
(3), the verb does not manifest any agreement with its subject. The main semantic
characteristic of counterfactual conditional-type (2) and contrastive imperatives
(3) is that they do not exhibit the typical illocutionary forces of imperatives (such
as command, instruction, request, warning, etc.), but rather, they convey a broader
range of meanings: (2) expresses the counterfactual conditional, and (3) has some
kind of contrastive interpretation (for a semantic analysis of these data see Jakab
2003a; in press).

Morphosyntactically, the examples in (2)–(3) differ from the regular uses of
imperatives in (1) in the following three ways: (i) The imperative verb form contains no distinctions of grammatical person or number, i.e., it is always the second
person singular. (ii) This unchangeable imperative verb form may be applied to a
subject in any of the three persons in both singular and plural. Consequently, there
is no agreement between the imperative verb and the subject of the clause. (iii) The
subject of the imperative must be overt, and, in (2), it must follow the imperative
verb whereas in (3) it must precede it.

Another goal is to show that Russian conjoined imperatives like (4a) and their English counterparts (translation of (4a)) are to be considered imperatives despite their partial conditional interpretation, whereas the Russian imperatives in (4b–b') are true conditionals. It is interesting to note that while a construction such as (4a) can be said to be a part of Universal Grammar (it exists in numerous languages), the structures in (4b–b'), which superficially appear to be very similar, are found only in Russian. It is, therefore, important to investigate this unique construction and explain the salient differences. Another reason why this phenomenon is essential to be examined is its relevance to one of the external systems, namely, its connection to semantics. As mentioned, these "noncanonical" uses of imperatives are not as unusual as they first appear: it is crosslinguistically quite common for imperatives to convey a conditional meaning. Despite this conditional interpretation (examples such as (4a)), however, they cannot be considered true conditionals. As Clark (1993) explains, the interpretation process of sentences such as (4a) gives the whole proposition (expressed by the imperative clause and indicative clause together) a form of conditionality; however, the imperative clause is an ordinary imperative and the declarative clause is an ordinary declarative. The strong tendency to attribute a conditional interpretation to such sentences derives from the fact that they refer to potential or possible worlds, a feature they share with real conditional sentences (cf. Jakab 2003a).

"Defective" conditional-type imperative (= regular imperative):

(4) a. *Skaži   komu-nibud' xot' slovo ob   ètom i   ja nikogda*
     say-imp3sg somebody   even word about this   and I   never
     tebja ne   prošču.
     you NEG will   forgive
     'Say one word to anyone about this, and I'll never forgive you.'

Conditional-type imperative:

(4) b. *Skaži   ty   komu-nibud' xot' slovo ob   ètom, ja*
     say-IMP2SG you-NOM somebody   even word about this   I
     nikogda by   tebja ne   prostil.
     never   COND you   NEG forgave
     'If you said one word to anyone about this, I would never forgive you.'

    b'. *Skaži   on   komu-nibud' xot' slovo ob   ètom, ja*
     say-IMP2SG he-NOM somebody   even word about this   I
     nikogda by   ego ne   prostil.
     never   COND him   NEG forgave
     'If he said one word to anyone about this, I would never forgive him.'

1.2 Proposal

It will be argued that the divergence in the agreement properties of the imperative verb can be derived from precisely determined configurational asymmetries (cf. Di Sciullo 2005). In particular, it will be shown to follow from the presence versus the absence of AgrP in the derivation and the position (movement vs. non-movement) of the subject. Thus, the derivation of regular imperatives contains an AgrP, which is missing from the derivation of non-canonical imperatives. Consequently, while the subject of regular imperatives has a case-feature, which is checked in Spec-AgrSP, the subject of counterfactual conditional-type and contrastive imperatives is caseless or it receives default case.

My arguments will be based on the following assumptions. Since the entire FinP is absent in the CP-field, in both constructions in (2)–(3): there is no TP, (ii) AgrSP is missing since the subject does not agree with the imperative verb which lacks phi-features, and (iii) the imperative moves to C to check its force features in accord with the general theory of imperatives (Rivero 1994; Zanuttini 1997; or Platzack & Rosengren 1998).

The difference, however, is that while C in (2) has a [cond] feature (i.e., the imperative verb functions like the conditional complementizer *esli* 'if', and, thus, it raises to C, which has the feature specification [cond]), C in (3) has a more general [mod] feature and it is able to attract the imperatives in (3), which also express some kind of modal meaning, such as obligation, for example. As we saw, the verbs in (2)–(3) bear imperative morphology, nevertheless they do not receive the reading commonly attributed to imperatives. In other words, imperative morphology in the present case is a necessary but not sufficient condition to produce imperative interpretation.

1.3 Organization

In Section 2, I compare Russian conditional-type imperatives, such as (4b–b′) with their "defective" conditional counterparts, such as (4a), and I show that the latter must be regarded as regular imperatives like (1) and not as imperatives like (2) that express true conditionals. Section 3 further elucidates the differences between the two non-canonical Russian imperatives, i.e., conditional-type imperatives (2) and contrastive imperatives (3): it explains the differences in their subject positions as they relate to the presence or absence of Agr and AGREE (cf. Chomsky 1998) in their derivation. Also, a similar analysis is given for root infinitives, a parallel construction to contrastive imperatives. A conclusion is provided in Section 4.

2.   Imperatives as "Defective" vs. full conditionals

2.1 Asymmetry in the appearance of the subject

There is a universal tendency for the subject not to be overt in imperative sentences. In many languages, like in Russian (cf. (1)), the verb form expresses the person and number of the subject, which is most often the second person singular or plural. The most striking difference between the Russian imperative sentences in (4b–b′), which express a conditional meaning, and the one in (4a) involves the presence or absence of an overt subject. The examples in (4b–b′) contain an overt subject, whereas the one in (4a) does not. The lack of an overt subject makes (4b–b′) more imperative-like than the examples in (4a), in which the subject is present. The type of Russian imperative that has a partial conditional interpretation, such as (4b–b′), exists in English as well (see Jakab 2003a for a detailed analysis).

For further illustration of the different syntactic properties of (4a) and (4b–b′), which act like full conditionals, consider the minimal pairs in (5)–(6) below. Besides a set of a- and b-examples, I include a set of b′-examples to illustrate that the subject can be any person in both singular and plural. The representation of the a-sentences is given in (7), and that of the b-sentences is seen in (8).

(5) a. *Mojsja   každyj den′ i   tvoja koža stanet   suxoj.*
         wash-IMP2SG every day and your skin will get dry
         'Wash yourself every day, and you skin will get dry.'

     b. *Mojsja   ty   každyj den′, tvoja koža stala   by*
         wash-IMP2SG you-NOM every day   your skin became COND
         suxoj.
         dry
         'If you washed yourself every day, your skin would become dry.'

     b′. *Mojsja   ja   každyj den′, moja koža stala   by*
          wash-IMP2SG I-NOM every day   my   skin became COND
          suxoj.
          dry
          'If I washed myself every day, my skin would become dry.'

(6) a. *Podojdi   bliže   i   ja tebja zastrelju.*
         come-IMP2SG closer and I   you   will shoot
         'Come closer and I'll shoot you.'

     b. *Podojdi   ty   bliže, ja by   tebja zastrelila.*
         come-IMP2SG you-NOM closer I   COND you   shot
         'If you came closer, I would shoot you.'

     b′. *Podojdi   oni   bliže, ja by   ix   zastrelila.*
          come-imp3pl they-NOM closer I   COND them shot
          'If they came closer, I would shoot them.'

(7)   (8)

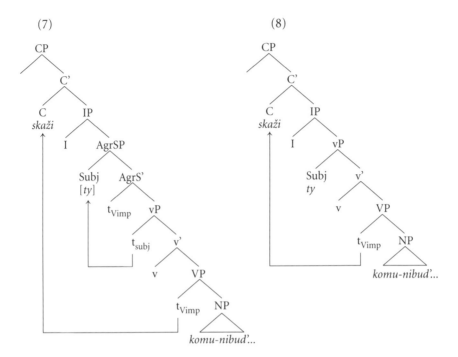

As the minimal pairs in (4)–(6) show, both a-examples and b-examples have a conditional interpretation. There are, however, several differences between them. (i) While the a-examples cannot have an overt subject, the b-examples are ungrammatical without an overt subject. (ii) The a-examples allow only second person subjects, whereas the b-examples can have a subject in any person (see b'-examples). (iii) While the subject in the a-examples agrees with the imperative verb (i.e., they contain an AgrSP), the subject in the b-examples does not (they lack an AgrSP). (iv) The subject in the a-examples has case, which is checked in Spec-AgrSP, whereas the subject of the b-examples has default case which does not need to be checked, or it is caseless since there is no position, which could attract it. (v) The a-examples are coordinated constructions, while the b-examples are subordinate sentences. (vi) The conjoined clause of the imperative in the a-examples does not contain a modal, whereas the superordinate clause in the b-examples must contain the modal particle *by*. These different syntactic properties suggest that the a-examples are more imperative-like, while the b-examples are more conditional-like.

According to the general theory of imperatives (Rivero 1994; Zanuttini 1997; or Platzack & Rosengren 1998), the imperative verb raises to C since it contains an operator that encodes illocutionary force. In other words, C has the illocutionary force feature [imp] that attracts the imperative verb. Platzack & Rosengren (1998), following Rizzi (1995), argue for a split-CP domain consisting of two parts. One is the "outward facing" ForceP, the highest projection of C, which stores the information on the type of the clause (whether it is indicative, interrogative or imperative). The other part is the "inward facing" FinP, which contains TP. Platzack and Rosengren argue that imperative clauses lack FinP, and hence also tense, in contrast with the other sentence types (indicatives and interrogatives). The lack of FinP accounts for the unique properties of the imperative's subject (which they call ImpNP). Although this ImpNP is usually absent, it always indicates the addressee (the covert ImpNP has the same properties as an overt second person pronoun). The lack of FinP, however, does not prevent the imperative verb from showing agreement morphology (cf. (1)). The relation regarding φ-features between the imperative verb and its subject (ImpNP) is expressed as a Spec-head relation in AgrSP, as (7) shows.

Proposal: in both a- and b-sentences in (4)–(6), too, the imperative verb moves to C, just like in regular imperative clauses. The difference between them is that while the a-sentences contain an AgrSP, thus making possible the agreement relation between the imperative and its subject, the b-sentences lack an AgrSP. The absence of AgrSP, shown in (8), accounts for the above outlined properties of conditional imperatives (i.e., the imperative never agrees with its obligatorily overt subject). Consequently, since there is no AgrSP (and no TP), the subject remains in its base-generated position, i.e., Spec-vP, where it receives its theta-role. It does not need to move because it does not need to check its features. Although it has φ-features, as seen in its semantic interpretation, they do not need to be checked since the φ-features of nominal elements are interpretable. Moreover, the imperative verb has no φ-features (as we saw, it never agrees with the subject), therefore no φ-feature checking needs to take place. On the other hand, the imperative verb of the a-sentences have φ-features which are properly checked since verbal φ-features are uninterpretable.

Given that the subject receives default case, no case-feature needs to be checked either and the subject is allowed to stay in situ in its base-generated position. Another option is to regard the subject as caseless. That the subject of imperatives lacks case is not a new idea. Platzack and Rosengren (p. 190) argue that since nominative case is checked in TP and since imperatives lack this projection, it is likely that imperative subject NPs lack case. Moreover, the subject of the imperative, when overt, never shows any case distinctions. The other option that they suggest is that the subject of imperatives checks its case in Spec-AgrSP. I adopt the latter suggestion since it emphasizes the difference between regular and conditional-type imperatives. In the conditional-type imperatives (see the b-examples of (4)–(6)), the subject, despite being always overt, does not ever agree with the imperative verb in either person or number, and it never shows case distinctions. Thus, while the subject of regular imperatives has a case-feature, which is checked in Spec-AgrSP (recall that the subject, covert or overt, always agrees with the second person imperative verb), the subject of conditional-type imperatives is caseless or it receives default case.

2.2 Evidence: Differences in embedding abilities

To provide additional support for the claim that the a-sentences of (4)–(6) are imperatives and that the b-sentences are conditionals, I shall present evidence from the restrictions on the embedding abilities of imperatives. It is a cross-linguistically well-established fact that imperative clauses cannot be syntactically embedded (cf. Jakab 2003a). This fact holds also for the canonical Russian imperatives such as (1), as (9) illustrates. Instead of the imperatives, languages tend to use infinitives or subjunctives in clauses embedded under directive verbs (verbs of volition and/or command) (for an extended discussion see Jakab 2003a).

> (9) *Ja prošu tebja, čto otkroj   okno.
>   I   ask   you   that open-IMP2SG window

However, when the imperative is used in a conditional sense (see (4)–(6)), we can find a contrast in the imperative's abilities to be embedded. Illustrated in (10)–(12) below, the a-examples of (4)–(6) behave like regular imperative clauses, given that they cannot be embedded. On the other hand, it is possible to embed the b-sentences. This fact is an additional piece of evidence for the claim that they are not imperatives, but rather conditionals. Notice, however, that although the b-sentences of (4)–(6) (shown in (10)–(12)) can be embedded, they cannot be embedded with a complementizer (čto 'that'). This further supports the claim that the imperative verb in the b-sentences behaves like a complementizer (it moves to C), and, as such, it does not tolerate the presence of another complementizer in the same position in the clause.

> (10) a. *Ja dumaju, skaži   komu-nibud' xot' slovo ob   ètom
>   I   think   say-IMP2SG somebody   even word about this
>   i   ja nikogda tebja ne   prošču.
>   and I never   you NEG will-forgive
>   b. Ja dumaju, (*čto) skaži   ty   komu-nibud' xot' slovo
>   I   think   that say-IMP2SG you-NOM   somebody   even word
>   ob   ètom, ja nikogda by   tebja ne   prostil.
>   about this I never   COND you   NEG forgave
>   'I think (*that) if you said one word to anyone about this, I would never forgive you.'

(11) a. *Ja dumaju, mojsja   každyj den' i   tvoja koža stanet*
     I think   wash-IMP2SG every day and your skin will get
     suxoj.
     dry

   b. *Ja dumaju, (*čto) mojsja   ty   každyj den', tvoja*
     I think   that   wash-IMP2SG you-NOM every day your
     koža stala   by   suxoj.
     skin became COND dry
     'I think (*that) if you washed yourself every day, your skin would become dry.'

(12) a. *Ja dumaju, podojdi   bliže   i   ja tebja zastrelju.*
     I think   come-IMP2SG closer and I you   will shoot

   b. *Ja dumaju, (*čto) podojdi   ty   bliže, ja by   tebja*
     I think   that   come-IMP2SG you-NOM closer I   COND you
     zastrelila.
     shot
     'I think (*that) if you came closer, I would shoot you.'

To further explain the difference in the embedding abilities of the a- and b-sentences in (4)–(6), illustrated in (10)–(12), I argue that it must be connected to the different modality that they express. It is a well-known fact that when we embed any type of sentence (indicative, interrogative or imperative), it loses its ability to express illocutionary force (cf. Jakab 2003a). Notice, however, that indicatives and interrogatives can be embedded, albeit they lose their illocutionary force, as in (13) and (14).

(13)   Mary is rich. → John believes that Mary is rich.

(14)   Is Mary rich? → John doesn't know whether Mary is rich.

On the other hand, imperatives simply cannot be embedded. I argue that this is the case because in imperatives, C contains the feature [imp] since CP accommodates an operator that encodes directive force (cf. Zanuttini 1997; Rivero 1994; Rivero & Terzi 1995; Han 1999). Thus the imperative verb, which inherently has the feature [imp], is attracted to C to check this feature. This theory would predict that both the a- and the b-examples in (4)–(6) should be disallowed from being embedded since the imperative verb occupies the C position in both. However, (10)–(12) show that only the a-examples are not allowed to embed, while the b-examples can be embedded. I suggest that, although the imperative occupies C in the b-examples in (4)–(6) as well, it is in this position for a different reason than the imperative in the a-examples. I propose that C of the imperative clauses in the b-examples has a different feature specification than C in the a-examples. C of the conditional-type imperatives (b-examples) contains a [cond] feature, and not an [imp] feature. Therefore the imperative verb is attracted to C to check its [cond] feature. That the imperative verb in the b-sentences contains a [cond] feature is supported by the fact that it behaves like the conditional complementizer *esli* 'if' since it triggers the presence of a conditional modal particle (*by*) in the superordinate clause. Notice that the imperative verb in the a-sentences does not trigger a conditional modal in its conjoined clause. The complementizer-like behavior of the imperative verb in the b-sentences becomes more obvious if we look at a conditional-type imperative such as (4b), repeated as (15) and its paraphrase in (16).

(15) *Skaži   ty   komu-nibud' xot' slovo ob   ètom, ja*
      say-IMP2SG you-NOM   somebody   even word about this   I
      nikogda by   tebja ne   prostil.
      never   COND you   NEG forgave
      'If you said one word to anyone about this, I would never forgive you.'

(16) *Esli ty   skazal by   komu-nibud' xot' slovo ob   ètom, ja*
      if   you   said COND somebody   even word about this   I
      nikogda by   tebja ne   prostil.
      never   COND you   NEG forgave
      'If you said one word to anyone about this, I would never forgive you.'

The fact that conditionals can be freely embedded (see the embedded version of (16) in (17)) explains why the b-examples of (4)–(6) can also be embedded. Notice that (16) can be embedded only without the complementizer *čto* 'that' just like the imperative in the b-sentences.

(17) *Ja dumaju, (*čto) esli ty   skazal by   komu-nibud' xot' slovo*
      I   tink-1sg (*that) if   you   said COND somebody   even word
      ob   ètom, ja nikogda by   tebja ne   prostil.
      about this   I never   COND you   NEG forgave
      'I think if you said one word to anyone about this, I would never forgive you.'

3.   Differences in the features of Russian imperatives

3.1 Difference in the feature specification of C

This section examines the other type of the non-canonical Russian imperatives, i.e., contrastive imperatives, given in (3), repeated as (18).

(18)   a.   *On   vsje   vremja   igrajet   v   karty   s   druz'jami,   a   ja*
        he   all   time   plays   in   cards   with   friends   but   I-NOM
        rabotaju   na   kuxne.
        work-IMP2SG   on   kitchen
        'He plays cards all the time with his friends, and I have to work in the
        kitchen.'   (Townsend 1970: 257)

    b.   *Prožili   oni   god   duša   v   dušu,   a   na   drugoj-to   god   ona*
        lived   they   year   soul   in   soul   but   on   second   year   she-NOM
        voz'mi   da   i   pomri.
        take-IMP2SG   PRT   and   die-IMP2SG
        'They lived for a year in full happiness, and then, in the second year,
        she takes it into her head and dies.'

We saw in the *Introduction* that contrastive imperatives divide into two groups: one
usually expresses an unpleasant obligation that is in contrast with the content of
the first clause, as in (18a). The other expresses a sudden action or abrupt behavior
with respect to the previous clause, as in (18b). Despite this difference in meaning
between the two groups of examples, I argue that they can be analyzed in the same
way syntactically. Both examples in (18) lack agreement between the nominative
subject NP and the following imperative verb since the imperative verb has no φ-
features. In other words, in these contrastive imperative constructions, the subject,
despite being always overt, does not ever agree with the imperative verb in either
person or number, and it never shows case distinctions. It will be thus argued that
while the subject of regular imperatives has a case-feature, which is checked in
Spec-AgrSP, the subject of contrastive imperatives is caseless or it receives default
case,[1] just like in the above discussed conditional-type imperatives. I propose that
the imperative verb raises to C in (18) similar to the conditional-type imperatives
like (2). The difference is that while C in (2) has a [cond] feature, C in (18) has a
[mod] feature that attracts the imperatives in (18), which also express some kind
of modal meaning.

3.2 Asymmetry in the position of the subject

We saw in the previous section that the subject of (2), which always follows the
imperative, stays in situ since it has no feature that needs to be checked (i.e., its
φ-features are interpretable and that its default case-feature needs no checking).
Conversely, the subject of (18), which comes immediately after the contrastive conjunction *a* 'but; on the other hand', obligatorily precedes the imperative verb. I
propose that the subject of (2), which always follows the imperative, stays in situ
since it has no feature that needs to be checked (i.e., its φ-features are interpretable
and that its default case-feature needs no checking). Conversely, the subject of (18),

which comes immediately after the contrastive conjunction *a* 'but; on the other hand', obligatorily precedes the imperative verb. Since the subject in (18) receives default case or no case (notice also that all the possible nominative case checking positions (Spec-TP and Spec-AgrSP) are missing), the subject in (18) moves only for one reason: it needs to be in a topic position in which it receives contrastive stress. The subject's clause-initial position also suggests that it moves to a topic position. The subject and the imperative verb end up in a Spec-head agreement re-lation in C; nevertheless, it does not follow from this relation that the subject gets case-marked since there is no Agr element in I (cf. Chomsky 1986:24). Moreover, case is checked under AGREE; since this relation is absent, there can be no case assignment to the subject (cf. Chomsky 1998). This prediction is borne out in the light of these Russian data.

The structure of the imperative clause in (18a) is given in (19).

(19)

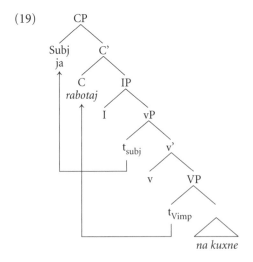

The representation in (19) thus shows that, besides the subject's location, the im-peratives in (18) have the same properties as the conditional-type imperatives like (2) in all other respects. That is, they lack TP (cf. Platzack & Rosengren 1998), i.e., the imperative verb never indicates tense distinctions. Moreover, they do not con-tain AgrSP, which accounts for the lack of agreement between the imperative and the subject. Since all the possible nominative case checking positions (Spec-TP and Spec-AgrSP) are missing, the subject of contrastive imperatives has no position where it could check its case features (it is also possible that the subject receives default case-marking which is not subject to case-feature checking). On the other hand, the subject of regular imperatives checks its case and agreement features in Spec-AgrSP.

3.3 A Similar non-agreeing construction: Root infinitives

There is a construction in Russian that exhibits similar properties with those of contrastive imperatives, namely the so called root infinitives such as (20). Both root infinitives and contrastive imperatives show lack of agreement between the obligatorily clause-initial nominative subject and the main predicate. Below, it will be shown how these two constructions can be accounted for in the same way.

> (20) *Ljudi   pirovat', a   my   gorevat'.*
>   people-NOM feast-INF but we-NOM grieve-INF
>   'People are off to feast, but we have to grieve.' (Greenberg 1991:353)

As (20) shows, root infinitives in Russian contain an infinitive, which is not a complement but the main predicate of the clause, and a nominative NP, which performs the action indicated by the infinitive. Besides the similarities mentioned above, there is one more: the verb in both constructions (18) and (20) is un-tensed: the infinitive[2] and the imperative predicates can occur only in the present tense. Consequently, it is essential to discuss the two constructions (root infinitives and contrastive imperatives) together, and optimally, to provide a similar explanation for both.

Departing from Greenberg's proposal for root infinitives (which will be outlined below), I argue that the topic position is not an adjoined CP projection, but the Spec of CP. In contrast with Greenberg, I suggest that the subject is not base-generated in the adjoined topic position since it cannot get its theta role there. Instead, I propose that the subject raises to Spec-CP from its base-generated Spec-vP position, where it can receive its theta role.

3.3.1   *Greenberg's (1991) analysis of root infinitives*
Greenberg suggests that the nominative NP in (20) is base-generated in a topic position, which he identifies as the Spec of the CP that is outside (i.e., adjoined to) the CP containing the infinitive, as in (21).

(21)

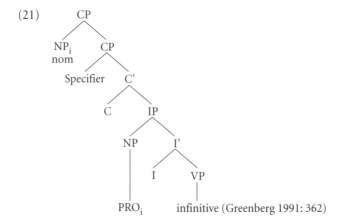

infinitive (Greenberg 1991: 362)

He argues that the nominative NP cannot move from the original subject position (Spec-IP in his framework) to Spec-CP because there is no subject-verb agreement in root infinitives, and because this nominative NP has a fixed clause-initial position. He explains the nominative case of the topicalized NP by a predication relation between the topic position and the clause containing PRO (given that (20) is not a control construction, the topic cannot control PRO). He suggests that nominative is a "Configurational Case", considered by him as a kind of default case,[3] which is automatically assigned to the position sister to CP (i.e., where the nominative NP is located). Given that this NP is coindexed with PRO, which is caseless, it receives the Configurational Case (i.e., nominative case) by default.

3.3.2   A new analysis of root infinitives

While I agree with Greenberg's analysis in placing the subject in a topic position given its permanent clause-initial location and its semantics, I propose a mechanism that diverges from his in the following respects. First, the subject cannot be base-generated in an adjoined position since it has to get its theta role from the verb. Therefore, I propose that the subject is base-generated in Spec-vP (where it receives its theta role), and it subsequently moves to Spec-CP. Second, if the topic position is an adjoined position in which the nominative NP is base-generated, there has to be some kind of a null element in the subject position to account for the case of the nominative NP. Greenberg indeed posits PRO in the subject position. It is, however, hard to justify the existence of PRO in non-control constructions such as root infinitives. Greenberg's configuration-based explanation for the assignment of nominative case seems stipulated since the indexing mechanism between the topicalized nominative NP and PRO is not clear. Moreover, if we posit PRO as the subject of infinitives in a clause without agreement (a description that fits root infinitives), we would expect the subject to appear in the dative case (cf. Babby 1998;

Moore & Perlmutter 1999, 2000). However, the subject in root infinitives can never be dative, as (22)–(23) show.[4]

(22)   *Princessa   xoxotat'.*
       princess-NOM laugh-INF
       'The princess started to laugh.'

(23)   *Ty   smejat'sja nado mnoj?*
       you-NOM laugh-INF above me
       'You dare to laugh at me?' (Greenberg 1991:353)

Therefore, I propose that in Russian root infinitives such as (22)–(23), the subject bears no case features similar to the subject of conditional and contrastive imperatives. It is not a stipulation to suggest that root infinitives lack a TP projection (the infinitive in (20) is "tenseless" in Avrutin's terms) because the infinitive does not express any tense distinction (see Fn. 2). There is no AgrSP in (20) either because the infinitive does not agree with the subject. Since the two potential nominative case checking positions, Spec-TP and Spec-AgrSP, are missing, the subject can be caseless or can receive the default nominative case in morphology (we saw that it cannot be dative, as would be expected with an infinitive predicate). Because the subject has no other features that need to be checked (the φ-features of the subject, being a nominal element, are interpretable and thus they do not need to be checked), it moves to the topic position only to account for the word order and meaning.[5] The infinitive, on the other hand, remains in situ because the derivation contains no element (lexical or functional) that could attract it. See the derivation of (20) in (24). (For more pieces of evidence cf. Jakab 2003b).

(24)

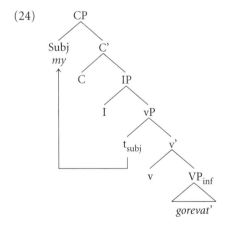

4. Conclusion

In this study I have analyzed conditional-type imperative and contrastive imperative constructions which represent instances in which the Russian imperative obtains an interpretation other than its typical illocutionary force. In contrast with regular imperatives, these non-canonical imperatives have no AgrSP, which accounts for the lack of agreement between the subject and the imperative. Following Platzack & Rosengren (1998), it was argued that imperatives do not contain a TP projection since they never show tense distinctions. I proposed that while the subject of canonical imperatives has case, which is checked in Spec-AgrSP, the subject of non-canonical imperatives is caseless or receives default case-marking (which is not subject to case-feature checking) since there is no projection which would be able to attract it (both potential nominative case checking positions, Spec-TP and Spec-AgrSP, are missing). Moreover, it was shown that since the φ-features of the subject, being a nominal element, are interpretable, they do not need to be checked.

Also, a unified analysis was given for contrastive imperatives and root infinitives that exhibit similar structural and semantic properties.

Notes

* This research has been partly supported by the Social Sciences and Humanities Research Council of Canada (grant # 412-97-0016), for the project entitled "Asymmetries in Natural Languages and their Treatment by the Performance Systems", awarded to professor Anna Maria Di Sciullo, in the Department of Linguistics at the Université du Québec à Montréal (UQAM).

1. There is independent evidence for syntactic caselessness in Russian, namely, in Russian bare copular sentences such as the one in (i).

(i) *Čexov   byl   pisatel'.*
     Chekhov-NOM was   writer-NOM
     'Chekhov was a writer.' (Pereltsvaig 2001: 1)

Following the hypothesis that only nominals that are arguments need to be case-marked, she argues that in a sentence like (i), the two nominative-marked noun phrases are in fact to be considered caseless because neither the pre-copular nor the post-copular phrase is an argument, given that they are not selected by a lexical head (they are DPs). Since they do not need case, they appear as morphological nominatives (ninative is the default or unmarked case in Russian) (cf. Chapter 4 of Pereltsvaig 2001).

2. Greenberg (1991) shows that the infinitive cannot occur with a copula in root infinitives, as in (ii).

(i) *Princessa   xoxotat'.*
    princess-NOM laugh-INF
    'The princess started to laugh.'

(ii) *Princessa *byla/*bylo/*budet xoxotat'.*

On the other hand, M&P (1999) argue that infinitives are always tenseless. They attribute the occurrence of the copula in sentences like (ii) to its "temporal particle" (i.e., non-verbal) status, which leads them to conclude that infinitives are tenseless (see M&P 1999) for an exhaustive discussion). While it is an attractive proposal, sentences like (ii) nevertheless contain an element (be it a copula or a temporal particle) that indicates tense. Root infinitives, however, can never occur with a tense-bearing element, as (i) demonstrates.

(ii) *Gruzovikam bylo/byvalo/budet   ne   proexat'.*
    trucks-DAT   wasN/used-toN/will NEG ride-through-INF
    'The trucks couldn't/used not to be able to/won't be able to get through.'
    (Moore & Perlmutter 1999:178)

3. "Configurational Case is the weakest form of case marking and imposes case only when no other method has been used during a sentence's derivation." (Greenberg 1991:363)

4. In the next section I further discuss the reasons why root infinitives and regular infinitives differ with respect to their subject's case.

5. Note that Spec-CP is an A-bar position, and as such, it cannot check case and φ-features on the nominal, exactly what is expected since the nominal does not need these features to be checked (cf. recursive CP-structures of Chomsky 2001).

References

Babby, L. H. (1998). Subject control as direct predication: Evidence from Russian. In Ž. Bošković, S. Franks & W. Snyder (Eds.), *Annual Workshop on Formal Approaches to Slavic Linguistics. The Connecticut Meeting 1997* (pp. 17–37). Ann Arbor, Mich.: Michigan Slavic Publications.

Barnetová et al. (1979). *Russkaja grammatika I* [Russian Grammar]. Prague: Academia.

Chomsky, N. (1986). *Barriers*. Cambridge, Mass.: MIT Press.

Chomsky, N. (1998). Minimalist inquiries: The framework. Ms. MIT.

Chomsky, N. (2001). Derivation by phase. In M. Kenstowicz (Ed.), *Ken Hale: A Life in Language* (pp. 1–52). Cambridge, Mass.: MIT Press.

Di Sciullo, A. M. (2005). *Asymmetry in Morphology*. In press. Cambridge, Mass.: MIT Press.

Greenberg, G. (1991). Analyzing Russian's actor-INFinitive construction. *Slavic and East European Journal, 35* (3), 352–367.

Han, C-H. (1999). The structure and interpretation of imperatives: mood and force in Universal Grammar. Doctoral dissertation. University of Pennsylvania.

Jakab, E. (2003a). The conditional expressed by Russian and English imperatives. In C. Beyssade, O. Bonami, P.C. Hofherr & F. Corblin (Eds.), *Empirical Issues in Formal Syntax and Semantics, 4* (pp. 275–290). Paris: Presses de l'Université de Paris-Sorbonne.

Jakab, E. (2003b). A unified analysis for Russian contrastive imperatives and root infinitives. In W. Browne, J-Y. Kim, B. Partee, & R. Rothstein (Eds.), *Annual Workshop on Formal Approaches to Slavic Linguistics: The Amherst Meeting 2002* (pp. 275–295). Ann Arbor: Michigan Slavic Publications.

Jakab, E. (forthcoming). Noncanonical uses of Russian imperatives. *Journal of Slavic Linguistics*. Bloomington, Indiana.

Moore, J. & Perlmutter, D. (1999). Case, agreement, and temporal particles in Russian infinitival clauses. *Journal of Slavic Linguistics, 7* (2), 171–198.

Moore, J. & Perlmutter, D. (2000). What does it take to be a dative subject? *Natural Language and Linguistic Theory, 18* (2), 373–416.

Pereltsvaig, A. (2001). On the nature of intra-clausal relations: a study of copular sentences in Russian and Italian. Doctoral dissertation. McGill University, Montreal, Quebec.

Platzack, C. & Rosengren, I. (1998). On the subject of imperatives: a minimalist account of the imperative clause. In K. Safir & G. Webelhuth (Eds.), *The Journal of Comparative Germanic Linguistics* (pp. 177–224).

Rivero, M-L. (1994). Clause structure and V-movement in the languages of the Balkans. *Natural Language and Linguistic Theory, 12,* 63–120.

Rivero, M-L. & Terzi, A. (1995). Imperatives, V-movement and logical mood. *Journal of Linguistics, 31,* 301–332.

Rizzi, L. (1995). The fine structure of the left periphery. In L. Haegeman (Ed.), *Elements of Grammar* (pp. 289–330). Dordrecht: Kluwer.

Townsend, C. (1970). *Continuing with Russian.* McGraw-Hill, Inc.

Zanuttini, R. (1997). *Negation and Clausal Structure.* Oxford: Oxford University Press.

Computational puzzles of conditional clause preposing

Nicola Munaro

University of Venice

In this article I will sketch an analysis of the ordering restriction constraining the relative order of protasis and apodosis when the former displays inversion between subject and inflected verb, on the basis of data from standard Italian and some North-Eastern Italian dialects: I will thereby try to provide an account for the fact that conditional clauses containing inversion must precede the main clause.

The analysis will turn out to shed light on the hierarchical articulation of the left periphery and on the conceptual issue as to whether it is preferable to distribute the burden of a single derivational step onto various interacting triggering factors or, in a more economical vein, to reduce the triggering forces to a minimum.[1]

1. Ordering restrictions on conditionals with respect to the main clause

In this section I present some evidence suggesting that in conditionals the main clause must follow the associated adjunct clause whenever inversion between the subject and the inflected verb obtains inside the latter.

I analyze the presence of subject (clitic) inversion inside the embedded clause as resulting from the raising of the inflected verb to some head position of the CP field,[2] as proposed in recent work (Munaro 2002a, 2002b). I take verb raising inside the adjunct clause to target an appropriate C° head in order to satisfy a clausal typing requirement.

1.1 Optative conditionals

In some North-Eastern Italian varieties the protasis can convey an optative reading whereby the speaker expresses his regret for the fact that a given situation did not take place.

In Friulian, where this kind of reading is attested, there is a rigid ordering restriction between the main clause and an optative conditional clause containing subject clitic inversion:

(1) a. *Vèssj-o korùt, no varès pjerdùt il treno in ke olte!*
     b. **No varès pjerdùt il treno in ke olte, vèssj-o korùt!*
         [Had-scl run] not would-have missed the train in that time [had-scl run]
         '[I wish I had run], I would not have missed the train on that occasion, [I wish I had run]!'

(2) a. *Fossj-o làt, al sarès stàt dut plui bièl!*
     b. **Al sarès stàt dut plui bièl, fossj-o làt!*
         [Were-scl gone] scl-would have been all more beautiful [were-scl gone]
         '[I wish I had gone], everything would have been better, [I wish I had gone]!'

(3) a. *Vèssj-o volùt studià, o varès podùt fa il profesor!*
     b. **O varès podùt fa il profesor, vèssj-o volùt studià!*
         [Had-scl wanted to study] scl-could have done the professor [had-scl wanted to study]
         '[I wish I had felt like studying] I could have become a professor [I wish I had felt like studying]!'

As these contrasts clearly show, the adjunct clause containing inversion between subject clitic and inflected verb must precede the main clause.

1.2 Counterfactual conditionals

In the unmarked case the protasis can express a counterfactual entailment, that is, the unrealized condition under which the event expressed by the main clause could have taken place.

In standard Italian a counterfactual conditional clause introduced by the subordinating complementizer *se* can either precede or follow the main clause:

(4) a. *Avremmo potuto uscire, se Gianni fosse arrivato in tempo.*
         'We could have gone out, if John had arrived in time.'
     b. *Se Gianni fosse arrivato in tempo, avremmo potuto uscire.*
         'If John had arrived in time, we could have gone out.'

On the other hand, whenever verb raising obtains inside the adjunct clause producing inversion between subject and auxiliary, the conditional clause obligatorily precedes the main clause:

(5) a. *Avremmo potuto uscire, fosse Gianni arrivato in tempo.
         'We could have gone out, had John arrived in time.'
     b. Fosse Gianni arrivato in tempo, avremmo potuto uscire.
         'Had John arrived in time, we could have gone out.'

The same restriction holds in a North-Eastern Italian dialect like Paduan:

(6) a. Garissimo podùo dirghelo, se el fusse vignù.
         Could have told-him-it, if scl-were come
         'We could have told him, if he had come.'
     b. Se el fusse vignù, garissimo podùo dirghelo.
         If scl-were come, could have told-him-it
         'If he had come, we could have told him.'

(7) a. *Garissimo podùo dirghelo, fùsse-lo vignù.
         Could have told-him-it, were-scl come
         'We could have told him, had he come.'
     b. Fusse-lo vignù, garissimo podùo dirghelo.
         Were-scl come, we could have told-him-it
         'Had he come, we could have told him.'

As is clear comparing (6) and (7), the subordinating complementizer *se* introducing the conditional clause is in this case in complementary distribution with subject clitic inversion.

1.3 Alternative concessive conditionals

The two alternatives expressed by a concessive conditional adjunct are evaluated by the speaker as irrelevant for the realization of the propositional content expressed by the main clause.

Again, the relative order of main clause and adjunct clause is immaterial when the complementizer *che* is realized, while in the presence of subject inversion the first position of the adjunct clause is mandatory:

(8) a. Che Gianni fosse venuto o meno/non fosse venuto, noi saremmo andati
         lo stesso.
         'Whether John had come or not, we would have gone in any case.'
     b. Noi saremmo andati (lo stesso), che Gianni fosse venuto o meno/non
         fosse venuto.
         'We would have gone (in any case), whether John had come or not.'

(9) a. Fosse Gianni venuto o meno, noi saremmo andati lo stesso.
         'Whether John had come or not, we would have gone in any case.'

b. *??Noi saremmo andati (lo stesso), fosse Gianni venuto o meno.*
   'We would have gone (in any case), whether John had come or not.'

The same pattern is displayed by Friulian, as witnessed by the contrast between (10) and (11):[3]

(10)   a.   *C'al sedi rivat o ca no'l sedi rivàt, jo o voi vie istés.*
      b.   *Jo o voi vie istés, c'al sedi rivat o ca no'l sedi rivàt.*
          [That scl-be arrived or that not-scl-be arrived] I scl-go away the same
          [that scl-be arrivedor that not-scl-be arrived]
          '[Whether he has arrived or not] I'm going in any case [whether he
          has arrived or not]'

(11)   a.   *Sedi-al rivàt o no sedi-al rivàt, jo o voi vie istés.*
      b.   *??Jo o voi vie, sédi-al rivàt o no sédi-al rivàt.*
          [Be-scl arrived or not be-scl arrived] I scl-go away the same [be-scl
          arrived or not be-scl arrived]
          '[Whether he has arrived or not] I'm going in any case [whether he
          has arrived or not]'

Summing up, the relative order of the main clause and an adjunct conditional clause is irrelevant when the adjunct clause is introduced by the complementizer, while the main clause must follow the adjunct clause whenever inversion between the subject and the inflected verb obtains inside the latter; more precisely, verb raising to the CP field inside the adjunct clause, producing subject inversion, induces a rigid order between the two clauses: I propose that the linear order results from the compulsory fronting of the conditional clause to a specifier of the left periphery of the main clause.[4]

2.   The landing site of conditionals

An analysis of the ordering restriction discussed in the previous section in terms of movement requires a precise determination of the position targeted by preposed conditionals. In this section I will try to identify the landing site of preposed conditionals with respect to other projections which have recently been argued to make up the richly articulated functional structure of the left periphery of the sentence.

2.1   Embedding conditionals in a split CP

Rizzi (1997) proposes for the CP-field the functional sequence in (12), that has been revised and further expanded by Benincà (2001) as in (13):

(12)   [ForceP [TopP [FocP [TopP [FinP]]]]]

(13)   [*DiscP* Hanging Topic [*ForceP* Excl-*wh* [*TopP* Left Disl [*FocP* Interr-*wh*/Focus [*FinP*]]]]]

On the basis of the sequence in (13), let us try to establish the relative order of a conditional clause with respect to the different kinds of constituents that can appear in the left periphery.

As shown by the Paduan and Italian examples in (14) and (15), a preposed conditional precedes both an interrogative *wh*-item and a focalized constituent:

(14)   a.   *Vegnisselo putacaso anca Mario, cossa ghe dirissito?*
       b.   **Cossa, vegnisselo putacaso anca Mario, ghe dirissito?*
            [What], came-scl suppose also Mario, [what] him tell-cond-scl?
            '[What], suppose Mario came, [what] would you tell him?'

(15)   a.   *Fossimo arrivati in tempo (o meno), MARIO avremmo dovuto avvertire.*
       b.   *?MARIO, fossimo arrivati in tempo (o meno), avremmo dovuto avvertire.*
            '[MARIO], had we arrived in time (or not), [MARIO] we should have warned'

Furthermore, a preposed conditional precedes both left-dislocated constituents and exclamative *wh*-items, as witnessed again by Italian and Paduan:

(16)   a.   *Fossimo arrivati in tempo (o meno), a Mario, avremmo dovuto dirglielo.*
       b.   *??A Mario, fossimo arrivati in tempo (o meno), avremmo dovuto dirglielo.*
            '[To Mario], had we arrived in time (or not), [to Mario], we should have told'

(17)   a.   *Vegnisselo putacaso anca Mario, quante robe no ghe dirissito!*
       b.   **Quante robe, vegnisselo putacaso anca Mario, no ghe dirissito!*
            [How many things], came-scl suppose also Mario, [how many things] not him tell-cond-scl!
            '[How many things], suppose Mario came, [how many things] you could tell him!'

Interestingly, a constituent functioning as hanging topic must precede the preposed conditional:

(18)   a.   *Mario, ci avessero telefonato (o meno), avremmo dovuto dirglielo.*
       b.   *??Ci avessero telefonato (o meno), Mario, avremmo dovuto dirglielo.*
            '[Mario], had they called us (or not), [Mario], we should have told'

We can conclude that conditional clause preposing targets a specifier position of the CP field higher than the one hosting interrogative *wh*-phrases, focalized constituents, left-dislocated constituents and exclamative *wh*-phrases, but lower than the one occupied by constituents functioning as hanging topics.

2.2 Two different targets

As we have seen above, conditional adjuncts can convey in some cases a desiderative reading; however, optatives occur generally as main clauses and, as such, one would a priori expect them to be compatible with a conditional clause; when functioning as apodoses they can marginally precede the *if*-clause, while the two clauses are more clearly incompatible when the *if*-clause precedes, as shown by the contrast between (19a) and (19b):

(19) a. ?*Trovasse almeno il coraggio di parlarle, se venisse anche lei!*
          'If only he dared to speak to her, if she came too!'
      b. ??*Se venisse anche lei, trovasse almeno il coraggio di parlarle!*
          'If she came too, I wish he dared to speak to her!'

Full ungrammaticality arises when both clauses display subject-verb inversion, irrespective of their relative order, as witnessed by the following Paduan examples:

(20) a. **Vegnisse-lo putacaso anca Mario, gavessela modo de parlarghe!*
      b. **Gavessela modo de parlarghe, vegnisse-lo putacaso anca Mario!*
          [Came-scl suppose also Mario], had-scl way of speaking-him,
          [came-scl suppose also Mario]!
          'Suppose Mario came, I wish she could speak to him!'

In the light of the morphosyntactic and semantic closeness of the optative and the hypothetical reading, it looks plausible to suggest that the relevant interpretive features are encoded by the same projection, labelled here for the sake of transparency *Hyp(othetical)P*;[5] adjunct clause preposing targets the specifier of *HypP*:

(21) [$_{\text{HypP}}$ [$_{\text{CP}}$ fùsse*lo* vegnùo anca Mario]$_x$ [$_{\text{Hyp}°}$] [$_{\text{ForceP}}$ [$_{\text{TopP}}$ [$_{\text{FocP}}$ [$_{\text{FinP}}$ [$_{\text{Agr-SP}}$ *pro* [$_{\text{Agr-S}°}$ gavaressimo]...podùo dìrghelo...t$_x$]]]]]!

Starting from the assumption that in main optatives the inflected verb raises itself to the head *Hyp°* for clausal typing purposes, the incompatibility witnessed by (19b) and (20) can be traced back to a constraint on checking preventing the activation of both the specifier and the head of the same projection, as long as they encode slightly different interpretations.[6]

On the other hand, concessive conditionals are compatible with (and precede) optatives, and either clause can contain inversion, as witnessed by Paduan and Friulian in (22a) and (22b) respectively:

(22) a. *Che'l vegna o che no'l vegna, telefonasse-lo almanco!*
          That scl-come or that not-scl-come, called-scl at least!
          'Whether he comes or not, I wish he called at least!'
      b. *Fossj-al vignùt o no fossj-al vignùt, s'al véss almancul clamàt!*
          Were-scl come or not were-scl come, if-scl-had at least called!
          'Had he come or not, if only he had called!'

Moreover, concessive conditionals are compatible with *if*-clauses and precede them, as shown again by Paduan and Friulian:

(23) a. *Che piova o che no piova, rivàsse-lo subito, podarissimo partire.*
          That rain or that not-rain, arrived-scl soon, could leave
      b. *??Rivàsse-lo subito, che piova o che no piova, podarissimo partir.e*
          Arrived-scl soon, that rain or that not-rain, could leave
          'Whether it rains or not, if he arrived soon, we could leave.'

(24) a. *Fossj-al vignùt o no fossj-al vignùt, s'al véssi clamaat, avaréssin podùt dìgilu.*
          Were-scl come or not were-scl come, if-scl-had called, could have told-him-it
      b. *??S'al vessi clamaat, fossj-al vignùt o no fossj-al vignùt, avaréssin podùt dìgilu.*
          If-scl-had called, were-scl come or not were-scl come, could have told-him-it
          'Had he come or not, if he had called, we could have told him.'

The same pattern is attested in standard Italian, as exemplified in (25) and (26):

(25) a. *(Che) venga o (che) non venga, se telefonasse, potremmo dirglielo.*
      b. *??Se telefonasse, (che) venga o (che) non venga, potremmo dirglielo.*
          'Whether he comes or not, if he called, we could tell him.'

(26) a. *?(Che) venga o (che) non venga, telefonasse, potremmo dirglielo.*
      b. **Telefonasse, (che) venga o (che) non venga, potremmo dirglielo.*
          'Whether he comes or not, called he, we could tell him.'

This leads to the postulation of a different (and higher) position as landing site for the alternative concessive conditional adjunct, which I take to be the specifier of a projection labelled *Conc(essive)P*.

Adapting the analysis of coordinated structures suggested by Kayne (1994) (in revising a proposal by Munn (1993)), I analyze the two members of the disjunctive cluster as occupying the specifier and the complement position of a *Disj(unction)P* headed by *o*, which raises as a whole to the [*Spec,ConcP*] position:

(27) [$_{DisjP}$ [$_{CP}$ sedial rivat] [$_{Disj°}$ *o*] [$_{CP}$ no sedial rivat]]

(28)   [$_{ConcP}$[$_{DisjP}$ sedi*al* rivat o no sedi*al* rivat]$_x$[$_{Conc°}$] [$_{HypP}$ [$_{ForceP}$ [$_{TopP}$ [$_{FocP}$ [$_{FinP}$ [$_{Agr-SP}$ jo [Agr-S°o voi vie] istés...t$_x$]]]]]]]]!

Given the ordering restrictions seen above, by embedding preposed conditionals in a layered CP we obtain, in the CP field, the following sequence of functional projections hierarchically organized in a fixed order:

(29)   [DiscourseP [*ConcessiveP* [*HypotheticalP* [ExclamativeP [TopicP [Focus/InterrP [FinP]]]]]]]

Within this outline of the left periphery, the two projections *ConcessiveP* and *HypotheticalP* could be regarded as encoding specific instantiations of clausal type; moreover, they define a sublayer located between the lower area, the target of phrasal constituents of the main clause, and *DiscourseP*, which is a sort of interface with the discourse domain; indeed, they can be characterized as codifying the relation between the main clause and adjunct clausal modifiers: in this perspective, the sequence in (29) reflects the intuitive fact that interclausal relations represent an intermediate level of linguistic representation between clause-internal relations and connections to the discourse.

2.3 On the hierarchical ordering of the relevant projections

If we excorporate from the identified sequence the positions relevant for clausal typing, we obtain the hierarchy in (30) where each projection can be seen as the syntactic codification of the typical mental attitude of the speaker with respect to the propositional content expressed by the clause:[7]

(30)   *ConcessiveP > HypotheticalP >>> ExclamativeP > InterrogativeP*

Conceptually, one can make sense of this sequence by saying that it expresses a right-to-left increasing degree of assertivity force, along the following lines.

The interrogative reading, intended as real request for new information, is associated with *InterrogativeP*; in *yes/no* questions the speaker asks the addressee to assign a truth value to the propositional content, while in *wh*-questions he requires the identification of an adequate referent for the *wh*-phrase;[8] interrogatives therefore express very weak, if any, assertive force.

ExclamativeP is associated with the exclamative reading; as is intuitively clear, exclamatives have greater assertive force than interrogatives: in exclamatives, the propositional content or the degree expressed by the *wh*-word is assigned by the speaker a certain relevance according to his or her (or to standard) expectations;[9] hence exclamatives, even if they have a presupposition, do not have themselves assertive force, since their content cannot be valued in terms of truth *vs.* falsity, as their function is to widen the range of alternatives under consideration.[10]

Consider now *HypotheticalP*, which encodes the optative and hypothetical reading; if accessible, this projection conveys a counterfactual entailment, in that both optatives and protases with subject inversion have a strong counterfactual flavour, as opposed to the corresponding structure with the complementizer.[11] In optatives with inversion the speaker expresses his or her own hope for the realization of a situation in which the propositional content were/had been assigned a counterfactual truth value; in this sense, optatives do have an assertive force of their own as they implicitly express, by contrast, that their propositional content is (or was) contrary to fact. In conditionals, on the other hand, the speaker makes the realization of the event expressed by the apodosis dependent on a situation in which the clausal content of the protasis were/had been assigned a counterfactual truth value; in this case, the assertive force is explicitly expressed through the matrix clause, which is in the unmarked case a statement.

Finally, *ConcessiveP* is associated with the alternative concessive conditional reading conveyed by the disjunctive cluster, where the speaker takes into account both truth values for the same propositional content, evaluating them as irrelevant for the realization of the event of the main clause.[12] The concessive conditional interpretation requires that a pair of antecedent conditions be evaluated in the structure, so that the consequent holds independently of their value; it is precisely in this sense that a concessive conditional, or, more precisely, the main clause associated with a concessive conditional, expresses the strongest degree of assertive force.[13]

3.   On the trigger of conditional clause preposing

At least three different factors can be identified as candidates for being the trigger of the mandatory displacement of the adjunct clause across the main clause; I will discuss each of these conditions in turn, trying to reduce them to just one.

3.1   Conditionals as clausal topics

As pointed out by von Fintel (1994) among others, the topic-focus status of the *if*-clause does play a role in determining the respective order of the two clauses;[14] he treats conditional clauses as correlatives, proposing that in *if-then* conditionals the *if*-clause is left dislocated and *then* functions as a resumptive element: the correlative structure *if-then* confers a topical status to the dislocated *if*-clause, which means that alternatives to the antecedent must be conceivable.[15]

Interestingly, both in standard Italian and in Paduan *if*-clauses with inversion can be resumed by *(al)lora*:

(31) a. *Fosse Mario arrivato in tempo, (allora) avremmo potuto partire.*
      b. *Fùsselo Mario rivà in tempo, (lora) garissimo podùo partire.*
          Were-scl Mario arrived in time, (then) could have left
          'Had Mario arrived in time, (then) we could have left'

With alternative concessive conditionals the resumption by an appropriate resumptive element is almost obligatory, as exemplified with Italian and Friulian:

(32) *Sia Gianni arrivato o meno, io me ne vado **comunque/in ogni caso/lo stesso**.*
      'Whether John has arrived or not, I'm going in any case/anyhow/all the same.'

(33) *Sédial rivàt o no sédial rivàt, jo o vai vie **istés**.*
      Be-scl arrived or not be-scl arrived, I scl-go away the same
      'Whether he has arrived or not, I'm leaving all the same.'

However, unlike conditional clauses introduced by a complementizer, conditionals with inversion have an intrinsically topical nature, which is witnessed by the fact that they cannot be used in isolation (like in (34) and (35)), focussed (in (36)) or modified by focussing elements (in (37)):

(34) *In quale caso non avrei ottenuto il diploma?*(Se) non avessi superato gli esami finali..*
      'In which case wouldn't I have obtained the certificate? If you hadn't passed the final exams.'

(35) a. *In quale caso lo rimprovererai?*
          'In which case will you scold him?'
      b. *(In ogni caso,) che l'abbia fatto o meno.*
      b'. ??*(In ogni caso,) l'abbia fatto o meno.*
          '(In any case,) whether he has done it or not.'

(36) a. *Glielo direi *(se) VENISSE, non *(se) TELEFONASSE.*
      b. **(Se) VENISSE, glielo direi, (non *(se) TELEFONASSE).*
          '[If he came] I would tell him [if he came], not if he called'

(37) a. *Potrei dirglielo **solo/proprio/persino** *(se) venisse.*
      b. ***Solo/Proprio/Persino** *(se) venisse, potrei dirglielo.*
          '[Only/just if he came], I could tell him [only/just if he came]'

Similar facts are pointed out for English inverted conditionals by Iatridou & Embick (1994), who explicitly propose that this kind of clauses cannot be focussed;[16] they suggest that the function of inversion is to establish a connection to previous discourse and, consequently, to indicate that the truth-value of the proposition in the antecedent is old or known information.

According to some recent analyses (e.g. Bayer (2001) among others), only main clauses, as opposed to (some types of) embedded clauses, have a node responsible for informational packaging. Also Haegeman (2002) argues that adverbial clauses, not being selected by the main predicate, lack a node encoding illocutionary force and have no straight connection path linking them to the speaker: their force remains unanchored, hence conditionals are part of the speech act of the main clause.

If topicalization is dependent on force in the sense that it expresses the speaker's topic, conditional clause preposing might be traced back to the necessity of getting in a local relation with the matrix node encoding force/speech act.[17]

3.2 Topicalization inside conditional topics

As shown by (38), internal topicalization is possible in conditional clauses in standard Italian:

(38)   a.   *Se queste cose non le sai, non supererai l'esame.*
           'If these things you don't know, you won't pass the exam.'
       b.   *Se di tutti questi argomenti non sai nulla, dovrai riprovare la prossima volta.*
           'If about all these subjects you don't know anything, you'll have to try again next time.'

The topicalization internal to the conditional antecedent is subject to restrictions; a constituent can be felicitously topicalized inside a conditional only when the *if*-clause precedes the main clause, that is, when it is itself a topic, as shown by the contrast between (39b1) and (40b2):

(39)   a.   *Cosa sarebbe successo se io non avessi superato gli esami finali?*
           'What would have happened if I hadn't passed the final exams?'
       b1. *Se gli esami finali tu non li avessi superati, non avresti ottenuto il diploma.*
       b2. *Se tu non avessi superato gli esami finali, non avresti ottenuto il diploma.*
           'If [the final exams] you hadn't passed [the final exams], you wouldn't have got the certificate'

(40)   a.   *In quale caso non avrei ottenuto il diploma?*
           'In which case wouldn't I have obtained the certificate?'
       b1. *Non avresti ottenuto il diploma se non avessi superato gli esami finali.*
       b2. #*Non avresti ottenuto il diploma se gli esami finali non li avessi superati.*
           'You wouldn't have obtained the certificate if [the final exams] you hadn't passed [the final exams].'

Following the spirit of Bayer's (2001) account of a similar phenomenon in Bavarian, I propose that internal topicalization is made possible by fronting of the adjunct clause to $[Spec,HypP]$ of the matrix clause.[18]

However, internal topicalization is impossible in a conditional displaying subject inversion:

(41)   a.   *Cosa sarebbe successo se Gianni non avesse superato gli esami finali?*
            'What would have happened if John hadn't passed the final exams?'
       b1. *Non avesse (Gianni) superato gli esami finali, (allora) avrebbe potuto ritentarli.*
       b2.?? *Non li avesse, gli esami finali, (*Gianni) superati, (allora) avrebbe potuto ritentarli.*
       b3.* *Gli esami finali non li avesse (Gianni) superati, (allora) avrebbe potuto ritentarli.*
            'If John hadn't passed the final exams, (then) he could have tried again'

As proposed above, subject-verb inversion entails internal raising of the inflected verb to the head $Hyp°$ for clausal typing purposes; given the sequence in (29), the sharp deviance of (41b2) can be accounted for under the assumption that verb raising through $Top°$ makes $[Spec,TopP]$ inaccessible;[19] as for the ungrammaticality of (41b3), in which the topicalized phrase precedes the inflected verb, it can be attributed to the absence of a $TopP$ above $HypP$.[20]

On the other hand, if the complementizer *se* is realized, the verb needn't raise, and $[Spec,TopP]$ remains accessible to phrasal constituents:

(42)   *Se gli esami finali tu non li avessi superati, non avresti ottenuto il diploma.*
       'If the final exams you hadn't passed, you wouldn't have obtained the certificate.'

If the proposed analysis is correct, the impossibility of topicalizing a constituent inside a protasis with inversion witnesses verb movement to the relevant head of the CP area, which can be seen as a second potential trigger for the mandatory fronting of the adjunct clause.

3.3 The structural deficiency of conditionals

As anticipated above, Haegeman (2002) distinguishes *event conditionals* from *premise conditionals*, and attributes to the former a structural representation like the one in (43b):

(43)   a.   John will buy the book if he finds it.
       b. $[_{CP} [_{IP}$ John $[_{I°}$ will$]$ $[_{vP} [_{vP}$ buy the book$] [_{CondCP}$ if he finds it$]]]$

Based on the observation that in English only adjuncts can undergo internal top-icalization, as witnessed by the contrast between (44a) and (44b), she proposes, modifying Rizzi's (2001b) proposal in (45a), that event conditionals lack both a Topic and a Focus projection, as represented in (45b), and that topicalized adjuncts target the specifier of the lower projection *ModP*:

(44) a. If the final exams you don't pass, you won't obtain the degree.
      b. If with these precautions you don't succeed, you should try again next
          week.

(45) a.   Force   *Topic Focus* Mod Fin
      b. Event-conditionals: Force/Sub   Mod Fin

As we have seen in the previous section, in standard Italian topicalization is pos-sible in conditionals introduced by *se*, hence a landing site must be available for internally topicalized constituents; following Benincà (2001), I will assume that, at least in standard Italian, no topic position is available below *FocusP*, and that, con-sequently, even in conditionals topicalized phrases target the specifier of *TopicP*.[21]

Differently, the hypothesis that event conditionals lack a *FocusP* is supported by the fact that in Italian they resist internal focalization, independently of the presence of inversion and of the respective order of the two clauses:

(46) a. *(Gianni) avrebbe superato l'esame, se IL MIO LIBRO fosse riuscito a
          leggere.*
      b. *Se IL MIO LIBRO (Gianni) fosse riuscito a leggere, avrebbe superato
          l'esame.*
          '[John would have passed the exam] if MY BOOK he had managed to
          read [John would have passed the exam]'

(47) a. *Paolo avrebbe superato l'esame, IL MIO LIBRO fosse Gianni riuscito a
          comprare.*
      b. *IL MIO LIBRO fosse Gianni riuscito a comprare, Paolo avrebbe superato
          l'esame.*
          '[Paul would have passed the exam] MY BOOK had John managed to
          buy [Paul would have passed the exam]'

This restriction can be captured by the assumption that the CP layer of event-conditionals (and possibly adjunct clauses in general) is deficient in that it lacks a Focus projection.

In the light of the alleged absence of both a *FocusP* and a node encoding information about the speech act, conditionals can be viewed as structurally de-ficient clauses as they have a reduced left periphery; adopting this perspective, one could try to account for the obligatory displacement of the protasis under Cardinaletti & Starke's (1999) theory of structural deficiency, according to which structurally poorer constituents tend to appear displaced from their base position to a higher site.

3.4 Reducing the triggering factors

Closer inspection reveals that the three conditions listed in the Sections 3.1 to 3.3 stay in a causal relation to each other, so that we can identify the following derivational path for conditional clause fronting.

If protases, as proposed, do have a *TopicP*, given the sequence in (29), verb raising to *Hyp°*, a relatively high head of the CP field, implies raising through the lower head positions, including *Top°* (and excluding *Foc°*, if the adjunct clause indeed lacks a Focus projection); the activation of the head *Top°*, a side effect of verb raising, results not only in blocking the access to [*Spec,Top*] (thereby excluding internal topicalization, as we have seen) but also in marking the whole clausal constituent as a topic; on the other hand, if topicality is codified in relation with a force node, this will trigger the compulsory preposing of the adjunct clause to target the appropriate specifier ([*Spec,HypP*] or [*Spec,ConcP*]) of the matrix CP field, where it enters a local relation with the matrix node responsible for informational organization, thereby determining the order in (48b):

(48) a. **Avremmo potuto partire, fosse Gianni arrivato in tempo.*
 b. *Fosse Gianni arrivato in tempo, avremmo potuto partire.*
  '[Had John arrived in time] we could have left [had John arrived in time]'

The complex interplay of different factors obscures the fact that the ordering restriction on inverted conditionals is derivable from a deeper formal condition, an independently motivated theory of structural deficiency predicting that structurally poorer constituents appear higher in sentence structure, which apparently drives a more general movement operation displacing unfocussed material to the left.

The proposed analysis suggests that the role of extra-syntactic factors relevant for the conceptual-intentional system, such as requirements tied to informational organization, can, at least in some cases, be traced back to constraints on first merge, which turn out to ultimately determine the legibility of interface representations.

4. Summary

In this paper I have argued that, in the absence of a subordinating complementizer, clausal typing can be achieved inside a conditional clause by verb raising to an appropriate head of the CP field; this results in activating the head of the *TopicP*, thereby determining the topical status of the clause, which in turn triggers raising of the clausal adjunct to the relevant specifier of the matrix CP field in order to enter a local relation with a force node.

The movement operation affecting conditionals targets the specifier of two functional projections located in the upper portion of the CP area, *ConcessiveP* for alternative concessive conditionals and *HypotheticalP* for counterfactual and optative conditionals; by encoding specific instances of clausal typing, these projections also codify interclausal relations.

Relying on previous work on the structural articulation of the left periphery, I have proposed that the projections devoted to clausal typing are hierarchically organized in a sequence which reflects a right-to-left increasing degree of assertive force:

(49)　*Concessive > Hypothetical >>> Exclamative > Interrogative*

Following some recent proposals on the internal shape of clausal adjuncts, I have also suggested that conditional clauses have a structurally deficient CP layer in that they lack both a node encoding informational structure and a node responsible for internal focalization of phrasal constituents.

Notes

1. This work has been presented at the *Language, Brain and Computation* conference held in Venice (October 3–5, 2002); some of the issues dealt with here have also been addressed in Munaro (2002a) and presented at the *XXV GLOW Colloquium* (Amsterdam, April 9–11, 2002) as well as at the *Ottava Giornata di Dialettologia* (Padua, July 2, 2002). Thanks are due to Paola Benincà, Guglielmo Cinque and Mario D'Angelo for extensive discussion and insightful suggestions; I also benefitted from discussions with Anna Cardinaletti and Cecilia Poletto, from the comments of an anonymous reviewer and from the remarks of the audiences at the above mentioned conferences; the usual disclaimers apply. Finally, I would like to thank P. Benincà and the Friulian team of Ph.D. students for patiently providing the Paduan and Friulian data.

2. At a high stylistic level, inversion between auxiliary and nominal subject is grammatical (and in complementary distribution with a complementizer) in standard Italian in the following contexts:

(i)   a.   *Avrebbe Gianni potuto aiutarci?*
           'Could John have helped us?'
     a′.   *Se Gianni avrebbe potuto aiutarci?*(echoing (ia))
           'If John could have helped us?'
      b.   *Quanti libri è Gianni riuscito a leggere!*
           'How many books John has succeeded in reading!'
     b′.   *Quanti libri che è riuscito a leggere Gianni!*
      c.   *Fosse Gianni arrivato in tempo!*
           'Had John arrived in time!'
     c′.   *Se Gianni fosse arrivato in tempo!*
           'If only John had arrived in time!'
      d.   *Fosse Gianni stato in grado di aiutarci, tutto questo non sarebbe successo.*
           'Had John been able to help us, all this would not have happened.'
     d′.   *Se Gianni fosse stato in grado di aiutarci, tutto questo non sarebbe successo.*
           'If John had been able to help us, all this would not have happened.'
      e.   *Sia Gianni in grado o meno di aiutarci, ce la faremo.*
           'May John be able to help us or not, we will succeed.'
     e′.   *Che Gianni sia in grado o meno di aiutarci, ce la faremo.*
           'Whether John can help us or not, we will succeed.'

(Some of) these cases have been analyzed by Rizzi (1982) as raising of the auxiliary verb to Comp°; Poletto (2000) equally takes subject-clitic inversion in these cases to follow verb raising to (a low head position of) the CP field to check a [-realis] feature, thereby inhibiting the realization of the complementizer. For the hypothesis that the enclitic subject pronoun is generated within a functional head of the CP field see also Munaro, Poletto & Pollock (2001).

3. A similar restriction is attested in Bellunese, a Northern Veneto dialect which displays compulsory preposing of disjunctive embedded *yes/no* questions with inversion:

(i)   a.   *No so dirte se'l gnen o se no'l gnen.*
           Not know tell-you whether scl-comes or whether not scl-comes
           'I can't tell you whether he comes or not.'
      b.   *Gnenlo (o) no gnenlo, no so dirte.*
           Comes-scl (or) not comes-scl, not know tell-you
           'Whether he comes or not, I can't tell you'
     b′.   *No so dirte, gnenlo o no gnenlo.*
           Not know tell-you, comes-scl or not comes-scl
           'I can't tell you whether he comes or not'

It is not implausible that in this case fronting of the embedded clause targets the specifier of the projection *Int(errogative)P* argued for by Rizzi (2001a).

4. The hypothesis that the attested order is produced by preposing of the conditional antecedent relies on the tacit assumption that in the basic order the main clause precedes the adjunct; empirical evidence that this is indeed the case is provided by Haegeman (2002), who gives a detailed analysis of the difference between event conditionals and premise conditionals (exemplified in (ia) and (ib) respectively):

(i) a.   If it rains we will all get terribly wet and miserable.
     b.   If – as you say – it is going to rain this afternoon, why don't we just stay at home?

Based on scope effects induced by scope bearing elements in the associated clause (such as tense, epistemic modality, adverbials, focus and quantifiers/bound pronouns) she proposes that event conditionals are more closely integrated with the associated clause than premise conditionals; in particular, she proposes that the structural integration of the former in the domain of the associated clause depends on their being generated in a position (right-)adjoined to the matrix vP or to a functional projection between vP and the surface subject position; interpretively, event conditionals form a complex predicate with the matrix vP and are therefore within the c-command domain of operators in the matrix CP.

5. As pointed out by Iatridou (2000), crosslinguistically, the morphological features of the verb in a counterfactual *if*-clause are the same as the ones found in the complement of a counterfactual wish, as exemplified in (ii) with standard Italian:

(i) a.   if....M1...then..M2
     b.   want M2 that...M1... (M = verbal morphology)

(ii) a.   Se *venisse*, me ne *andrei*.
          'If he *came*, I would go.'
     b.   *Vorrei* che *venisse*.
          'I wish he *came*.'

6. The relevant projection has been labelled *Counterf(actual)P* and *Hyp(othetical)P* in Munaro (2002a) and (2002b) respectively.

7. The correctness of the relative order between *HypotheticalP* and *InterrogativeP* in the sequence in (30), that is, of the hypothesis that the former occupies a structurally higher position, is confirmed by Iatridou and Embick's (1994) generalization according to which, crosslinguistically, languages exhibiting counterfactual/conditional inversion display inversion in interrogatives as well; they also point out that the set of languages allowing indicative inversion (which I have not taken into account here) constitutes a proper subset of those allowing counterfactual inversion. Furthermore, they observe that in some syntactic environments the verb movement to C° associated with conditional inversion is differentiated from other cases of verb movement.

8. The reader is referred to Obenauer (1994) for a detailed analysis of different kinds of *wh*-questions.

9. According to Zanuttini & Portner (2000), Portner & Zanuttini (2002), exclamative clauses have two basic semantic properties: (a) *factivity*, as the propositional content of the exclamative is presupposed to be true; (b) *widening*, as exclamatives are always uttered against a background of a set of alternative propositions. The compatibility with the speaker's expectations depends crucially on the presence of negation, which triggers a presuppositional implication both in *yes/no* exclamatives and in *wh*-exclamatives, as thoroughly discussed in Portner & Zanuttini (1996).

10. As observed by Sadock & Zwicky (1985:164), "exclamations are intended to be expressive, whereas declaratives are intended to be informative [...] in an exclamation the speaker emphasizes his strong emotional reaction to what he takes to be a fact [...] exclamations are, like interrogatives, non-assertive...".

11. This is supported by the fact that subject inversion in standard Italian leads to uncancelability of counterfactuality, as pointed out to me by Guglielmo Cinque:

(i)   a.   *Se Gianni avesse bevuto del vino, avrebbe le guance rosse...ed infatti ce le ha.*
       b.   **Avesse Gianni bevuto del vino, avrebbe le guance rosse...ed infatti ce le ha*
             'If Gianni had drunk some wine, his cheeks would be red...indeed they are.'

Moreover, in protases with subject clitic inversion with a verb in a non-compound tense, an adverb like *suppose* is required in Paduan to achieve full grammaticality, as opposed to the corresponding structure with the complementizer:

(ii)   a.   [?]*Vignisse-lo anca Mario, podarìssimo partire.*
       b.   *Vignisse-lo putacaso anca Mario, podarìssimo partire.*
             Came-scl [suppose] also Mario, could leave
             'Suppose Mario came as well, we could leave.'

In the North-Eastern Italian dialects considered here the inflected verb of inverted conditionals appears in the (imperfect or pluperfect) subjunctive. Portner (1992) states that conditionals with subjunctive antecedents implicate that their antecedents are false (and that pluperfect subjunctive tends strongly to be viewed as contrary to fact); similarly, Giorgi & Pianesi (1997) propose that subjunctive conditionals are always counterfactual and that counterfactuality requires some attitude of the speakers toward the truth of the protasis.

12. According to Quer (1998), concessive conditionals relate a set of antecedents to a consequent either by a disjunction of a conditional and its negation – *alternative concessive conditionals* – or by a focus particle or scalar expression that modifies a conditional – *polar concessive conditionals*; the two types of concessive conditionals are exemplified by the Catalan examples in (i) and (ii) respectively:

(i)   a.   *Li agradi o no (li agradi), se'l prendrà.*
             'Whether he likes-subj it or not, he will drink it.'
       b.   *Et posis aquì o (et posis) allà, em molestes.*
             'Whether you come-subj stand here or you go-subj stand there, you disturb me.'

(ii)   a.   *Fins i tot si m'ho paguessin, no hi aniria.*
             'Even if they paid-subj it for me, I would not go.'
       b.   *Encara que no em convidi a la festa, li faré un regal.*
             'Even if he does not invite-subj me to the party, I will buy him a present.'

Quer points out that concessive conditionals are licensed in modal environments and involve a non veridical model of evaluation that contains a set of worlds.

13. As for the presence of disjunction in concessive conditionals, Higginbotham (1991) views every *or* as an *either/or*, i.e. as part of a larger constituent including *either* or its interrogative counterpart *whether*, so that (ia) is semantically equivalent to (ib):

(i)   a.   If you (either) marry her or don't marry her, you will regret it.

b.   If you marry her, you will regret it, and if you don't marry her, you will regret that too.

14. He observes that *if*-clauses can either be topical (more commonly) or express new information, depending on the context, as highlighted by the contrast between (i) and (ii):

(i)   a.   What will you do if I give you the money?
       b1.   If you give me the money, I'll buy this house.
       b2.   #I'll buy this house if you give me the money.

(ii)   a.   Under what conditions will you buy this house?
       b1.   #If you give me the money, I'll buy this house.
       b2.   I'll buy this house if you give me the money.

The conditional adjunct can precede the main clause only when it conveys known information (like in (i)), functioning informationally as a topic.

15. According to this view, (ia) is structurally assimilated to (ib):

(i)   a.   *If it rains, then we will stay at home.*
       b.   *In Hamburg, da bin ich gestern gewesen.*
               'In Hamburg, there I've been yesterday.'

An example like (iia) is assigned the structural representation in (iib):

(ii)   a.   *Wenn es regnet, dann werden wir zu Hause bleiben.*
               'If it rains, then we will stay at home.'
       b.   [CP Wenn es regnet [CP dann [C° werden] [IP wir zu Hause bleiben]]]

16. Their descriptive generalization is based on the following evidence. First, both in English and Dutch, unlike *if*-conditionals, inverted conditional antecedents may not be modified by adverbs like *even/only*:

(i)   a.   *Only* if Peter had come would Susan had left
       b.   *Even* if she had been allergic to dill, he would (still) have served the stuffed grape leaves

(ii)   a.   **Only* had I thought that he was sick would I have called him
       b.   *?(?)Even* had Joe served truffles Kathy would not have been happy

Secondly, unlike regular *if*-clauses, V1 adjuncts may not be clefted:

(iii)   a.   It is if John had come that Mary would have left
        b.   *It is had John come that Mary would have left

Thirdly, unlike conditional antecedents introduced by *if*, inverted conditionals may not be used as answers to questions, as witnessed by the following contrasts in Dutch and English:

(iv)   a.   *Wanneer heeft een schepsel een neus?*
               'When does a creature have a nose?'
       b.   *Als het een mond heeft.*
               'If it has a mouth.'

b'. #*Heeft het een mond.*
    'Has it a mouth.'

(v) a. When/under what circumstances would Mary have come?
      b. If she had been offered many artichokes
      b'. #Had she been offered many artichokes

The authors propose that these contrasts result from a more general property of inverted conditional adjuncts, namely, that they may not be focussed, and suggest assessing a correlation between inverted antecedents and old information.

17. According to Iatridou & Embick (1994), antecedents with counterfactual inversion are crosslinguistically less restricted in their distribution than their indicative counterparts, in that they may follow the main clause more frequently; this fact, which requires more careful investigation, is beyond the scope of this paper. For recent proposals on the syntactic codification of speech act and clausal type the reader is also referred to Portner & Zanuttini (2002) and Tenny & Speas (2002).

18. The constraint on *emphatic* topicalization in Bavarian discussed by Bayer (2001) and Bayer et al. (2001) is based on contrasts such as the one between (ia) and (ib), which show that the topicalization of the subject is licit only when the *if*-clause precedes the main clause:

(i) a. *Da Xaver wenn hoam kummt kriagt-a wos z'essn.*
        'As for Xaver, if he comes home, he will get something to eat'
    b. **Da Xaver kriagt wos z'essn der wenn hoam kummt.*
        'As for Xaver, he will get something to eat, if he comes home'

More generally, it is possible to topicalize the subject of the embedded clause only when it precedes the main clause:

(ii) a. *Da Xaver daB an mantl kafft hot hot neamad glaubt.*
        'As for Xaver, nobody believed that he bought a coat.'
     b. *Da Hans ob kummt woaB-e ned.*
        'As for Hans, I don't know if he will come.'

For an analysis of a similar constraint in Bangla see also Bhattacharya (2001).

19. This hypothesis is independently supported by the fact that in English, conversely, a constituent in [*Spec,Top*] blocks verb movement to Top°, as pointed out in Haegeman & Guéron (1999):

(i) a. I promise that *on no account will* I write a paper during the holidays
    b. *I promise that *during the holidays will* I on no account write a paper

20. Note that the following sequence is grammatical:

(i) *Gli esami finali, non li avesse (?Gianni) superati, avrebbe potuto ritentarli.*
    'The final exams, hadn't (John) passed them, he could have tried again.'

This sequence could be interpreted as a case of topicalization targeting a specifier of the matrix CP, external to the adjunct clause; the fact that the dislocated constituent resists being preceded by the preposition shows that it functions as hanging topic and occupies [*Spec,DiscP*] (as predicted by the sequence in (29)):

(ii) a.   *Mario, fossi arrivato in tempo, avrei potuto dirglielo.*
   b.   ??*A Mario, fossi arrivato in tempo, avrei potuto dir(glie)lo.*
       '(To) Mario, had I arrived in time, I could have told.'

Furthermore, the fact that the hanging topic needs a resumptive dative clitic inside the main clause shows that the position it occupies is external to the conditional clause:

(iii) a.   *Mario, gli avessimo telefonato, avremmo potuto dirglielo.*
   b.   *?*Mario, gli avessimo telefonato, avremmo potuto andarcene.*
       'Mario, had we called him, we could have told him/gone away.'

21. The contrast reported in (44), exemplifying the impossibility of internal topicalization for argumental constituents in English, can possibly be accounted for adopting a finer-grained analysis of left dislocation and topicalization such as the one proposed by Cinque (1990).

References

Bayer, J. (2001). Asymmetry in emphatic topicalisation. In C. Féry & W. Sternefeld (Eds.), *Audiatur Vox Sapientiae* (pp. 15–47). Berlin: Akademic Verlag.

Bayer, J., Bader, M., & Meng, M. (2001). Morphological underspecification meets oblique case: Syntactic and processing effects in German. *Lingua, 111*, 465–514.

Benincà, P. (2001) The position of Topic and Focus in the left periphery. In G. Cinque & G. Salvi (Eds.), *Current Studies in Italian Syntax Offered to Lorenzo Renzi* (pp. 39–64). Elsevier: North-Holland Linguistic Series.

Bhattacharya, T. (2001). The puzzle of Bangla Comp-internal clauses. *Snippets, 3*, 6–7.

Cardinaletti, A. & Starke, M. (1999). The typology of structural deficiency: A case study of the three grammatical classes. In H. van Riemsdijk (Ed.), *Clitics in the Languages of Europe Empirical Approaches to Language Typology, 20* (5) (pp. 145–233). Berlin-New York: Mouton de Gruyter.

Cinque, G. (1990). Types of A'-dependencies. *LI Monographs 17*. Cambridge, Mass.: MIT Press.

von Fintel, K. (1994). Restrictions on quantifier domains. Ph.D. Dissertation. University of Massachusetts – Amherst.

Giorgi, A. & Pianesi, F. (1997). *Tense and Aspect: From Semantics to Morphosyntax*. Oxford: Oxford University Press.

Haegeman, L. (2002). Anchoring to speaker, adverbial clauses and the structure of CP. In S. Mauck & J. Mittelstaedt (Eds.), *Georgetown University Working Papers in Theoretical Linguistics Vol. 2– Fall 2002* (pp.117–180).

Haegeman, L. & Guéron, J. (1999). *English Grammar: A Generative Perspective*. Oxford: Blackwell.

Higginbotham, J. (1991). Either/Or. In *Proceedings of NELS 21* (pp. 143–155). Université du Québec à Montréal.

Iatridou, S. (2000). The grammatical ingredients of counterfactuality. *Linguistic Inquiry, 31* (2), 231–270.

Iatridou, S. & Embick, D. (1994). Conditional inversion. In M.Gonzàlez (Ed.), *Proceedings of NELS 24* (pp. 189–203). Amherst: University of Massachusetts.

Kayne, R. (1994). The antisymmetry of syntax. *LI Monographs* 25. Cambridge, Mass.: MIT Press

Munaro, N. (2002a). Splitting up subject clitic-verb inversion. In C. Beyssade, R. Bok-Bennema, F. Drijkoningen, & P. Monachesi (Eds.), *Romance Languages and Linguistic Theory 2000* (pp. 233–252). Amsterdam/Philadelphia: John Benjamins.

Munaro, N. (2002b). The microvariation of non-veridicality: On the role of morpho-syntax in clausal typing. Talk delivered at GLOW XXV, Amsterdam.

Munaro, N., Poletto, C. & Pollock, J. Y. (2001). *Eppur si muove*! On comparing French and Bellunese *Wh*-movement. In P. Pica & J. Rooryck (Eds.), *Linguistic Variation Yearbook* 1 (pp. 147–180). Amsterdam/Philadelphia: John Benjamins.

Munn, A. (1993). Topics in the syntax and semantics of coordinate structures. Ph.D. Dissertation. University of Maryland.

Obenauer, H.-G. (1994). Aspects de la syntaxe A-barre. Effets d'intervention et mouvements des quantifieurs. Thèse de Doctorat d'État. Université de Paris VIII.

Poletto, C. (2000). *The Higher Functional Field*. Oxford: Oxford University Press.

Portner, P. (1992). Situation theory and the semantics of propositional expressions. Ph.D. Dissertation. University of Massachusetts, Amherst.

Portner, P. & Zanuttini, R. (1996). The syntax and semantics of scalar negation: Evidence from Paduan. *Proceedings of NELS 26* (pp. 257–271). University of Massachusetts – Amherst.

Portner, P. & Zanuttini, R. (2002). Clause types: Form and force in grammatical theory. Talk delivered at the Workshop on Syntax and Semantics of CP, Berlin ZAS.

Quer, J. (1998). *Mood at the Interface*. The Hague: Holland Academic Graphics.

Rizzi, L. (1982). *Issues in Italian Syntax*. Dordrecht: Foris.

Rizzi, L. (1997) The fine structure of the left periphery. In L. Haegeman (Ed.), *Elements of Gramma* (pp. 281–337). Dodrecht: Kluwer.

Rizzi, L. (2001a). On the position *Int(errogative)* in the left periphery of the clause. In G. Cinque & G. Salvi (Eds.), *Current Studies in Italian Syntax offered to Lorenzo Renzi* (pp. 287–296). Elsevier: North-Holland Linguistic Series.

Rizzi, L. (2001b). Locality and left-periphery. Ms. University of Siena.

Sadock, J. & Zwicky, A. (1985). Speech act distinctions in syntax. In T. Shopen (Ed.), *Language Typology and Syntactic Description* (pp. 155–196). Cambridge: Cambridge University Press.

Tenny, C. & Speas, P. (2002). Grammaticization at the left periphery. Talk delivered at the Workshop on Syntax and Semantics of CP, Berlin ZAS.

Zanuttini, R. & Portner, P. (2000). The characterization of exclamative clauses in Paduan. In N. Munaro (Ed.), *Quaderni di lavoro dell'ASIS 3: Frasi esclamative e strutture correlate* (pp. 1– 12). Padua: Istituto di Fonetica e Dialettologia – CNR.

Clefts and tense asymmetries*

Manuela Ambar
Universidade de Lisboa

In this work we first review some relevant literature on clefts; two perspectives seem to cover the analyses observed: (i) the cleft element starts as predicate of a sentential subject (Akmajian 1970; Frascarelli 2000; Costa & Duarte 2001); (ii) the cleft element is generated in a full clause starting as subject or complement of *be* from where it moves to a peripheral position (Emonds 1976; Chomsky 1977; Obenauer 1976, 1981, 1994; Kiss 1996; Ambar 1996, a.o).

We then present evidence drawn from selection, from tense in Portuguese clefts, from the distribution of wh-words and from focus vs. topic relations for distinguishing clefts from identificational structures involving a relative clause, whose surface structure may be misleading confused with clefts, and for defending a perspective of type (ii) above. We tentatively propose a system for that-clefts that aims at deriving the properties described, namely the presence in Portuguese vs. its absence in other languages of what we have called *infl-less clefts* and *tense identity* between the copula and the lexical embedded verb. It is claimed that the parameter responsible for this opposition relies in particular properties of the copula and of Tense. It is then hypothesized that clefts in languages of the French type are nothing but identificational structures with an adjoined CP, much in terms of Clech-Darbon, Rebuschi & Rialland (1999) and Munaro & Pollock (2001).

Introduction

Our main goal in this work is to describe the use of the clefts and pseudo-clefts in Portuguese, in order to capture the relevant properties of these structures before proposing a system able to derive them in a unified way.

In Section 1, we present the crucial contexts of clefts in the traditional view. In Section 2, we review some literature on the issue. In Sections 3, 4, and 5, we analyze the distribution of clefts and pseudo-clefts in European Portuguese. In Section 6, we outline a system for deriving *that*-clefts and in Section 7, we present a brief conclusion. From the systematic description of the facts emerges a property of clefts not considered in the literature:[1] clefts in Portuguese require *tense identity* between the copula and the lexical embedded verb. This behavior of tense in clefts is then used as a diagnostic to distinguish clefts from restrictive and free relatives and is related to another particular behavior of clefts in Portuguese, manifested in the existence of what we call *Infl-less clefts*.

This work constitutes a step in research on these structures, which are complex and on which converge different aspects of the grammar. This is why we just outline an analysis for *that*-clefts in this article. Limitations of space preclude the presentation of an analysis extended to clefts having recourse to wh-words (some included in the group of clefts, others in the group of the pseudo-clefts in the traditional classification) and to clefts in the context of wh-questions. Although these structures have been input for the analysis outlined, they don't behave uniformly and there is a subset of wh-clefts that we will consider as being not (pseudo-)clefts. The argumentation for that distinction would lead us to the study of phenomena that are not in the scope of this paper. The results described represent then part of a work that has started in the past and will continue in the future.

1.   The different types of clefts

Clefts have been considered to belong to different types. The *criteria* followed in the classification are traditionally based on the different positions the cleft constituent occupies in the sentence and the arrangements the structure has to undergo in each case. The following classification is usually established. Under the label 'clefts' are structures exemplified in 1.; sentences in 2. exemplify the *so-called* pseudo clefts:

1. *Clefts*

> (1)   *Foi o livro que o João comprou.*
> it was the book that John bought

> (2)   *Foi o livro o que João comprou.*
> it was the book what John bought

2. *Pseudo-clefts*

> (3)   *O que o Pedro comprou foi o livro.*
> what Peter bought was the book

> (4)   *O livro foi o que o Pedro comprou.*
> the book was what Peter bought

Besides these structures, available in languages of the French or English type, Portuguese displays another construction we have correlated with (pseudo-)clefts exemplified above. Departing from other more complex classifications (cf. Casteleiro 1977; Costa & Duarte 2001, among others), we have called them *be_focus* structures (Ambar 1996, 1999); henceforth we will call them *that-less clefts*, in order to clearly capture the relation with (pseudo-)clefts:

3. *That-less clefts*

> (5) *O João comprou foi o bolo.*
>   John bought was the book.

On the other hand, clefts in (1) can be modified in European Portuguese in a way with no parallel in other languages – the cleft constituent can precede the copula, but then the inflection on the copula has to be 3rd person singular, present tense. We will call these structures *Infl-less-clefts*:

4. *Infl-less-clefts*

> (6) a. *O livro(s) é que o João comprou.*
>   the book(s) is that John bought
>   b. **O livro(s) foi (são/foram) que o João comprou.*
>   the book(s) was (are/were) that John bought

Structures of the cleft type appear combined with interrogative wh-phrases. These structures are similar to *Infl-less-clefts* in that both allow a constituent to precede the copula, a DP or a wh-phrase in each case and both may require adjacency between the copula and the complementizer, but they differ in that wh-question clefts allow variation in tense[2] whereas *Infl-bare-clefts* do not. Wh-questions combined with clefts may be fronted or *in situ* as illustrated in (7) and (8) respectively:

5. *Wh-question clefts*:

> (7) a. *(O) que é que o João comprou ?*
>   (The) what is that the John bought?
>   b. *Quem é que tu encontraste ?*
>   Who is that you met?
>   c. *(O) que / quem / ? que amigo foi que o João encontrou ?*
>   (The) what / who / what friend was that the John met?
>
> (8) a. *Foi o quê que o João comprou ?*
>   Was what that the John bought?
>   b. *Foi quem que o João encontrou ?*
>   was who that the John met
>   c. *?Foi que livro que o João comprou ?*
>   It was what book that the John bought

2. Different accounts of clefts

Let us start by three analyses of clefts developed in the 70's – Akmajian (1970), Emonds (1976) and Chomsky (1977).[3]

Akmajian (1970)
    In this work clefts of the type exemplified in (2) are derived from pseudo-clefts, through cleft extraposition of the free relative structure starting as subject of *be*:

(9)   a.   [$_{CP}$ who is sick] is me → 'cleft extraposition'
      b.   it$_i$ is me [$_{CP}$ who is sick] $_i$

Akmajian's proposal does not successfully account for clefts of type (1), where a complementizer instead of a relative pronoun heads the sentential subject:

(10)   a.   *[that I spoke] was to John
       b.   it was to John [that I spoke]

In (10a) 'that I spoke' is clearly not a complete phrase that could be subject of a predicate. Furthermore the derivation of (10b) has recourse to rightward movement – extraposition. Assuming, in the spirit of Kayne (1994) and Ambar (1988), that there is no rightward movement, this operation becomes banned from our system.

Emonds (1976)
In Emonds's (1976) clefts are derived from the underlying structure illustrated in (11):

(11)   [that I spoke to John] was

The derivation proceeds as follows: the element undergoing the cleft operation, say *John* in (11), moves from the clause headed by *that* to a focus position at the right (12a) – this movement can optionally leave a pronoun behind (12b):

(12)   a.   [that I spoke to –] was John
       b.   [that I spoke to him] was John

When (12b) has been derived, a wh-feature is attached to the NP or PP dominating the pronoun (13a), and the wh-phrase is fronted (13b):

(13)   a.   [that I spoke to him^{+wh}] was John
       b.   [who I spoke to –] was John

Finally, the clause headed by the wh-phrase undergoes 'cleft extraposition'. Cleft extraposition yields representations (14a) and (14b), derived from (12a) and (13b) respectively:

(14) a. It was John that I spoke to
  b. It was John who I spoke to

One might wonder why the first underlying structure (11) does not correspond to a possible structure in the language. On the other hand, being rightward movement operations focus movement and extraposition are unavailable in our framework as referred to above.

Chomsky (1977)
In Chomsky (1977) clefts result from topicalization, as illustrated in (15)–(16):

(15) It is [$_{XP}$ me$_i$ [$_{XP}$ 0$_i$ that [t$_i$ is sick]]]

(16) It is [$_{XP}$ me$_i$ [$_{XP}$ who$_i$ 0 [t$_i$ is sick]]]

(15) derives structures of type (1), (16) structures of type (2). Therefore clefts illustrated in (1), problematic for Akmajian's analysis, are easily derived under this proposal and the problem raised by rightward movement does not arise.

  However, comparing (15)–(16) with other topicalization structures, we conclude that the latter do not involve either visible wh-movement or a visible complementizer.

Obenauer (1981)

(17) C'est [$_{XP}$ Max$_i$ [$_{XP}$ t$_i$ que$_i$ [t$_i$ is est malade]]]

Obenauer (1981) proposes for French an analysis in the line of Chomsky (1977).
  The analysis successfully accounts for that-t effect in French. Assuming that this is a topic-like structure we find the same problem as in Chomsky (1977), referred to above. Furthermore, as we will see, tense restrictions that will prove to exist in clefts are not considered in these analyses.

Kiss (1996)
Kiss (1996) derives clefts from the FP theory (Brody 1995). It is assumed that the F head of a Focus projection does not subcategorize a VP in every language; in some languages, e.g. in English, it takes a CP complement that blocks V movement to F; therefore F is lexicalized by the expletive *be* and the cleft element – a focus operator – moves from the embedded VP into Spec,FP through Spec,CP:

(18) [$_{CP}$ [[$_{IP}$ it [$_I$ past [$_{FP}$ to John$_i$ [$_F$ be [$_{CP}$ t$_i$ [$_C$ that [$_{IP}$ I [$_I$ past [$_{VP}$ speak [$_{PP}$ t$_i$]]]]]]]]]]]]

Alternatively, the cleft phrase is base generated in Spec,FP and co-indexed with what the author considers a resumptive wh-pronoun in the embedded CP:

(19) [$_{CP}$ [[$_{IP}$ it [$_I$ past [$_{FP}$ John$_i$ [$_F$ be [$_{CP}$ who$_i$ [$_C$ [$_{IP}$ I [$_I$ past [$_{VP}$ speak [$_{PP}$ to [t]]]]]]]]]]]]]

The analysis does not consider agreement and tense restrictions either.

Ambar (1996)

Having observed that clefts are submitted to restrictions on tense and agreement, Ambar (1996) proposes a system whose main goal is to account for those restrictions. The different positions of the cleft constituent in the structure result from tense checking requirements combined with focus and topic checking, the first underlying structure being the following:

(20)   [TopicP [Topic' [Topic_FocusP [Topic_Focus' [IP pro é (is) [CP [C' que (that) [IP os meninos ouviram as sonatas (the kids listen at the sonatas)]]]]]]]]

It is assumed that *be*, being defective for lexical features, cannot check tense by itself. It can however do it if it is related with lexical elements or receives this property from another tense associated to a lexical tensed verb through co-indexation. Raising of the cleft element to the subject position of *be*, inducing agreement with the copula, is followed by movement of *be* to the focus head (lexicalizing TopicFocus^0), after licensing of tense. The constituent moved to the selected Spec,IP is in a projection adjacent to the focus projection and can therefore receive Focus (Rizzi 1997 & Ambar 1996, 1999). It was also proposed that the embedded CP, being a projection not adjacent to the Focus projection (TopicFocusP) cannot receive Focus. It is then interpreted as a topic of a certain type.

To explain absence of tense and Agr in Portuguese clefts exemplified in (6) (*infl-less clefts*) the analysis had to stipulate a tense movement operation at LF. It was claimed that the tense (also in Comp) of the embedded domain raises to the matrix tense, in the context of *present*, 3rd person singular in the copula (zero tense, zero agreement), though not in the context of *past* (a strong tense fills the position, blocking movement of another tense). *É que* would then lexicalize focus. In the present work we will assume that movement is always visible, in the spirit of Kayne (1998); we will therefore abandon this hypothesis of having recourse to movement in LF.

Frascarelli (2000)

For Frascarelli (2000), *be* also lexicalizes focus, as in Kiss (1996) and Ambar (1996), but, differently from these analyses, it takes a small clause as complement, as in (21):

(21)   [IP [I' [FP [F' be [SC [DP [CP (whom) OP i [C' (that) [IP I [VP saw [DP twh [e]i]]]]] [DP Mary i]]]]]]

Costa & Duarte (2001)

Costa & Duarte (2001), in the spirit of Duarte (2000) and Frascarelli (2000), also propose for Portuguese that *be* takes a small clause as complement:

(22) [$_{IP}$ ser [$_{SC}$ [$_{CP}$ o que (what) / OP que o João comeu (that John ate)] [$_{DP}$ o bolo (the cake)]]]]

This structure allows deriving wh-pseudo-clefts and wh-clefts by moving either the subject or the predicate of the small clause to the left (Moro 1997; Hoekstra & Mulder 1990).

Costa & Duarte assume these structures to be of the identificational type (Heycock & Krock 1999), as illustrated in:

(23) a. *A festa é na 6ᵃa feira.*
          the party is on Friday
      b. *Na 6ᵃ feira é a festa.*
          in the Friday is the party
      c. *O João é simpático.*
          the John is kind

Note however that in cleft structures the DP predicate of the small clause must be of the same category as the complement selected by the verb in the relative clause, i.e. if the verb in the relative selects for a PP, then the predicate of the small clause has to be a PP, if the verb selects for a DP, the predicate has to be a DP, and so on. Note further that this *categorial identity* requirement is not normally satisfied in small clauses, as confirmed by the examples provided by Costa & Duarte in (23), where the subject is a DP and the predicate either a PP (23a) or AP (23c). Thus, we see no reason why in (22) the predicate (the DP) has to inherit the *categorial* status of the subject (the CP) – more precisely of the wh-phrase or category bound by the operator heading the CP subject –, even assuming that subject and predicate are coindexed, as should also be the case in (23), where, however, this categorial identity is not observed. Moreover in these analyses tense restrictions are not considered.

A different approach is proposed for French by Clech-Darbon, Rebuschi & Rialland (1999) and by Munaro & Pollock (2001). In both analyses CP is adjoined to the identificational structure, but as (24) and (25) below show there are crucial differences in each proposal:

Clech-Darbon, Rebuschi & Rialland (1999)
For these authors clefts are identificational structures to which a CP is right-adjoined:

(24) [$_{IP}$ [$_{IP}$ C'est $_v$ [$_{VP}$ t $_v$ [$_{NP}$ le petit]]] [$_{CP}$ Op$_i$ [$_{C'}$ qui [$_{IP}$ t$_i$ est tombé]]]]

Munaro & Pollock (2001)

(25) a. $[_{ForceP}$ $[_{CopP}$ est $[_{SC}$ que ce $]]$ F° $[_{Op1}$ O$_i$ que $[_{IP}$ Marie voulait rencontrer t$_i$$]]]$

  b. $[_{Op2}$ que$_i$ $[_{ForceP}$ $[_{CLP}$ t$_i$ $[_{CopP}$ est $[_{SC}$ t$_i$ ce $]]]$ F° $[_{Op1}$ O$_i$ que $[_{IP}$ Marie voulait rencontrer t$_i$$]]]$

In Munaro and Pollock's proposal the identificational structure is a small clause where *ce* is one of the terms, as is not the case in (24).

With these analyses in mind let us turn to the particular behavior of clefts in Portuguese.

3. Tense restrictions

3.1 Two types of restrictions

Restriction I

As (6) shows, in clefts of type (1) (with complementizer *que*) the cleft constituent may precede the copula in Portuguese, but then the copula will always be 3rd person singular, present tense, irrespective of the tense in the embedded domain. Any other tense or agreement marks on *be* will lead to ungrammaticality:

(6) *O livro(s) é que o João comprou.*
  the book(s) is that the John bought

(26) **O livro foi que o João comprou.*
  the book was that the John bought

(27) **Os livros são/foram que o João comprou.*
  The books are/were that the John bought

Assuming present is a *zero* tense (Giorgi & Pianesi 1992; Kayne 1993) and 3rd person singular is a default agreement, I will consider that the copula in structures of type (6) has to be uninflected.

In order for the copula to be inflected in tense in this context a wh-word has to replace the complementizer *que*, the result being what has been called pseudo-clefts of type (4) above, illustrated here in (28)–(29):

(28) *O livro foi o que o João comprou.*
  the book was what the John bought

(29) *O João foi quem o Pedro encontrou.*
  the John was who the Peter met

Restriction II

Another type of restriction shows up in (pseudo-)clefts: the tense in the copula has to be identical to the tense in the embedded lexical verb, as is the case in the pseudo-clefts (28)–(29) above.

This matching condition on tense, which will be clearer in what follows, is also observed in clefts exemplified in (1) and (2), repeated here as (30)–(31) for ease of exposition:

(30) a. *Foi o livro que o João comprou.*
          was the book that the John bought
      b. **Foi o livro que o João vai comprar/comprará/ comprava.*
          was the book that John is going to buy / will buy /bought (imperfect)

(31) a. *Foi o livro o que o João comprou.*
          was the book what the John bought
      b. **Foi o livro o que o João vai comprar/compra/comprava/comprará.*
          was the book what John is going to buy / buys / bought (imperfect)/will buy

3.2 Clefts vs. restrictive relatives

Note that there are well-formed structures apparently identical to (30b) where this *tense identity* is not obligatory, as exemplified in (32) below:

(32) *Foi o livro que o João vai oferecer / oferecerá à Ana.*
      was the book that the John is going to offer / will offer to Ana

However, (32) should not be confused with (30b), as the following tests show.

Let us take clefts of type (30a) – where there is tense identity – and structures of type (32) – where there is no tense identity – and observe in what contexts they can be produced.

Consider question (33) and answers (a–e) in (33):

(33) *Que livro custou 45 euros ?*
      what book cost 45 euros

      a. **Foi o livro.*
          it was the book
      b. *Foi o livro que o João comprou.*
          it was the book that John bought
      c. *Foi o livro que o João vai oferecer / oferecerá à Ana.*
          was the book that John is going to offer /will offer to Ana

    d. *Foi o livro o que o João **comprou.***
       was the book what John bought

    e. *Foi o livro o que João **vai oferecer / oferecerá à Ana.***
       was the book what John is going / will offer to Ana

(33a) is not an appropriate answer to question in (33). Both (33b), exhibiting the same form as (30a), where the tense in the copula is identical to the tense in the lexical verb, and (33c), equivalent to (32), where the tenses are not identical, are adequate answers to (33). It seems then that both identical and different tenses are possible in this context, in contradiction with what we are claiming: clefts in Portuguese require *tense identity*.

In what follows we will see that this contradiction is only apparent and that the permission for both identical and disjoint tenses in (33b–c) results from the fact that these structures are not clefts. Clefts do require *identity of tense* between the copula and the embedded lexical verb. We will then conclude that (33b) (= (1), (30a)) is ambiguous: it can be a cleft or a relative. As a cleft it requires *tense identity*, as a relative *tense identity* is not obligatory.

Observe that in (33) the requested information is on some given *properties of book*, normally supplied by adjectival phrases, prepositional phrases or relative clauses. In (33b–c) the constituent that transmits the new information requested by the question is the whole complex DP, i.e. focus has scope not on *o livro* (the book) itself, the cleft element in structures like (1), but on the entire complex DP that includes the relative clause – it is this relative that identifies the variable of the wh-phrase in the question in (33); this is why (33a) is not an appropriate answer to (33): the constituent identifying the variable is missing (the relative clause) – there is something like vacuous focus, the focused element has no phonetic content. In answers in (33) the *cleft reading* is then lost. Inversely, in a cleft focus would have scope over the simple DP *o livro* (the book), but not over the clause headed by *que* – thus concerning focus in clefts the DP (the cleft element) is divorced from the embedded clause, in relatives not.

Being relatives (not clefts), the embedded clauses in (33b–c) do not require tense identity.

Interestingly, as the contrast between (33b–c) and (33d–e) shows, wh-words are ruled out from this context, i.e. contrary to what happens in *cleft* structures exemplified in (1)–(2), a wh-word cannot substitute for complementizer *que* in paradigm (33).

The ungrammaticality induced by the presence of a wh-word becomes then a diagnostic for distinguishing a cleft DP from a DP antecedent of a relative. Wh-words are ruled out from context (33) for the same reason they are ruled out from restrictive relative clauses when not preceded by a preposition, as illustrated by (34):

(34)   a.   *O livro que o João comprou foi caro.*
            the book that John bought was expensive

       b.   **O livro o que o João comprou foi caro.*
            the book what John bought was expensive

       c.   *O rapaz que ama a Maria é simpático.*
            the boy that loves Mary is kind

       d.   **O rapaz quem ama a Maria é simpático.*
            the boy who loves Mary is kind

       e.   *O rapaz a quem a Ana falou é meu amigo.*
            the boy to whom Ana spoke is my friend.

Summarizing, the clauses headed by *que* (that) in sentences (33b, c) are restrictive relatives, (1) is a cleft, not a relative. This is why: (i) commutation with a wh-word is impossible in the first context (33d–e) but possible in the latter (2); (ii) *tense identity* is not obligatory in the first context, but it is in the latter; (iii) focus has scope on ihe embedded clause in the first context but not in the latter – i.e. in clefts there are two informational and prosodic units, henceforth graphically separated by the double slash // – e.g. in clefts like (1) and *(2) o livro* (the book) is focus, the clauses headed by *que* in (1) or *o que* in (2) are topics of a certain type:

(1)   **Foi** o livro // que o João **comprou**.
      it was the book that John bought

(2)   **Foi** o livro o // que o João **comprou**.
      it was the book what John bought

To make clearer what we have just observed, note that in the appropriate informational context, (33b), though not (33c), could receive a cleft reading, i.e., abstracting from the prosodic differences ((33b) (= (1)) is ambiguous. Observe question (35):

(35)   *O que foi que o João comprou ?*
       what was it that Peter bought?

       a.   *Foi o livro.*
            it was the book

       b.   *Foi o livro // que o João comprou.*
            it was the book that John bought

       c.   *Foi o livro // o que o João comprou.*
            it was the book what John bought

       d.   **É o livro (o) que o João comprou.*
            it is the book what/ that John bought

       e.   **Foi o livro (o) que o João comprará, compra, ...*
            it was the book what / that that John will buy

    f. *Foi o livro que o João ofereceu/ oferecerá à Ana.*
       it was the book that João offered / will offer to Ana
    g. **Foi o livro o que o João ofereceu / oferecerá à Ana.*
       it was the book what João offered / will offer to Ana

First, (35a), contrary to (33a), is well formed, showing that in this context a relative clause is not missing for an adequate answer to the question and that focus is assigned to the simple DP *o livro (the book)* – the identification of the variable of the wh-phrase (*o que* in the question) has to be accomplished by a DP, not by a relative clause as in (33). The clause headed by *que* or *o que* in (35b–c) does not receive focus, as confirmed by the fact that it already appears in the question; it is then independent (cleft) from the DP *o livro* – in other terms this DP is not the antecedent of the embedded clause; they do not constitute a unit for focus, as confirmed by the two distinct prosodic units, specific of clefts and graphically represented by //. As expected, the tense identity requirement shows up – cf. (35b–c) vs. (35 d–e) – and again contrary to paradigm (33), wh-words can substitute for complementizer *que* – observe the grammaticality of (35c). Note that (35f), where there is no tense identity, is well formed; we predict then that the embedded clause is a relative, not a cleft. The ungrammaticality of (35g) confirms this prediction: a wh-word cannot occur in this context just as it cannot in relative clauses. In sentence (35f) focus has scope over the complex DP, not on the simple DP, or, in other terms, here the embedded clause is not a topic – actually it does not appear in the question.

    Another argument for claiming that relatives, exemplified in (33b,c) and (35f) are not clefts of type illustrated by (1)–(2), is provided by the fact that the entire complex DP including the relative can itself be cleft, in the appropriate context for clefts, as (36a–b) and (36c) show, respectively:

(36) a. *Foi o livro que o João comprou // que **custou** 45 euros.*
         it was the book that John bought that cost 45 euros
      b. *Foi o livro que o João vai oferecer / oferecerá à Ana // que **custou** 45 euros.*
         was the book that John is going to offer /will offer to Ana that cost 4 euros
      c. *Foi o livro que o João ofereceu / oferecerá à Ana // que o João **comprou**.*
         was the book that John offered / will offer to Ana that John bought

Then both properties of clefts – (i) tense identity and (ii) substitution for a wh-word – reappear, as illustrated by the bold past verbal forms in (36) and bold wh-words in (37), respectively:

(37) a. *Foi o livro que o João comprou // o **que** custou 45 euros.*
         it was the book that John bought that coasted 45 euros

b. *Foi o livro que o João vai oferecer / oferecerá à Ana // o **que** custou 45 euros.*
was the book that John is going to offer /will offer to Ana that cost 4 euros

c. *Foi o livro que o João ofereceu / oferecerá à Ana // o **que** o João comprou.*
was the book that John offered / will offer to Ana what John bought

Now consider statement (38) and the contrastive comments (38a–d):

(38)   O João comprou a revista (, não comprou ?)
        John bought the magazine (,didn't he?)

a. **(Não..,) foi o livro.*

b. *(Não..,) foi o livro // que / o que o João comprou.*
(no... ,) it was the book that John bought

c. **(Não..,) foi o livro que o João comprará / oferece/ oferecerá à Ana.*
(no..,) it was the book that John will buy / offers / will offer to Ana

d. **(Não..,) é o livro que o João comprou.*
(no..,) it is the book that John bought

Note first that (38a) is not a felicitous sentence for contrastive focus on *o livro* (the book). Comparing (38a) with (38b) we conclude that in order to have contrastive focus the presence of a phonetically realized topic-like constituent is needed – *o João comprou* (John bought) is already in the statement (38), it constitutes then shared information. Note further that, with respect to this behavior, (38a) contrasts with (35a), where absence of the topic-like element is not only possible, but rather preferable for getting *full* presentational focus interpretation.

Thus, in (38a) contrastive focus is assigned to the DP *o livro* (the book) vs. *a revista,* (the magazine), not to the CP headed by *que* (that). In other words, with respect to focus-topic interpretation *o livro* (the book) is divorced (cleft) from the embedded CP. The cleft reading obtains – the former (*o livro,* the book) receives Focus, the latter (CP headed by *que*) receives Topic-like interpretation. Consequently, *tense identity* is again at stake; (38b) respects that condition; (38c–d) not – these are therefore excluded.

At the same time a wh-word can substitute for *que* in (38b) giving (39a), though not in (38c–d), which go on ungrammatical as shown in (39b–c):

(39)   a. *(Não..) Foi o livro o que o João comprou.*
        (no..) it was the book what John bought

b. **(Não..) Foi o livro o que o João comprará/vai oferecer à Ana.*
it was the book what John will buy / is going to offer to Ana

c. **(Não) É o livro o que o João comprou.*
it is the book that John bought

Summarizing:

- in clefts focus is assigned to a constituent with autonomy (+ cleft) *wrt* the embedded clause e.g. a simple DP (this DP is not the antecedent of that clause); in relatives focus is assigned to a constituent that has no autonomy (– cleft) *wrt* the embedded clause e.g. a complex DP (the DP is the antecedent of the relative clause);
- clefts are broken structures with 2 informational and prosodic units: a focus + a topic;
- in clefts the tense in the copula has to be identical to the tense in the embedded clause and this embedded clause is not a relative, it is a sentential complement of *be* (plausibly of tense in *be*); if the embedded clause is a relative this condition is not observed;
- there are ambiguous structures, allowing either a cleft reading or a relative-type interpretation (33b);
- tense becomes a diagnostic for distinguishing these two types of structures: clefts require identical tenses in Portuguese; restrictive relatives do not;
- wh-words (not introduced by a preposition), cannot occur in restrictive relatives in general; in clefts they can; wh-words constitute then another diagnostic for distinguishing clefts from relatives;
- clefts are not restrictive relatives.

3.3   Clefts vs. free relatives

Let us now test the hypothesis that clefts and pseudo-clefts are free relatives.
Consider question (40):

(40)   *Quem chegou ?*
who arrived

As paradigm (41) below shows, *tense identity* between the copula and the lexical verb is again required – only sentences where the tense in the copula is identical to the tense in the lexical verb (41a,c) are adequate answers to (40):

(41)   a.   *Quem chegou // foi o Pedro.*
who arrived was Peter
b.   **Quem chegou é o Pedro.*
who arrived is Peter
c.   *Foi o Pedro // quem chegou.*
it was Peter who arrived
d.   **É o Pedro quem chegou.*
it is Peter who arrived

However this *tense identity* is not obligatory in small clauses having a free relative as subject:

(42) a. *Quem chegou é meu amigo.*
     who arrived is my friend

 b. *Quem trabalhou seriamente um dia verá os resultados.*
    who worked seriously, one day will see the results

 c. *Quem chegou é de Coimbra.*
    who arrived is from Coimbra

 d. *Quem chegou é simpático.*
    who arrived is kind

Categorial identity between the subject and the predicate of a small clause having a free relative as subject is not obligatory, as it isn't in small clauses in general. In clefts that *categorial identity* is obligatorily required. The contrasts (a–b) and (c–d) in (43) are due to selection – the verb *gostar de* (to like) selects the preposition *de:*

(43) a. *É de linguistica que o Pedro gosta*
     it is of linguistics that Peter likes

 b. **É linguistica que o Pedro gosta*
    it is linguistics that Peter likes

 c. *De quem o Pedro gosta é da Ana*
    of whom Peter likes is of+the Ana

 d. **Quem o Pedro gosta é da Ana*
    who Peter likes is of+the Ana

Thus, assuming that (pseudo-)clefts are derived from small clauses having a free relative as subject, one had to stipulate two idiosyncratic conditions for the well-formedness of small clauses entering cleft structures: on the one hand, *categorial identity* between the predicate (the cleft element) and the constituent heading the free relative, on the other hand, *tense identity* between the tense in the lexical verb of the free relative and the tense in the copula.

Therefore we exclude the hypothesis of deriving clefts from an initial structure of this type.

Summarizing:

- the tense in free relatives is not necessarily identical to the tense in the matrix clause; in clefts it is;
- there is no *categorial identity* between the subject and the predicate of a small clause having a free relative as subject; in clefts there is;
- clefts are not free-relatives.

3.4 That-less clefts

In our previous works on focus (Ambar 1996, 1999) we observed that Portuguese displays a special construction that has in common with clefts the presence of *be*, but differs from them in different aspects, namely in the absence of the complementizer. We have called these structures *be-focus structures*, we henceforth will call them *that-less clefts*, for a clearer relation with clefts. Although these structures contrast with regular clefts in different respects, the tense identity and the categorial identity we have described behave similarly.

As sentences in (44) show, the copula has to have the same tense as the lexical verb:

(44)   a.   *O João comprou foi o livro.*
                  John bought was the book
          b.   **O João comprou é o livro.*
                  John bought is the book

So, as in regular clefts, the copula can be inflected in tense, but this tense has to be identical to the tense in the lexical verb. However, contrary to regular clefts, which accept agreement between the cleft element and the copula in some cases, *that-less clefts* do not.

(45)   a.   **O João comprou foram os livros.*
                  John bought were the books
          b.   *O João comprou foi os livros.*
                  John bought was the books

Casteleiro (1977) and Kato & Raposo (1996) derive these structures from pseudo-clefts, through deletion of the wh-pronoun. Ambar (1999) deals with them in terms of remnant IP movement and Costa & Duarte (2001) consider them to involve non-maximal VPs. We will not pursue this question here. Our goal was just to point out that *tense identity* is required in these structures. For the time being we will go on assuming the proposal outlined in Ambar (1996, 1999).

In next section we will look at agreement restrictions in regular clefts. However, we will not get conclusive results due to the hesitation found among the speakers concerning overt agreement in these constructions. I will leave for future work part of these facts.

Summarizing:

–   tenses have to be identical in *that-less clefts*;
–   bad results with overt agreement in the copula.

4. Agreement restrictions

We have already observed that in *infl-less clefts* both the tense and the agreement marks in the copula have to be, respectively, present (a zero tense) and 3rd person singular (a zero person). Consequently there is neither tense identity nor agreement identity with the embedded inflection.

Let us briefly see the restrictions on agreement.

As exemplified in (46), irrespective of the object (46a) or subject (46b) status of the pre-copula constituent, overt agreement between this constituent and the copula is impossible:

(46) a.   *Os bolos de chocolate é /*são que o João comeu.*
           the chocolate cake(s) is /are that John ate
      b.   *Os meninos é / *são que comeram o bolo de chocolate.*
           the kids is / are that ate the chocolate cake

In the pseudo-clefts, exemplified in (47) for cleft subject and in (48) for cleft object, agreement vs. non-agreement produces the following contrasts:

(47) a.   *Os meninos ? foi / (?) foram quem comeu o bolo de chocolate.*
           the kids was / were who ate the chocolate cake
      b.   *Quem comeu o bolo de chocolate ?? foi / foram os meninos.*
           who ate the chocolate cake were the kids

(48) a.   *Os bolos de chocolate foi / ? foram o que o João comeu.*
           the chocolate cakes was / were what John ate
      b.   *O que o João comeu ? foi / foram os bolos de chocolate.*
           what John ate was / were the chocolate cakes

In pseudo-clefts (47)–(48), it seems that agreement is better with the subject than with the object, and still better if the DP is in post copula position.

Observe now clefts with complementizer *que* and with wh-words, first for the subject (49) and then for the object (50):

(49) a.   *Foram/ *? foi os meninos que comeram os bolos.*
           were / was the kids that ate the chocolate cake
      b.   *Foram / *? foi os meninos quem comeu o bolo.*
           were / was the kids who ate the cake

(50) a.   *Foram / *? foi os bolos que os meninos comeram.*
           were / was the cakes that the kids ate
      b.   *Foram / *? foi os bolos o que os meninos comeram.*
           were / was the cakes what the kids

In clefts (49)–(50), whenever the cleft element is a DP overt agreement between the copula and the cleft element is preferred:

- agreement seems to be better with subjects than with objects;
- agreement seems to be better when the cleft element is in post-copula position;
- agreement seems to be better with clefts than with pseudo-clefts

5.   More on clefts and focus

In the structures described so far, the cleft elements considered – the ones that receive focus – have been constituents that move from CP. Let us observe now other cases of *focus scope* in clefts.

Consider (51):

(51)   *Foi o João que partiu o copo.*
       it was John that broke the glass

(51) can be an adequate answer, or comment, to (52), (53), (54):

(52)   *Que aconteceu ?*
       what happened?
       a.   *Foi o João que partiu o copo.*
            it was John that broke the glass
       b.   **Foi o João quem partiu o copo.*
            it was John who broke the glass
       c.   **Foi o copo que o João partiu.*
            it was the glass that John broke
       d.   **Foi o copo o que o João partiu.*
            it was the glass what John broke

(52) is a question requiring a whole sentence as focus in the answer. What paradigm (52) shows is that in order to have focus on the whole sentence, the clause has to be headed by *que* (the complementizer) preceded by the subject; a wh-word prevents focus to have scope over the entire clause. On the other hand the contrast between (52a) and (52c) shows that, in sentences where the *subject* precedes the complementizer, the whole clause (CP) can be assigned focus, but in those where the element preceding *que* is different from the subject focus cannot be assigned. There is then a subject-object asymmetry.

Inversely, focus on the DP is insensitive to the subject-object asymmetry and to the presence vs. absence of wh-words:

(53)   *Quem partiu o copo ?*
       who broke the glass?

     a.   *Foi o João // que/quem partiu o copo.*
        it was John // ..that/who broke the glass
     b.   *Quem partiu o copo // foi o João.*
        who broke the glass was John

(54)   *O António partiu o copo...*
       António broke the glass...

     (Não) foi o João// .. que/quem partiu o copo.
     (no) it was John//..that/who broke the glass

As general conclusions, the contrasts above have shown that:

a.   clefts are not to be confused with restrictive relatives: restrictive relatives can have tense different from the tense in the main verb, clefts do not; in clefts wh-words can occur, irrespective of the presence or absence of a preposition preceding it; in restrictive relatives they cannot;

b.   clefts are not to be confused with free relatives: free relatives allow a tense different from the tense in the main clause; in clefts there is tense identity;

c.   the predicate of the small clause having a free relative as subject is not necessarily of the same category as the gap in the relative, in clefts it is;

d.   cleft sentences have two distinct informational and intonational units: a focus and a topic; relatives not;

e.   cleft sentences may be ambiguous: they can surface with the same form as restrictive relatives, free relatives and even when they are clefts they can satisfy either presentational focus on a given constituent, or contrastive focus, or presentational focus on the whole sentence. This is the case of sentences like: *Foi o João que partiu o copo*, it was 'John that broke the glass'. Then a subject/object asymmetry shows up.

6.   Towards an analysis

In this section we will try to answer the following questions:

(i)   why is there tense identity in Portuguese?

(ii) why has Portuguese inlf-less clefts?

(iii) why do clefts always have focus? What is the relation of *be* with focus and topic?

(iv) is it possible to give to clefts a unified treatment, accounting for the facts described?

We will just consider *that*-clefts, i.e. clefts with complementizer *que* (that).

The idea that a structure having a small clause is involved in the derivation of clefts makes sense, given the copular status of *be*. However we have seen that clefts exhibit properties that the analyses based on the assumption that clefts and pseudo-clefts are derived from a small clause having a (free) relative-type structure as subject do not consider: the tense identity requirement in languages of the Portuguese type, the categorial identity requirement – related to selection –, or the different behavior of wh-words in clefts vs. relatives.

Suppose we maintain Frascarelli's (2000) and Costa & Duarte's (2001) idea of a small clause underlying cleft structures, given the properties of *be*, but that we reject their hypothesis,[4] either for the subject – it cannot be a relative – or for the predicate of that small clause – the cleft element is not the predicate of the small clause, it originates in the full clause, due to the restrictions observed in the preceding sections. Let us hypothesize that the initial structure is of the type represented in (55), where *ser* (be) selects a small clause whose subject is empty and whose predicate is the full clause – CP:

(55) $[_{IP} [_{I'} [_{vP} \text{ser (be)} [_{SC} \text{e} [_{CP} \text{que} [_{IP}]]]]]]$

We come back to the idea that the cleft element originates in the embedded clause, from where it moves to the final cleft position, as in the proposals by Chomsky (1977), Emonds (1976), Obenauer (1981), Kiss (1996) and Ambar (1996, 1999), among others. With this hypothesis we solve the problem of selection, raised in the preceding sections.

Recall two crucial contrasts between Portuguese and other languages: *tense identity* in regular clefts and pseudo-clefts and the availability of *infl-less clefts* in Portuguese vs. its unavailability in other languages, say French, English or Italian.[5]

Tense identity seems to be not obligatory either in French or in Italian:

(56)   *C'est Jean qui est parti.*

(57)   *È Gianni che ha comprato il libro.*

In (56) and (57) the copula is in the *present* and the lexical verb in the *past*, an unavailable option in Portuguese – recall that to the question *quem partiu?* (who left) the answer has to be *foi o João que partiu* (it was John that left), not * *é o João que partiu* (it is John that left).

And *infl-less clefts* are excluded:

(58)   **Gianni è / è stato che ha comprato il libro.*

(59)   **Jean est que/qui a acheté le livre.*

(60)   *John is that bought the book.

Thus, (56)–(57) in Portuguese are not well-formed clefts, but (58)–(60) are. Note that the hypothesis of deriving the contrast from the pro-drop parameter is immediately excluded – Italian is a pro-drop language and has no *infl-less clefts*. On the other hand it would be desirable that the same parameter is responsible for both differences.

It is tempting to claim that the parameter differentiating Portuguese to French and Italian relies on the particular properties of *ser* (be), combined with differences in the behavior of Tense in Portuguese vs. the other languages. Portuguese has two verbs – *ser* and *estar* – for expressing what English or French do with one – *be* or *être* respectively:

(61) a. *O João é simpático.*
          John is kind.
      b. *O João está feliz.*
          John is happy.

Assume that *ser* (be) is defective for lexical features; in Portuguese it cannot check Tense by itself, unless it is related to lexical elements or receives this property from another tense associated to a lexical verb through coindexation.

Consider then (62). *Ser* (be) will be unable to check the features of tense, due to its lexical defectiveness, which is plausibly to be seen in unvalued features of Event (vP) for Portuguese, though not for French or English. But the empty position in the small clause has a relation with its predicate – CP. Assume it Agrees with it; therefore it is coindexed with its head – C^0 –, which in turn is related to Tense in the embedded IP:

(62) $[_{IP} [_{I'} [_{vP}$ foi $[_{SC}$ e$_i$ $[_{CP} [$ que$_i$ $[_{IP}$ o João$_i$ T$_i$ comprou o livro $]]]]]]]$
              was   that   the John bought the book

Now e$_i$ has tense / Event features, but not phonetic content. Assume it incorporates in v (vP) of the matrix clause,[6] the copula's domain. The copula will agree in tense with the embedded lexical verb. Note that this hypothesis leads to the intuitive observation that in these structures it is tense that plays the crucial role – we would say that it is tense that selects the embedded domain. Actually clefts are nothing but the identification of an event combined with a strategy for focusing one or another of the intervening parts.

Suppose now that some features – plausibly those related with Past, Present, Event[7] –, but not all, are checked through the strategy described; then, by hypothesis, the other features – plausibly person, EPP, normally checked by some argument of the predicate, that in the case is *be*, also defective for that – need to be legitimated.

Assume that in order to achieve checking of these features, some lexical constituent has to move to the domain of *be*, for checking of the person feature or

EPP feature. Suppose further that it first raises to spec, vP, ending the process of endowing *be* with all features normally present in regular lexical verbs and yielding representation (63a). Then, feature checking of matrix T – tense features and person, EPP – will be accomplished by further movement of the copula and of the DP in vP to I (T) and to spec, I (T), respectively, as illustrated by (63b):

The resulting structure would be (63c):

(63) a. $[_{IP} [_{I'} T [_{vP} o João_i [_{v'} foi_{ik} [_{VP} t_{cop} [_{SC} e_k [_{CP} t_i [que_k [_{IP} t_i T_{ik}$ comprou o livro]]]]]]]]]]

   b. $[_{IP} o João_i [_{I'} foi_{ik} [_{VP} t_{cop} [_{SC} e_k [_{CP} t_i [que_k [_{IP} t_i T_{ik} comprou o$ livro]]]]]]]]

   c. *O João foi que comprou o livro
       the John was that bought the book

In (63) the constituent moved to spec, IP is a DP, with the appropriate person feature. Then visible agreement between the DP and the copula will show up.

However the output of the derivation (63a–b) – is ungrammatical.[8] For the time being I will assume that this is due to lacking one type of feature checking – focus. More precisely I will hypothesize that *ser* (be) has a focus feature[9] and that this feature is active only when it is Event related, in the unmarked case through tense;[10] *foi* (was) has then to raise to the head of FocusP:

(64)

$[_{FP} foi_{ik} [_{IP} o João_i [_{I'} t_{ik} [_{VP} [_{SC} t_{ik} [_{CP} [que_k [_{IP} t_i T_{ik} comprou o livro]]]]]]]]$
was   the John   that   bought the book

We will assume what we have proposed in our works on Focus. The unmarked position for Focus is post-verbal, for Topic it is pre-verbal (Ambar 1988, 1996, 1999; Costa 1996, 1998). In Ambar (1999) it was claimed that the FocusP should be rather considered TopicFocusP; the head of this projection had two features – *t(opic)* and *f(ocus)* features – the *f* feature had to be checked by an Event related element – the verb raised to the head of the projection in the unmarked case – the result being presentational focus over the lexical elements at the right; once this *f* feature was checked the remaining unchecked feature (*t*-feature) had to be checked by some XP (normally discourse linked) in Spec, TopicFocusP – this element would then be interpreted as a topic of a certain type (the subject of focus); if the *f*-feature was not checked in that way – by verb raising – then some XP could move to Spec and check both features, giving rise to contrastive focus on the moved phrase. We also claimed that all the remnant material separated from the focused element, e.g. by traces, would be interpreted as a topic-like element. For concreteness, in (64) *que comprou o livro* (that bought the book) has to be interpreted as a topic-like element, due to the fact that a lexical focus head does not immediately dominate it. Limitation of space precludes going through the argumentation here.[11]

Thus, in (64), *o João* (the John) is focus (presentational) and the lexical material under CP (*que comprou o livro*, that bought the book) is a topic of a certain type – which we have suggested to call *appendix* elsewhere. This focus/topic opposition has effects on the prosody, as ahead noted (see its graphic representation in (65) – //). The *contrastive flavor* of these constructions will then be due to the presence of both focus and topic constituents phonetically realized in the structure (recall the contrast between (35a) and (38a) above).

We derive structures of type (65), which can enter presentational focus as we have seen above (recall that they are appropriate answers to wh-questions – cf. (35):

(65) a. *Foi o João // que saiu*
          it was John that left
      b. *Foram os meninos // que saíram*
          it were the kids that left

In languages of the French type the copula is able to check the tense features of Tense. It is why the identity of tenses required in Portuguese is not a condition for well-formedness of clefts in French. As (66) shows we can have *present* in the copula and *past* in the embedded lexical verb:

(66) *C'est Jean qui est parti*

Keeping the differences of both analyses, it is then plausible that Clech-Darbon, Rebuschi & Rialland (1999) and Munaro & Pollock (2001) are right when they assume that clefts in French are nothing but identificational structures with a CP adjoined to them. I will not pursue this question here.

Let us turn now to *Infl-less clefts*, repeated below:

(67) a. *O João é que saiu.*
          the John is that left+AGR 3rd SG
      b. *Os meninos é que saíram.*
          the kids is that left+AGR 3rd PL

Compare again structures in (67) with those in (65). We conclude that the former systematically differ from the latter in the following aspects. Contrary to (65), in (67): (i) the tense identity is not respected, (ii) there is no visible agreement between the element receiving focus and the copula and (iii) the moved XP precedes the copula. A fourth observation is that (65) vs. (67) also contrasts concerning the intervention of lexical material between the copula and the complementizer. Whereas in (65) it is possible to have intervening lexical material between the copula and the complementizer, in (67) it isn't:

(68)   *Foram os meninos realmente que saíram.*
       it were the kids actually that left

(69)   **Os meninos é realmente que saíram.*
       the kids is actually that left

Assume the claim made in the introduction: present is a zero tense, 3rd person singular a default agreement (or establishing the parallelism, a zero agreement). On the other hand *ser* (be) is defective for lexical features. Suppose now that in this situation *que* incorporates in *é*, forming a unitary complex, an idea already present in Casteleiro (1977), in Ambar (1996) and in Costa & Duarte (2001). We are then reinterpreting our 1996's proposal, where this move was accomplished at LF. The reanalysis of *é* and *que* in *é que* will have the effect of lexicalizing the higher domain. The ungrammaticality of (69) is then predicted – no lexical material can intervene between *é* and *que*. Note that if there is no Infl (no Tense, no Agr) and if *be* is lexically defective, plausibly then, on the one hand, the incorporation strategy used in regular clefts for checking the tense features of Infl is unnecessary here – thus it does not apply – and, on the other hand, *be* is inactive for selection.[12] Consequently, in *Infl-less clefts* the IP domain does not play any role; the same is true for the empty subject in the small clause. One could tentatively hypothesize that these nodes – IP and SC – do not project in these constructions.

The resulting structure would look like (70b) rather than (70a):

(70)   a.

$[_{FP} [_{IP} - [_{vP} \text{é-que}_k [_{SC} [-] [_{CP} [t_k [_{IP} \text{o João T}_k \text{comprou o livro }]]]]]]]]$
               is that   the John   bought the book

       b. $[_{FP} [_{vP} \text{é-que}_k [_{CP} [t_k [_{IP} \text{o João T}_k \text{comprou o livro }]]]]]]$
               is that   the John   bought the book

Now different questions arise. What about focus? We assumed above that *ser* (be) has a focus feature that is active when related to Tense. It was why in (64) *foi* (was) had to raise to FocusP or why the probe Focus could match a valued focus feature in the copula (see fn. 9). Given that in (70) there is no tense in the copula, one may conclude that this focus feature is inactive. Consequently *é que* doesn't have to raise to FocusP. However one could think of *que* as being able to transmit Event properties to *é que*, – being the complementizer of the embedded CP, *que* (that) has Event properties. We will therefore assume that *é que* does not need to raise to FocusP due to inactiveness of the focus feature in *be*, but the complex *é que* can check focus due to Event properties in *que*.[13]

Consider again *infl-less* clefts in (67). There are facts leading to the conclusion that *é que* does not raise to check Focus in these structures. First, the study of Focus in Portuguese led us to conclude that either the verb raises to the head of FP, giving rise to presentational focus, or a XP, say a DP, raises to Spec, Focus providing contrastive focus, as referred to above. It is possible to test that just one position is filled (Ambar 1999). Second, sentence (71) below shows that this is probably true: an adverb, for instance, can intervene between the pre-copula XP and the complex *é que*. If *o João* were in Spec, FP and *é que* in F^0, (71) should be excluded:

(71)   *O João realmente é que sabe isso.*
        John actually is that knows that

Finally, the interpretation available for *o João* can only be contrastive focus, which is exactly the interpretation assigned to elements in Spec,FocusP. It is then desirable to have the same procedure here than in similar focus structures. We will therefore conclude that *é que* does not raise to FocusP in *infl-less clefts* of type (67, 71) and that some XP raises or is merged in Spec,FocusP to check contrastive focus:[14]

(72)   [$_{FP}$ o João$_i$ [$_{IP}$ [$_{I'}$ [$_{vP}$ é-que $_k$ [$_{CP}$ [t$_k$ [$_{IP}$ t$_i$ T$_{i\,k}$ comprou o livro]]]]]]]
        the John   is that   bought the book

We derive what we have called an *infl-less cleft*.

   We also derive absence of agreement and of tense identity with the embedded lexical verb – on the one hand *é* has zero tense and zero agreement (this is why *que* can raise) and on the other hand *que* has no such spelt out features – consequently, there is no reason to raise the subject to Spec,IP, which plausibly is not projected as suggested in (70b) – see fn. 13.

   Notice then that *é* (is) seems to do nothing in *é que* (is that).[15] We would then expect it to be null. This is precisely the case of Brazilian Portuguese where sentences like (73) are possible with the interpretation of (67, 72) (Kato et al. 1996; Modesto 2001):

(73)   *João que comprou o livro.*
        John that bought the book

The reason why sentences of type (73) are possible in Brazilian Portuguese, though not in European Portuguese, is unclear for me at the moment and requires further research, namely on Tense and on the copula in both varieties of Portuguese. However, thinking of the different behavior of Agr and Tense in both languages, the suspicion is that Tense is the responsible for the contrast (Galves 1993, 1998, 2001; Rouveret 1996; Ambar, Gonzaga & Negrão 2002, among others).

   Observe again (70). If nothing else happens to (70), one might wonder whether its output is grammatical. (70) seems to correspond to structures like (74):

(74)   *É que as crianças gostam de chocolates.*
        It is that my kids love chocolates

These sentences are produced in a situation like:

(75) a. *Comprei muitos chocolates ...*
          I bought lots of chocolates....
      b. *É que as crianças gostam de chocolates...*
          It is that my kids love chocolates

I will assume that the proposal made above (70) for *é que* also applies to (74)–(75b), i.e. also in these structures *é que* is a complex resulting from incorporation; also here no lexical material can intervene between the copula and the complementizer:

(76) *É realmente que as crianças gostam de chocolates.*
      It is really that my kids love chocolates

Note however that the output of (70) is possible if and only if it receives the interpretation obtained in context (75), i.e. the structure is possible just in case it is somehow Discourse linked. I will assume that *é que* raises to the head of FocusP (as we have seen it can check focus due to the Event properties in *que*) and that a Discourse topic null operator is merged in Spec, FP, more precisely spec,TopicFocusP, checking the *t*-feature of this projection (see discussion under (64)). The required interpretation can then be seen as the effect of the combination of these two operations, the null topic operator having the function of relating the discourse with the focused proposition introduced by *é que*:

(77) [$_{FP}$ Op [$_{F'}$ é-que $_k$ [$_{vP}$ t $_k$ [$_{CP}$ [t$_k$ [$_{IP}$ as crianças gostam de chocolates]]]]]]
          is that   the kids   like   chocolates

Note, on the one hand, that focus has scope on the entire embedded IP because there is no intervention of lexical material between the focus head and the constituent receiving focus – IP; on the other hand the null operator is topic not focus, confirming what we have assumed before: topic can be null, focus not and the focus projection is filled by just one focus element. Interestingly then we see, through example (78) below, that no lexical material can precede the null topic operator:

(78) a. **Realmente é que as crianças gostam de chocolates.*
          Really is that the kids like chocolates
      b. *É que realmente as crianças gostam de chocolates.*
          It is that really the kids like chocolates.

We will tentatively consider that the ungrammaticality of (78a) is due to an intervention effect – the presence of the adverb in (78a) blocks the identification of the null topic operator by the Discourse.

Concerning clefts with complementizer *que* (that), in Section 5. we observed a subtle contrast that we have not considered in the analysis outlined so far. I repeat it in (79):

(79)   Que aconteceu ?
       what happened

    a.   *Foi o Pedro que partiu o copo.*
       it was Peter that broke the glass

    b.   **Foi o copo que o Pedro partiu.*
       it was the glass that Peter broke

    c.   **Foi o Pedro quem partiu o copo.*
       it was Peter who broke the glass

    d.   **Foi o copo o que o Pedro partiu.*
       it was the glass what Peter broke

Sentence (79a) is ambiguous – it can be an answer to (i) *who broke the glass?* or to (ii) *what happened?* In the interpretation (i) – focus on the subject – it would have derivation (80) below, as we saw above in (64):

(80)

$[_{FP}$ foi $_{ik}$ $[_{IP}$ o João$_i$ $[_{I'}$ t $-$ e $_{ik}$ $[_{VP}$ $[_{SC\ ik}$ $[_{CP}$ [que$_k$ $[_{IP}$ t$_i$ T$_{ik}$ comprou o livro $]]]]]]]$
    was   the John   that   bought the book

Observe the following. First, in the chains formed in (80) an intervening index different from the one in the subject, which is related to inflection (79b), or an intervening wh-phrase (79c, d) would block percolation of Focus to CP. Second, we wouldn't like to have the same derivation for the two interpretations – (i) focus on the subject, as represented in (80) (= (64)) and (ii) focus on CP, the interpretation available in (79a).

    Suppose then that when focus is on CP, the subject is not in the position it is in structures where focus has scope just on it – (80). Instead, suppose that whenever focus is on the whole CP, the subject has to be in Spec,CP as in (81):

(81)

$[_{FP}$ foi $_{ik}$ $[_{IP}$ $[_{I'}$ t $-$ e $_{ik}$ $[_{VP}$ $[_{SC\ ik}$ $[_{CP}$ o João$_i$ [que$_k$ $[_{IP}$ t$_i$ T$_{ik}$ comprou o livro $]]]]]]]]$
    was   the John that   bought   the book

Then we should have to slightly modify what we observed under (64): when the head of FP is filled by a tensed verb, Focus is assigned to the first lexical unit dominated by FP. In (80, 64), that unit is *o João* (John), which is separated from the next lexical unit – CP – by different traces; therefore, this CP cannot be interpreted as focus; it will be interpreted as topic. In (81), CP is the first lexical unit – then it will receive Focus. We still have to explain why the subject – *o João* – does not remain in Spec, spec of the embedded IP, giving rise to an ungrammatical sentence. We would assume that *que*, heading CP, is not sufficiently lexical to receive focus. Thus, the subject – a lexical XP – has to raise to the CP domain. If the constituent that raises to Spec,CP is different from the subject, an intervention effect will be produced – having an index different from inflection this constituent will block focus assignment to IP – the result being that the focus scope will not be on the whole sentence. Note that Kayne (1994, Fn. 6, pp. 153) suggests that in cleft structures like (82a) the cleft phrase is in Spec, CP (82b) – as in relatives, the difference being that in clefts CP is complement of *be*, whereas in relatives it is complement of D^0:

(82)   a.   It is linguistics that we are studying.
        b.   It is [$_{CP}$ linguistics$_i$ [that [$_{IP}$ we are studying e$_i$]]]

Also Modesto (2001) proposes a structure like (82b) for *that*-clefts of type (64), (80) in Brazilian Portuguese.[16]

Different questions arise however. I have raised two of them under the discussion of Chomsky's (1977) analysis in Section 2; now others emerge from what we have observed: (i) sentences in (79a), (81) don't have the same interpretation as those in ((64), (80)), (ii) a wh-word in Spec,CP blocks the interpretation required for (79a), (81). Moreover, if a wh-phrase replaces the DP *o João* (the John) in (79a), (81), then the sentence becomes a wh-question, not a cleft of type (2) in Section 1, i.e. not a cleft with a –Q wh-word, as the opposition between the paraphrases in (83b–c) vs. (84b–c) shows – a –Q wh-word may be replaced by DP – que as in relatives, but not by que –N', as in questions; a +Q wh word has the opposit behaviour:

(83)   a.   *Foi quem que comprou o livro ?*
             it was who that bought the book
        b.   **Foi a pessoa que que comprou o livro.*
             it was the person that that bought the book
        c.   *Foi que pessoa que comprou o livro.*
             it was what person that bought the book

(84)   a.   *Foi o João quem comprou o livro.*
             it was John who bought the book
        b.   *Foi o João a pessoa que comprou o livro.*
             it was John the person that bought the book
        c.   **Foi o João que pessoa que comprou o livro*
             it was John what person that bought the book

The answers to these questions are not in the scope of this article. We would have to go through the study of –Q wh-(pseudo)clefts and +Q wh-(pseudo)-clefts. In that study the nature of wh-words, in the line of Di Sciullo's (1996, 1999, 2001, 2005) proposals, will be of crucial relevance. As announced in the introduction, limitations of space have required restricting the analysis to *that*-clefts. We will soon extend our analysis to a larger domain. We will then try to find solutions for the problems raised.

7. Conclusion

In this work I have described the behavior of clefts in Portuguese. My main concern was to shed some light on the particular behavior of tense in these constructions in Portuguese, a fact that has not been observed in the literature.

The comparison of clefts with relatives was important in this testing. Then, another conclusion emerged from that compared description: *that*-clefts seem to be not relatives.

Finally I have tentatively presented an analysis whose main goal was to relate the *tense identity* found in regular clefts with another idiosyncrasy of Portuguese – *infl-less clefts* – and with the facts observed with respect to focus.

I hope that the next step, with a systematic study of (pseudo)-clefts with wh-words and of *that-less clefts,* will lead to a unified account of clefts in a system more elegant than the one presented now.

Notes

* This work was presented at the conference *Language, Brain and Computation*, held at Venice in October 2002. I am especially grateful to its director Anna-Maria Di Sciullo for relevant support, subtle comments and help. I thank that audience for their comments.

1. In our 1996 ms. paper on Focus we had already pointed out this *tense identity*, though not all the argumentation presented here.

2. In this case adjacency is not required.

3. The paradigm of clefts is not always complete in those works. This is the case of Chomsky (1977), for example, – a not surprising fact given that this article deals with other phenomena. In the absence of other credible judgements on English clefts, I use in part Kiss's (1996) exemplification of the analyses referred to.

4. On par with Akmajian's proposal of deriving pseudo-clefts from an underlying structure having a free relative as subject of *be*, with subsequent derivation of clefts from pseudo clefts, through extraposition.
Alternatively one could maintain Kiss's (1996) and Ambar's (1996) proposal and assume that *be* selects CP (or Tense). But then the whole story about small clauses would have to be revisited.

5. Unfortunately I couldn't systematically test all the data with a representative number of native speakers. So I limit the examples to the languages and to the sentences whose judgements are unequivocal.

Note that in (56) there is *tense identity* between the main copula and the embedded auxiliary *(est, ha* in French and Italian respectively). On the other hand in Portuguese in the context of other tenses, e.g. future, apparently the *tense identity* requirement is weakened: *Quem comprará o livro ?* (who will buy the book?) – *É / será o Pedro que comprará* (it is/will be Peter that will buy). However, *future* is plausibly not a different tense – in fact it is the infinitive + *(h)a*, the present of *haver*, with consequences also on other phenomena, e.g. clitic positioning. As we claimed elsewhere, plausibly then *past* is the only true tense. Limitations of space preclude going through this matter here.

6. There are different ways of implementing this strategy where $[e_i]$ looks like a sort of null clitic. Note that the features transmitted are Tense features related to Event. Plausibly then $[e_i]$ passes through small vP – defective for Event, given the properties of *be*. One could think that $[e_i]$ in vP enables *be* with the necessary features for checking Tense, but see discussion under (63) and fn. 9. For simplification of the representation I will use either vP or VP for the projection dominating the copula.

7. Note that these are the features of Tense related to Comp.

8. Note that movement of the subject to Spec,IP is an improper movement assuming that this is an A-position – the ungrammaticality of (64) would then be explained. However other constituents different from DPs can occupy the position; consequently Spec,IP seems to be an A'-position in these constructions (cf. Hoekstra & Mulder 1990; Barbosa 1998 and Costa & Duarte 2001).

9. Plausibly the only feature *be* has.

An alternative analysis would consist of considering that movement of the cleft DP – o *João* in (63) – ends up in vP, as in (63a), and that the tense and person or EPP features of T are valued through Agree, i.e. much in terms of Chomsky (2001), rather than in Chosmky's (1995) view. Then, *focus* would also be valued through Agree – the probe focus in FP seeking for a goal would match the now valued focus feature in the copula in vP. This hypothesis would explain why the contrast concerning presentational focus with regular lexical verbs opposing French to Portuguese *(comeu o João* (ate John) vs. * *a mangé Jean)* disappears in clefts. Note that if *be* has a focus feature, as we are claiming, then we also explain why focus is obligatory in clefts, either assuming the analysis in the text or the one suggested here.

10. For the need of Event in Focus checking, see Zubizarreta (1998), Ambar (1996, 1999), among others.

11. The main goal of this proposal was to account for the complementary distribution observed between presentational vs. contrastive focus, concerning, for example, verb movement. The proposal also captured the different interpretation of each type of focus – contrastive focus would have a *mixed* reading, with *t*(opic) and *f*(ocus) properties; presentational focus a *pure f*(ocus) interpretation. A distinction was also made between this topic-like element in Spec,TopicFocusP and other topic elements – a *t*-phrase in this projection was considered as the element (the subject) introducing focus (the predicate). In most cases this *t*-phrase is null and discourse linked; focus can never be null. But see Ambar (1999) for details.

12. We return to the observation under (62): plausibly it is Tense that selects the embedded domain. We should then wonder whether this embedded domain is a small clause as we have been assuming for the clefts considered so far. Note that the consideration of a small clause in these structures was motivated by the behavior of *be* in other constructions. I will not pursue this question here.

13. Note that, contrary to *be*, *que* has no intrinsic focus feature in need to being checked – this is why *é que* can raise to check focus, given the Event properties of *que*, but doesn't have to. This property of *be* is intended to cover the traditional intuition that *be* relates concepts – plausibly a topic with a focus. As we will see below *é que* raises to focus whenever the proposition headed by *que* is assigned focus; being the head of this proposition *que* has then this focus feature. Wrt focus, the difference between *be* and *que* is then that the focus feature is an intrinsic feature in the former, whereas an optional feature in the latter (in the sense that focus can be assigned, but it is not always assigned, as in other structures).

14. Note that, as we observed in the preceding footnote, *é que* raises to FP when *que*, more precisely the proposition headed by *que*, bears a focus feature. This is not the case in these structures – here what bears focus is the XP in Spec,Focus, not the embedded CP – this is topic. An alternative hypothesis would be to consider that *que* (that) transmits to *é que* its EPP feature. Then, some element would have to fill Spec,FP, i.e. a given XP would have to raise or to be merged in that position. However it is not the case that Spec,CP is always filled – on the contrary there is the whole story of Double Filled Comp effects.

15. Actually it must still do in European Portuguese though not in Brazilian Portuguese.

16. Modesto (2001) derives the impossibility of occurring a wh-phrase in Spec,CP in (79b) from the combination of the features ± predicative and ±QU.

References

Akmajian, A. (1970). On deriving cleft sentences from pseudo-cleft sentences. *Linguistic Inquiry, 1,* 149–168.

Ambar, M. (1988). *Para uma Sintaxe da Inversão Sujeito-Verbo em Português.* Ph.D. dissertation. 1992. Lisboa: Colibri.

Ambar, M. (1996). The syntax of focus – a unified approach. Ms. U. Lisbon. Talk delivered at International Workshop on Focus, Paris.

Ambar, M. (1999). Aspects of focus in Portuguese. In L. Tuller & G. Rebuschi (Eds.), *The Grammar of Focus* (pp. 23–53). Amsterdam: John Benjamins.

Ambar, M., Gonzaga, M. & Negrão, E. V. (2002). Tense, quantification and clause structure in EP and BP – evidence from a comparative study on *sempre*. In *Proceedings of Going Romance 2002* (pp. 28–30). Amsterdam: John Benjamins.

Barbosa, P. (1998). On inversion in wh-questions in romance. Ms. to appear in A. Hulk & J-Y. Pollock (Eds), *Romance Inversion.* New York: Oxford University Press.

Brody, M. (1995). Focus and checking theory. In I. Kenesei (Ed.), *Approaches to Hungarian V. Levels and Structures* (pp. 29–44). Szeged: JATE.

Casteleiro J. M.(1977), *Sintaxe Transformacional do Adjectivo. Regência das Construções Completivas*, Dissertação de Doutoramento, Faculdade de Letras, Universidade de Lisboa.

Chomsky, N. (1977). On wh-movement. In P. Cullicover, T Wasow & A. Akmajian (Eds.), *Formal Syntax* (pp. 71–132). New York: Academic Press.

Chomsky, N. (1995). *The Minimalist Program*. Cambridge, Mass.: MIT Press.

Chomsky, N. (2001). Derivation by Phase. In Michael Kenstowicz (Ed.), *Ken Hale: A life in language*. Cambridge, Mass.: MIT Press.

Clech-Darbon, A., Rebuschi, G. & Rialland, A. (1999). Are there cleft sentences in French? In L. Tuller & G. Rebuschi (Eds.), *The Grammar of Focus* (pp. 83–119). Amsterdam: John Benjamins.

Costa, J. (1996). Positions for subjects in European Portuguese. Ms. to appear in *WCCFL XV Proceedings*.

Costa, J. (1998). *Word Order Variation. A Constrained Based Approach*. Haia: HIL.

Costa, J. & Duarte, I. (2001). Minimizando a estrutura: uma análise unificada das construções de clivagem em Português. *Actas do XVI Encontro Nacional da Associação Portuguesa de Linguística* (pp. 627–638). Lisboa: APL.

Di Sciullo, A-M. (1996). Modularity and X^0/XP asymmetry. *Linguistic Analysis, 26*, 1–26.

Di Sciullo, A-M. (1999). Local asymmetry. *WPL MIT, 35*, 23–67.

Di Sciullo, A-M. (2001). P and the operator shell. Talk delivered at IGG, Trieste.

Di Sciullo, A-M. (2005). *Asymmetry in Morphology*. In press. Cambridge, Mass.: The MIT Press.

Duarte, I. (2000). Sobre interrogativas –Q em Português Europeu e Português Brasileiro. Ms. U. Lisboa.

Emonds, J. (1976). *A Transformational Approach to English Syntax*. New York: Academic Press.

Frascarelli, M. (2000). Cleft constituents as small clauses heads: A new proposal. Talk delivered at XXVI Incontro di Grammatica Generativa, Roma.

Galves, C. (1993). O enfraquecimento da concordância no Português Brasileiro. In I. Roberts & M. Kato (Eds.), *Português Brasileiro, uma viagem diacrônica* (pp. 387–408). Campinas: Editora da Unicamp.

Galves, C. (1998). Tópicos e Sujeitos, pronomes e concordância no Português Brasileiro. *Cadernos de Estudos Linguísticos, 34*, 7–21.

Galves, C. (2001). *Ensaios sobre as gramáticas do Português*. Campinas: Editora da Unicamp.

Giorgi, A. & Pianesi, F. (1992). For a syntax of tense. Ms. University of Catania and IRST, Trento.

Heycock, C. & Krock, A. (1999). Pseudocleft connectedness: Implications for the LF interface level. *Linguistic Inquiry, 30*, 365–397.

Hoekstra, T & Mulder, R. (1990). Unergatives as copular verbs; locational and existential predication. *The Linguistic Review, 7*, 1–79.

Kato, M., Braga, M. L., Corrêa, V.,. Rossi, M. A. L & Sikanski, N. S. (1996). As construções –Q no Português Brasileiro falado: perguntas, clivadas e relativas. Ms. to appear in *Gramática do Português Falado. Volume VI: Desenvolvimentos*. Campinas: Editora da UNICAMP.

Kato, M. & Raposo, E.(1996). European and Brazilian Portuguese word order: Question, focus and topic constructions. In C. Parodi, C. Quicoli, M. Saltarelli & M. L. Zubizarreta (Eds.), *Aspects of Romance Linguistics* (pp. 267–277). Washington: Georgetown University Press.

Kayne, R. (1993). Toward a modular theory of auxiliary selection. *Studia Linguistica, 47,* 3–31.

Kayne, R. (1994). *The Antisymmetry of Syntax.* Cambridge: MIT Press.

Kayne, R. (1998). Covert vs. overt movement. Ms. New York – Cuny.

Kiss, K. (1996). The focus operator and information focus. Ms. Budapest University.

Modesto, M. (2001). *As construções clivadas no Português do Brasil: relações entre interpretação focal, movimento sintáctico e prosódia.* São Paulo: Humanitas.

Moro, A. (1997). *The Raising of Predicates.* Cambridge: Cambridge University Press.

Munaro, N. & Pollock, J-Y. (2001). Qu'est-ce que (qu)-est-ce que? – A case study in comparative Romance interrogative syntax. Ms. Venice, Amiens.

Obenauer, H-G. (1976). *Etudes de syntaxe interrogative du Français.* Tübingen.

Obenauer, H-G. (1981). Le principe des catégories vides et la syntaxe des interrogatives complexes. *Langue Française, 52,* 100–118. Paris: Larousse.

Obenauer, H-G. (1994). Aspects de la syntaxe A-Barre. Thèse de Doctorat d'Etat. Université de Paris VIII.

Rizzi, L. (1997). The fine structure of the left periphery. In L. Haegeman (Ed.), *Elements in Grammar: Handbook of Generative Syntax* (pp. 281–337). Dordrecht: Kluwer.

Rouveret, A. (1996). Clitics, subjects and tense in European Portuguese. *Revue des Langues Romanes, XCIII* (2): 337–373.

Zubizarreta, M-L. (1998). *Word order, Prosody and Focus.* Cambridge, Mass.: MIT Press.

Generating configurational asymmetries in prosodic phonology*

Evan W. Mellander
University of Leipzig

The paper examines a number of asymmetries in the types of internal configurations permitted in prosodic entities cross-linguistically, including consonantal and diphthongal moraicity and the *Iambic / Trochaic Law*. It is demonstrated that when these restrictions are analysed in terms of rhythmic constituency, striking parallels emerge with respect to the position of strong beats within the relevant metrical domain. A unified analysis for the attested patterns is proposed in the framework of Optimality Theory (Prince & Smolensky 1993), exploiting an asymmetric set of rhythmic well-formedness constraints (Van de Vijver 1998). The strong cross-linguistic preference for initial prominence in binary domains is explained through a conspiracy effect in constraint interaction, whereby different rankings converge on a single output (cf. Trochaic Default: McCarthy & Prince 1986).

1. Introduction

While the parsing of the speech signal into prosodic units is a universal property of natural language, individual grammars differ with respect to the structural properties of these constituents. Cross-linguistically, certain properties appear to be strongly favoured over others, resulting in asymmetric sets of preferred configurations for prosodic constituents. While prosodic theory has developed a number of mechanisms to account for asymmetric configurational restrictions in specific types of prosodic entities such as moraic consonants, diphthongs, and metrical feet, these devices are formally unconnected, and often lack independent motivation entirely. The present paper sketches out a unified alternative to such mechanisms by appealing to general principles of rhythmic well-formedness (Van de Vijver 1998), and accounts for configurational asymmetries in several types of prosodic constituents through constraint interaction in Optimality Theory (Prince & Smolensky 1993). On this view, surface configurational asymmetries in prosodic constituents can be predicted on the basis of quantity-prominence relations that follow from the interaction of asymmetric rhythmic constraints. The analysis illustrates how seemingly opaque configurational patterning can be generated straightforwardly if asymmetric relations are exploited as primitives of Universal Grammar.

1.1 Configurational restrictions on consonantal moraicity

At an abstract level, syllable quantity can be measured in terms of *weight units* or *moras*, where a light syllable contains a single mora and a heavy syllable contains two moras (e.g. Hyman 1985; Hayes 1989). Many languages distinguish between heavy and light syllables for purposes of stress assignment and other prosodic phenomena, and consonants often play a role in determining syllable weight. In the vast majority of such systems, however, only those consonants in the syllable coda (i.e. tautosyllabic *postvocalic* consonants) can bear a mora, while those in the syllable onset cannot.[1] A well-known example is the stress rule of Latin, which can be stated (slightly simplified) as follows: "stress the penult if heavy, otherwise the antepenult". Examples of Latin stress are given in (1) below. (Data from Hayes 1995: 50, cf. Mester 1994.)

(1)   Stress in Latin
     a. *penult = CVV*   a.mí:.kus   'friend, kind'
                       gu.ber.ná:.bunt   'they will reign'
     b. *penult = CV*   i.ni.mi:.kí.ti.a   'hostility'
                       do.més.ti.kus   'belonging to the house'
     c. *penult = CVC*   or.na.mén.tum *or.ná.men.tum 'equipment'
                       sa.pi.én.te:s   *sa.pí.en.te:s   'wise' nom. pl.

In (1a), stress falls on the CVV penult due to the presence in that syllable of a long vowel, rendering it heavy. This contrasts with (1b), where a CV penult counts as light, resulting in antepenultimate stress. In (1c), the presence of a coda consonant in the penult draws stress onto that syllable despite the fact that the vowel is short. This demonstrates that the presence of a coda consonant is a sufficient cndition for a syllable to be counted as heavy in Latin, while the presence of an onset consonant is not. The moraic structure of consonants in Latin can thus be represented as in (2) below, where the syllables /at/ and /ta/ are compared.

(2)   Consonantal moraicity   *Heavy*   *Light*

   Trochaic   a.   (a̱ t)$_{Syll}$ b.   *(a̱ t)$_{Syll}$

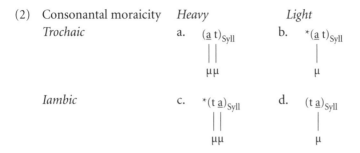

   Iambic   c.   *(t a̱)$_{Syll}$ d.   (t a̱)$_{Syll}$

Notice that the restrictions in (2) are asymmetric. Taking the vowel as the syllable head (<u>underlined</u>. cf. *Sonority Sequencing*: Clements 1990), only *trochaic* or left-headed configurations can be heavy, as in (2a) (cf. (2c)), while *iambic* or right-headed configurations must be light, as in (2d) (cf. (2b)). The moraic status of consonants is thus contingent on a particular configurational relationship with the syllable head. This relationship is known in the literature as *Weight-by-Position* (e.g. Hayes 1989; see Section 2.1 for discussion).

   Similar restrictions obtain in the moraic structure of diphthongal sequences, which we will turn to presently.

1.2   Configurational restrictions on diphthongal moraicity

Diphthongs, or bipartite vocalic nuclei, can be broadly classified into two types, those with a rising sonority profile from left to right (hereafter *rising diphthongs*,[2] e.g. that in French *bois* [bua] 'wood') and those with a falling sonority profile from left to right (hereafter *falling diphthongs*, e.g. that in English *cow* [kau]).

   Cross-linguistically, rising diphthongs generally behave as light while falling diphthongs behave as heavy (cf. Kaye 1985; Hayes 1985; Hyman 1985; Schane 1987, 1995; Rosenthall 1994; Mellander 2003). Empirical motivation for this generalisation can be found in a number of languages. Consider the data in (3) below from Vata (Eastern Kru), a language where rising diphthongs are tolerated but falling diphthongs are not. (Data from Kaye 1985: 291 with tonal patterns omitted.)

(3)   Monomoraic syllables in Vata

		Monomoraic		*Bimoraic*	
Monophthongs	a.	di	'villages'	b. –	*diː
		vɛdɛ	'manioc'		*vɛːdɛː
		ɔ	'he/she'		*ɔː
Diphthongs	c.	cɪa	'study'	d. –	*caɪ
		sɪɔ	'snail'		*sɔɪ
		yuʌ	'children'		*yʌu

Kaye analyses vowel sequences in Vata as diphthongal constituents rather than onset-nucleus sequences on the basis of a ban on branching onsets in the language.[3] If Vata is assumed to enforce a ban on all bimoraic syllables as one might infer from the absence of long vowels in the language (3b), the absence of falling diphthongs in (3d) (cf. rising diphthongs in (3c)) can be explained straightforwardly provided a bimoraic structure is assumed.

In Spanish, rising diphthongs can occur in word-medial closed syllables while falling diphthongs cannot, as illustrated in (4) below.[4] (Data from Rosenthall 1994: 135–9.)

(4)   Diphthongs by syllable type in Spanish

		Rising Diphthongs		*Falling Diphthongs*	
Open Syllables	a.	dia.blo	'devil'	b. frai	'friar'
		fue.ro	'law'	au.to	'car'
		kuo.ta	'quota'	pei.ne	'comb'
Closed Syllables	c.	muer.te	'death'	d. –	*meur.te
		sies.ta	'siesta'		*seis.ta
		puer.ta	'door'		*peur.ta

If falling diphthongs – and crucially not rising diphthongs – are assumed to be heavy, this gap follows straightforwardly from a maximally bimoraic rimal constituent (cf. Rosenthall 1994; Selkirk 1984). Given a monomoraic representation for rising diphthongs, the inclusion into the syllable of a moraic coda consonant (via *Weight-by-Position*, see Section 2.1) is unproblematic with respect to a maximally binary rime. The same does not hold, however, in the case of a (bimoraic) falling diphthong, where the inclusion of a tautosyllabic moraic coda consonant would result in an illicit trimoraic syllable.[5]

On this view, a diphthongal offglide *must* be moraic, while a diphthongal onglide *must* be nonmoraic. This is exemplified in (5) below, for the diphthongal sequences /au/ and /ua/.

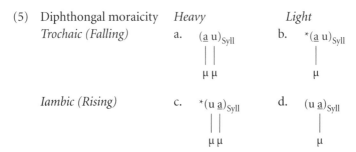

(5)   Diphthongal moraicity

The syllable head again falls on the most sonorous melody. As we saw in the case of moraic consonants (cf. (2)) trochaic structures must be heavy or bimoraic while iambic structures must be light or monomoraic. From a configurational stand-point, therefore, the restrictions on moraic consonants and diphthongal moraicity are identical. This observation suggests that both phenomena could be accounted for with the same mechanism.

In the following section we consider a slightly more complicated set of configurational restrictions – those on metrical feet.

1.3 Configurational restrictions on metrical feet

Many languages parse strings of syllables into iterative prosodic constituants called *metrical feet*, which are normally disyllabic and are manifested in one of two forms: trochaic feet (e.g. in Fijian, Mohawk), or iambic feet (e.g. in Choctaw, Hixkaryana). The two system types with representative examples are given in (6) below. (Fijian data in this paper are taken from Hayes 1995: 143–5, attributed to Schütz 1978, 1985 and from Dixon 1988; Choctaw data in this paper are taken from Hayes 1995: 210, attributed to Munro & Ulrich 1984; Ulrich 1986; Nicklas 1975.)

(6) Trochee: $(\acute{\sigma}\,\sigma)$ Iamb: $(\sigma\,\acute{\sigma})$
     Fijian: $(^{n}\underline{\text{di}}.\text{ko})(\underline{\text{ne}}.\text{si})$ *Choctaw:* $(\text{t}\int\!\text{i}.\underline{\text{pi:}})(\text{sa}.\underline{\text{li}})$
                 'deaconess' S78   'you (obj.)-see-I (subj.)' N:242

A number of persistent asymmetries obtain between the trochaic and iambic systems. The most well-known of these asymmetries stems from the *Iambic / Trochaic Law* (hereafter ITL), a set of generalisations bearing on how humans perceive rhythmic constituency in alternating beats with differing acoustic properties (Woodrow 1909, 1951). These are summarized in (7) below.

(7) Iambic/Trochaic Law (Hayes 1995: 71)
     a. Elements contrasting in intensity naturally form groupings with initial prominence.
     b. Elements contrasting in duration naturally form groupings with final prominence.

In recent years, scholars have linked these generalisations to asymmetric quantitative processes and parsing phenomena in iambic and trochaic systems (Hayes 1985, 1987, 1995; Kager 1993, 1995, 1999; McCarthy & Prince 1986; Mester 1994; Prince 1992). On this view, trochaic systems differ from iambic systems as in (8) below.

(8) Iambic/Trochaic Law (Kager 1993: 382)
     a. Trochaic systems have durationally even feet.
     b. Iambic systems have durationally uneven feet.

The preferred configurations for quantitative feet under the ITL are thus as in (9) below.

(9)   Quantity-sensitive feet *Even*   *Uneven*

    Trochaic ($\underline{\sigma}\ \sigma$)   a.   b.

                            $(\underline{\sigma}\ \sigma)_{Ft}$ $^*(\underline{\sigma}\ \sigma)_{Ft}$

                            | | ∧|

                            $\mu\ \mu$ $\mu\mu\mu$

    Iambic ($\sigma\ \underline{\sigma}$)   c.   d.

                            $^*(\sigma\ \underline{\sigma})_{Ft}$ $(\sigma\ \underline{\sigma})_{Ft}$

                            | | |∧

                            $\mu\ \mu$ $\mu\mu\mu$

While the quantitatively even trochee in (9)a is licit under (8), the quantitatively uneven trochee in (9)b is not. Conversely, while the quantitatively uneven iamb in (9)d is well-formed under (8), its quantitatively even counterpart in (9)c is illicit.

    These restrictions are supported by evidence from quantitative processes in a range of languages. Two such processes are given in (10), and exemplified in (11) and (12) below.

(10)   Quantitative Processes Enforcing Conformity with the ITL

    a. *Iambic lengthening*

        (Choctaw, Kari'ña) $\sigma\ \sigma$ $(\sigma\ \underline{\sigma})_{Ft}$

                              | | ⇒ |∧

                              $\mu\ \mu$ $\mu\mu\mu$

    b. *Trochaic Levelling*

        (Fijian, Middle English) $\sigma\ \sigma$ $(\underline{\sigma}\ \sigma)_{Ft}$

                                  ∧| ⇒ | |

                                  $\mu\mu\mu$ $\mu\ \mu$

(11)   Iambic Lengthening in Choctaw

    a. /sa-litiha-tok/ (sa.<u>li:</u>)(ti.<u>ha:</u>)(<u>tok</u>) *(sa.<u>li</u>)(ti.<u>ha</u>)(<u>tok</u>)

        /$\sigma_\mu\sigma_\mu\sigma_\mu\sigma_\mu\sigma_{\mu\mu}$/ ($\sigma_\mu\ \underline{\sigma}_{\mu\mu}$)($\sigma_\mu\underline{\sigma}_{\mu\mu}$)($\underline{\sigma}_{\mu\mu}$) *($\sigma_\mu\underline{\sigma}_\mu$)($\sigma_\mu\underline{\sigma}_\mu$)($\underline{\sigma}_{\mu\mu}$)

        'I was dirty' M&U:192

    b. /oktʃa -li-li-h/ (<u>ok</u>)(tʃa.<u>li:</u>)(<u>lih</u>) *(<u>ok</u>)(tʃa.<u>li</u>)(<u>lih</u>)

        /$\sigma_{\mu\mu}\sigma_\mu\sigma_\mu\sigma_{\mu\mu}$/ ($\underline{\sigma}_{\mu\mu}$)($\sigma_\mu\underline{\sigma}_{\mu\mu}$)($\underline{\sigma}_{\mu\mu}$) *($\underline{\sigma}_{\mu\mu}$)($\sigma_\mu\underline{\sigma}_\mu$)($\underline{\sigma}_{\mu\mu}$)

        'I woke him up' U:54

(12)   Trochaic Levelling in Fijian

    a. /^{m}bu:-$^\eta$gu/ (^{m}<u>bú</u>. $^\eta$gu) *(^{m}<u>bú:</u>. $^\eta$gu) 'my grandmother'

        /$\sigma_{\mu\mu}\sigma_\mu$/ ($\underline{\sigma}_\mu\sigma_\mu$) *($\underline{\sigma}_{\mu\mu}\sigma_\mu$) S85:528

b. /siːvi/ (sí.ßi   *(sí:.ßi)   'exceed'

/σ_{μμ}σ_{μ}/ (σ̱_{μ}σ_{μ}) *(σ̱_{μμ}σ_{μ})   D:26-7

In (11), underlyingly short vowels undergo lengthening in the second syllable of iambic feet forming uneven ($σ_{μ}σ̱_{μμ}$) iambs, while in (12) underlyingly long vowels undergo shortening in the initial syllable of trochaic feet, forming even ($σ̱_{μ}σ_{μ}$) trochees.

These quantitative processes are not symmetrically attested across the world's languages, however. As illustrated in (13) below, Iambic Lengthening occurs in 21 languages while Trochaic Levelling is found in only five – this despite the fact that there are many more trochaic languages than iambic ones.

(13)   Quantitative Processes Driven by the ITL (Hayes 1995:83, 148)[6]

Iambic Lengthening: /σ_{μ}σ_{μ}/ → (σ_{μ}σ̱_{μμ})		Trochaic Levelling: /σ_{μμ}σ_{μ}/ → (σ̱_{μ}σ_{μ})	
Cariban:	Hixkaryana	Austronesian:	Fijian
	Macushi		Hawaiian
	Carib		Tongan
	Tiriyó	W. Germanic:	Middle
	Kari'ña		English
Muskogean	Choctaw/Chicasaw	Romance:	Abruzzese
Algonquian:	Menomini		Italian
	Potawatomi		
	Munsee/Unami		
Lake Iroquoian:	Cayuga		
	Onondaga		
	Seneca		
Eskimo:	St. Lawrence Island Yupik		
	Central Alaskan Yupik		
	Pacific Yupik		
	Steward Peninsula Inupiaq		
N. California:	Kashaya		
	Maidu		
	Sierra Miwok		
Southern Paiute			
Yidiny			

In Section 3.4 an explanation will be offered for the pervasiveness of iambic lengthening in iambic systems relative to Trochaic Levelling in trochaic systems.

In the preceding sections evidence has been presented for three configurational asymmetries in prosodic constituents: consonantal moraicity, diphthongal moraicity, and the ITL. We will now briefly review previous approaches to these asymmetries.

2.   Previous analyses of configurational asymmetries

2.1 Syllables

Previous accounts of *Weight-by-Position* and the moraicity of diphthongal sequences suffer from two distinct weaknesses. Firstly, they do not provide an adequate explanation for the asymmetric nature of these restrictions, and secondly they fail to link the configurational parallels between consonantal and diphthongal moraicity with respect to syllable weight.

In serial frameworks, *Weight-by-Position* has been analysed in terms of the rule in (14) below, where a mora is assigned to a consonant in coda position. More recently, *Weight-by-Position* has been expressed as a constraint, as exemplified in (15).

(14)   Weight-by-Position (Hayes 1989)

(15)   WEIGHT-BY-POSITION (Kager 1999: 147)
       Coda consonants are moraic.

In both approaches, the asymmetric nature of *Weight-by-Position* follows from the absence of a corresponding requirement that onset consonants bear a mora.

With respect to the moraicity of diphthongal sequences, Rosenthall (1994) analyses these restrictions by appealing to the constraints in (16) and (17) below, which correctly eliminate undesirable diphthong types in accordance with the observed distributional facts: SONFALL ((16)) rules out bimoraic diphthongs with rising sonority while SONRISE ((17)) rules out monomoraic diphthongs with falling sonority.

(16)   SONFALL (Rosenthall 1994:19; Casali 1998:57)

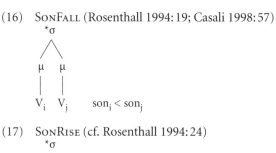

(17)   SONRISE (cf. Rosenthall 1994:24)

As with *Weight-by-Position*, the asymmetric nature of these restrictions is explained formally through the stipulation that there are no corresponding constraints militating against the mirror-image configurations, in this case against heavy falling and light rising diphthtongs, respectively.

More importantly, these analyses miss the generalisation, mentioned above, that precisely the same configurational restrictions obtain with respect to consonantal and diphthongal moraicity: trochaic structures contain two moras while iambic structures contain one mora (cf. (2) and (5) above). An account expressing these asymmetries in terms of general restrictions on the moraic structure of *syllables* would already constitute an improvement over these approaches. As we will see below, however, the relevant constraints are more general still, and generate a particular set of configurational restrictions in syllables due to the maximally binary nature of these constituents at the moraic level.

2.2 Feet

In standard OT (Prince & Smolensky 1993), the formal distinction between iambic and trochaic systems is captured in terms of the relative ranking of two symmetric constraints, given in (18) and (19) below.

(18)   RHTYPE=T (cf. Prince & Smolensky 1993)
       Feet are left-headed.

(19)   RHTYPE=I (cf. Prince & Smolensky 1993)
       Feet are right-headed.

In grammars where RHTYPE=T outranks (hereafter '>>') RHTYPE=I, feet are trochaic. This is illustrated in tableau (20a) below, cf. the opposite ranking in (20b), i.e. RHTYPE=I >> RHTYPE=T.

(20)

a. /σσ/	RHTYPE=T	RHTYPE=I	b. /σσ/	RHTYPE=I	RHTYPE=T
☞ i. (σ̠ σ)		*	i. (σ̠ σ)	*!	
ii. (σσ̠)	*!		☞ ii. (σσ̠)		*

Candidate (20a.*ii*) – representing the iambic parse – incurs a fatal violation of RHTYPE=T, and is thus ruled out in favour of candidate (20a.*i*). Candidate (20a.*i*) – representing the trochaic parse – is thus the optimal output (indicated by the pointing hand), despite a violation of lower-ranking RHTYPE=I. In the grammar represented in tableau (20b), however, the constraint ranking is reversed. Consequently, the violation of RHTYPE=I incurred by candidate (20b.*i*) is fatal, leaving candidate (20b.*ii*) as optimal despite a violation of RHTYPE=T.

In order to account for ITL effects, this mechanism is supplemented by other constraints which militate against specific configurations. Examples of such constraints are given below.

(21)   RHYTHMIC HARMONY (Prince & Smolensky 1993:59)

$^*(\sigma_{\mu\mu}\ \sigma_\mu)$

(22)   UNEVEN-IAMB (Kager 1999:151)

$(\sigma_\mu\underline{\sigma}_{\mu\mu}) >> (\sigma_\mu\underline{\sigma}_\mu),\ (\underline{\sigma}_{\mu\mu})$

(23)   IAMBIC/TROCHAIC LAW (Alber 1997:6)

a.   The components of a trochaic foot must be quantitatively equal.

b.   The components of an iambic foot must contrast in quantity.

While the constraint in (21) bans uneven trochees outright, that in (22) expresses a preference for uneven iambs over other possible iambic foot shapes, and the formulation in (23) combines both restrictions into a single constraint. While such approaches are consistent with (aspects of) the perceptual evidence underlying the ITL, they do little to enhance our understanding of the forces that shape the asymmetric preferences in foot shape given in (9) above.

In the following section an alernative will be proposed to the symmetric conception of rhythm represented by RHTYPE=T/I, exploiting an asymmetric pair of rhythmic primitives whose outcomes are conditioned not only by constraint ranking but also by the size of the rhythmic domain. The proposed analysis accounts for asymmetric configurational restrictions in feet and syllables alike.

3.   Analysis: Rhythmic constraints in prosodic constituents

As discussed in the previous section, many standard OT analyses for configurational asymmetries in prosodic phonology are *ad hoc* and miss the deeper generalisation that cross-linguistically well-formed prosodic constituents share configurational properties. Specifically, well-formed trochaic constituents are strictly
bimoraic – trochaic feet, closed syllables, and falling diphthongs. Well-formed
iambic constituents, on the other hand, are generally *non-binary* at the moraic
level – canonical iambic feet (trimoraic), open syllables and rising diphthongs
(monomoraic).

3.1 Rhythmic constraints

Van de Vijver (1998) derives a number of interesting effects through the interaction
of a different set of rhythmic constraints. A central aspect of Van de Vijver's analysis is the idea that iambic systems are characterized by the avoidance of metrical
prominence at the edges of prosodic words. This effect is formalized by means of
*Edgemost, which is assumed to be highly ranked in iambic languages. Given in
(24) below, *Edgemost militates against prominence at the left and right domain-
edges.

   (24) *Edgemost (Van de Vijver 1998)[7]
         Edge-adjacent elements may not be prominent.

In certain grammars, satisfaction of *Edgemost is limited by Peak-First, a competing rhythmic constraint (given in (25) below) which demands that prominence
occur initially in metrical groupings.

   (25) Peak-First (Mellander 2003; cf. Trochee: Van de Vijver 1998)
         Prominence is manifested on initial elements.

Since the two constraints have conflicting requirements with respect to domain-
initial elements, atisfaction of *both* Peak-First and *Edgemost is impossible
within a single stress domain, and their effects are mediated through constraint
interaction.

   In prosodic words, the ranking of *Edgemost >> Peak-First forces a left-
aligned foot to have an iambic prominence profile and accounts for the general
absence of final stress in iambic systems, as illustrated in (26) below.[8]

(26)   No stress at the right edge (cf. Van de Vijver 1998: 45)[9]

Input:	σσσσ	*Edgemost	Peak-First	Parse-Head
a.	| * . * . |PWd (σ̱ σ)(σ̱ σ)	*!		
b.	| . * . * |PWd (σ̱ σ)(σ̱ σ)	*!	*	
c. ☞	| . * . . |PWd (σ̱ σ)(σ̱ σ)		*	*

Candidates (26a) and (26b) each incur a fatal violation of *Edgemost due to prominence on a syllable adjacent to a prosodic word-edge – the left edge in candidate (26a) and the right edge in candidate (26b). This leaves candidate (26c) as optimal, despite violations of lower-ranking Peak-First for non-initial prominence in the prosodic word and of Parse-Head, the constraint demanding overt realisation of foot-heads.

By reversing the relative ranking of *Edgemost and Peak-First, stress is realised on the initial syllable resulting in trochaic rhythm, as demonstrated in (27) below.

(27)   Stress at the left edge

Input:	σσσσ	Peak-First	*Edgemost	Parse-Head
a. ☞	| * . * . |PWd (σ̱ σ)(σ̱ σ)		*	
b.	| . * . * |PWd (σ̱ σ)(σ̱ σ)	*!	*	
c.	| . * . . |PWd (σ̱ σ)(σ̱ σ)	*!		*

Candidates (27b) and (27c) incur fatal violations of Peak-First due to the absence of prominence on the word-initial syllable. This leaves candidate (27a) as optimal despite a violation of lower-ranking *Edgemost.

In the case of binary domains, Peak-First and *Edgemost invariably generate a trochaic rhythmic profile regardless of their relative ranking. This is demonstrated in the tableaux in (28) below, where trochaic and iambic parses of a bimoraic constituent are evaluated against both possible rankings of *Edgemost and Peak-First.

(28)

a. /μμ/	Peak-First	*Edgemost
☞ *i.* (* .)		*
ii. (. *)	*!	*

b. /μμ/	Peak-First	*Edgemost
☞ *i.* (* .)	*	
ii. (. *)	*	*!

Candidate (28a.*ii*) fatally violates Peak-First due to non-initial prominence and is thus ruled out in favour of candidate (28a.*i*). In (28b), both candidates violate *Edgemost, since both contain a stressed syllable adjacent to a foot-edge. Candidate (28b.*ii*) is eliminated by Peak-First, however, due to non-initial prominence leaving candidate (28b.*i*) as optimal. The tableaux illustrate how both rankings converge on the same output candidate – a trochaic rhythmic profile (cf. Trochaic Default: McCarthy & Prince 1986). It is precisely this mechanism which accounts for the overwhelming cross-linguistic preference for trochaic rhythm in constituents which are binary at the moraic level.[10] The significance of this result for consonantal and diphthongal moraicity will be taken up in the following section.

3.2 Rhythmic constraints and Weight-by-Position

Since in most languages syllables are limited to a maximum of two moras, we expect the internal rhythmic organisation of heavy syllables to mirror the rhythmic structure of other bimoraic configurations, i.e. to display an invariant trochaic pattern. *Weight-by-Position*, which assigns moras exclusively to *postvocalic* consonants within a syllable, can be understood as a monifestation of rhythmic wellformedness at the subsyllabic level (cf. Prince 1983). Since the *configurational* aspect of *Weight-by-Position* can be accounted for in terms of independentlymotivated rhythmic constraints, it is unnecessary to re-encode this information in a separate constraint. Instead, we appeal to the following general requirement, demanding that consonants be associated with a mora. (For alternative views see Broselow et al. 1997; Rosenthall & Van der Hulst 1999.)

(29)   Moraic-C (cf. *Weight-by-Position*)
       Consonants are moraic.

Moraic-C expresses a preference for all consonants to project prominence onto the metrical grid, i.e. to be moraic (cf. Sherer 1994). This constraint differs from Weight-by-Position (15) solely in that it does not stipulate a specific (asymmetric) configurational relationship (coda position) with respect to syllable structure. This is unnecessary, since configurational restrictions on moraic consonants follow from rhythmic well-formedness under Peak-First and *Edgemost.

   In languages where Moraic-C >> Dep-μ, consonants may surface as moraic. This is illustrated in (30a) below, which evaluates moraic representations of a VC syllable. Candidate (30a.*ii*) fatally violates Moraic-C due to a nonmoraic consonant, leaving candidate (30a.*i*) as optimal despite a violation of low-ranking Dep-μ for mora insertion. The opposite ranking is given in (30b).

(30)

a.	/at/	Moraic-C	Dep-μ
☞ *i*	[*.] μ μ | | a t		*
ii	[*] μ | a t	*!	

b.	/at/	Dep-μ	Moraic-C
i	[*.] μ μ | | a t	*!	
☞ *ii*	[*] μ | a t		*

Candidate (30b.*i*) fatally violates Dep-μ due to mora insertion leaving candidate (30b.*ii*) as optimal despite a violation of low-ranking Moraic-C. The potential for moraic consonants thus arises when Moraic-C is ranked above Dep-μ.

Even in languages which allow for moraic consonants, however, those in onset position are consistently nonmoraic. This effect follows from the interaction of *Edgemost and Peak-First, as shown in (31) below.

(31)   No moraic onsets[11]

Input:	/ta/	*Edge	Pk-First	Moraic-C	Dep-μ
a.	[.*] μ μ | | t a	*	*!		*
b. ☞	[*] μ | t a	*		*	

While both candidates incur offsetting violations of *Edgemost, candidate (31a) fatally violates Peak-First due to non-initial prominence, leaving candidate (31b) as optimal. Thus, in systems where rhythmic constraints are highly ranked, onset consonants surface as nonmoraic.

3.3   Rhythmic constraints and diphthongal moraicity

The interaction of rhythmic constraints also provides an explanation for the weight typology of diphthongs in (5). Following standard moraic theory (Hayes 1999), I assume vowels to be underlyingly moraic. As a result, when an underlying sequence of two vowels surfaces as a light diphthong, MAX-μ is violated. To avoid this, a falling diphthongal sequence is parsed as bimoraic, as illustrated in (32) below.

(32)   Heavy falling diphthongs

Input: /au/	*EDGEMOST	PEAK-FIRST	MAX-μ
a. ☞ [*.] μ μ | | a u	*		
b. [*] μ | a u	*		*!

Candidate (32b) fatally violates MAX-μ due to mora loss, leaving candidate (32a) as optimal. This is not the case in rising diphthongal sequences, however, as illustrated in (33) below.

(33)   Light rising diphthongs

Input: /ua/	*EDGEMOST	PEAK-FIRST	MAX-μ
a. [.*] μ μ | | u a	*	*!	
b. ☞ [*] μ | u a	*		*

While candidate (33a) satisfies MAX-μ because both vocalic moras are present in the output, it is dispreferred on rhythmic grounds to the monomoraic output in (33b). Specifically, candidate (33a) incurs a fatal violation of PEAK-FIRST, leaving candidate (33b) as optimal.

If rhythmic constraints are highly ranked, the satisfaction of MAX-μ through full realisation of underlying moraic content is subordinated to the demands of rhythmic well-formedness. Falling and rising diphthongal sequences yield different quantitative outputs because satisfaction of rhythmic constraints in a bimoraic parse is possible *only* with the trochaic rhythmic profile of a falling diphthong, and crucially not with the iambic rhythmic profile of a rising diphthong. In a falling diphthong (32), rhythmic constraints do not express a preference between monomoraic and bimoraic parses, allowing full satisfaction of faithfulness to the underlying representation through a bimoraic parse. In a rising diphthong (33), however, rhythmic constraints prefer a monomoraic parse over a bimoraic one at the expense of faithfulness. Mora loss in rising diphthongs thus follows straight-forwardly from the enforcement of rhythmic constraints which are generalisable to other phenomena, eliminating the need for an *ad hoc* solution like SonFall.

3.4 Rhythmic constraints and metrical feet

Metrical feet differ crucially from syllables in that the size of the rhythmic domain is not limited to two moras, e.g. the (trimoraic) uneven iamb. The foot-internal rhythmic structure of an iambic foot is that of a *moraic amphibrach* – a tri-moraic domain with prominence on the second mora (Kager 1993). Such a struc-ture satisfies *Edgemost, since neither the initial mora nor the final mora bears prominence. Augmentation through iambic lengthening can thus be viewed as a functionally-motivated process which creates rhythmically optimal feet in gram-mars where *Edgemost is ranked highly. This solution is particularly attractive since the ranking of *Edgemost >> Peak-First in iambic systems is indepen-dently motivated by the distribution of stressed syllables within the prosodic word as demonstrated in (26) and (27) above. Iambic lengthening through satisfaction of high-ranking *Edgemost is illustrated in (34) below.

(34)   Iambic Lengthening[12]

Input:	$\sigma_\mu \, \sigma_\mu$	*Edgemost	Peak-First	Dep-μ
a.	(. *) μ μ | | σ σ	*!	*	
b. ☞	(. * .) μ μ μ | V σ σ		*	*
c.	(* .) μ μ | | σ σ	*!		

Candidate (34a) incurs a fatal violation of *Edgemost due to prominence on the rightmost mora. Candidate (34c), is likewise eliminated, as it fares no better on *Edgemost than candidate (34a). The violation of *Edgemost is avoided in candi-date (34b), however, since the prominent mora is not adjacent to a foot-edge. This candidate consequently emerges as optimal, despite one violation of PEAK-FIRST for non-initial prominence, and one violation of DEP-μ for mora insertion.

The absence of lengthening in word-final feet in iambic systems (e.g. the un-lengthened final vowel in (6)) is understood as a consequence of the fact that these feet lack stress (see tableau (26)).[13] The lack of prominence in these feet means that *EDGEMOST is satisfied without lengthening, as illustrated in tableau (35) below.

(35)   No Iambic Lengthening in final position

Input:	$\sigma_\mu\ \sigma_\mu$ |$_{PWd}$	*EDGEMOST	PEAK-FIRST	DEP-μ
a. ☞	(. .)|$_{PWd}$ μ μ | | σ σ		*	
b.	(. . .)|$_{PWd}$ μ μ μ | V σ σ		*	*!

Candidate (35b) is ruled out by a fatal violation of DEP-μ, leaving (35a) as the optimal output. Since mora insertion would yield no gain in rhythmic well-formedness, such a move constitutes a gratuitous violation of faithfulness. On this view, iambic systems are those which avoid peripheral prominence in two distinct metrical domains: prosodic words and feet.

In grammars where *EDGEMOST is highly ranked, the rhythmic superiority of the uneven iamb over even trochaic and iambic feet follows straightforwardly from its trimoraic structure. It is not immediately obvious, however, why a moraic am-phibrach must necessarily take the shape of an iamb; indeed, one can easily imagine a trimoraic trochaic foot as well. This possibility is illustrated in (36b) below, cf. the uneven iamb in (36a). With respect to foot boundaries, both configurations in (36) are equally well-formed. What then accounts for the fact that it is the uneven iamb rather than the uneven trochee that is consistently selected as optimal in grammars where *EDGEMOST >> PEAK-FIRST?

(36)   Iambic and trochaic trimoraic feet with medial prominence

   a. (. * .)   b. *(. * .)
       μ μ μ   iamb   μ μ μ   trochee
       \| V   V \|
       σ σ   σ σ

The answer is rhythmic well-formedness at the syllabic level. Since an uneven foot must by definition contain a heavy syllable, the preference for the uneven iamb rather than the uneven trochee in satisfaction of *EDGEMOST follows from maximal satisfaction of rhythmic constraints with respect to *syllable* boundaries. This is illustrated in (37) below.

Both candidates in (37) incur one violation of *Edgemost for prominence adjacent to the syllable-edge and one violation of Peak-First for the absence of prominence on the foot-intital mora. Candidate (37b) incurs an additional and fatal violation of Peak-First, however, for the absence of prominence on the *syllable-intital* mora. Recall from previous sections that a heavy syllable is a binary domain and invariably emerges as rhythmically trochaic. The requirement that heavy syllables be trochaic translates into a requirement that trimoraic feet be iambic under constraint interaction.

(37)   Rhythmic well-formedness within the foot *and* syllable

		*Edgemost	Peak-First
a. ☞	(. [* .]) μ μμ | V σ σ	*	*
b.	([. *] .) μμ μ V | σ σ	*	**!

The extreme pervasiveness of Iambic Lengthening in iambic systems also falls out of this account. Imagine a nominally iambic system, i.e. *Edgemost >> Peak-First, but without Iambic Lengthening, i.e. Dep-μ >> *Edgemost. Such a system is represented in (38) below.

(38)   "Iambic" system without Iambic Lengthening

Input:	σ_μ σ_μ	Dep-μ	*Edgemost	Peak-First
a.	(.*) μ μ | | σ σ		*	*!
b.	(. * .) μ μ μ | V σ σ	*!		*
c. ☞	(*.) μ μ | | σ σ		*	

Candidate (38b) is ruled out immediately by high-ranking DEP-μ, while both remaining candidates incur a single violation of *EDGEMOST for prominence adjacent to a foot-edge – the right edge in the case of candidate (38a), and the left edge in the case of candidate (38c). Candidate (38a) is finally eliminated by PEAK-FIRST, however, due to non-initial prominence, leaving candidate (38c) as the optimal output. Yet candidate (38c) is not an iamb at all but rather an even trochee. The unavailability of Iambic Lengthening through the promotion of DEP-μ above *EDGEMOST has the additional effect of eliminating iambic rhythm altogether by rendering it suboptimal to a trochaic parse. The reason that Iambic Lengthening is so common in iambic systems, therefore, is that iambic systems are only rhythmically permissible if even iambic feet are avoided.[14]

This account also provides an explanation for why iambic systems are crosslinguistically less common than trochaic ones. With respect to rhythmic constraints, trochaic systems arise in all grammars where PEAK-FIRST outranks *EDGEMOST, as well as in grammars like that in (38) above, where *EDGEMOST outranks PEAK-FIRST but where DEP-μ also outranks *EDGEMOST. Conversely, iambic systems arise uniquely in grammars where *EDGEMOST outranks both PEAK-FIRST *and* DEP-μ. Consider the stress typology in (39) below.

(39)   Stress typology of rhythmic constraints
　　　　PEAK-FIRST >> *EDGEMOST >> DEP-μ   *trochaic*
　　　　PEAK-FIRST >> DEP-μ>> *EDGEMOST   *trochaic*
　　　　DEP-μ>> PEAK-FIRST >> *EDGEMOST   *trochaic*
　　　　*EDGEMOST >> PEAK-FIRST >> DEP-μ   *iambic*
　　　　*EDGEMOST >> DEP-μ>> PEAK-FIRST   *iambic*
　　　　DEP-μ>> *EDGEMOST >> PEAK-FIRST   *trochaic*

In (39) we see that four of the six possible grammars in the factorial typology generated on the basis of these three constraints generate trochaic rhythm, while only two of the six possible grammars generate iambic rhythm. This typology correctly predicts the relative infrequency of iambic systems cross-linguistically.

4.   Summary

This paper has attempted to demonstrate that configurational asymmetries in prosodic constituents can be accounted for in a unified manner if asymmetric rhythmic primitives are assumed. Asymmetric restrictions on consonantal and diphthongal moraicity as well as the *Iambic / Trochaic Law* are explained in terms of the interaction of rhythmic constraints in Optimality Theory. The strong cross-linguistic preference for trochaic configurations in binary rhythmic domains such as heavy syllables is explained by the fact that a trochaic rhythmic profile is preferred in bimoriac domains regardless of the relative ranking of the rhythmic constraints. This is not the case on the standard analysis, where other devices are needed to eliminate iambic configurations in these contexts. The rhythmically-based analysis also accounts for why Iambic Lengthening is so pervasive in iambic systems, relative to Trochaic Levelling in trochaic systems, and for the infrequency of iambic systems generally.

Notes

* I am grateful to Jonathan Bobaljik, Colleen Fitzgerald, Tracy Alan Hall, Glyne Piggott and Ruben van de Vijver for generous and constructive feedback on aspects of this analysis. All errors and omissions are my own. This research was supported by a DFG postdoctoral fellowship.

1. See Davis (1988) for discussion on a number of exceptions.

2. The term *falling diphthong* has also been used to describe such structures, in reference to falling vowel height or falling syllabicity (Schane 1987; Booij 1989).

3. Tautosyllabic CLV sequences do occur in Vata, but Kaye analyses LV clusters as nuclear constituents analogous to rising diphthongs. This analysis is motivated by two pieces of evidence: firstly, putative CL onset clusters do not respect sonority sequencing, e.g. [wlɪ] 'fingers', [ylʊ] 'sun'; secondly, there are no *CLGV sequences in Vata, as one would expect if both branching onsets and branching nuclei were allowed.

4. Citing Harris (1983), Rosenthall (1994: 139) notes three exceptions to this generalisation, *vein.te, trein.ta* and *aun.que*. José Alvarez (p.c.) notes two additional exceptions: *seis.cien.tos* and *pleis.to.ce.no.*

5. There are a number of exceptions to the ban on trimoraic syllables. See Kager (1999) for a formulation of this constraint and discussion.

6. Tiriyó from Van de Vijver (1998); Kari'ña from Alvarez (2000, to appear). The present list includes vocalic as well as consonantal Iambic Lengthening through gemination. A slightly different type of Trochaic Levelling is the process of *Brevis Brevians* in Pre-Classical Latin (Allen 1973; Prince 1992; Prince & Smolensky 1993; Mester 1994; Mellander 2001).

7. The avoidance of domain-peripheral prominence is a common property of languages. Examples include peninitial and penultimate stress (cf. Nonfinality: Prince & Smolensky 1993), as well as V2 effects in syntax which have been argued to be phonological in nature (Rice & Svenonius 1998; Bošković 2001). Thanks to Loren Allen Billings for pointing this out to me.

8. This also accounts for the absence of *right-to-left* iambic systems, which would have final stress. Van de Vijver (1998) argues that putative cases of final stress in iambic systems can be renanlysed as intonational phenomena.

9. Another possibility is stress on the first syllable of the final foot, i.e. |. * * .|, as exemplified by Southern Paiute (Sapir 1930; Halle & Vergnaud 1987; Prince & Smolensky 1993). Such structures are assumed generally to be ruled out by other constraints, notably a ban on adjacent stressed syllables.

10. This also explains the fact that in so-called 'quantity-insensitive' systems – where binarity is enforced at the syllabic level – feet are universally trochaic (Hayes 1995).

11. Here and in the following tableaux we abstract away from the relative ranking of *EDGEMOST and PEAK-FIRST, since both possibilities yield the same output in binary (and unary) domains (see the previous section).

12. Van de Vijver (1998) appeals to a different mechanism to account for iambic lengthening. Following Revithiadou & Van de Vijver (1997), iambic lengthening is assumed to arise through the convergence of two processes: lengthening of stressed elements and lengthening of domain-final elements.

13. Van de Vijver (1998) takes the same position, although for different reasons; since lengthening is interpreted as a phonetic manifestation of stress, the absence of stress entails the absence of lengthening.

14. There are a small number of systems where Iambic Lengthening does not occur (see Hayes 1995:266–8). Such systems can be accounted for by ranking alignment constraints above rhythmic constraints (McCarthy & Prince 1993).

References

Alber, B. (1997). Quantity sensitivity as the result of constraint interaction. In G. Booij & J. van de Weijer (Eds.), *Phonology in Progress – Progress in Phonology*. The Hague: Holland Academic Press. *HIL Phonology Papers, III*, 1–45.

Allen, W. S. (1973). *Accent and Rhythm*. Cambridge: Cambridge University Press.

Alvarez, J. (2000). Syllable reduction and mora preservation in Kari'ña. Paper presented at the *Annual Meeting of the Society for the Study of the Indigenous Languages of the Americas*, Chicago.

Alvarez, J. (2003). Syllable reduction and mora preservation in Kari'ña. *Amérindia, 28* (Langues caribes), 55–82.

Booij, G. (1989). On the representation of diphthongs in Frisian. *Linguistics, 25*, 319–332.

Bošković, Z. (2001). *On the Nature of the Syntax-Phonology Interface: Cliticization and Related Phenomena*. Elsevier.

Broselow, E., Chen, S. I, & Huffman, M. (1997). Syllable weight: Convergence of phonology and phonetics. *Phonology, 14*, 47–82.

Casali, R. F. (1998). *Resolving Hiatus*. New York & London: Garland Publishing.

Clements, G. N. (1990). The role of the sonority cycle in core syllabification. In J. Kingston & M. Beckman (Eds.), *Papers in Laboratory Phonology I: Between the Grammar and Physics of Speech* (pp. 283–333). Cambridge: C.U.P.

Davis, S. M. (1988). Syllable onsets as a factor in stress rules. *Phonology, 5*, 1–19.

Dixon, R. M. W. (1988). *A Grammar of Boumaa Fijian*. Chicago: University of Chicago Press.

Halle, M. & Vergnaud, J.-R. (1987). *An Essay on Stress.* Cambridge, Mass.: MIT Press.

Harris, J. W. (1983). *Syllable Structure and Stress in Spanish: A Nonlinear Analysis.* Cambridge, Mass.: MIT Press.

Hayes, B. (1985). Iambic and trochaic rhythm in stress rules. In *Proceedings of the Berkeley Linguistics Society, 11,* 429–446.

Hayes, B. (1987). A revised parametric metrical theory. *Northeastern Linguistic Society, 17,* 274–89.

Hayes, B. (1989). Compensatory lengthening in Moraic phonology. *Linguistic Inquiry, 20,* 253–306.

Hayes, B. (1995). *Metrical Stress Theory: Principles and Case Sudies.* Chicago: University of Chicago Press.

Hayes, B. (1999). Phonetically-driven phonology: The role of optimality theory and grounding. In M. Darnell et al. (Eds.), *Functionalism and Formalism in Linguistics, Volume I: General Papers* (pp. 243–286). Amsterdam: John Benjamins.

Hyman, L. (1985). *A Theory of Phonological Weight.* Dordrecht: Foris.

Kager, R. (1993). Alternatives to the iambic-trochaic law. *Natural Language and Linguistic Theory, 11,* 381–432.

Kager, R. (1995). On foot templates and root templates. In M. den Dikken & K. Hengeveld (Eds.), *Linguistics in the Netherlands* (pp. 125–138). Amsterdam: John Benjamins.

Kager, R. (1999). *Optimality Theory.* Cambridge, U.-K.; New York: Cambridge University Press.

Kaye, J. (1985). On the syllable structure of certain West African languages. In D. Goyvaerts (Ed.), *Essays in Memory of M.W.K. Semikenke* (pp. 285–308). Amsterdam: John Benjamins.

McCarthy, J. J. & Prince, A. (1986). Prosodic morphology. RUCCS Technical Report 32. Piscataway, NJ.

McCarthy, J. J. & Prince, A. (1993). Generalized alignment. RUCCS Technical Report 7. Piscataway, NJ.

Mellander, E. W. (2001). Quantitative processes in trochaic systems. In K. Megerdoomian & L. A. Bar-el (Eds.), *Proceedings of the Twentieth West Coast Conference on Formal Linguistics* (pp. 414–427). Somerville, Mass.: Cascadilla Press.

Mellander, E. W. (2003). A prosodic theory of prominence and rhythm. Unpublished Ph.D. dissertation (2002). McGill University, Montreal. [Revised version distributed by McGill Working Papers in Linguistics Thesis Series.]

Mester, R. A. (1994). The quantitative trochee in Latin. *Natural Language and Linguistic Theory, 12,* 1–61.

Munro, P. & Ulrich, C. (1984). Structure preservation and Western Muskogean rhythmic lengthening. In M. Cobler, S. MacKaye, & M. T. Wescoat (Eds.), *Proceedings of the Third West Coast Conference on Formal Linguistics 3* (pp. 191–202). Stanford, California: Stanford Linguistics Association.

Nicklas, T. D. (1975). Choctaw morphophonemics. In J. M. Crawford (Ed.), *Studies in Southeastern Indian Languages* (pp. 237–250). Athens: University of Georgia Press.

Prince, A. (1983). Relating to the grid. *Linguistic Inquiry, 14,* 19–100.

Prince, A. (1992). Quantitative consequences of rhythmic organization. In K. Deaton, M. Noske, & M. Ziolkovski (Eds.), *CLS 26-II: Papers from the Parasession on the Syllable in Phonetics and Phonology* (pp. 355–398). Chicago: Chicago Linguistic Society.

Prince, A. & Smolensky, P. (1993). Optimality theory: Constraint interaction in generative grammar. Technical Reports of the Rutgers Center for Cognitive Science 2. Piscataway, NJ.

Revithiadou, A. & van de Vijver, R. (1997). Durational contrasts and the iambic/trochaic law. In V. Samiian (Ed.), *Proceedings of the Western Conference on Linguistics* 9.

Rice, C. & Svenonius, P. (1998). Prosodic V2 in Northern Norwegian. Paper delivered at WCCFL 17.

Rosenthall, S. (1994). Vowel/glide alternation in a theory of constraint interaction. Ph.D. Dissertation. University of Massachusetts, Amherst.

Rosenthall, S. & van der Hulst, H. (1999). Weight-by-position by position. *Natural Language and Linguistic Theory, 17,* 499–540.

Sapir, E. (1930). Southern Paiute, a Shoshonean language. In *Proceedings of the American Academy of Arts and Sciences* 65 (pp. 1–296).

Schane, S. (1987). The resolution of hiatus. In A. Bosch, B. Need, & E. Schiller (Eds.), *CLS 23: Parasession on Autosegmental and Metrical Phonology* (pp. 279–290). Chicago: Chicago Linguistic Society.

Schane, S. (1995). Diphthongization in particle phonology. In J. A. Goldsmith (Ed.), *The Handbook of Phonological Theory* (pp. 586–608). Cambridge, Mass.: Blackwell.

Selkirk, E. (1984). *Phonology and Syntax: The Relation Between Sound and Structure.* Cambridge, Mass.: MIT Press.

Schütz, A. J. (1978). English Loanwords in Fijian. In A. J. Schütz (Ed.), *Fijian Language Studies: Borrowing and Pidginization* (pp. 1–50). Bulletin of the Fiji Museum 4. Suva, Fiji Museum.

Schütz, A. J. (1985). *The Fijian Language.* Honolulu: University of Hawaii Press.

Sherer, T. (1994). Prosodic phonotactics. Ph.D. Dissertation, University of Massachusetts, Amherst.

Ulrich, C. (1986). Choctaw morphophonology. Ph.D. Dissertation, UCLA.

van de Vijver, R. (1998). The iambic issue: Iambs as a result of constraint interaction. HIL dissertations 37. Holland Institute of Generative Linguistics. Leiden.

Woodrow, H. (1909). A quantitative study of rhythm. *Archives of Psychology, 14,* 1–66.

Woodrow, H. (1951). Time perception. In S. S. Stevens (Ed.), *Handbook of Experimental Psychology* (pp. 1224–1236). New York: Wiley.

Brain

Language learnability and the forms
of recursion*

Thomas Roeper and William Snyder

University of Massachusetts at Amherst / University of Connecticut

The usual assumption is that learning is not required for recursive operations, because they are provided by UG. Fundamental operations like Merge are recursive and universal. Yet, grammar-particular choices must be made: in each language, certain forms of recursion are permitted, and others excluded. We advance the following general hypothesis: A primary task of the language-learner is to identify recursive (hence productive) grammatical processes. Different types of recursion define different acquisitional stages, and may also be distinguished in parsing and neurological computation. A case study of root compounding is presented, with reference to English, Swedish, and French.

Introduction

Recursion has been recognized as a fundamental property of human language throughout the history of Generative Grammar. Indeed, in a recent article, Hauser, Chomsky, & Fitch (2002) argue that recursion is what distinguishes human language from the communication systems of nonhuman animals. In this paper we take up the following question: What is the role of recursion in children's acquisition of language?

Our starting point is the fact that across different languages, the precise set of recursive operations that are available actually varies. Hence, questions of language learnability arise immediately. How does the child know what is recursive and what is not? We begin by demonstrating variation in the recursive operations available for complex word formation; our remarks are stated in terms of the Abstract Clitic Hypothesis of Keyser & Roeper (1992).[1] We then turn to questions of language learnability, and argue for the following proposal: Explicit evidence of recursion, in the form of self-embedded structures, plays a central role in language acquisition.

1.   The Abstract Clitic Hypothesis

Endocentric compounding is a domain where recursion can take several different forms.[2] In this section we set out three such forms, using the framework of Keyser & Roeper (1992). We distinguish between root compounds with a monomorphemic modifier (1a), root compounds with a branching modifier (1b), and synthetic compounds (1c). All three compound-types freely permit a constituent (such as an N) to be contained within a larger constituent of the same type. In subsequent sections we will see that the grammatical availability of these different compound-types is subject to cross-linguistic variation.

(1)   a.   [restaurant$_N$ [coffee$_N$ cup$_N$]$_N$]$_N$
      b.   [[gourmet$_N$ coffee$_N$]$_N$ cup$_N$]$_N$
      c.   [[pen$_N$ hold$_V$] -er$_N$]$_N$

Moreover, the availability of recursive root compounding, as in (1a) or (1b), has important consequences for sentence-level syntax. Keyser & Roeper (1992) have presented detailed arguments from English for a close grammatical relationship among phenomena including resultatives (*hammer the metal flat*), particles (*lift the box up*), and compounding. Snyder (1995, 2001) has similarly argued, on comparative and acquisitional grounds, that the operation of endocentric root compounding is a necessity, in order for a language to permit certain complex predicates such as particle constructions and resultatives: Many of the world's languages disallow root compounding as a grammatical operation, and such languages systematically lack the (Germanic-style) particle and resultative constructions.[3] Similarly, for any given child acquiring English, the point when V-NP-particle constructions begin to appear in the child's speech is consistently the same as the point when novel N-N compounds begin to appear ($r = .98$, $t(8) = 12.9$, $p < .001$).[4] We will return to these issues below. For the moment, however, it is useful to point out that Keyser & Roeper's approach will permit us to make a direct connection between compounding and complex predicates.[5]

Following Keyser & Roeper, we assume the following derivation for an English root compound such as *coffee cup*:

(2)   a.

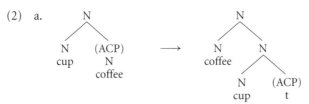

Here we assume that in English, each of the lexical categories (N, V, A, P) can have the Abstract Clitic Position (ACP) as its complement.[6] This is a significant but natural generalization of the ACP across categories. Such a claim is theoretically welcome inasmuch as it suggests, as does derivational morphology, that grammatical generalizations should not be sensitive to node labels. In (2a), the modifier *coffee* is first introduced into the ACP, and then must move and adjoin to the left of *cup*.[7]

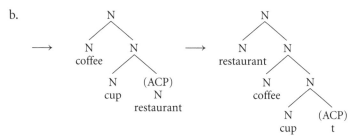

As in Keyser & Roeper, we assume that a (non-argument) trace left in the ACP can be deleted, and that the ACP can then be used to introduce another modifier.[8] Thus, in (2b) we extend the derivation in (2a) to form the compound *restaurant coffee cup*, or 'coffee cup of the kind associated with restaurants'.

A second type of root compound can be formed in English by inserting a *compound* into the ACP. Thus, in (3a, b) we derive *[gourmet coffee] cup*.

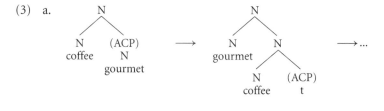

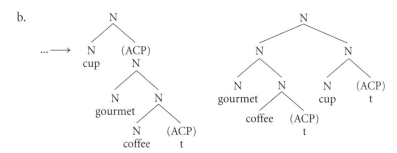

In (3a) we first create the compound *gourmet coffee*. In (3b) we insert the result into the ACP of the N *cup*, to obtain *gourmet coffee cup*, or 'cup of the kind associated with gourmet coffees'.

One final type of compounding will be relevant for our discussion: synthetic compounding, as in *pen-holder*, or 'device that holds pens'. The derivation we assume for this example is illustrated in (4).

(4)   a.

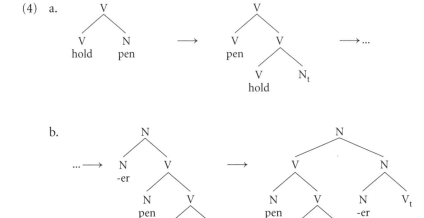

b.

In (4a) we first derive the complex V *pen-hold*. The N *pen* is the complement and logical object of the V *hold*. Then, the compound-formation rule applies to move and adjoin *pen* to the left of *hold*. The trace left by *pen* is an argument trace; following Keyser & Roeper, we assume that this trace is undeletable. In (4b) the resulting complex V is inserted as the complement to the nominal suffix *-er*. Once again, the compound-formation rule applies, and we obtain the surface form *pen-holder*.[9]

In contrast to Keyser & Roeper, we will assume that no ACP is involved in (4). We take the ACP to be associated specifically with modifiers, rather than arguments. In (4) the V *hold* takes the N *pen* as an argument. Likewise, the suffix *-er* takes complex V *pen-hold* as its argument. Thus, the ACP plays no role.[10]

2.   Cross-linguistic variation: Swedish

Swedish differs from English in the following crucial respect: In Swedish, a branching constituent cannot be inserted into the ACP. As a result, root compounds are strictly right-branching. Consider the examples in (5).

(5)   a.   barn [bok klub] 'child [book club]', or 'book club for children'
      b.   *[barn bok] klub '[child book] club', or 'club for (collectors of) children's books'

   c.   [barn bok]-s klub' [child book]'s club', or 'club for (collectors of) children's books'

In (5a), *bok* 'book' modifies *klub* 'club', and *barn* 'child' in turn modifies the entire compound *bok klub*. The compound *barn bok* 'child book', however, cannot modify the N *klub* in (5b). To obtain this reading, the infix *-s* must be used, as in (5c).

The derivation for (5a) is illustrated in (6).

(6) a.

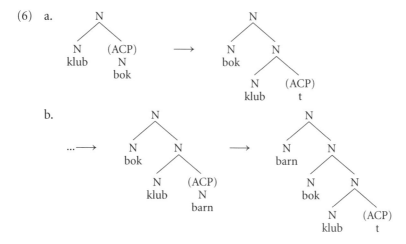

Precisely as in (2a, b), the ACP is first used to introduce the simplex modifier *bok* in (6a). The trace of *bok* is deleted, and the ACP is used again, to introduce the simplex modifier *barn* in (6b).

The (disallowed) derivation for the form in (5b) is illustrated in (7).

(7) a.

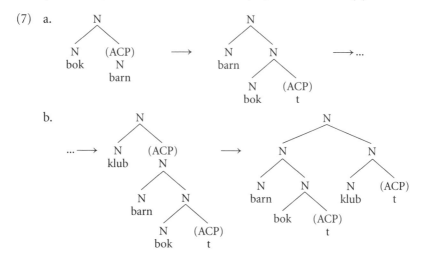

The derivation is exactly parallel to that of English *[gourmet coffee] cup* in (3a, b). The problem comes in the first step of (7b), when the branching constituent *barn bok* is inserted into the ACP. In Swedish the ACP cannot host a constituent with internal structure.

The alternative in (5c) obeys this constraint, as illustrated in (8).

(8) a.

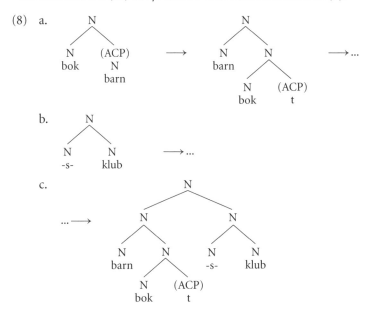

The compound *barn bok* is constructed in (8a), and in (8b) a parallel derivation combines *klub* with the infix *-s-*.[11] This infix requires a second argument, and the compound *barn bok* is inserted into its external-argument position. Crucially, the only ACP involved in this derivation in that of the N *bok*, and its only occupant is the simplex constituent *barn*.

Thus far we have seen that the proposed constraint on the ACP in Swedish correctly excludes branching modifiers from root compounds, as in (5b), while correctly allowing the alternative form in (5c). A prediction of our approach is that the exception in (5c) will be general: As long as the ACP is not involved, the left branch of a complex word can hold a branching constituent. A dramatic confirmation of this prediction comes from synthetic compounds, as shown in (9).

(9) a. pen+hål+are   'pen+hold+er'
      b. [pen+hål+ar]+hål+are '[pen+hold+er]+hold+er'
            (or 'device to hold pen-holders')

Swedish allows a direct counterpart to the English example *pen-holder*. As illustrated in (4a, b), the derivation of this compound does not involve the ACP, because *pen* is an argument of *hold*, and the complex V *pen-hold* is an argument of the nominal suffix -*er*. The ACP is never involved in predicate-argument relations, but only in relations of modification.[12]

In our approach, the complex V *pen-hold* (or its Swedish equivalent *pen-hål*, in (9a) is an example of a branching constituent hosted in the left branch of a complex word, and thus supports our contention that the constraint operative in Swedish is specifically tied to the ACP. A skeptic might object, however, that the constituency of this word could be *pen-[hold-er]* instead of *[pen-hold]-er*.[13] To answer this concern, we point to the more complex example in (9b), which is also grammatical in Swedish. Whatever the hierarchical structure of *pen+hål+ar(e)* is, there can be little doubt that it is morphologically complex. The fact that this complex form can itself appear in the left branch of the larger compound *[pen+hål+ar]+hål+are* shows quite clearly that the constraint on branching constituents in Swedish compounds applies only to those modifiers that pass through the ACP.

3.   Cross-linguistic variation: French

French contrasts with both Swedish and English in that novel endocentric, root compounds cannot be created at will (as discussed in detail by Bauer 1978; cf. also Di Sciullo & Williams 1987:83). While numerous frozen examples exist in the French lexicon (e.g. *homme grenouille* 'underwater diver', lit. 'man frog'), creating a new endocentric, root compound is comparable to inventing a novel morpheme; its intended meaning must be explained to the listener.

On our account, French differs from English and Swedish in that it altogether lacks the ACP. As a consequence, a bare root cannot automatically enter into a modification relation with another root, to form an endocentric compound. Where endocentric root compounding is an automatic, *syntactic* process in Germanic, it is only a pattern for conscious word-coinage in French.

In contrast to endocentric root compounding, complex word-formation with closed-class, bound morphemes is fully productive in French. Representative examples appear in (10).

(10)   a.   *l' achet+eur* 'the purchas+er' (masc.)
       b.   *la vend+euse* 'the sell+er' (fem.)

The forms in (10) are lexicalized, but the suffixes -*eur* and -*euse* can be applied quite generally to create an agent or instrument nominal from an existing V.[14] Given that the ACP's role lies in general modification relations, not predicate-argument relations of the kind found with derivational suffixes, the latter are unaffected by the absence of the ACP in French.[15]

4. Learnability and recursion

The points of cross-linguistic variation encountered above can be stated in parametric terms, as follows:

(11)   The language {does, does not} permit the ACP as the complement to a lexical category.
(Does: English, Swedish; Does not: French)

(12)   The language {does, does not} permit branching constituents to occupy the ACP.
(Does: English; Does not: Swedish; N/A: French)

The point of variation in (12) perhaps reflects a much more general property of human language, which we can state as follows:

(13)   Recursion Constraint: The output of a given operation (such as endocentric root compounding) cannot serve as the input to the same operation.

The Recursion Constraint would then apply everywhere, except when the child's linguistic input provides evidence to the contrary. The constraint makes predictions far beyond root compounding. As a putative deep principle of grammar, it offers a perspective from which to examine all recursive structures. Accordingly, it serves to define a *set* of narrow-UG parameters, to be evaluated through examination of a wide variety of recursive structures.

Returning to the more narrowly stated parameters in (11) and (12), the first question is how the learner can set these parameters correctly, using evidence available from child-directed speech. The existence of numerous lexical compounds (such as *revue mode*, literally 'magazine fashion', for 'fashion magazine') in French means that the simple presence of endocentric root compounds in the input is not a reliable indicator that the language takes the positive setting of (11). Namiki (1994), however, notes that *recursive* compounds (that is, endocentric root compounds properly containing another such compound) are extremely rare in languages of the French type. Further, Roeper, Snyder, and Hiramatsu (2002) have shown that recursive root compounds such as *Christmas tree cookie* and *peanut butter sandwich* are well-represented in English samples of child-directed speech in the CHILDES database MacWhinney (2000).

Given that recursive lexical compounds in French are both few in number and low in frequency of use (the one clear example of which we are aware is *gateau forêt-noire* 'black-forest cake'), we retain the learnability account of Roeper et al. (2002) for the parameter in (11). Significantly, the child is listening for a self-embedded structure (an endocentric root compound *within* an endocentric root compound), and only if she encounters such evidence for *recursive* application of

the compounding operation, will she conclude that endocentric root compounding is among the grammatical operations available in her language. Without clear
evidence of recursion, individual examples of root compounds will simply be
stored in the lexicon as isolated cases.

Learnability of the setting for the parameter in (12) can likewise be accomplished by having the child listen for a particular self-embedded structure. This
time, the relevant evidence will come from an endocentric root compound containing another such compound as the *modifier*. Again, the samples of child-
directed speech examined by Roeper et al. (2002) indicate that such forms are
well-attested (consider once again *[[Christmas tree] cookie]* and *[[peanut butter]
sandwich]*, for example).

Returning to Hauser, Chomsky, & Fitch's (2002) proposal that recursion is the
defining characteristic of the human faculty of language, narrowly construed (the
"FLN"), we advance the following strong claims:

(14)   Parametric variation in the FLN amounts to variation in the set of (poten-
       tially) recursive operations that are available in each language.

(15)   Children's acquisition of grammar is based on their finding clear evidence
       that particular grammatical operations have applied recursively.

In present terms, the availability of the ACP, in (11), determines whether endocentric root compounding is available to the language as a potentially recursive, grammatical operation. Likewise, the possibility of inserting a branching constituent
into the ACP, in (12), determines whether the left-branching form of recursive
root compounding is grammatically available to the language. In both cases, clear
evidence to the learner will come from recursive compounds in the input.

One may ask whether a parameter such as (11) constitutes a "global" parameter of the FLN, with widespread consequences for the shape of the language.
We submit that it does. As argued in Roeper et al. (2002), the availability of the
ACP not only gives rise to recursive root compounding, but is also a prerequisite
for complex predicates such as V-NP-Particle constructions and transitive resultatives. The acquisitional evidence in Snyder (1995, 2001) also supports a close
connection to English double-object dative constructions (*give Mary the book*) and
make-causatives (*make John buy the book*). The detailed investigation of English in
Keyser & Roeper (1992) indicates further connections, to bare-V/N idioms (*pay
attention*), middles (*This book reads easily*), and null-P constructions (*jump (over)
the fence*), for example. Hence, the syntactic effects of the parameter in (11) are
indeed widespread.[16,17]

A further question is whether the trigger for a parameter such as (11) is *necessarily* an instance of recursion. An alternative, in the particular case of (11), could
be hearing an example of a V-NP-particle construction, for example. While there

are non-recursive triggers available for (11), this turns out not always to be the case. Consider the example of the Saxon genitive in German, as illustrated in (16).

(16)   Maria-*s* Auto 'Maria's car'

The morpheme -*s* in (16) serves to mark possession, and at first glance appears comparable to the English possessive marker -'*s*. An important difference, however, is that the English possessive is potentially recursive (17a), while the Saxon genitive is not (17b).

(17)   a.   [John-'s car]-'s motor
       b.   *[Hans-*ens* Auto]-*s* Motor

The English possessive has a grammatical basis in the phrase structure (the -'*s* is plausibly a D^0), while the Saxon genitive in German is lexical in nature – not formed in the syntax. Crucially, the child acquiring German must avoid misanalyzing the Saxon genitive as an English-like possessive. As far as we are aware, the *only* way the child can correctly decide whether the -*s* is part of the FLN (as in English) is by waiting for a recursive form, as in (17). In the absence of such evidence, the child will treat the -*s* as lexical, rather than syntactic.[18]

What, then, are the forms of recursion that are subject to cross-linguistic variation? They include at least the following: self-embedding, iterative, and scopal recursion. The first type, self-embedding recursion, refers to cases of a structural constituent embedded within a larger constituent of the same type. In addition to endocentric root compounding (with either monomorphemic or polymorphemic modifiers), the X-bar structure of phrase-level syntax belongs to this category. Choices to be made will include setting the X-bar parameters themselves (for example, whether a head precedes or follows its complement), and also deciding whether particular forms (such as the Germanic -*s* suffix) are to be handled syntactically or lexically.

By "iterative" recursion, we mean cases such as *very, very, [...] happy*, where a lexical item is repeated for emphasis; relative-clause sequences such as *This is the cat [that ate the rat [that ran out ...];* and coordination of (arbitrary numbers of) sentences with conjunctions like *and* and *or*. In all these cases, the relevant grammatical operations can be (and usually are) expressed by recursive rules, but the result is what computer scientists call "tail recursion" – a type of recursion for which simple iteration is a computationally more efficient substitute (compare "This is a cat, and the cat ate a rat, and the rat ran out..."). Finally, by "scopal" recursion we mean cases such as variable binding and negative polarity, naturally described in terms of the c-command relation. This relation is formally equivalent to the propagation of information downward, recursively, through a tree.

In summary, points of cross-linguistic variation include both the set of recursive operations employed by the FLN, and the particular surface forms that are handled by the FLN (as opposed to the lexicon) in a given language. For the child, an especially reliable source of evidence about language-particular properties of the FLN will be examples of recursion in the linguistic input. The strongest hypothesis, then, is that the inventory of recursive operations is the sole point of parameterization within the FLN, and that evidence of recursive application of these operations is what drives children's acquisition of syntax.

Notes

* We are grateful to Bob Berwick, Anna Maria Di Sciullo, Sonja Eisenbeiss, Sandiway Fong, Robbie Moll, and the audience at the 2002 Conference on Brain, Language, and Computation for stimulating discussion; and to Anders Holmberg and Anders Löfqvist, for the Swedish data in Section 2 Snyder's contributions were supported by NIH grant DCD-00183.

1. More recent work in the spirit of the Abstract Clitic Hypothesis includes Hale & Keyser (2002, Ch. 6) and van Hout & Roeper (1998).

2. In this paper we focus on "endocentric" compounds as in (1), where one part of the compound is clearly the head. We will set aside "exocentric" compounds such as French *essui-glace* 'windshield wiper' (lit. 'wipe(s)-windshield'). The latter forms are treated by Di Sciullo & Williams (1987) as a VP located under an N, and are there classified as "syntactic words."

3. Here a word of caution is in order. Our precise claim is that *"Germanic-style"* resultatives and verb-particle constructions are available only in languages that freely permit the creation of endocentric root compounds. Ultimately, this generalization should be explained in terms of a point of parametric variation much more abstract than the surface constructions themselves. Thus, even to the extent that we can give an operational definition of "Germanic-style verb-particle constructions," for example, this is merely a rough diagnostic for the nature of the underlying grammar. Di Sciullo (1999, 2002) correctly observes that Italian sometimes permits constructions that resemble the Germanic resultative and verb-particle constructions, even though it disallows endocentric root compounding as a creative process. Yet, the underlying grammar of Italian clearly must be different, as illustrated by the following examples (provided by Andrea Calabrese, p.c.).

(i)   a.   John has beaten the metal (flat).
      b.   Gianni ha battuto il metallo (*piatto).

(ii) a.   John has lifted the box (up).
      b.   Gianni ha alzato la scatola (*su).

Thus, while the relevant similarities of Italian to Germanic certainly merit investigation, the differences are also considerable, as expected under the present proposals.

4. For acquisitional evidence linking novel N-N compounds and resultatives, see Sugisaki & Isobe (2000).

5. For reasons of space, however, discussion of Keyser & Roeper's approach to complex predicates will be limited to brief remarks in Section 4.

6. The term *clitic*, like all central terms of grammar, is used in both descriptive and explanatory ways. Careful analysis leads to more refined concepts, and it is unsurprising that a given term cannot be defined adequately to cover all cases. The use of the word *clitic* in *Abstract Clitic Hypothesis* is intended to capture two notions: a) that the projection is less than a Maximal Projection, and b) that it involves lexical drift together with a verb. Thus *give up* is not a compositional result of combining *give* and *up* together. The use of the term means nothing beyond these claims. How far it can connect to other uses of *clitic* – to capture, say, the phonological behavior of pronouns in French – is left open. The two primary points, non-maximality and the lexical connection, are quite important and warrant the use of the term. Though one might invent another term, it does not seem useful.

7. Note that movement of the modifier to the left of the compound's head is taken here to be the result of an independent morphological property of English. In general, material inserted into the ACP can remain *in situ*.

8. The deletion of an *argument* trace would lead to a violation of Full Interpretation (or of the Theta Criterion, in earlier formulations), but the deletability of certain non-argument traces has been proposed, for example, in Lasnik & Saito (1984). In the present proposal, the deletion of non-argument traces from the ACP appears to be necessary to capture both the restrictive nature of the position – that it cannot be filled overtly twice – and the possibility of recursion (*re-re-read*, *over-reinvest*) for elements of the same category. On the other hand, Merce Coll-Alfonso (p.c.) has suggested to us that trace-deletion could be avoided, if the NP node that is created by leftward movement projects a new clitic position of its own, where an additional modifier can then be inserted. We will leave this as an intriguing direction for future research.

9. See Fu, Roeper, & Borer (2001) for extensive discussion and further derivational processes for nominalizations.

10. In present terms, the First Sister Principle (FSP) of Roeper & Siegel (1978) appears to be a general constraint on the rule of compound formation, because it applies both to modifiers inserted through the ACP, and to arguments in synthetic compounds, which undergo compounding from a non-ACP position. The FSP accounts for contrasts such as the following:

(i)   a.   well-made
      b.   *well-maker
      c.   well-sung
      d.   *well-singer

These facts illustrate both that adverbial modifiers *well* can undergo compounding, and that such modifiers must be immediately adjacent to the verb when compound-formation applies. Thus, in (ii), the direct object *boat* is immediately adjacent to *make*, and is the only element that can be compounded with *make*.

(ii)   make [boat] well ⇒ boat-maker/*well-maker

Yet, if the passive applies, the modifier can be treated as the first sister:

(iii)   [The boat was] made well. ⇒ well-made

Note that there are interesting intricacies here. Implicit objects, unlike the passive's under-lying objects, block compounding:

(iv)   He behaves well. ⇒ *well-behaver

In (iv) there is an implicit reflexive present, and this appears to count as the V's first sister. In (iv), like (v), *well* cannot participate in compounding.

(v)   He behaves himself well.

11. We tentatively treat the Swedish infix -*s*- as a lexical head, rather than a functional head, on the grounds that functional material is more typically excluded from compounds.

12. A novel proposal of this paper, and a departure from earlier work, is that the ACP is specifically a position for *modifiers*. Arguments, under this approach, must occupy a conventional complement position, rather than the ACP.

13. The alternative analysis, as in *pen [hold-er]*, does occur (at least in English), but it delivers a different reading:

(i)   a.   truck-driver
       b.   gypsy driver

In the synthetic compound (i.a), there continues to be a verb-object relation, where the verb *drive* directly dominates the object. In the root compound (i.b), however, the N *gypsy* functions as a modifier of the whole word *driver*. A related example is *silver holder*, which can mean, as a synthetic compound, 'thing that holds silver'; or as a root compound, 'holder made of silver'. In Roeper & Siegel (1978) it was pointed out that "apparent synthetic compounds" can be identified by whether the second element can occur by itself. For instance, we have (ii.a, b).

(ii)   a.   type-setter
        b.   *he is a setter

The -*er* in (ii.a, b) is possible only when an object has been incorporated into the verb. In contrast, *driver* in (i.b) is an independent word, and can combine with other N's through root compounding.

14. Agent/instrument nominals formed with -*er* in English are discussed in some detail in van Hout & Roeper (1998). The fine-grained semantics of the French nominals in -*eur* may be slightly different, but we leave this to future research.

15. Note also that the ACP is only *one* source of recursion, even in the languages that have it. In French, where the ACP is unavailable, recursion is nonetheless possible with derivational morphology, in exocentric compounds, and in phrasal syntax.

16. More precisely, we assume that the ACP provides a derivational point of insertion for the modifier, in a root compound; for the particle, in a separable-particle construction; and for null morphemes required in each of the English double-object dative, middle, and null-P constructions.

17. The effects of (12) should similarly be widespread. A direction of current research is a comparative study of complex predicates in English and Swedish. If the ACP in Swedish is never occupied by a branching constituent, then (for example) we expect that English forms such as (i) will be systematically absent:

(i)   John lifted the box [*right* up].

In English, the modified particle *[right up]* can be inserted into the ACP, although it is necessarily extraposed before spell-out (as discussed in Keyser & Roeper 1992). In Swedish such forms are predicted to be altogether impossible, although we have not yet checked them with our Swedish consultants.

18. See Gentile (2001) for preliminary evidence that children of 3.5 years understand that *[John's sister]'s picture* is acceptable in English, and refers to a picture of John's sister, not of John. As discussed there, recursive possessives in the adult input are rare but do occur. Representative examples from transcript data are "[Donna's dog]'s name is Tramp" and "What's [the hopperoo's friend]'s name?".

References

Bauer, L. (1978). *The Grammar of Nominal Compounding, with Special Reference to Danish, English, and French.* Odense: Odense University Press.

Di Sciullo, A.-M. (1999). Verbal structures and variation. In E. Treviño & J. Lema (Eds.), *Semantic Issues in Romance Syntax (Current issues in Linguistic Theory, Vol. 173)* (pp. 39–57). Amsterdam: John Benjamins.

Di Sciullo, A.-M. & Williams, E. (1987). *On the Definition of Word.* Cambridge, Mass.: The MIT Press.

Di Sciullo, A.-M. (2002). Symmetry, antisymmetry and tractability. Paper presented at the Second International Conference of the Federation on Natural Language Processing, *Language, Brain and Computation.* University of Venice. Italy.

Fu, J., Roeper, T., & Borer, H. (2001). The VP within process nominals: Evidence from adverbs and the VP anaphor *do-so. Natural Language & Linguistic Theory, 19,* 549–582.

Hale, K. & Keyser, S. J. (2002). *Prolegomenon to a Theory of Argument Structure.* Cambridge, Mass.: MIT Press.

Hauser, M. D., Chomsky, N., & Fitch, W. T. (2002). The faculty of language: What is it, who has it, and how did it evolve? *Science, 298,* 1569–1579.

Keyser, S. J. & Roeper, T. (1992). Re: The abstract clitic hypothesis. *Linguistic Inquiry, 23,* 89–125.

Lasnik, H. & Saito, M. (1984). On the nature of proper government. *Linguistic Inquiry, 15,* 235–289.

MacWhinney, B. (2000). *The CHILDES Project: Tools for Analyzing Talk.* Mahwah, New Jersey: Lawrence Erlbaum Associates.

Namiki, T. (1994). Subheads of compounds. In S. Chiba (Ed.), *Synchronic and Diachronic Approaches to Language: A Festschrift for Toshio Nakao on the Occasion of his Sixtieth Birthday* (pp. 269–285). Tokyo: Liber Press.

Roeper, T. & Siegel, M. (1978). A lexical transformation for verbal compounds. *Linguistic Inquiry, 9,* 199–260.

Roeper, T., Snyder, W., & Hiramatsu, K. (2002). Learnability in a Minimalist framework: Root compounds, merger, and the syntax-morphology interface. In I. Lasser (Ed.), *The Process of Language Acquisition.* Frankfurt: Peter Lang Verlag.

Snyder, W. (1995). Language acquisition and language variation: The role of morphology. Ph.D. Dissertation, MIT.

Snyder, W. (2001). On the nature of syntactic variation: Evidence from complex predicates and complex word-formation. *Language, 77,* 324–342.

Sugisaki, K. & Isobe, M. (2000). Resultatives result from the compounding parameter: On the acquisitional correlation between resultatives and N-N compounds in Japanese. In R. Billerey & B. D. Lillehaugen (Eds.), *Proceedings of WCCFL XIX* (pp. 493–506). Somerville, Mass.: Cascadilla Press.

van Hout, A. & Roeper, T. (1998). Events and aspectual structure in derivational morphology. *MIT Working Papers in Linguistics, 32,* 175–220.[18]

The autonomous contribution of syntax and pragmatics to the acquisition of the Hebrew definite article

Sharon Armon-Lotem and Idit Avram
Bar Ilan University

This paper investigates the autonomous contribution of syntax and pragmatic to the acquisition of the Hebrew definite article. Hebrew-speaking children get conflicting input on the content of D, since Hebrew has only a definite article and it is not obligatory with non-discourse-related definite nouns, like the sun. Hebrew-speaking children were tested for their use of the definite article in definite discourse-related and non-discourse-related contexts and in indefinite referential and non-referential contexts. Children of all age groups used the definite article. The twos added the definite article, but only in referential contexts. Children continued to drop the definite article in definite contexts, up to the age of four. The definite article was dropped at a higher rate with non-discourse-related definite nouns. These findings suggest that the pragmatic principle of non-shared knowledge is acquired by the age of three but syntactic knowledge is mastered only by the age of five. They also suggest a separation of linguistically related pragmatic principles like the concept of non-shared knowledge from cognitively related ones.

1. Introduction

Definiteness is a grammatical marker of the coordination and differentiation relation between a speaker, a hearer, and their knowledge about a referent. In other words, definiteness is concerned with the grammaticalization of identifiability and nonidentifiability of referents on the part of a speaker or a hearer. Thus, the use of definiteness depends on acquiring syntactic, semantic, and pragmatic knowledge. The present study investigates the autonomous contribution of syntax and pragmatics to the acquisition of the Hebrew definite system.

According to Chesterman (1991), a definite NP has a referent which is assumed by the speaker to be unambiguously identifiable by the hearer (i.e. a known referent); and an indefinite NP has a referent which is assumed by the speaker not to be unambiguously identifiable by the hearer (i.e. an unknown referent). The referent of the NP can be identified if the speaker introduces a referent to the hearer, or if the speaker instructs the hearer to locate the referent in some shared set of objects (Hawkins 1978). Some examples of such shared sets are (a) previous discourse between speaker and hearer, (b) the immediate situation of utterance, or (c) the larger situation of shared general knowledge (i.e. definite non-discourse-related objects such as *the sun* or *the moon*).

Different languages mark definiteness in typologically different ways. In English all singular nouns require an article, definite or indefinite, preceding the whole noun-phrase (e.g. *a/the big boy*). In Hebrew, definiteness is marked by a definite prefix on every definite noun and any adjective modifying it (e.g., <*ha->yeled* (<*ha->gdol)* the-boy the-big). In both English and Hebrew, unlike German, for example, the definite marker does not agree in gender or number with the head noun.

2.   The definite system

2.1 Definiteness in English

Syntactically, every singular count noun in English requires an indefinite or definite article (e.g., *(a/the) boy)*. Plural count nouns and mass nouns require the definite article whenever pragmatically appropriate (e.g., *(the) boys, (the) sugar)*. The choice of articles depends on the knowledge of the speaker of her own knowledge and of others' knowledge as well.

Schaeffer (1997) discusses three different aspects of definiteness in adult English. The referential definite 'the' is used when the referent is known to both speaker and hearer, as in (1):

(1)   There is a car and a ball on the carpet. The car is red.

The object in the world that 'the car' refers to is known by both speaker and hearer, due to the fact that it was mentioned in the previous discourse. The referent can also be part of world knowledge shared by both speaker and hearer, as in (2):

(2)   The sun is out.

There is only one object in the world that is known as 'the sun'.

The referential indefinite 'a' is used when the referent is known only to the speaker, as in (3):

(3) I bought a book yesterday.

The indefinite nominal 'book' does have a referent, but only the speaker knows it. The non-referential indefinite 'a' is used when the referent is unknown to both speaker and hearer, as in (4):

(4) I haven't seen a movie for ages.

There is no movie in the world that could be the referent for 'a movie'. Schaeffer concluded from the above that in adult English the form of the definite article is based on definiteness rather than referentiality, since the latter relies solely on speaker's knowledge, while in fact both speaker's and hearer's knowledge are crucial for definiteness.

Schaeffer proposes that definiteness and referentiality should be syntactically marked by features such as [speaker] and [hearer] on the D-head of the DP, as in Figure 1:

	Article	Speaker	Hearer
Referential definite	the	+	+
Referential indefinite	a	+	−
Non-referential indefinite	a	−	+

Figure 1. Definiteness, referentiality and the speaker & hearer features

Figure 1 shows that:

1. A referential definite nominal expression is marked only with the features [speaker] and [hearer].
2. A referential indefinite nominal expression is marked with the feature [speaker].

Schaeffer further claims that non-referential indefinite nominal expressions are NumPs, without a D-head, and are not marked with [speaker] or [hearer] features. Consequently, the pragmatic distinction between speaker and hearer is crucial to the acquisition of the properties of D.

2.2 Definiteness in Hebrew

Definiteness marking in Hebrew is less uniform than in English or German, but resembles other Semitic languages, such as Arabic (Wintner 2000). The only definite marker in Hebrew, 'ha-', is a nominal prefix that does not inflect, as in (5), rather than a function word marking a whole phrase. It is used in agreement both on nouns and on the adjectives modifying them, as shown in (6). In the direct object position, definite NPs are introduced by the definite accusative case marker 'et' which has the characteristics of a preposition, as shown in (7):

(5) a. Indefinite NP: *yeled shata mic*
             boy drank juice
             'A boy drank some juice'
     b. Definite NP: *raiti yeled. ha-yeled shata mic*
             I-saw boy. the-boy drank juice
             'I saw a boy. The boy drank some juice'

(6)   Agreement: *raiti yeled gadol. ha-yeled ha-gadol shata mic*
             I-saw boy big. The-boy the-big drank juice
             'I saw a big boy'.'The big boy drank some juice'

(7)   Direct Object: *kaniti mic. yeled shata *(et) ha-mic*
             I-bought juice. Boy drank acc the juice
             'I bought some juice. A boy drank the juice'

Non-discourse-related definite (generic) nouns in Hebrew, unlike English, may appear without the definite article 'ha', depending on their syntactic position and semantic reading, as in (8):

(8) a. *Yesh   (*ha-)shemesh ba-xuc*
             cop(exist) (*the-)sun   outside
             'It's sunny outside' (literally: the sun exists outside)
     b. *Hine (ha-)shemesh*
             Here (the-)sun
             'Here is the sun'
     c. *Ani roe (et ha-)shemesh*
             I see (acc the-)sun
             'I see the sun'
     d. *Ani mistakelet al *(ha-)shemesh*
             I look at (the-)sun
             'I look at the sun.'

In (8a), with the existential copula *yesh*, the definite article is ungrammatical with all nouns. Sentences (b) and (c) have an existential reading too, reflected in the possibility of replacing the optional definite article *ha-* in (b) by the existential copula *yesh*. Thus, the article is optional. In sentence (d), the article is syntactically obligatory since it follows a preposition which takes a DP as its complement. These characteristics of the definite system in Hebrew make it less uniform and more sensitive to a variety of syntactic and semantic factors.

3.   The acquisition of definiteness

The acquisition of the definiteness system poses a hard and complex communicative problem to the child (Zur 1983). A proper use of the definiteness system is a combination of a syntactic task and a pragmatic task. The latter requires an ability to consider the hearer's knowledge, overriding the speaker's egocentric tendency in order to create a coherent referent system for the hearer. The speaker needs to know that her knowledge is different from the hearer's own knowledge, in order to share her knowledge with the hearer. She also needs to know about general knowledge shared with the hearer. This means that the child has to distinguish between objects that exist in reality and those which exist only in his or her mind.

According to Piaget (1959), the communicative ability of a child is limited, since his or her speech is egocentric and is not directed at the hearer. Children seem to lack the ability to differentiate speaker from hearer at the first stages of language acquisition, and have to compensate for this deficit by other means. By the end of the first year, the child might compensate by gestures, pointing, nodding his or her head, etc. Later on, he or she might use demonstratives such as *this*. The most complex form is the anaphoric use of definiteness, which means a specific linguistic reference.

Between two and three, children start using the definiteness markers, but they do not have an adult-like control (Zur 1983: 10). At first, the child uses definiteness markers in relation to objects, which relate to his or her close surrounding. In most cases, he or she does not yet appreciate correctly the communicative status of that referent. Only at a later stage does the child develop the ability to relate to other objects, which are not close to him or her. With this latter development, he or she also develops the ability to draw away from his or her egocentric point of view and to take into consideration the hearer's knowledge as well.

Definiteness, expressed by the use of determiners, is one of three syntactic aspects which are obligatory in adult English, but are optionally expressed in the child's early grammar (Hoekstra & Hyams 1996), the other two being the use of root infinitives and certain types of null subjects. Hoekstra and Hyams claim that the interpretation of the 'dropped' elements should be analyzed by an appeal to pragmatic principles in the child's system. Moreover, they state that the option of direct discourse interpretation, and hence root infinitives and determiners drop, disappears with the development of the pragmatic system.

3.1   Acquisition of definiteness in Hebrew

Zur (1983), looking at children from two to twelve years old, found that just as in English, definite markers are already used by the age of two. Performance, however, improves along with the age. Many errors in the use of definiteness were detected until the age of 3;6. At the age of three to five there was an overgeneralization of the rules, and lack of knowledge of the constraints limiting the application of the rules. Moreover, age five was found to be critical for the acquisition of the definite system.

Syntactically, children initially use bare nouns, which are extended within the earliest word combinations into full NPs, where quantifiers and determiners are used in [Spec, NP] (Armon-Lotem 1996). Since there is not enough space to host more than one modifier, the projection is extended into NumP and DP. This syntactic structure makes it possible for the child to extend the number of possible features which are identified. The productive use of the definite article *ha-* is partly a proof of the above.

3.2 Acquisition of definiteness in English

Schaeffer (1997) conducted a study on the acquisition of definiteness by English-speaking children. She argues that while the use of articles is close to adult-like by the age of four, at 2 and 3, children make some syntactic errors. She claims that children initially rely on referentiality in their choice of articles, since referentiality is a semantic notion that does not rely on the hearer's knowledge, but solely on the speaker's knowledge. Thus, the syntactic errors result from the lack of a pragmatic principle, 'the concept of non-shared knowledge', which differentiates the knowledge of the speaker and the hearer. She further claims that development within the pragmatic component will lead to a development within syntax. More specifically, she argues that non-referential indefinite nominal expressions are NumPs, without a D-head, and are not marked with [speaker] or [hearer] features. Consequently, the pragmatic distinction between speaker and hearer is crucial to the acquisition of the properties of D.

Schaeffer (1997) predicts that children will overgenerate the definite referential article *the* to contexts which require the indefinite referential *a*, indicating lack of pragmatic knowledge about the speaker/hearer differentiation. On the other hand, children will drop the definite article *the* in definite contexts, and the indefinite article *a* in referential indefinite contexts due to lack of syntactic knowledge about the use of D. This lack of knowledge could either be the outcome of a structure without a D, or a structure in which the features of D are not specified, as has been suggested for other functional categories in early child grammar (Bohnacker 1997; Clahsen, Sonja & Vainikka 1994). She found that English-speaking 2-year-olds, and to a lesser extent 3-year-olds drop articles in referential contexts and overgenerate definite articles in indefinite referential contexts. Schaeffer suggests that these errors result from the child's lack of the concept of non-shared knowledge, a pragmatic concept which indicates that speaker's knowledge and hearer's knowledge are always independent. Once this concept has been acquired, the child distinguishes the two features and marks them on D.

4.   The concept of non-shared knowledge and the Theory of Mind

The concept on non-shared knowledge "expresses an obligation for the speaker to consider the hearer's knowledge as a separate entity and therefore as something that is principally different from the speaker's knowledge. However, in certain cases, speaker's and hearer's knowledge may coincide" (Schaeffer 1997:2). If the concept of non-shared knowledge is missing, then the speaker automatically attributes his or her own knowledge to the hearer, overgenerating the use of definite articles.

This concept has been associated with some aspects of Theory of Mind. Malle claims that theory of mind "refers to the ability to represent, conceptualize, and reason about mental states" (2001:3) of self and others. Piaget was the first to investigate children's understanding of the mind, and conclude that children are egocentric and make no attempt to understand the other's point of view. Lately, Theory of Mind has been related to the development of intentionality from 'zero-order' level, when the child has no beliefs and desires, to 'first-order' level, when the child has beliefs and desires, but does not recognize the other's beliefs, and finally to 'second-order' level, when the child has beliefs and desires of his or her own, and of others (Brentano 1960, from Astington 1993). Between age two and age five children are claimed to move from first order level to second order level. By the age of two, their conceptual understanding of desires grows. An understanding of beliefs emerges by the age of three and the differentiation between thoughts and things, and false belief by the age of four. At this point children understand, according to Malle (2001), that different people represent the world in different ways and therefore can believe or know different things. Pragmatic concepts, such as the concept of shared knowledge, also rely on such understanding.

5.   Methodology

The current research is an adaptation of Schaeffer (1997) to Hebrew. The aim of the study was to see if Hebrew, despite the typological differences in structure (e.g., prefix vs. function word) and acquisition (i.e., definiteness is mastered later in Hebrew than in English), will show the same discrepancy between syntax and pragmatics as English does, and whether the findings will lend themselves to an analysis that ties the pragmatic aspects of definiteness to the Theory of Mind.

The following predictions emerge from Schaeffer's findings (1997), taking into account typological differences:

1. Children will drop the definite article 'ha-' in referential definite contexts, due to limited syntactic knowledge.
2. Children will overgenerate the definite article 'ha-' in contexts which require the indefinite referential article (in Hebrew- zero article), until they acquire the concept of non-shared knowledge.
3. Children will drop the definite article for non-discourse-related definite NPs, until they acquire the relevant world knowledge.

The data were collected using a toy elicitation task (Crain & Thornton 1998; Thornton 1996). The experimenter manipulated the toy props while a blindfolded puppet was listening to the story. Being blindfolded, the puppet needed the child's help to understand the story. The child could not use deictics like 'this' to identify the objects. Therefore, the only way the child could correctly identify the objects for the puppet was by naming them.

The experiment consisted of up to eighteen game-stories, at least three in each of the following categories:

(a) The referential definite existent.
(b) The non-discourse-related definite NP.
(c) The referential indefinite existent.
(d) The referential indefinite non-existent.
(e) The non-referential indefinite.

An example of the task in the definite – referential context is illustrated in (9):

(9)   Situation: Mr. Bunny is blindfolded.
      There is a ball and a car on the table.
      Mr. Lion enters.

      Mr. Bunny: Who is it
      Mr. Lion: It's me Mr. Lion
      Mr. Bunny: What's on the table
      Mr. Lion: A ball and a car. I have an idea

      Situation: Mr. Lion pushes the car.

      Mr. Bunny: What did Mr. Lion do?

      Child: *hu daxaf et ha-oto* / 'he pushed the car'
               **hu daxaf oto* / '*he pushed a car'

All the stories were piloted with an adult control group. Stories were presented in a random order, over two to three sessions. The first session started with up to six 'warm-up' stories containing a personal pronoun, in order to verify that the children understand the task. Warm-up stories were used in the following sessions only when necessary.

5.1 Categories of analysis

The five aforementioned contexts were analyzed into four categories, collapsing together the two indefinite referential contexts since the results were identical. The four categories were:

1. Definite discourse-related contexts.
2. Definite non-discourse-related contexts.
3. Indefinite referential contexts.
4. Indefinite non-referential contexts.

Data in each category were analyzed, per age group, regarding the number of errors and type of errors, the omission or addition of the definite article.

5.2 Subjects

32 Hebrew-speaking children aged 2–5, divided into three groups, and an adult control group were tested. The children, all from middle socioeconomic status (SES), attended different preschools across Israel. Table 1 shows the age range, mean age, and number of subjects in each group:

Table 1. Subject

	Age	Mean Age	Total Num.
Twos	2;0–2;11	2;26	11
Threes	3;2–3;10	3;37	11
Fours	4;1–5;0	4;48	10
Adults	—	—	5
Total			37

Most interviews took place at the preschool in a quiet room with one or two experimenters. Some of the sessions, however, took place at the subject's home. All sessions were tape-recorded and later on transcribed.

5.3 Findings

Children of all age groups used the definite article, with a very few errors. There were hardly any additions of the definite article in the indefinite context, but there

Wrong use of the definite system

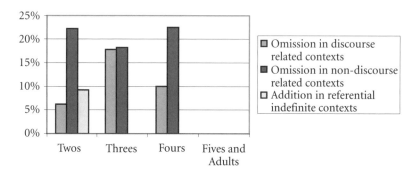

Figure 2. Error rate across categories (by age)

were some omissions of the definite articles in both obligatory contexts. Analyzing the types of errors, it was found that the addition of the definite article was limited to the twos (M 2;3). It occurred in 10% (5/54) of the referential indefinite contexts, but never in the non-referential contexts. Dropping of the definite article was found in 13% (9/70) of discourse-related definite context, up to age 4 (M 4;6), with the twos showing the lowest error rate (1/15) and the threes showing the highest error rate (18%–5/28). Dropping of the definite article was found in 21% (21/100) of non-discourse-related definite contexts, up to age 4 (M 4;6), the fours' error rate being as high as the twos'. This is shown in Figure 2.

In sum, omission of definite articles is more frequent than addition of the article, and remains a problem for a longer period. The use of definiteness in non-discourse-related contexts seems to pose a consistent problem as late as the age of four, whereas the use of definiteness in referential indefinite contexts is problematic only for the twos.

6.   Discussion

The Hebrew findings are consistent with Schaeffer's findings for English as far as additions are concerned. In both languages, two-year-old children overgeneralize the definite article to indefinite referential contexts. This looks as if they used the definite article to mark referentiality rather than definiteness. From a pragmatic perspective, it seems that they do not distinguish between speaker and hearer features. Since they never overgeneralize in the non-referential context, it seems safe to assume that in this context no feature is available and D is not used at all. Around the age of three they learn the pragmatic concept of non-shared knowledge and start using the definite article only in definite referential contexts.

In English, however, the system stabilizes both pragmatically and syntactically by the age of three, whereas in Hebrew, omissions of the definite article are found as late as four, and the question is why. Schaeffer argues that omissions around the age of two are due to lack of syntactic knowledge which makes it possible to use NumPs rather than DPs. These omissions were bound to disappear once children acquire the concept of non-shared knowledge, which enables them to mark the features 'hearer' and 'speaker' on D.

The Hebrew-speaking children seem to have acquired the concept of non-shared knowledge, as is evident from the absence of overgeneralizations of the definite article beyond the age of three. The question is whether we can attribute lack of syntactic knowledge to the Hebrew-speaking four-year-olds. As noted earlier, most omissions occur in the non-discourse-related definite context, a context which requires world knowledge, rather than unique syntactic knowledge. It seems that while Hebrew-speaking children clearly differentiate the speaker's knowledge from the hearer's knowledge before the age of three, they do not know, by the age of four, which beliefs can be attributed to the hearer based on shared world knowledge, that is, they are lacking the pragmatic concept of shared world knowledge.

Why is the type of pragmatic knowledge which is acquired by the age of three enough to stabilize the acquisition of definiteness in English, but not in Hebrew? The answer seems to lie within the domain of syntax, or more specifically in the syntactic uniformity of the definiteness paradigm. Definiteness in English is a uniform paradigm. Articles are obligatory and are used systematically in both definite and indefinite contexts. In Hebrew, however, definiteness is a non-uniform paradigm with only a definite article, and even this article is optional in some of the contexts where it is obligatory in English, e.g., in non-discourse-related definite context.

Being optional, the use of the definite article is more sensitive to a wider range of syntactic, semantic, and pragmatic factors. One possible semantic factor is that the English indefinite article *a* has a referential interpretation and a quantifier interpretation (Fodor & Sag 1982), while indefinite bare nouns in Hebrew lack the quantifier interpretation (Y. Greenberg, p.c.). For example, while the use of the indefinite article in '*a sun*' indicates that there is more than one sun, the bare noun *shemesh* (sun in Hebrew) does not have this reading. Therefore, in English, the use of a definite article with such nouns is semantically obligatory, in order to avoid the 'one of many' reading. In Hebrew, since the bare nouns do not have this reading, non-discourse-related definite nouns, like the *sun* or the *moon*, do not necessarily require a definite article and its use relates to particular syntactic structures (e.g., after a phrasal verb), and the different pragmatic aspects of definiteness. This complexity influences the use of the definite article in definite discourse-related contexts, causing a marginal instability. To sum, Hebrew-speaking children acquire the concept of non-shared knowledge by the age of 3, but master the system only when they acquire the concept of shared world knowledge, i.e., when they learn what the other thinks.

7. Conclusion

The Hebrew findings support Schaeffer's findings regarding the separate contribution of pragmatic principles and syntactic principles to the acquisition of definiteness, and add to them a second distinction between the contribution of different pragmatic principles to the acquisition of definiteness. These findings, while answering some questions, raise many others. Does this second distinction mirror the child's cognitive development? Is the concept of non-shared knowledge a linguistic manifestation of self-other differentiation? Is the concept of shared knowledge a linguistic manifestation of self-other coordination? Is shared world knowledge related to the Theory of Mind?

Further research is needed in order to answer these questions and find out how the pragmatics of definiteness relate to the Theory of Mind. Several age-related conceptual correlations lend themselves to it. The acquisition of the concept of non-shared knowledge (before age 3) follows the conceptual understanding of desire (age 2), but precedes the conceptual understanding of belief (age 3), whereas understanding of belief (age 3) and false belief (age 4) seems to facilitate the acquisition of the concept of shared world knowledge (age 4–5). These correlations call for further research, testing the same children on Theory of Mind tasks while they are tested for linguistic knowledge of definiteness.

References

Armon-Lotem, S. (1997). The minimalist child: parameters and functional heads in the acquisition of Hebrew. Ph.D. Dissertation, Tel-Aviv University.

Astington, J. W. (1993). *The Child's Discovery of the Mind*. New York: Harvard UP.

Bohnacker, U. (1997). Determiner phrase and the debate on functional categories in early child language. *Language Acquisition, 6,* 49–90.

Brentano, F. (1960). The distinction between mental and physical phenomena. In R. M. Chisholm (Ed.), *Realism and the Background of Phenomenology* (pp. 39–61). New York: Free Press.

Chesterman, A. (1991). *On Definiteness: A Study with Special Reference to English and Finnish*. New York: Cambridge University Press.

Clahsen, H., Sonja, E., & Vainikka, A. (1994). The seeds of structure. A syntactic analysis of the acquisition of case marking. In E. Hokstra & B. Schwartz (Eds.), *Language Acquisition Studies in Generative Grammar* (pp. 85–118). Amsterdam: John Benjamins Publishing.

Crain, S. & Thornton, R. (1998). *Investigations in Universal Grammar*. Cambridge, Mass.: MIT Press.

Fodor, J. D. & Sag, I. A. (1982). Referential and quantificational indefinites. *Linguistics and Philosophy, 5*, 355–398.

Hawkins, J. (1978). *Definiteness and Indefiniteness: A Study in Reference and Grammaticality Prediction*. London: Croom Helm.

Hoekstra, T. & Hyams, N. (1996). The syntax and interpretation of dropped categories in child language: A unified account. In Camacho J., Choueiri, L., & Watanabe, M. (Eds.), *The Proceedings of the Fourteenth West Coast Conference on Formal Linguistics* (pp. 123–136). United States: CSLI Publications.

Malle, B. F. (2001). The relation between language and Theory of Mind in development and evolution. Presented at the symposium on The Evolution of language out of Pre-language, Institute of Cognitive and Decision Sciences. University of Eugene: Oregon.

Piaget, J. (1959). *The Language and Thought of the Child*. London: Routledge and Kegan Paul.

Schaeffer, J. (1997). Articles in English child language. Paper presented at the Linguistic Society of America, Los Angeles.

Thornton, R. (1996). Elicited production. In D. McDaniel, C. McKee, & H. S. Cairns (Eds.), *Methods for Assessing Children's Syntax* (pp. 77–101). Cambridge, Mass.: MIT Press.

Wintner, S. (2000). Definiteness in the Hebrew Noun Phrase. *Journal of Linguistics, 36* (2), 319–363.

Zur, B. (1983). On the acquisition of definiteness by Hebrew-speaking children. Ms. Paper, Tel-Aviv University, (In Hebrew).

D(iscourse)-linking and question formation

Comprehension effects in children and Broca's aphasics

Helen Goodluck
University of York, U.K.

Recent studies of the comprehension of d(iscourse)-linked questions by children and Broca's aphasics show a subject-object asymmetry: d-linked object questions are harder than d-linked subject questions. A similar asymmetry is not found for non-d-linked questions. This study provides evidence that this asymmetry may be linked to the lexical content of the d-linked question. This calls into question one previous account of the subject-object asymmetry and suggests that part of the difficulty with d-linked questions may derive from perceptual factors in the set-up of the experiment.

1. Introduction

It has long been observed that d(iscourse)-linked wh-phrases such as *which man* (Pesetsky 1987) exhibit different behavior from non-d-linked phrases such as *who* or *what*, for example, permitting obviation of superiority effects (1b) vs. (1d) and the relaxation of island constraints (2a) vs. (2b),[1]

(1) a. Mary asked who read what.
     b. *Mary asked what who read.
     c. Mary asked which man read which book.
     d. Mary asked which book which man read.

(2) a. ??*A chi   ti   chiedi quanti   soldi   hai dato?* (Italian)
         To whom do you wonder how much money you gave
     b. *A quale dei tuoi   figli   ti   chiedi   quanti*
         To which one of your children do you wonder how much
         soldi   hai dato?
         money you gave

One of the earliest psycholinguistic studies of d-linking is Hickok & Avrutin's (1996) study of the comprehension of d-linked questions by two Broca's aphasics. Their subjects responded to questions following scenarios acted out by the experimenter. The basic form of the scenarios was that an animal of type A performs an action on another animal, which then performs the same action on a second animal of type A (e.g. pig 1 pushes a tiger, which then pushes pig 2). Either the subject or object position was questioned (3a, c vs. 3b, d) and the question word was either d-linked or not (3a, b vs. 3c, d).

(3) a. Who pushed the tiger?
     b. Who did the tiger push?
     c. Which pig pushed the tiger?
     d. Which pig did the tiger push?

For their aphasic subjects Hickok and Avrutin observed a striking subject-object asymmetry. Subjects performed well on subject questions, regardless of whether or not the question word was d-linked, and they also did well on non-d-linked object questions (70–80% correct). However, when the object question was d-linked, performance dropped to chance level. Avrutin (2000) observed the same effect for 4-6-year-old English-speaking children, as did De Vincenci, Arduino, Ciccarelli, & Job (1999) with a picture identification study with Italian-speaking children.

In a subsequent study of Broca's aphasics, Tait, Thompson, & Ballard (1995) observed a more mixed pattern, with only two of four Broca's aphasics showing the pattern of greater difficulty with d-linked than with non-d-linked object questions.

2.   Accounts of the subject-object asymmetry

Various accounts have been put forward for the asymmetrical d-linking deficit in comprehension. Hickok & Avrutin (1996) follow the linguistic analysis of Cinque (1990), who proposed that d-linked questions can involve binding chains rather than movement (government) chains. On this account the deficit of Broca's aphasics can be put down to an impairment in the ability of these patients to form binding chains. The subject-object asymmetry observed can be accounted for by the use of a first NP = agent strategy, which will result in correct answers for subject d-linked questions, but not object d-linked questions (Grodzinsky 1995).

Noting the controversial nature of Cinque's claim that d-linked phases are associated with binding chains, Tait et al. (1995) consider two different possible explanations of the asymmetrical d-linking effect. First, in the spirit of Chomsky's (1995) bare phrase structure analysis, they suggest that the type of category moved – X^0 (head movement, in the case of *who*) vs. XP (phrasal movement, in the case of *which*) – may account for the difference. Second, they suggest that the semantics of the two different types of question is different, with the representation of d-linked phrases being more complex, with an additional predication relation:

(4) a. Who/what pushed the tiger? For which x : (kick-elephant (x))
    b. Which pig kicked the elephant? For which x : (pig (x) and kick-elephant (x))

Tait et al. argue that this means that d-linked questions are computationally more complex than non-d-linked phrases. This semantic proposal fits the fact that Tait et al. did not find a d-linking effect when the d-linked phrase was *which one*, as opposed to a more specific phrase such as *which pig*.

Avrutin (2000) objects to Tait et al.'s syntactic proposal concerning head movement vs. phrasal movement on the ground that this alone cannot account for the asymmetry between subject and object d-linked questions.

Avrutin is sympathetic to the processing complexity account based on semantic representations, but proposes that the processing difficulty lies rather with "the integration of syntactic and discourse-related knowledge" (p. 302). Avrutin proposes that while the interpretation of a non-d-linked phrase can be achieved by establishing an operator-variable relationship in the syntax, d-linked phrases require the introduction of a discourse referent. De Vincenzi et al. (1999) also favor a processing account, although they are non-committal about the source of the processing difficulty. In addition to Avrutin's response to Tait et al.'s proposals, a reviewer of this paper argues that Tait et al.'s semantic account is flawed, in that non-d-linked phrases do involve a semantic restriction. The reviewer's point is that representation of a *who* such as (4a) must be along the lines in (5).

(5) For which x: (animate (x) and kick-elephant (x))

3. New experiments

I carried out two new experiments with 4-6-year-old children, aiming to replicate and extend the work of Hickok & Avrutin (1996) and Avrutin (2000).

3.1 Experiment 1

The materials and procedure for this experiment followed closely that of Hickok and Avrutin, with the addition of a new object question condition, in which there were three different animals and two different actions. For example, a tiger first pats a cow and then pushes a pig, followed by the question,

Table 1. Percentage correct responses. Experiment 1

Subject Questions H & A format		Object Questions H & A format		Object Questions New format	
–DL	+DL	–DL	+DL	–DL	+DL
88	83	88	62	93	88

Table 2. Percentage correct responses. Experiment 2

Subject Questions H & A format		Object Questions H & A format		Object Questions New format	
–DL	+DL	–DL	+DL	–DL	+DL
93	95	98	95	100	98

(6)   a.   Who did the tiger push?
      b.   Which animal did the tiger push?

Each subject responded to four tokens of each sentence type (3a–d and 6a–b). Fifteen 4–6-year-old children were tested (mean age: 67 months). The results are given in Table 1.

It is clear from Table 1 that the basic result of Hickok and Avrutin and of Avrutin is replicated for their materials. The difference between the non-d-linked and d-linked Hickok and Avrutin's object questions is significant ($t(14) = 3.23$, $p = .006$). Nine of the fifteen children had more correct responses to the non-d-linked object questions than to the d-linked object questions in the Hickok and Avrutin format and no child showed a reverse pattern. However, for the new object question condition, no effect of d-linking is found.

3.2 Experiment 2

This experiment was identical to experiment 1, except that the d-linked phrase in conditions (3c) and (3d) contained the phrase *which animal*, rather than, for example, *which pig*. The subjects were fourteen 4–6-year-olds (mean age: 58 months). The results are given in Table 2. In this experiment, performance was near-perfect for all conditions.

4. Discussion

The present experiments contribute two pieces of evidence to the debate on the processing of d-linked questions. First, the success that children had with the new format d-linked object questions in both experiments and with the Hickok and Avrutin format object questions in Experiment 2 shows that a deficit with d-linking is not universally found for children, complementing Tait et al.'s observation that such a deficit is not universally found with Broca's aphasics. It can be objected to the new format questions that all a child has to do to get the question right is to point to the animal that receives the action of the verb in the question. This objection does not hold, however, for the Hickok and Avrutin format questions with *which animal*. Second, the fact that we found a high performance with d-linked phrases such as *which animal* argues against Tait et al.'s semantic account of the d-linking deficit – the phrase *which animal* requires a two-predication semantic representation of the type proposed by Tait et al. (for which x [animal (x) and V-NP (x)]). Thus the objection mentioned above that non-d-linked question words such as *who* in fact require a semantic restriction is bolstered by the fact that we obtained a high level of performance for some d-linked phrases that also clearly require a semantic restriction.

Having eliminated the semantic processing complexity account, let us consider again the other two accounts of the d-linking asymmetry given in Section 2. I do not agree with Avrutin's assertion that the difference between X^0 movement and XP movement cannot account for the observed subject-object asymmetry. Let us assume that movement of a phrase is psycholinguistically more taxing than movement of an X^0, and that extraction from object position is more taxing than extraction from subject position (the latter claim being supported by much experimental evidence). Under these assumptions the combination of XP movement and object extraction can be taken to be sufficiently difficult to trigger an interaction effect. This would be more convincing if the data showed some effect of d-linking for the subject position, but nonetheless it may be that the subject questions are just not challenging enough for any d-linking effect to show up. Note that Avrutin's alternative theory that it is the necessity of integrating syntactic and discourse representations for d-linked *wh*-phrases that results in the deficit for d-linked phrases is also subject to the objection that it does not in and of itself account for the subject-object asymmetry, and Avrutin deals with this by appealing to the first NP = agent strategy to explain the absence of a d-linking effect for subject questions, just as Hickok and Avrutin did. Thus so far it appears that it's a draw between the X^0/XP and discourse integration accounts of the special difficulty of d-linked object questions – both need to appeal to some extra factor to explain why subject *which* questions are not harder than subject *who* questions.

Avrutin argues in support of his account also in terms of the fact that integrating discourse and syntax is known to cause children difficulty, citing evidence such as the fact that children have greater difficulty with pronouns, which can – and in some cases must – take a sentence external referent, than with reflexives, which always refer sentence internally. I believe that it is correct to claim that integrating syntax and discourse causes children difficulty and have suggested that this may be a consequence of the overall architecture of the human sentence processor (Goodluck 1990). However, I am not convinced that discourse integration is the source of the difficulty children have with d-linked questions. My reason for this is that while Avrutin correctly cites De Vincenzi 1991 as evidence that d-linking may require extra computational resources, we also have some evidence that d-linking may in some sense ease processing. The same children who took part in Experiments 1 and 2 above also did an experiment in which we compared d-linked and non-d-linked questions such as (inter alia),

(7) a. Who/which animal did the elephant ask to help?
     b. Who/which animal did the elephant ask if she should help?

The questions were posed following short stories in which two candidate answers were provided: the object of asking and the object of helping. Children were more likely to take the embedded clause as the site of the wh-phrase when the phrase was d-linked than when it was not. This suggests that d-linking helps the child to maintain the question phrase as active and hence to discharge it at the more deeply embedded position.

5. Summary and conclusion

This study has replicated and extended the finding that d-linked object questions can cause special difficulty for children, although such questions can also be comprehended very well. The results with phrases such as *which animal* (experiment 2) argue against one account of the difficulty of d-linking (Tait et al.'s semantic complexity account). Both Tait et al.'s syntactic complexity (X^0/XP) account of the difficulty of d-linking and Avrutin's discourse integration account must recruit an additional factor to explain children's success with d-linked subject questions (this factor on Avrutin's account being a first NP = subject strategy). I believe too little is known at the moment about the psycholinguistics of d-linking to say that the discourse complexity account should be preferred in terms of falling within a general model in which access to the discourse causes children (and aphasics) trouble. Nor do I think that it is necessarily right to seek out a single factor as the source of difficulty with d-linking. There is no reason why both syntactic complexity and discourse demands should not both play a role, with the challenge being to tease the two apart. Moreover, the result that changing a more specific phrase such as *which pig* to *which animal* eliminates the d-linking effect suggests that some of the effect may derive from perceptual factors related to the set-up of the experiment, since it is not obvious on linguistic grounds why a search of the complete array of animals presented in the senario should be easier than a search of a subset of the array.[2] That is, the mention of a specific animal may set off a comparison process that – in combination with questioning of the object position – triggers errors. This is the topic of experiments currently in progress.

Acknowledgments

This research was supported by Social Sciences and Humanities Research Council of Canada grant # 410-2001-0458. I am very grateful to Nicole Tapajna for her help in running subjects, and to a reviewer, Paul Hirschbuhler, and audiences at the Venice Language Brain and Computation Conference, the University of Essex and the University of Ottawa for their comments. As always, many thanks to the subjects in the experiments for taking part

Notes

1. The examples in (1) are from Pesetsky (1987), who attributes them to Chomsky (1980), who in turn attributes them to R. Kayne (Pesetsky, fn. 8); the examples in (2) are from Cinque 1990.

2. It should be noted that Hickok and Avrutin (1996) retested one of their patients with non-specific d-linked phrases and still obtained the d-linking deficit for object questions.

References

Avrutin, S. (2000). Comprehension of discourse-linked and non-discourse linked questions by children and Broca's aphasics. In Y. Grodzinsky, L. Shapiro & D. Swinney (Eds.), *Language and Brain: Representation and Processing* (pp. 295–312). San Diego: Academic Press.

Chomsky, N. (1980). On binding. *Linguistic Inquiry, 11,* 1–46.

Chomsky, N. (1995). *The Minimalist Program.* Cambridge, Mass.: MIT Press.

Cinque, G. (1990). *Types of Ā-Dependencies.* Cambridge, Mass.: MIT Press.

Goodluck, H. (1990). Knowledge integration in processing and acquisition. In L. Frazier & J. de Villiers (Eds.), *Language Acquisition and Language Processing* (pp. 369–382). Dordrecht, The Netherlands: Kluwer.

Grodzinsky, Y. (1995). Trace deletion, theta-roles and cognitive strategies. *Brain and Language, 51,* 469–497.

De Vincenzi, M. (1991). *Syntactic Parsing Strategies in Italian.* Dordrecht, The Netherlands: Kluwer Academic.

De Vinzenci, M., Arduino, L. Ciccarelli, L., & Job, R. (1999). Parsing strategies in children's comprehension of interrogative sentences. *Proceedings of the 1999 European Conference on Cognitive Science* (pp. 301–308). Istituto de Psicologia, Siena, Italy.

Hickok, G. & Avrutin, S. (1996). Comprehension of wh-questions in two Broca's aphasics. *Brain and Language, 52,* 314–327.

Pesetsky, D. (1987). Wh-in situ: Movement and unselective binding. In E. Reuland & A. ter Muelen (Eds.), *The Representation of (In)definiteness* (pp. 98–129). Cambridge, Mass.: MIT Press.

Tait, M., Thompson, C., & Ballard, K (1995). Subject-object asymmetries in agrammatic comprehension of four types of wh-question. *Brain and Language, 51,* 77–79.

Evidence from ASL and ÖGS for asymmetries in UG

Ronnie B. Wilbur

Purdue University

In syntax, configurational asymmetry can provide an explanation for the merging, dependency, and word order of linguistic categories (Di Sciullo 2002). The inclusion of data from two sign languages demonstrates that asymmetry is not limited to spoken languages, but is a more general phenomenon deserving a place in Universal Grammar (UG). This paper (1) reviews evidence documenting argument asymmetries in American Sign Language (ASL); (2) identifies structural asymmetries of headedness and at the peripheries for ASL and Austrian Sign Language (ÖGS); and (3) documents domain asymmetries in ASL, specifically c-command versus Spec-head agreement (checking domain/residual) for clause-level facial marking. Together these data provide solid support for the universality of argument and structural asymmetries in UG.

1. Introduction

The goal of this paper is to provide arguments from two signed languages for the hypothesis that configurational asymmetry is part of Universal Grammar (UG). Di Sciullo (2002) argues that asymmetry is basic to grammar, is instantiated in each component, and is the optimal configuration for interpretation. In syntax, it can provide an explanation for the merging, dependency, and word order of linguistic categories with each other (Chomsky 1995; Kayne 1994), and Di Sciullo (2002) extends the investigation of asymmetry to morphology. Because the arguments for asymmetry and UG in general have been based on spoken languages, the inclusion of sign language arguments represents a significant source of additional support for the fundamental hypotheses.

Three types of syntactic asymmetries will be discussed here. First, the evidence documenting argument asymmetries in American Sign Language (ASL) will be reviewed. Second, structural asymmetries related to the peripheries and headedness of configurations will be identified for ASL and Austrian Sign Language (ÖGS). Third, domain asymmetries, specifically c-command versus spec-head agreement, will be documented for ASL. Finally, the implications of these asymmetries for sign language research and UG theory will be discussed.

1.1 Background regarding ASL

ASL is known to be an SVO language (Liddell 1978). Unlike English, which allows stress to move to different locations within a sentence, ASL has fixed focus prominence in final position of the main CP (Wilbur 1997). This means that the word order in ASL is variable so as to accommodate the fixed focus requirements, and it can be observed that the surface word order is primarily driven by discourse relations rather than grammatical relations (Wilbur 1997; Kiss 1995). Further discussion of ASL phrase structure will be postponed until the various argument asymmetries have been discussed

2. Evidence for argument asymmetries

In this section, several types of data will be presented in support of argument asymmetries in ASL. These include behavior with respect to (1) different verb categories (transitive, unaccusative, unergative); (2) negation and distributivity; (3) genericity; and (4) stage versus individual level predicates.

2.1 Internal vs. external arguments

The first argument asymmetry of interest is the distinction between subject and (direct) object, or more specifically, between external and internal arguments. Kegl (1990) identified predicate-argument structures (PAS) for ASL. These include transitives (both external x and internal <y>; example (1)), unaccusatives (internal only; example (2)), and unergatives (external only; example (3)). In the following examples, subscripted letters {a, b} refer to locations in space that are established for particular noun referents; for example, in (1) MARY_a JOHN_b $_b\text{HIT}_a$, Mary is established at point a in space; the movement of the verb HIT is started at that location and moves to the location b that was established when John was introduced into the conversation; that is, HIT is an agreeing verb for both external and internal arguments. Subscripted numerals refer to arbitrary points in space; a subscripted 0 refers to a neutral location, that is, one not intended to be referred back to. 'cl:' refers to a classifier handshape; after the colon the handshape for one or both hands is identified.

(1) transitive x<y>

    a. MARY$_a$ JOHN$_b$ $_b$HIT$_a$ 'John hit Mary.'

    b. JOHN$_a$ SCARE MARY$_b$ 'John scared Mary.'

    c. STICK JANE$_0$ cl:hand+BREAK   'Jane broke the stick.'

(2) unaccusative <y>

    a. BOX$_e$ cl:s/s+EXPLODE   'The box exploded.'

    b. STICK$_{10}$ cl:G+BREAK (inchoat) 'The stick broke.'

(3) unergative x< >

    a. JOHN$_f$ cl:B+DIED   'John died.'

These data provide the classic examples to show that external arguments are differentiated from internal ones. Consequences of this differentiation can be clearly seen by comparing (1c) and (2b), which both contain the verb 'break'. In both examples, the classifier handshape used in the formation of the verb sign is dependent on the internal argument. In (1c) the 'handling' classifier 'cl:hand' is chosen to show both that there is an agent 'Jane' manipulating the stick in order to break it (Kegl 1990), and that there is an object 'stick,' shown by the degree of closure of the fist indicating information about the circumference of the object being handled. In contrast, in (2b) the descriptive classifier handshape 'cl:G' is chosen to reflect the fact that the stick which breaks is a 'long thin object' ('G' is the handshape made with the index finger extended from a closed fist); no agent is included (no external argument is projected).

2.2 Argument differentiation by negation and distributive

Internal and external arguments are further distinguished by their asymmetrical behavior with respect to the negative sign NOTHING. Wood (1999) argued that NOTHING is an operator that can only have scope over internal arguments (Wood 1999), as in (4):

(4) TEACHER CUT PAPER NOTHING

    'The teacher didn't cut any paper'

    *'No teacher cut paper.'

Thus, NOTHING can negate the subject of unaccusatives, but not the external arguments in unergatives or transitives. Benedicto & Brentari (2004) use this test to separate classifiers in ASL into two groups – those taking internal arguments and those taking external arguments. For example, they show that 'limb' classifiers participate in unergative predicates with a single external argument and alternate with 'whole entity' (e.g. vehicle) classifiers which occur in unaccusative predicates with a single internal argument. Another alternation is seen between transitive predicates with handling classifiers and intransitive (unaccusative) predicates with whole entity classifiers.

They also observe that [distributive] predicates only scope with respect to internal arguments (Benedicto & Brentari 2004).[1]

(5)   GIRL DRESS BUY+[distr]
    girl   dress   buy+[distributive]
    'The girl bought each of the dresses.'
    #'Each of the girls bought a dress.'

2.3 Argument differentiation by genericity and brow raise

Wilbur (1998) demonstrated that ASL external arguments may be bound by the generic operator GEN, whereas internal arguments cannot be. Generic subjects occur with the nonmanual brow raise marking, whereas no other subjects do. The correlation between generic subjects and brow raises can be seen from the fact that subjects of individual-level predicates, which are generic, have the brow raise marking, whereas subjects of stage-level predicates, which are plural but not generic, do not. Similarly, in object position, bare NPs are interpreted as plurals, not generics, and do not have brow raise over them. An example from English would be "She ate (some) eggs for breakfast." Examples for ASL will be discussed below (9 & 10).

2.3.1   Introduction to brow raise
Brow raise is used in many different structures in ASL. Those in Table 1 were identified over 20 years ago (Liddell 1978, 1980; Coulter 1978), but have been until recently treated as a (partially) unrelated set. The headings in Table 1 indicate whether the brow raise occurs over 'old' or 'new' information (Wilbur 1994b); the fact that both old and new occur eliminates the possibility of a discourse-functional explanation (Wilbur 1999).

Table 1. Structures with 'br' in ASL

'background' information	'assertion'
Topic	Topicalization/Focalization
Left Dislocation	Focused Modals
Yes/No question	Focused Predicate Adjectives
Relative clause	THAT-clefts
Wh-clause in wh-cleft	Focus Particles ('even', 'only')
Conditional clause	
Material preceding focused negative	

Wilbur (1999; Wilbur & Patschke 1999) argues that "brow raise 'br' occurs on structures headed by restrictive [-wh]-operators". Specifically, brow raise covers the material in the specifier that is in a spec-head agreement relation with a restrictive operator. These restrictive operators (or, alternatively, their respective features) may occur either in C^0 or D^0 in ASL.[2]

2.3.2   *Generics provide an independent test of the hypothesis*
The inclusion of generics resulted from my search for a [-wh]-operator not included in Table 1, to provide an independent test of the Wilbur (1999) hypothesis. Carlson & Pelletier (1995) argue that generics theoretically have the [-wh]-operator GEN that binds generic subjects. Chierchia (1995), Krifka (1995), and Krifka et al. (1995) discuss how GEN fits into the framework of (adverbs of) quantification viewed as an operator with a restriction and a nuclear scope. Chierchia (1995) extends this analysis of GEN to individual-level predicates and predicate NPs (the latter are discussed in Section 2.3.3). In ASL, the bare singular NP is used for generics, as seen in (6) and (7), both of which occur with individual-level predicates:

(6) $\overline{\text{br}}$
       LION TEND #TAIL POOFY-ON-END TEND[3]
       'A lion/the lion/lions usually has/have a bushy tail.'

(7) $\overline{\text{br}}$
       POTATO SELF WOW DIGEST EAT DIGEST EASY WOW[4]
       'The potato is highly digestible.'

Certain relative clause constructions, namely those that introduce new information (see Footnote 4), can also serve as the generic subject of an individual-level predicate (8).

(8) $\overline{\text{br}}$ $\overline{\text{hn}}$
       RULE GENERAL MAN SELF(cl:G) FIREMAN TEND   INTELLIGENT[5]
       'As a general rule, firefighters (men who are firefighters) are (really) intelligent.'

There is however no brow raise on subjects of stage-level predicates because they are not generic, as seen in (9):[6]

(9)   FIREMAN ALWAYS TEND AVAILABLE 24 HR ALL-TIME, NO-MATTER TIME
       AVAILABLE MUST
       'For the public safety, (some) firefighters are available all the time.'

Example (10) provides another occurrence of the bare singular FIREMAN with no brow raise and is ambiguous between singular and plural readings:[7]

(10)   <u>   br   </u>
YOU WANT HELP PT HAVE FIREMAN PT READY AVAILABLE HELP CAN PT...
'If you need some help, there is/are (a/some) fireman/firemen available at
the loading dock.'

The construction HAVE NP is the existential 'there is/are' (Wilbur 1998). Thus, the
NP FIREMAN is in the nuclear scope bound by existential closure and is unavailable
to GEN. What this means is that the actual interpretation is dependent on other
factors, such as whether the verb shows agreement (in this case it does not) or
other information provided in the sentence that can narrow the possible readings
(Petronio 1993). In (10) not enough information is available to identify which is
the preferred reading. But in (9) our knowledge of the fact that a single fireman
cannot be available 24 hours a day all the time leads to a preference for the plural
reading. Thus, (9) is not a true generic, and FIREMAN has a 'plural but not generic'
interpretation, as it does in the plural reading of (10). The plural reading of (10)
can be forced by the presence of an overt quantifier such as MANY or FEW, as in (11).
When a bare singular appears with an overt quantifier such as MANY, there still is
no brow raise, reflecting the fact that overt adjectives/adverbs of quantification and
inherent restrictive operators are different types of modification/predication:

(11)   <u>   br   </u>
KNOW #HELLABRUN ZOO PT, HAVE MANY LION THERE.
know   Hellabrun Zoo def exist
MANY OOH! ESCAPED++ #ZOO YESTERDAY
    wow escape[distrib]
'You know the Hellabrun Zoo has many lions. Many (lions) of them es-
caped from the zoo yesterday.'

2.3.3   Predicate nominals

Wilbur (1995) showed that brow raise appears on the first nominal of predicate
nominals, as predicted by Chierchia's (1995) analysis. However, unlike English
(12), predicate nominals are not 'reversible' in ASL (13).

(12)   a. 'Bronze is a metal.'   (plain)
      b. 'A/one metal is bronze.'   (reversed)

(13)   a. <u> br   </u>
      BRONZE METAL   (plain)

      b. <u>   br   </u>
      *METAL BRONZE   (reversed)

      c. <u> br   </u>
      *METAL BRONZE   (reversed)

Thus, the data from ASL predicate nominals are consistent with the behavior of GEN predicted by Chierchia on semantic grounds. The marking of GEN in ASL by brow raise provides independent evidence for the Wilbur (1999; Wilbur & Patschke 1999) claim regarding the role of brow raise as an overt marker of the presence of [-wh]-operators based on those structures in Table 1. Furthermore, ASL can be seen to provide independent support for Carlson & Pelletier's (1995) initial postulation of the GEN operator.

3. Evidence for structural asymmetries

This section will address the evidence for various structural asymmetries in ASL. A comparison with spoken Catalan provides insights into why ASL behaves the way it does as well as a contrast with behaviors that it does not display.

3.1 Asymmetrical behavior with respect to the peripheries

I have argued elsewhere that even though ASL basic word order is SVO, its surface word order is primarily determined by what information is in focus and the fact that ASL has fixed phrasal stress assignment in matrix CP final position (Wilbur 1995, 1996a, 1997). Catalan provides a language comparison, in that it also has basic SVO word order and fixed matrix CP final stress. However, there are significant distinctions between ASL and Catalan in how they accomplish the goal of putting focus in main clause final position: ASL prefers leftward movement (preposing) to remove non-focused material from final position to certain projections in the CP field, while Catalan prefers rightward movement (right detachment or dislocation) to accomplish the same task. Also, ASL allows greater freedom of constituent ordering in the main clause, while Catalan preserves much of its SVO ordering (Vallduví 1991).

Vallduví argues that the basic strategy for achieving focus in matrix clause final position in Catalan is by multiple right detachment, that is, by moving non-focused material rightward outside of the main CP to (unstressed) adjunction positions. This leaves the final position of the main clause occupied by the element(s) in focus. In (14), 'al calaix' is in focus; the pause after it is represented by a comma. Note that all possible orderings of non-focused information can occur:

(14)   [*Al calaix*,]   ficara   el ganivet el Juli.
        In-the drawer, put-future the knife   Juli
        [*Al calaix,*] *ficara, el ganivet, el Juli.*
        [*Al calaix,*] *ficara, el Juli, el ganivet.*
        [*Al calaix,*] *el Juli, el ganivet, ficara.*

> [*Al calaix,*] *el Juli, ficara, el ganivet.*
> [*Al calaix,*] *el ganivet, el Juli, ficara.*
> [*Al calaix,*] *el ganivet, ficara, el Juli.*
> 'Juli will put the knife [in the DRAWER.]'

The right dislocated phrases contain old information. The actual ordering of these phrases is discourse dependent, but these possibilities illustrate another aspect of Catalan, namely that when the non-focused material is moved rightward out of the core clause, the strict SVO word order seen in main clauses is no longer maintained. Vallduví argues that the first right-moved phrase serves the function of indicating that the focus information should be substituted by the hearer for what the speaker believes the hearer has in knowledge store. Subsequent right-moved phrases are presumably redundant for this function. Although recent analyses have argued for a node in the CP field responsible for information packaging (e.g., Bayer 2001; Haegeman 2002; Munaro 2002), it is not clear how the *right* dislocated elements in Catalan should be treated. Nor is Catalan an isolated case; French also displays right dislocation, although it also projects CP fields for left dislocation.

Unlike Catalan, ASL relies on leftward preposing (or deletion) of non-focused material to ensure that the focus phrase appears in CP-final position. In fact, ASL does not use true right dislocation at all (Wilbur 1996a); on the right, only standard Tag questions may appear. Thus whatever projections are seen on the right in Catalan and French (other than Tag) are lacking in ASL, whereas the left periphery in ASL can host (among others) a topic slot, a left dislocation slot, and [spec, CP] as the topicalization landing site (Wilbur 1996a; Wilbur & Patschke 1999; *contra* Neidle et al. 2000).[8]

The above discussion of fixed focus at the end of the main CP shows that ASL does assign a function to the right CP edge. The result of this, however, is another set of disallowed structures, namely those that would put non-focused material after the focus. Thus, in ASL wh-clefts allow (15a) but not (15b).[9]

                    <u>   br   </u>

(15)   a. BILL EAT WHAT, SAUSAGE
           'What Bill ate was a sausage.'

                 <u>   br   </u>

       b. *SAUSAGE WHAT BILL EAT
          *'A sausage is what Bill ate.'

Consequences of this restriction can also be seen in the grammaticality of conditional "if X. . .Y" constructions but the absence of right-adjoined "Y if X," and their counterparts with "when" and "because" (see Munaro 2002 for further discussion of conditionals and CP fields). In fact, all brow raise marked structures are either CP-left peripheral or DP-left peripheral (relative clauses). Further evidence for left peripheral phenomena in ASL is the behavior of wh-phrases in wh-questions. Example (16a) illustrates a wh-question with the standard brow furrow 'bf' marking. The wh-phrase 'which computer' has been moved leftward to [spec, CP] from its original position as the object of 'buy'. The head of the wh-phrase has been doubled to the right and is attached to C^0 (recall that [+wh] is, by definition, focus).

$$\overline{\qquad\qquad\qquad\qquad\text{bf}\qquad\qquad\qquad\qquad}$$

(16) a. WHICH COMPUTER PHIL BUY *t* WHICH
      b. *WHICH PHIL BUY WHICH COMPUTER
      c. *WHICH COMPUTER PHIL BUY WHICH COMPUTER
          'Which computer did Phil buy?'

The reverse movement, with the wh-phrase to the right and the wh-head to the left, is not permitted (16b). Also, doubling of the entire wh-phrase to the right is not permitted (16c). However, the same sequence of signs in (16c) is permissible (only) if there is a clear pause before the second occurrence of the wh-phrase, indicating that the second occurrence is in a different CP from the first (17). Such sequences are optimally consistent with the ASL lack of tolerance for redundancy of non-focused material and its other preference for repetition (doubling) of focused information.

(17) WHICH COMPUTER PHIL BUY? WHICH COMPUTER?
      'Which computer did Phil buy? Which computer?'

Pausing also plays a significant role in our understanding of the phrase structure of ÖGS (Section 4.2) and its different possibilities compared to ASL. We turn now to headedness differences within and across the two sign languages.

4.   Structural asymmetries: Mixed headedness[10]

In this section, a comparison will be made of the "doubling" process in ASL and ÖGS. In the two languages, there are both similarities and significant differences in what categories of signs may participate in doubling and where the double may appear. These differences are attributed to constituent structure, in how the relevant phrases are headed (initial or final), which affects the syntactic places where doubled items can then appear. The observed differences reflect the fact that ASL has two locations for doubling, whereas ÖGS has only one. This difference results from the fact that ASL has initial heads on all its lexical and functional phrases except for CP, which is head-final, while ÖGS has head-initial CP but head-final VP. Petronio (1993) argues that true doubles are base-generated in C, which is generally agreed to be on the right in ASL, and no alternate analysis has yet been attempted. Other so-called "doubles" are either tags or separate questions. Wilbur (1999) provides further evidence that the pronoun double is in C and identifies a category of predi-cates (those with experiencer subjects) which show partial handshape assimilation that indicates they are in the process of reanalyzing the final pronoun doubles as subject agreement affixes on the verb. ÖGS does not have C on the right, and the head it does have on the right (V) is not known to be host for doubles in any other sign language.

ÖGS and ASL both allow "doubling" to Tag Phrases, with a required pause before the tag material in both languages.[11] However, ASL is also able to use head-final C for doubled material (as seen in examples (6), (7), and (16)) but ÖGS, which has head-initial C, cannot. It is final C doubling that allows ASL to have "doubling" without a pause before the doubled material. Thus, ASL "doubling" has two options, tag question with a pause and true doubling in final C without a pause, whereas ÖGS has only one, tag question with a pause. This structural difference is further reflected in which categories the two languages allow to double. In ÖGS, only those lexical categories that are allowed to appear in Tag Phrases may double, whereas in ASL, other categories that do not appear in Tags are also allowed to double (e.g., verbs, numbers).

4.1 Mixed headedness in ASL

In ASL, all phrases are head-initial except for CP, which has its head C on the right (Figure 1). It has been speculated that this may be a leftover from the ear-lier stages of development of ASL as a creole, in which the predominant order was SOV (Fischer 1975, 1990). All specifiers are on the left (Wilbur 1995; Wilbur & Patschke 1999; Petronio & Lillo-Martin 1997; contra Neidle et al. 2000 claims to the contrary).

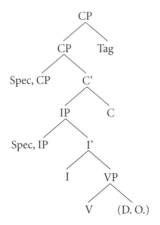

Figure 1. Tree for ASL

4.2 Mixed headedness in ÖGS

The ÖGS data come from 1.5 hours of elicited and naturalistic signing of 5 deaf Styrian dialect signers and 3 hours of naturalistic signing from published video-tapes of other ÖGS dialects.

Understanding of ÖGS phrase structure begins with the behavior of modals, which is both similar to, and different from, German. An intensive investigation of these modals confirms that modals occur in second position in ÖGS or, if the subject pronoun has been dropped, in initial position (Hunger et al. 1999, 2000). When signers are given scripted German interrogatives with modals in initial position (18a), they produced equivalents in ÖGS that never put the modal in initial position (18b). Indeed the only occurrences of modals in initial position are those that result from omission of subject pronouns.

(18) a. German *Darfst du Fußball spielen?*
      b. ÖGS PT$_2$ DÜRFEN FUSSBALL SPIELEN?
      c. English Are you allowed to play soccer?

Scripted German sentences with modals in final position (19a) are consistently translated into ÖGS with modals in second position (19b).

(19) a. German *Ich glaube, daß das Kind im Garten spielen <u>mag</u>.*
      b. ÖGS ICH DENKEN KIND$_a$ PT$_a$ <u>MÖGEN</u> DRAUSSEN GARTEN SPIELEN
      c. English I think the child wants to play in the garden.

In the structural analysis of the German sentence (19a), the verb '*spielen*' is in the head-final position V in the VP, and the modal '*mag*' is in the head-final I of the IP showing the inflection for number and tense characteristics of this structural location; see Figure 2a for German. In main clauses in German, this inflected form moves to verb-second position, which is the position of head-initial C. If no modal or auxiliary is present, the verb itself would have to move from V to I, where it would obtain its inflections, and then from I to C in order to have a grammatical structure. In the embedded clause in (19a), raising from I to C is not required, thus '*mag*' remains at the end of the sentence in the I slot after the verb.

Like ASL, the data from ÖGS show all specifiers on the left. Unlike ASL, with respect to heads, ÖGS has C and I on the left, and V on the right – the opposite of ASL (Wilbur 2002). In the ÖGS sentence (19b), the verb SPIELEN is head-final in the VP. However, in contrast to spoken German, in (19b) the modal MÖGEN has moved from its starting position as the head of IP (parallel to the spoken German) to the verb-second position head-initial C.[12] That is, ÖGS seems to require the verb-second position to be filled in both main and embedded clauses (as compared to ASL, which requires neither). In essence, ÖGS does not display the split nature of spoken German, which shows different word order preferences for main and em-

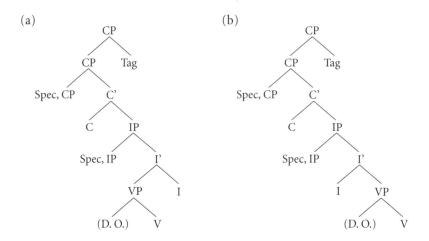

Figure 2. Trees for German (a) and ÖGS (b)

bedded clauses. Furthermore, ÖGS allows null copula (like ASL), whereas German does not. These data provide solid evidence of the separate nature of ÖGS as an independent language that does not merely mimic the syntax of the surrounding spoken language (as signed German would do).[13] It also shows that there is a limit to how much the surrounding spoken language can influence an indigenous sign language through language contact.

In the investigation of modal behavior, sentences were scripted to determine if doubling is permissible in ÖGS. There were two types involving modals, those with initial and final modals (20a), and those with medial and final modals (20b).

(20)   a. Initial/final: MÖGEN BUB FUSSBALL SPIELEN MÖGEN?
       b. Medial/final: BUB KÖNNEN FUSSBALL SPIELEN KÖNNEN?

In production, all of the doubled modals in final position were preceded by a pause. Pausing is one of a few measurable variables that is independent of modality; that is, whether signed or spoken, pausing is measured in units of time (milliseconds). Further investigation confirmed that pauses are required for doubling in ÖGS (Hunger, Schalber & Wilbur 2000). These data reflect the basic structure of ÖGS: it has SOV word order, meaning that the VP is head-final (refer to Figure 2b). Modals, which start in head of IP, are moved to second position, which is head-initial C. Hence, head-initial C is *not a possible doubling site*. This leaves ÖGS with only one site for doubling – Tag Phrase, which is outside/adjoined to the main CP and thus is in a separate Intonational Phrase (Wilbur 1994a). This is borne out by the data in (21), where in (21a) doubling of the modal to TagP with a pause before it is grammatical and in (21b) doubling of the modal without a pause is ungrammatical. Consider where the double with a pause before it would have to be – adjoined to IP. There appears to be no syntactic justification for this possibility.

(21) a. BUB WOLLEN LERNEN, WOLLEN
     b. *BUB WOLLEN LERNEN WOLLEN
       'Bub will learn.'

4.3 Further evidence for the differences in headedness

There is one additional data set that supports the argument that ASL has C on the right and ÖGS has C on the left. This comes from the difference in what lexical categories can be doubled in both languages. The argument that ÖGS only permits doubling to TagP entails that only categories that are eligible to appear in Tag Phrases may be doubled. This is indeed the case, in that ÖGS only permits doubling of modals, subject pronouns, and negatives.[14] In contrast, ASL permits doubling of these categories, as well as wh-words, quantifiers, and numerals. These additional categories adjoin to C in ASL, an option that is not available in ÖGS. Thus, the proposed headedness asymmetries, within each language and across the two, account for the observed differences in what categories are eligible to be doubled.

5. Structural asymmetry: Spreading domains

In this section, I will consider one more asymmetry in ASL, namely the difference in behavior between c-command domain and specifier-head agreement or 'checking' domain. The c-command domain is typically the head-complement domain, also referred to by Chomsky (1995) as the 'internal domain' because it typically contains the internal arguments of the verb. Specifier-head agreement is where the verb picks up its inflections and consists of a heterogeneous set of phrasal types that can be included in the specifier.[15] In ASL, the two marked brow positions, raised and furrowed, are associated with different domains and consequently spread over different constituents. Neutral brow occurs in non-operator positions, leaving brows available for affective use if desired.

Brow furrow is associated with the [+wh]-operator and spreads over its c-command domain (cf. example (16); Wilbur 1995, 1997, 2000, 2005). In contrast, brow raise is associated with [-wh]-operators and is limited to the checking domain of the operator with which it is associated (topic, relative clause, focus, topicalization, left dislocation, yes/no question, conditional clause, when clause, GEN, etc.), thereby permitting more than one brow raise per sentence, each with a different operator. In (22), examples from Boster (1996) are given, illustrating that brow raise does not spread over its c-command domain, and that there may be more than one brow raise in a sentence. Example (23) illustrates three brow raises, the first associated with Left Dislocation (a type of topic), the second with Topic, and the third with IP material that has been moved out of CP-final position to [spec, CP]; the main verb 'refuse' is focused in C, that is, it is in CP-final position.

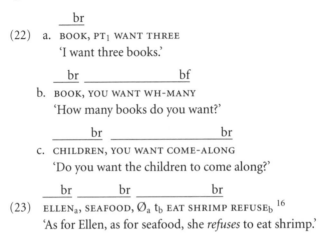

(22) a. $\overline{\text{br}}$
          BOOK, PT$_1$ WANT THREE
          'I want three books.'

      b. $\overline{\text{br}}$ _____ $\overline{\text{bf}}$
          BOOK, YOU WANT WH-MANY
          'How many books do you want?'

      c. _____ $\overline{\text{br}}$ _____ $\overline{\text{br}}$
          CHILDREN, YOU WANT COME-ALONG
          'Do you want the children to come along?'

(23) $\overline{\text{br}}$ _____ $\overline{\text{br}}$ _____ $\overline{\text{br}}$
      ELLEN$_a$, SEAFOOD, $\varnothing_a$ t$_b$ EAT SHRIMP REFUSE$_b$ [16]
      'As for Ellen, as for seafood, she *refuses* to eat shrimp.'

Thus, the ASL nonmanual behavior of brow raise and brow furrow provide strong support for the theoretical postulation of structural domain differences within and across XPs. It should also be noted that the ASL negative headshake also spreads across its c-command domain (Veinberg & Wilbur 1990), providing further support for Haegeman's (1995) attention to the similarities between the Negative Criterion and the Wh-Criterion. [17]

6. Conclusion

This paper has provided a variety of data from ASL to demonstrate that asymmetry in syntax is not limited to spoken languages, but is rather a more general phenomenon deserving a place as part of Universal Grammar. The evidence from ASL shows argument asymmetries, structural asymmetries (left vs. right with respect to peripheries, focus, clause order; spec-head agreement vs. c-command domain), and mixed headedness (*pace* Kayne 1994). The evidence from ÖGS demonstrates that these asymmetries are not unique to ASL, and that the settings for the structural asymmetries and mixed headedness are language specific, possibly parameterized.

There are two highlights of the arguments reported here that should be emphasized. One is that the linguistic analysis is based on a comparison of two signed languages, ÖGS and ASL, as opposed to the more traditional analyses based on comparison of a signed and a spoken language. This type of signed-based comparative analysis is a necessary component of the development of a sign language typology and, indeed, a comprehensive linguistic typology (Wilbur 1997). It has been suggested that signed languages may show less typological diversity than spoken languages, possibly the result of a modality effect. In their discussion of this issue, Newport & Supalla (2000) note that there is "no reason from available evidence to believe that there is special similarity among sign languages in their syntactic structure..." This report has provided clear crosslinguistic differences between ASL and ÖGS in their headedness of CP, IP, and VP. From these differences we have derived an explanation for the differences in doubling behavior, both in terms of requirements on pausing and what may or may not double.

The second highlight is that the ASL-ÖGS comparison has been based on an easily measureable and judgeable prosodic characteristic, pausing, that is known to correlate with constituent structure in both spoken and signed languages (Grosjean & Lane 1977). Thus there is independent data, in addition to judgments of grammaticality, providing strong validation for the claims regarding phrase structure of these languages. Together these data provide solid support for the universality of argument and structural asymmetries in Universal Grammar.

Acknowledgments

The group responsible for the ÖGS research includes Katharina Schalber, Barbara Hunger, Dr. Nadja Grbič, Elke Mutschlechner, Arnold Morascher, and Deaf associate Christian Stalzer, associated with Karl-Franzens-Universität, Graz, Austria; and Tamara Alibasič and Ninoslava Šarac, University of Zagreb, Croatia, who all came together in conjunction with my teaching at Graz in 1998, 1999, and 2000. Katharina, Tamara, and Nina have since earned MA degrees in Linguistics from Purdue University, and now work on a project comparing Austrian and Croatian SLs with ASL and others. This project was partially funded by NSF grant No. 99-05848-BCS, and now 0345314-BCS, and in part by NIH DC005241.

Notes

1. Wilbur (2002a, b, 2003) provides further support and analysis for this observation.

2. When the operator is [+wh], brow furrow shows up to mark wh-questions. When there is no operator, the brows are in neutral position (except for affective functions, such as happy, puzzled, etc). Other sign languages do not necessarily use brow position in this way.

3. TEND is a lexical marker of habitual aspect, translated here as 'usually'. It may also be considered as the marker of 'characterizing' sentences (Wilbur 1998). Doubling of modals, subject pronouns, quantifiers, and negatives at the end of the main CP is a common feature in ASL. Inherent possession is not overtly marked with the verb 'have' which is typically used in existentials. #GLOSS means the sign is a lexical borrowing from English through fingerspelling. 'br' refers to brow raise, and the underline shows the extent of the brow raise, in this case the one sign LION, and in (6) over both POTATO and SELF.

4. Note that there is no use of TEND; generic and habitual are separate features. Specifically, generic takes individual 'i' variables, whereas habitual takes time 't' variables (Wilbur 1998). The use of SELF is a separate issue, marking functions such as reflexive, emphatic focus, agent, factive, definite, copula, and relative clauses introducing new information (Fischer & Johnson 1982; Wilbur 1996b). The recurrence of wow before and after 'digest eat digest easy' frames the predicate in the same way that TEND does in example (5), a process called 'copying' or 'doubling'.

5. 'hn' is a single head nod, which is believed to function as an emphasis marker (Wilbur 1991).

6. The absence of brow raise is consistent with the interpretation of firemen in (7) as plural but not generic.

7. PT is the gloss for pointing, in this case to a point in space not previously identified in the discourse (that is, not having been previously established, it has no antecedent). The subsequent PTS may or may not be directed at exactly the same spot as the first one; since no NP has been established and co-indexed with the first point, these subsequent points are not required to be co-indexed either. Thus, their actual location in space should be similar to the first point, but identity of spatial location is not required because identity of reference is not involved.

8. Pollock (2001) argues for a projection AssertiveP to account for presupposed information. Significantly, Ambar (2001) argues that languages in which AssertiveP is 'prominent' display a tendency to move constituents to that projection. Thus, it could be said that ASL is 'AssertiveP prominent'. Space considerations preclude further discussion.

9. Furthermore, in ASL only wh-clefts that identify the value of the open variable, indicated by 'what' in (i), are permitted. Those which predicate something of that variable but do not identify the variable, known also as free relatives, are not allowed, as in (ii). (iii) shows that this restriction is not related to the use of an adjective in focus position, but is directly a requirement on identification. There is, then, an asymmetry in the functions of the wh-clefts, which can only identify, and the predicate nominals, which can only predicate.

	_____br_____	
(i)	BILL EAT WHAT, SAUSAGE	'What Bill ate was sausage.'
	_____br_____	
(ii)	*BILL EAT/DO WHAT, STUPID	'*What Bill ate/did was stupid'
	_____br_____	
(iii)	BILL FLUNK TEST WHY, STUPID	'The reason why Bill flunked the test is he's stupid.'

10. I am deliberately avoiding the question of how to achieve the desired surface order from a universal spec-head-comp phrase structure. First, our understanding of ASL syntax is woefully inadequate to attempt this at this time; moreover, our understanding of ÖGS syntax is limited to the facts observed here. Second, I do not want to distract from the impact of the general comparison between the two languages.

11. Here Tag refers to the formulaic type of tag question seen in English, which may contain a pronominal copy of the main clause subject, the same tense, a copy of the main clause auxiliary or modal, and the opposite polarity. In ASL, opposite polarity is not required. ÖGS appears to follow ASL (they are unrelated languages however).

12. Note that both languages require [spec, CP] to be filled. Thus in (18b) the subject KIND PT 'the boy' moves up from [spec, IP]. Note also that our transcription of ÖGS uses the German infinitive as a gloss.

13. This same separation is clearly observed when comparing ASL to English (Neidle et al. 2000).

14. This conclusion raises another question: if ÖGS doubling is to TagP only, then is this really doubling, or is it what is traditionally called Tag Formation (by whatever mechanisms are theoretically selected to account for it)? If what is observed in ÖGS is simply Tag Formation, then ÖGS should not be said to have doubling at all.

15. Chomsky (1995) originally included adjuncts as part of the checking domain. I argued against this overly broad definition using data from ASL (Wilbur 1995). I thank Howie Lasnik (p.c.) for informing me that Chomsky subsequently changed the definition to this narrower one, now referred to as spec-head agreement.

16. In this example, 'refuse' has moved right to C for focus; 'Ellen' is a base-generated Left Dislocation (adjunct) that controls the null pronoun subject (Lillo-Martin 1986, 1991). 'Seafood' is in a whole-part topic (adjunct) relationship with the direct object 'shrimp.'

17. Ignoring the asymmetries arising in multiple negative and wh cases, which she discusses as potential barriers to collapsing the two into one general condition.

References

Ambar, M. (2001). Wh-asymmetries. In Di Sciullo, A. M. (Ed.), *Asymmetry in Grammar Vol. 1: Syntax and Semantics* (pp. 209–250). Amsterdam/Philadelphia: John Benjamins.

Bayer, J. (2001). Asymmetry in emphatic topicalization. Ms., University of Konstanz.

Benedicto, E. & Brentari, D. (2004). Where have all the arguments gone? Argument changing properties of classifiers in ASL. Ms. in revision, Natural Language and Linguistic Theory.

Boster, C. T. (1996). On the quantifier-noun phrase split in ASL and the structure of quantified noun phrases. In W. H. Edmondson & R. B. Wilbur (Eds.), *International Review of Sign Linguistics* (pp. 159–208). Hillsdale, New Jersey: Lawrence Erlbaum Associates.

Carlson, G. N. & Pelletier, F. J. (1995). *The Generic Book*. Chicago: University of Chicago Press.

Chierchia, G. (1995). Individual predicates as inherent generics. In G. N. Carlson & F. J. Pelletier (Eds.), *The Generic Book* (pp. 224–237). Chicago: University of Chicago Press.

Chomsky, N. (1995). *The Minimalist Program*. Cambridge, Mass.: MIT Press.

Coulter, G. (1978). Raised eyebrows and wrinkled noses: The grammatical function of facial expression in relative clauses and related constructions. In F. Caccamise & D. Hicks (Eds.), *ASL in a Bilingual, Bicultural Context. Proceedings of The Second National Symposium on Sign Language Research and Teaching* (pp. 65–74). Coronado, California: National Association of the Deaf.

Di Sciullo, A. M. (2002). Asymmetry, antisymmetry and tractability. Paper presented at the *Second Conference of the Federation on Natural Language Processing: Language, Brain, and Computation*, University of Venice, Italy.

Fischer, S. D. (1975). Influences on word order change in ASL. In C. Li (Ed.), *Word Order and Word Order Change* (pp. 1–25). Austin: University of Texas Press.

Fischer, S. D. (1990). The head parameter in ASL. In W. Edmondson & F. Karlsson (Eds.), *SLR '87: Fourth International Symposium on Sign Language Research* (pp. 75–85). Hamburg: SIGNUM.

Fischer, S. D. & Johnson, R. (1982). *Nominal markers in ASL*. LSA annual meeting.

Grosjean, F. & Lane, H. (1977). Pauses and syntax in American Sign Language. *Cognition, 5,* 101–117.

Haegeman, L. (1995). *The Syntax of Negation*. Cambridge: Cambridge University Press.

Haegeman, L. (2002). Anchoring to speaker: Adverbial clauses and the structure of CP. Ms., Université de Lille III.

Hunger, B., Schalber, K., & Wilbur, R. B. (2000). *Bub wollen lernen, wollen?* Further investigations into the modals in the Styrian dialect of Austrian Sign Language with a particular focus on repetition and pauses. Theoretical Issues in Sign Language Research 7, Amsterdam (poster).

Hunger, B., Schalber, K., Alibašić, T., Šarac, N., & Wilbur, R. B. (1999). About the position of modals in the Styrian dialect within the Austrian Sign Language (ÖGS): *Bub Fussball spielen kann*? International Conference on Early Communication and Language Development, Dubrovnik, Croatia.

Kayne, R. (1994). *The Antisymmetry of Syntax*. Cambridge, Mass.: MIT Press.

Kegl, J. (1990). Predicate argument structure and verb classes in the ASL lexicon. In C. Lucas (Ed.), *Sign Language Research: Theoretical Issues* (pp. 149–175). Washington, DC: Gallaudet University Press.

Kiss, K. É. (1995). *Discourse Configurational Languages*. Oxford: Oxford University Press.

Krifka, M. (1995). Focus and the interpretation of generic sentences. In G. N. Carlson & F. J. Pelletier (Eds.), *The Generic Book* (pp. 238–264). Chicago: The University of Chicago Press.

Krifka, M., Pelletier, F. J. , Carlson, G. N., ter Meulen, A., Chierchia, G., & Link, G. (1995). Genericity: An introduction. In G. N. Carlson & F. J. Pelletier (Eds.), *The Generic Book* (pp. 1–124). Chicago: University of Chicago Press.

Liddell, S. K. (1978). Non-manual signals and relative clauses in American Sign Language. In P. Siple (Ed.), *Understanding Language Through Sign Language Research* (pp. 59–90). New York: Academic Press.

Liddell, S. K. (1980). *American Sign Language Syntax*. The Hague: Mouton.

Lillo-Martin, D. (1986). Two kinds of null arguments in ASL. *Natural Language and Linguistic Theory, 4,* 415–444.

Lillo-Martin, D. (1991). *Universal Grammar and American Sign Language*. Dordrecht: Kluwer.

Munaro, N. (2002). Computational puzzles of conditional clause preposing. Paper delivered at the *Second Conference of the Federation on Natural Language Processing: Language, Brain, and Computation*, University of Venice, Italy. In this volume.

Neidle, C., Kegl, J., MacLaughlin, D., Bahan, B., & Lee, R. (2000). *The Syntax of American Sign Language*. Cambridge, Mass.: MIT Press.

Newport, E. & T. Supalla (2000). Sign Language Research at the Millennium. In K. Emmorey & H. Lane (Eds.), *The Signs of Language Revisited: An Anthology to Honor Ursula Bellugi and Ed Klima* (pp. 103–114). Mahwah, New Jersey: Lawrence Erlbaum Associates.

Petronio, K. (1993). Clause structure in American Sign Language. Ph.D. Dissertation, University of Washington, Seattle.

Petronio, K. & Lillo-Martin, D. (1997). Wh-movement and the Position of Spec-CP: Evidence from American Sign Language. *Language, 73,* 18–57.

Pollock, J.-Y. (2001). Wh-questions and wh-exclamatives. *Conference on Asymmetry*, University of Quebec at Montreal.

Vallduví, E. (1991).The role of plasticity in the association of focus and prominence. In Y. No & M. Libucha (Eds.), *ESCOL '90: Proceedings of the Seventh Eastern States Conference on Linguistics* (pp. 295–306). Columbus, Ohio: Ohio State University Press.

Veinberg, S., & Wilbur, R. B. (1990). A linguistic analysis of the negative headshake in American Sign Language. *Sign Language Studies, 68,* 217–244.

Wilbur, R. B. (1991). Intonation and focus in American Sign Language. In Y. No & M. Libucha (Eds.), *ESCOL '90: Proceedings of the Seventh Eastern States Conference on Linguistics* (pp. 320–331). Columbus, Ohio: Ohio State University Press.

Wilbur, R. B. (1994a). Eyeblinks and ASL phrase structure. *Sign Language Studies, 84,* 221–240.

Wilbur, R. B. (1994b). Foregrounding structures in ASL. *Journal of Pragmatics, 22,* 647–672.

Wilbur, R. B. (1995). What the morphology of operators looks like: A formal analysis of ASL brow raise. In L. Gabriele, D. Hardison, & R. Westmoreland (Eds.), *FLSM VI: Formal Linguistics Society of Mid-America: Vol. 2. Syntax II & semantics/pragmatics* (pp. 67–78). Bloomington, Indiana: Indiana University Linguistics Club Publications.

Wilbur, R. B. (1996a). Evidence for function and structure of wh-clefts in ASL. In W. H. Edmondson & R. B. Wilbur (Eds.), *International Review of Sign Linguistics* (pp. 209–256). Hillsdale, New Jersey: Lawrence Erlbaum Associates.

Wilbur, R. B. (1996b). Focus and specificity in ASL structures containing SELF. *Linguistic Society of America*, San Diego.

Wilbur, R. B. (1997). A prosodic/pragmatic explanation for word order variation in ASL with typological implications. In K. Lee, E. Sweetser, & M. Verspoor (Eds.), *Lexical and Syntactic Constructions and the Construction of Meaning, Vol. 1* (pp. 89–104). Philadelphia: John Benjamins.

Wilbur, R. B. (1998). Generic and habitual structures in ASL: The role of brow raise. *Theoretical Issues in Sign Language Research, 6.* Gallaudet University, Washington, D.C.

Wilbur, R. B. (1999). A functional journey with a formal ending: What do brow raises do in American Sign Language? In M. Darnell, E. Moravscik, M. Noonan, F. Newmeyer, & K. Wheatly (Eds.), *Functionalism and Formalism, Volume II: Case studies* (pp. 295–313). Amsterdam: John Benjamins.

Wilbur, R. B. (2000). Phonological and prosodic layering of non-manuals in American Sign Language. In H. Lane & K. Emmorey (Eds.), *The Signs of Language Revisited: Festschrift for Ursula Bellugi and Edward Klima* (pp. 213–241). Hillsdale, New Jersey: Lawrence Erlbaum Associates.

Wilbur, R. B. (2002). Phrase structure in ASL and ÖGS. In R. Schulmeister & H. Reinitzer (Eds.), *Progress in Sign Language Research: In Honor of Siegmund Prillwitz* (pp. 235–248). Hamburg: Signum.

Wilbur, R. B. (2005). A reanalysis of reduplication in American Sign Language. In B. Hurch (Ed.), *Studies in reduplication*. Berlin/New York: Mouton de Gruyter.

Wilbur, R. B. & Patschke, C. (1999). Syntactic correlates of brow raise in ASL. *Sign Language & Linguistics, 2,* 3–40.

Wood, S. (1999). Semantic and syntactic aspects of negation in ASL. MA thesis, Purdue University.

Acquisition of phonological empty categories

A case study of early child Dutch

Ning Pan and William Snyder
University of Louisiana at Lafayette / University of Connecticut

Levelt, Schiller & Levelt (2000) propose that Dutch-learning children acquire the earliest four syllable types in the order (1) CV, (2) CVC, (3) V, and (4) VC. Yet, re-examination of the data (Fikkert 1994; Levelt 1994; MacWhinney & Snow 1990) using frequency-based modified sign tests shows that CV can be acquired genuinely earlier than CVC/V/VC, but the latter three syllable-types are actually acquired together. Two new parameters in Government Phonology (Kaye, Lowenstamm & Vergnaud 1990) are proposed: [+/− empty onset] and [+/− empty nucleus]. These make accurate predictions for the syllable-type inventories of adult languages, and account for the acquisitional evidence from Dutch.

1. Introduction

In this paper we discuss the early stages of syllable acquisition, based on the data of 12 children who acquired Dutch as their first language (Fikkert 1994; Levelt 1994; MacWhinney & Snow 1990). We define the early stages of syllable acquisition as the stages before any branching constituents (branching onsets or branching rhymes) appear. This leaves us with the earliest four syllable types – CV, CVC, V and VC. We first review earlier studies of the Dutch data, in Section 2. In Section 3, we present new findings from our re-examination of the Dutch data. In Section 4, we offer a preliminary proposal to explain our observations. We then extend our proposal to account for the available cross-linguistic data, in Section 5. Section 6 concludes the paper.

2. Earlier studies

Fikkert (1994) provided an extensive and detailed discussion of syllable acquisition by Dutch children within the *Principles-and-Parameters* model (Chomsky 1981, 1986). The development of onsets and the development of rhymes were studied separately. For example, Fikkert claimed that initially, onsets are obligatory, then they become optional, and finally complex onsets appear. For rhymes, she found that initially there is no coda, then codas appear, and finally coda clusters appear. Yet, it is not clear from Fikkert (1994) how the syllable as a whole develops.

Based on the same data as in Fikkert (1994), Levelt, Schiller & Levelt (1999) attempted to explore how the syllable as a whole develops, within the framework of Optimality Theory (OT) (McCarthy & Prince 1993; Prince & Smolensky 1993). They aligned the children's data on a Guttman scale, and deduced the order of appearance of different syllable types. The order of early syllable types is shown in (1), in which an arrow means "appeared before."

(1)   CV → CVC → V → VC
(adapted from Levelt, Schiller & Levelt 1999:242)

Levelt, Schiller & Levelt (1999) interpreted this order as a genuine developmental order. The earliest four syllable types were claimed to be acquired in the order in (1), one after the other. The developmental order was analyzed as the result of an initial ranking, and subsequent re-rankings of a number of proposed constraints.

3. Our findings

We re-examined the Dutch data used by Levelt's group; the corpora for their 12 subjects are available in the Levelt-Fikkert section of CHILDES (Fikkert 1994; Levelt 1994; MacWhinney & Snow 1990). Different from Levelt, Schiller & Levelt's (1999) finding in (1), our reanalysis shows that the last three types, CVC, V and VC, are in fact acquired at the same time. Their order of appearance is merely a reflection of their relative frequency in the child's speech.

Of these 12 children, three (Jarmo, Noortje, Tom) have corpora beginning before the full array of CVC/V/VC syllables had appeared. To assess whether order of appearance reflects ordered acquisition or simply relative frequency, we performed modified sign tests based on frequency of the syllable-types in a slightly later transcript. For example, Jarmo's corpus contains 41 CV syllables before his first CVC syllable. In a later sample of Jarmo's speech (containing 67 spontaneous utterances), Jarmo produced 40 CV syllables, and 9 CVC syllables. Under the null hypothesis that CV and CVC syllables entered Jarmo's speech at the same age, and had the same relative frequency found in the later transcript, the likelihood of sampling 41 or more CV syllables simply by chance, before the first occurrence of CVC, is $p = (40/49)^{41} < .001$. We conclude that Jarmo indeed acquired CVC later than CV. Yet, Jarmo's acquisition of CVC/V/VC syllables showed no significant ordering ($p > .05$ for CVC vs. V, and for V vs. VC).

The corresponding analysis for Noortje revealed that CV was again significantly earlier than CVC ($p = (21/31)^{18} = .001$), but the remaining syllable-types (CVC vs. V, V vs. VC) were not significantly different ($p > .05$). Finally, Tom's corpus showed no significant ordering among the four syllable-types. Thus, our fine-grained analysis of the Dutch data indicates that CV can be acquired genuinely earlier than CVC/V/VC; but that the latter three syllable-types are actually acquired as a group, at least by the three Fikkert-Levelt children for whom relevant data are available.

A question that arises is why the syllable types CVC, V and VC should be acquired as a group. That is, what single property, common to all three syllable types, are the children discovering?

4. Seeking a solution

Here we want to take a closer look at the syllable structure of CVC, V and VC to see if we can find a solution. There are two major views on how human speech sounds are ordered and structured. We will begin with the standard view, in which human speech sounds are organized into rising and falling sonority sequences, with each sonority peak defining a unique syllable. (See Blevins 1995 for an overview.) According to this view, a string of human speech sounds is made up of a string of syllables. A standard view of syllable structure is given in (2). The syllable dominates the onset and the rhyme, and the rhyme dominates the nucleus and the coda. The final consonant in a CVC syllable is analyzed as a coda.

(2)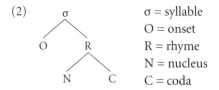

σ = syllable
O = onset
R = rhyme
N = nucleus
C = coda

Under the syllable-oriented view, it has long been realized that there is a sharp asymmetry between the two margins of the syllable – the onset and the coda. The most unmarked syllable type, CV, contains an onset but no coda. There are languages where onsets are obligatory, but there are no languages where codas are obligatory. There are no languages that disallow onsets, but there are languages that forbid codas. All these points indicate that the coda is more marked than the onset. Even in OT, we have constraints like "ONSET" and "NO-CODA". These two constraints, while descriptive rather than explanatory, also assign a different status to the onset and the coda. Yet, the observed disparity between the onset and the coda is not clearly revealed in the structure in (2).

Furthermore, a word-final coda has also been observed to behave differently from a word-internal coda. For example, there are languages (e.g. Luo and Yucatec Maya) where the CVC sequence appears only word-finally. There are also languages (e.g. Italian and Telugu) where the CVC sequence appears only word-internally (Harris & Gussmann 1998). Moreover, it is found that in stress assignment, a word-final coda sometimes cannot contribute to the weight of the preceding sylla-ble (Hayes 1982), while a word-internal coda certainly can. Finally, closed syllable shortening only takes place word-internally, not word-finally, for example in En-glish (Harris & Gussmann 1998). All these points suggest that the word-final coda and the word-internal coda do not have the same status either. The standard view of syllable structure in (2) does not seem to have a satisfactory explanation for this inconsistency between the word-internal coda and the word-final coda.

An opposing view can be found in Government Phonology (GP) (Kaye, Lowenstamm & Vergnaud 1990; Kaye 1990, 1993), which treats a string of human speech sounds simply as a string of onset-rhyme pairs, rather than a string of sylla-bles. We can call this the "onset-rhyme view", as opposed to the "syllable-oriented view". A CVC syllable is structured as in (3), according to the onset-rhyme view.

(3)
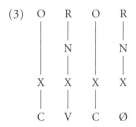

In the onset-rhyme view, there is no coda at all. The final consonant in a CVC sequence is analyzed as an onset followed by an empty nucleus (e.g. Kaye 1990; Lowenstamm 1996; Harris & Gussmann 1998; Szigetvári 2000).

The GP structure for the CVC sequence provides a possible and natural expla-nation for the different status of the onset and the coda. The onset is followed by an overt nucleus, while the 'coda' is actually an onset followed by an empty nucleus. The cross-linguistic evidence can be interpreted as showing that an onset followed by an empty nucleus is more marked than one followed by an overt nucleus. Like-wise, the inconsistency between the word-internal coda and the word-final coda is no longer mysterious under the onset-rhyme view. The two structures in (4) clearly show the different status of the so-called word-internal coda and the word-final coda. The word-internal coda is in a true coda position, while the so-called word-final coda is in an onset position which is followed by an empty nucleus.[1]

(4) a.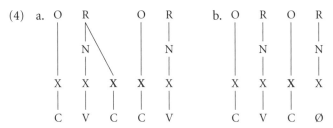

Finally, evidence from early child language also supports the structure in (3). Goad (1998) has shown that children initially syllabify final consonants as onsets of empty-headed syllables.

Comparing the syllable-oriented and onset-rhyme views of phonological constituent structure, the latter can better explain the observed phenomena. If we adopt the onset-rhyme view, CVC, V and VC can be represented as follows:

(5) a.

In the above representation, CVC, V and VC syllables all contain empty categories, either an empty onset or an empty nucleus or both. Therefore, containing an empty category could be the common property shared by all three syllable types. An initial proposal we can make at this point is that the availability of empty C/V elements is determined by a single phonological parameter:

(6) *Empty Category Parameter*
     Empty categories are allowed.   [No/Yes]

The underlined value is the default value of this parameter. The child starts with the default setting [– empty category], and only produces CV syllables. When the child discovers that Dutch is [+ empty category], the CVC, V, and VC syllables all become available. Any ordering among CVC, V, and VC simply reflects their relative frequency of use.

The proposed Empty Category Parameter can also shed light on the phenomenon of *final consonant deletion*, a very common error for both normal and language-disordered children, which as yet lacks any satisfactory explanation. The common understanding is that children delete the final consonant because they "want to avoid" the final consonant. Yet, this is simply a restatement of the question. Another possibility is that deleting final consonants makes pronunciation "easier" (Grunwell 1997), but this likewise offers little insight.[2]

In contrast, the proposed Empty Category Parameter provides a reasonable explanation. When a child cannot produce the final consonant in a CVC syllable, the reason is that her grammar does not yet allow the (marked) option of an onset followed by an empty nucleus. The following data from both disordered and normal children further support this hypothesis.

(7)   Disordered speech: Jamie (7:2)

    a.   [kæː] 'cab'   [dɔː] 'dog'   [dʌ] 'duck'
    b.   [kæːbi] 'cabby' [dɔgi] 'doggie' [dʌki] 'duckie'
                                                    (Dinnsen, Elbert & Weismer 1981)

The examples in (7b) show that Jamie did not have any problem producing the consonants [b], [g] or [k]; he simply could not produce these consonants when they were followed by an empty vowel, as in (7a). Thus, in Jamie's grammar, the Empty Category Parameter was still in its unmarked setting.

(8)   Normal speech: Mollie (18 months)

    a.   [bɛ] 'bed'   [gu] 'good'
    b.   [buki] 'book' [bɪbi] 'bib' [waki] 'walk'
                                                    (Holmes 1927, cited by Goad 1998)

In (8), Mollie had difficulty producing CVC syllables. She sometimes completely deleted the onset-rhyme pair that contained an empty rhyme, as in (8a); and sometimes repaired the problematic onset-rhyme pair by inserting a vowel, as in (8b). This pair of strategies clearly points to a problem in producing an onset followed by an empty nucleus.

Although *final consonant deletion* is a very common child error, children seldom make errors of initial consonant deletion. This is seen in (7) and (8). Jamie and Mollie deleted final consonants, but they never deleted an initial consonant. Researchers often discuss the error of *final consonant deletion*, but they pay little attention to the uniformly correct use of the onset. The proposed Empty Category Parameter directly relates the correct use of initial consonants and the mistaken deletion of final consonants. The child's grammar initially disallows an onset-rhyme pair with an empty position. Hence, she avoids the "final" consonant, which is actually followed by an empty vowel. The child does not delete initial consonants, however, because they are allowed in her grammar.

5. A modified proposal

We have seen that the proposed Empty Category Parameter (6) can account for the data from child Dutch, and that it also provides an explanation for the common child error of *final consonant deletion*. A problem arises, however, when we consider its predictions for cross-linguistic variation. Syllable structure presumably involves several parameters, and if all the parameters are in their unmarked settings, the language allows only CV syllables. If the earliest four syllable types involve the Empty Category Parameter, we expect that a language has either all of the three syllable types with empty categories (CVC, V and VC), or none of them. This prediction is false. Thargari has only CV and CVC syllables, and Cayuvava has only CV and V syllables (Levelt & van de Vijver 1998). To account for the typology of syllable-type inventories, we propose to split the Empty Category Parameter into two parameters, as in (9).

(9)   a.   *Empty Onset Parameter*
         Empty onsets are allowed.   [No/Yes]
      b.   *Empty Nucleus Parameter*
         Empty nuclei are allowed.   [No/Yes]

In both parameters, the underlined value is the default value. These two parameters can account for the following syllable-type inventories (data from Levelt & van de Vijver (1998)):

(10)   [–EO, –EN]: CV   (Hua)
       [–EO, +EN]: CV, CVC   (Thargari)
       [+EO, –EN]: CV, V   (Cayuvava)
       [+EO, +EN]: CV, CVC, V, VC   (Mokilese)

The two parameters in (9) also predict three possible sequences of acquisition:

(11)   a.   Stage I: [–EO, –EN]   – CV
           Stage II: [+EO, +EN]   – (CV), CVC, V, VC

       b.   Stage I: [–EO, –EN]   – CV
           Stage II: [+EO, –EN]   – (CV), V
           Stage III: [+EO, +EN]   – (CV), (V), CVC, VC

       c.   Stage I: [–EO, –EN]   – CV
           Stage II: [–EO, +EN]   – (CV), CVC
           Stage III: [+EO, +EN]   – (CV), (CVC), V, VC

6.   Conclusions

We have re-examined the Dutch data for acquisition of early syllable types, and provided a parametric account of syllable acquisition in the early stages. The children examined in this study (Jarmo, Noortje, Tom) provide support for the possibility in (11a) – Jarmo and Noortje acquired CV significantly earlier than the other syllable types, but none of the children showed a significant gap within the CVC/V/VC cluster. A prediction for future research is that (11b) and (11c) will be the only additional patterns attested, when more children's corpora are examined. In particular, acquisitional sequences in which VC is acquired significantly earlier than CVC, or in which VC is acquired significantly earlier than V, are predicted to be impossible.[3]

The phonological approach explored in this paper – GP (Kaye, Lowenstamm, & Vergnaud 1990; Kaye 1990, 1993) – is interesting for its *parametric* character.[4] The idea that the child might be setting *independent* parameters, rather than changing *relative* rankings within a single list of constraints, leads to sharp, testable predictions for the time course of language acquisition.

Notes

1. GP does not recognize *coda* as a constituent. The term *coda* used in GP is just a short and convenient form for *post-nuclear rhymal position* (Kaye 1990:311).

2. We thank Dr. Martin Ball for this point.

3. This prediction is consistent with the implicational patterns reported in Harris (1994: 162–163): "the existence of final VC] sequences in a language implies the existence of V] but not vice versa; ... and in languages permitting both V] and VC] the former is acquired before the latter."

4. A reviewer asks how GP handles epenthesis in Spanish borrowings such as (i). In particular, how does GP account for the position of the epenthetic vowel?

(i)   a.   espagueti   'spaghetti'
      b.   esprey   'spray'
      c.   esfera   'sphere'

In GP, the *s* in an *s* + *C* sequence is always in a post-nuclear rhymal position, rather than an onset position. This is so even in initial *s* + *C* clusters, which are represented as follows:

(ii)

(Kaye 1992:293)

English differs parametrically from Spanish in the availability of "Magic Licensing": The empty nuclear position before *s* is magically licensed in English, and receives no phonetic interpretation (Kaye 1992:306). In Spanish, however, the nucleus of the initial rhyme must be filled with a vowel.

References

Blevins, J. (1995). The syllable in phonological theory. In J. A. Goldsmith (Ed.), *The Handbook of Phonologica Ttheory* (pp. 206–244). Oxford: Blackwell.

Chomsky, N. (1981). Principles and parameters in syntactic theory. In N. Hornstein & D. Lightfoot (Eds.), *Explanation in Linguistics: The Logical Problem of Acquisition* (pp. 32–75). London: Longman.

Chomsky, N. (1986). *Knowledge of Language: Its Nature, Origin and Use*. New York: Praeger.

Dinnsen, D., Elbert, M., & Weismer, G. (1981). Some typological properties of functional misarticulation systems. In W. O. Dressler (Ed.), *Phonologica 1980* (pp. 83–88). Innsbruck: Innsbruck Beiträge zur Sprachwissenschaft.

Fikkert, P. (1994). On the acquisition of prosodic structure. Ph.D. Dissertation. Leiden University, The Netherlands.

Goad, H. (1998). On the status of final consonants in early child language. In A. Greenhill, M. Hughes, H. Littlefield, & H. Walsh (Eds.), *Proceedings of the 22nd Annual Boston University Conference on Language Development* (pp. 269–280). Somerville, Mass.: Cascadilla Press.

Grunwell, P. (1997). Natural phonology. In M. J. Ball & R. D. Kent (Eds.), *The New Phonologies* (pp. 35–75). San Diego: Singular.

Harris, J. (1994). *English Sound Structure*. Oxford: Blackwell.

Harris, J. & Gussmann, E. (1998). Final codas: Why the West was wrong. In E. Cyran (Ed.), *Structure and Interpretation in Phonology: Studies in Phonology* (pp. 139–162). Lublin: Folia.

Hayes, B. (1982). Extrametricality and English stress. *Linguistic Inquiry, 13*, 227–276.

Kaye, J. D. (1990). Coda licensing. *Phonology, 7*, 301–330.

Kaye, J. D. (1992). Do you believe in magic? The story of *s* + *C* sequences. *Working papers in Linguistics and Phonetics, 2*, 293–313. School of Oriental and African Studies, University of London.

Kaye, J. D. (1993). Derivations and interfaces. *SOAS Working Papers in Linguistics and Phonetics, 3*, 90–126. Reprinted in J. Durand & F. Katamba (Eds.) (1995), *Frontiers of Phonology: Atoms, Structure, Derivation* (pp. 289–332). London and New York: Longman.

Kaye, J. D., Lowenstamm, J., & Vergnaud, J.-R. (1990). Constituent structure and government in phonology. *Phonology, 7* (2), 193–231.

Levelt, C. (1994). *On the Acquisition of Place*. The Hague: Holland Academic Graphics.

Levelt, C., Schiller, N. O., & Levelt, W. J. (2000). The acquisition of syllable types. *Language Acquisition, 8*, 237–264.

Levelt, C. & van de Vijver, R. (1998). Syllable types in cross-linguistic and developmental grammar. Paper presented at the Third Biannual Utrecht Phonology Workshop, Utrecht, The Netherlands.

Lowenstamm, J. (1996). CV as the only syllable type. In J. Durand & B. Laks (Eds.), *Current Trends in Phonology: Models and Methods* (pp. 419–442). European Studies Research Institute, University of Salford Publications.

McCarthy, J. & Prince, A. (1993). Prosodic morphology I: constraint interaction and satisfaction. Ms., University of Massachusetts, Amherst, and Rutgers University, New Brunswick, New Jersey.

MacWhinney, B. & Snow, C. (1990). The child language data exchange system: An update. *Journal of Child language, 17,* 457–472.

Prince, A. & Smolensky, P. (1993). Optimality theory: constraint interaction in generative grammar. Ms., Rutgers University, New Brunswick, New Jersey, and University of Colorado at Boulder.

Szigetvári, P. (2000). Dismantling syllable structure. In H. Bartos (Ed.), *Papers on the Mental Lexicon* (pp. 177–209). Budapest: Research Institute of Linguistics, Hungarian Academy of Sciences.

Prosodic cues during online processing of speech
Evidence from stress shift in American English*

Matt Bauer

Georgetown University

Two experiments were designed to test whether speakers of American English use cues from stress shift to facilitate parsing decisions. Stress shift occurs when initially stressed words follow words with final stress, but it does not occur across intonation boundaries, as in (b) compared to (a).

a. When linguists discuss Japanese dialects, they never agree.
b. When linguists discuss Japanese, dialects always come up.

The predictability of when stress shift applies might help the parser to determine phrase endings. However, experimental results failed to confirm that the parser uses stress shift to mark intonational boundaries. Possibly, experimental design introduced a confound. Alternatively, cues from stress shift, though acoustically perceptible, are unavailable or not useful to the parsing mechanism.

Introduction

This paper reports findings from two experiments that addressed the role prosody plays during online sentence processing.[1] The goal of the experiments was to investigate whether speakers make immediate use of acoustic information from one particular prosodic phenomenon, stress shift in American English, to facilitate speech processing in real time. Results from both experiments indicated stress shift was not an important cue.

The paper is organized as follows. First, I discuss research on sentence processing, and its domains of evidence. Then, I discuss stress shift and why it might be interesting for psycholinguistics, and finally, I present the results of the experiments.

1.   Overview

One noticeable difficulty with grammaticality judgments is that sometimes an otherwise perfectly grammatical sentence is incomprehensible. For example, all the sentences in (1) are grammatical in the technical sense that they each are well-formed English sentences, but only (a) is acceptable. Sentence (b) is marginal, and (c) is almost impossible interpret.

(1)   a.   The cat ate the mouse.
    b.   The cat the dog chased ate the mouse.
    c.   The cat the dog the horse kicked chased ate the mouse.

Upon reflection, one can see that (c) means that *the cat that ate the mouse is the one that the dog chased, and the same dog that chased the cat is the one that the horse kicked*, but when a speaker is listening to this sentence, the meaning is difficult to recover. Early work in language processing used the differences among sentence like (a–c) as evidence that there exists a mechanism independent of the grammar that is devoted to understanding speech in real time (see Townsend & Bever 1999 for a general discussion). Mostly, the parsing mechanism is successful in recovering an interpretation, but sometimes, like with reactions to (b) and especially (c), the parser fails. By one account, the fact that the parser fails is "a gift from nature" because it allows investigators to determine what factors play an important role in language processing in real time (Trueswell et al. 1999).

Studies of on-line processing of speech typically attempt to address questions such as (2a–b).

(2)   a.   How sensitive are speakers to linguistic information?
    b.   How do they use such information to parse sentences on-line?

It stands to reason that speakers can only use linguistic information that they have access to, so the answer to (2a) will have implications for (2b). And the answer to (2b) will provide a clue as to what linguistic information is useful during sentence processing and what information is not.

Initial investigation into the parser suggested that parsing preferences were based solely on the attachment site of a phrase (Frazier 1987). For example, (3a) is ambiguous. It can mean *the man used a telescope to see the woman*, or *the man saw a woman who was carrying a telescope*. In the first reading, with a telescope attaches to the VP, as in (b), and in the second it attaches in the NP, as in (c).

(3)   a.   The man saw the woman with a telescope.
    b.   The man VP[saw the woman with a telescope].
    c.   The man saw NP[the woman with a telescope].

Taraban & McClelland (1988) found that speakers listening to sentences like (3a) tend to immediately parse it with an instrumental reading, (b), without even considering the modifier reading, (c). Taken together with an assumption that VP attachment is structurally "simpler" than NP attachment by some measure, they concluded that the parser tends toward (b) over (c) because the parser prefers to assign as simple a structure as possible to a string. Subsequent research has revealed that the parser takes into account a wealth of linguistic information to help it determine an interpretation of a sentence – not just attachment site.

1.1 Syntactic and semantic effects

Most of the work on parsing preferences during online speech processing addresses either syntactic or semantic effects (see Frazier 1987 or Townsend & Bever 2001 for a comprehensive overview).

These studies rely on garden path effects to determine what linguistic cues speakers use to parse sentences. In a garden path sentence, speakers arrive at a wrong interpretation precisely because their expectations of what the structure of a sentence might look like are not met. For example, sentence (4a) is a garden path and (4b) is not. *The old man washed the boat* is easy to understand, but *the old man the boat* requires a little effort to figure out. *It is the old who are the ones who guard the boat: the old man the boat.* Notice that both sentences are ambiguous up to the point of *man*. In either sentence, *old* could be a noun or an adjective. Only when speakers come to *the* in (4a) or *washed* in (4b) is the ambiguity resolved. Such a word is referred to as the *disambiguating word*.

(4) a.   The old man the boat.
     b.   The old man washed the boat.

In these studies investigating sentences like in (4), participants sat in front of a computer terminal and were presented with each sentence, one word at a time, represented in brackets in (5).

(5) a.   [The]$_1$ [old]$_2$ [man]$_3$ *[the]$_4$* [boat.]$_5$
     b.   [The]$_1$ [old]$_2$ [man]$_3$ *[washed]$_4$* [the]$_5$ [boat.]

Participants pressed the space bar to advance through the sentence. Reaction time from when the stimulus was displayed to when the participant pressed the space bar was measured for each response. The results showed that reaction time following the disambiguating word is significantly greater for the garden path than for the normal sentence.

What makes *the old man the boat* so difficult is that speakers prefer to parse *old* as an adjective, not a noun, and *man* as a noun, not a verb. Speakers hear *the* and think, "ok, an adjective or a noun will follow." And then they hear *old* and they parse it as an adjective. Why? Because the frequency by which old is an adjective following *the* is far greater than the frequency by which *old* is a noun following *the*. The conclusion is that speakers are sensitive to category frequency of a word and use that information to make predictions about phrase structure of a linguistic stream (see Jurafsky 1996 for more detail on category-frequency effects).[2]

The sentences in (6) showing a semantic effect work the same way. Speakers are sensitive to frequency by which a polysemous word exhibits a single meaning in a given context and use it to parse a sentence.

(6)   a.   Jingling his coins, the boy went to the bank to <u>cash</u> his check.
      b.   Jingling his coins, the boy went to the bank to <u>catch</u> some fish.

In (6), *coins* primes *bank* to mean the building, not a patch of land near a stream. In (6b), speakers expect a building-type reading of *bank*, and must reevaluate their prediction when they come to *catch*. The result is a delay in response time after *catch* compared to after *cash*.

Similar semantic and syntactic effects on parsing have been shown for using the frequency by which verbs take certain arguments to make parsing predictions (Trueswell & Kim 1998) and for using thematic roles to disambiguate between a reduced relative and a main clause (Trueswell & Tanenhaus 1991), among many, many others. Again, I refer the interested reader to Townsend & Bever (1999) for an extensive review of the psycholinguistics literature.

1.2 Prosodic effects

Looking back at the research question in (2), it is worth questioning whether other linguistic cues, such as prosody, play a role in determining parsing preferences. In her discussion of psycholinguistic research addressing prosody and parsing, Nicol (1996) points out that, while prosodic constituents do not always map neatly onto syntactic boundaries, they do demarcate edges of domains. She suggests that edge boundaries might be useful for a parser in determining syntactic closure of a phrase. In an otherwise ambiguous context, prosodic cues may favor one interpretation over another.

So far, there is a substantial body of evidence showing that prosody plays an important role in parsing sentences (see Warren 1996; Nicol 1996; Beckman 1996 for overview). But at the same time, there is a handful of studies that suggest that some prosodic cues are not useful (see Watt & Murray 1996; McAllister et al. 1995 for examples).

In one study citing positive effects, Nagel et al. (1996) used a cross splicing technique to determine the effect of prosodic contours on predicting a verb's argument structure. They drew from the fact that certain verbs have an equal frequency of taking clausal or nominal complements. For example, in (7a–b) from Nagel et al., *promise* can have a nominal complement as in (7a) or a clausal complement as in (7b).

(7) a. The company owner promised the wage increase <u>to the workers.</u>
     b. The company owner promised the wage increase <u>would be substantial.</u>

Crucially, at the point of *the wage increase*, there is an ambiguity as to whether the complement of *promise* is an indirect object of the verb or a subject of the following clause. Nagel et al. investigated whether speakers would rely on prosodic cues from the sentence leading up to the point of disambiguation to predict the verb's argument structure. To test for this, they recorded sentences such as (7a–b), and then cross-spliced material after *the wage increase* from sentences like (a) with the initial part of sentences like (b), and vice versa. The result was four conditions:

(8) a. Sentences with the prosodic contour of having <u>nominal</u> complements, and in fact have <u>nominal</u> complements.
     b. Sentences with the prosodic contour of having <u>clausal</u> complements, and in fact have <u>clausal</u> complements.

(9) a. Sentences with the prosodic contour of having <u>clausal</u> complements, but in fact have <u>nominal</u> complements.
     b. Sentences with the prosodic contour of having <u>nominal</u> complements, but in fact have <u>clausal</u> complements.

The logic of these conditions is that sentences such as (8a–b) have a naturally-occurring prosodic contour, but those like (9a–b) do not. Any differences in processing (9a–b) compared to processing (8a–b) would be due to the manipulations performed on the naturally-occurring sentences. The authors argue that, provided cross-splicing would not introduce significant confounds, if prosodically natural sentences are in some measurable way easier to process than unnatural sentences, then prosody must play an important role in making immediate parsing decisions about a verb's argument structure.

In the study, participants were exposed to all four conditions, and at the point of ambiguity resolution (the word following the ambiguous NP, *the wage increase*), they were asked to respond to a lexical decision task, word or non-word. Nagel et al. found that participants responded significantly faster to lexical decision tasks during naturally-occurring sentences than with non-natural ones. They interpreted the results as an indication that speakers use prosodic information on-line to facilitate parsing decisions. In their view, speakers used the prosodic information leading up to the point of disambiguation in the unnatural sentence condition to make false predictions about what type of complement the verb will take. When their predictions failed, speakers reevaluated the structure, and the result was an increase in processing effort compared to when speakers listened to natural sentences.

Similarly, Watt & Murray (1996) also tested if intonational contour is a useful parsing cue for predicting verb argument structure, but they found no effect, despite known acoustic differences which speakers are sensitive to and despite using several techniques known to have revealed positive effects. They attributed the difference in results between their study and Nagel et al. (1996) to the "manipulation" of the experiment materials. They suggest that a more "robust" but less "natural" altering of the prosodic contour "might have influenced parsing decisions." They concluded, citing Cutler & Isard (1980), that much of prosody might be "like the 'sauce' of the sentence." It "enhanc[es] and subtly chang[es]" a string but is of no real consequence to the parser, which is "more concerned with the underlying morphosyntactic 'meat'".

It seems natural, then, to ask whether all prosodic phenomena that speakers are sensitive to are useful prosodic cues. Perhaps many are, but some others are not. Indeed, it is common for researchers to publish papers whose results show positive effects. This tendency, known as the file-drawer phenomenon, has the effect of skewing the results of a set of literature in favor of a general process. In this case, it might seem reasonable to conclude that prosody does in fact contribute to the parsing mechanism in the same way that semantic and syntactic cues do.

1.3   Stress shift in American English

One fairly well-studied prosodic phenomenon is stress shift in American English (Selkirk 1984; Shattuck-Hufnagel, Ostendorf & Ross 1994; Grabe & Warren 1996). Stress shift is the perceived shift of primary stress from word-final position to an earlier syllable with a full vowel. It is triggered by a preceding, initially-stressed word. For example, in (10a), *thirteen* has word-final stress, but when it precedes *women* in (10b), which has word-initial stress, speakers perceive a shift of stress in *thirteen* from TEEN to THIR, as shown in (10c).

(10)   a.   thirTEEN
       b.   WOmen
       c.   thirTEEN WOmen → THIRteen WOmen

The readjustment of stress in (8c) is generally viewed to arise from clashing stress peaks in adjacent syllables (Selkirk 1984). Languages such as English that ban clashes avoid it by altering the stress of the first offending peak, thus preserving a rhythmic stress-no stress alternation.

Stress shift does not apply across the board. It occurs within intonational boundaries, but never across, so stress shift will occur in (11a) but not in (11b). In (11a), stress is T̲V. In (11b), stress is TV̲. Commas mark the intonation boundary.

(11)   a.   When my father watches TV soaps, they're his favorite.
      b.   When my father watches TV, soaps are his favorite.

Recent work on stress shift indicates that the perception of the shift is actually due to a reduction pitch and shortening of duration in the final rhyme, [i], of the stress shift word, *TV*, not due to any real shifting of stress (Vogel, Bunnel, & Hoskins 1994).

Nevertheless, stress shift involves an acoustic cue to which speakers are sensitive by some measure, and it is worth asking if they make good use of their perception of it to help parse sentences on-line. The present study addressed this issue directly.

2.   Experiment 1

2.1 Participants

Nine (9) native speakers of English participated in the study. The participants were recruited from the population of friends and acquaintances of the researcher.

2.2 Procedure

A reader recorded 8 minimally-paired sentences similar to (10a–b). One sentence of the pair exhibited stress shift; the other did not (see appendix for a list of sentences used – all of the sentences were taken directly from or altered slightly from Grabe & Warren (1996)). The sentences were digitized and segmented into sound-files grouped by words or phrases. For example, (11a) was converted into 6 files:

(12)   [When my]$_1$ [father watches]$_2$ [TV]$_3$ [soaps]$_4$ [are his]$_5$ [favorite]$_6$

For each sentence pair, the potential stress shift word from one sentence was cross-spliced with the stress shift environment of the other. The result was 32 sentences separated into four sentence conditions: (a) stress shift within an intonational boundary, (b) non stress shift across an intonational boundary, (c) non stress shift within an intonational boundary, and (d) stress shift across an intonational boundary. For example, sentences (13)–(14) show how sentences (11a–b) were cross-spliced to generate the four conditions. Phrases enclosed in brackets indicate stress shift, and phrases separated by brackets indicate no stress shift. Commas mark an intonational boundary. Crucially, the sentences in (13) are natural, and in (14) are cross spliced.

(13)   a.   When my father watches [TV soaps], *Stress shift,*
             they're his favorite.   *expected*
       b.   When my father watches TV], [soaps *No stress shift,*
             are his favorite.   *expected*

(14)   a.   When my father watches TV] [soaps, *No stress shift,*
             they're his favorite.   *unexpected*
       b.   When my father watches [TV, soaps] *Stress shift,*
             are his favorite.   *expected*

Participants sat in front of a computer terminal, and listened to the sentence materials. For each sentence, they listened to it one sound-file at a time. After each sound-file was played, participants used the keyboard as an input device and pressed the space bar to advance to the next sound-file. Response times were measured for how long it took participants to press the space bar after each sound-file was played. When the entire sentence was played, participants were asked a secondary-task question. They used the keyboard to respond with either "yes" or "no." After each response, they pressed the space bar to advance to the next trial. The experiment took about 15 minutes. The study was conducted between April and May 2002.

2.3   Expected results

Up to the point of *TV* in (15a–b), it is ambiguous whether the following word begins or ends an intonational phrase.

(15)   a.   When my father watches TV soaps, they're his favorite.
       b.   When my father watches TV, soaps are his favorite.

If the parser uses stress shift to make immediate parsing decisions, then following stress shift (*TV* in 15a), speakers will expect a trigger (*soaps*) within the same intonational phrase. By extension, they will predict that the trigger is in the same syntactic phrase. Following non-stress shifted words (*TV* in 15b), speakers will not expect a stress shift trigger (*soaps*) within the same phrase. Instead, they will assume any potential trigger will be the subject of the next syntactic phrase.

If this is the correct view of how the parser interacts with acoustic cues from stress shift environments, I expected one of two possible results. In sentences where stress shift occurred in an inappropriate environment, I expected participants to be surprised when they learned the trigger exhibited the prosodic contour of the *beginning* of an intonational phrase. That "surprise" would emerge as increased processing effort and result in a significant delay in response after the potential stress shift trigger compared to natural sentences. I expected the same result after the trigger word in sentences where stress shift failed to apply but should have.

Alternatively, speakers might hold off reevaluating their predictions until they have syntactic reasons to do so. In other words, speakers might ignore the cues from the potential trigger. In such cases, the effects of cross splicing would not be evident until the word following the potential trigger. In an environment where stress shift did not apply but should have, speakers will assume the potential stress shift trigger to be the subject of the next syntactic phrase (that would be *soaps* in 14a). However, when speakers are confronted with the actual subject of the sentences (*they're*), they will be forced to reevaluate their predictions. The result will be a delay in response time in cross spliced sentences compared to natural ones. I expected the same result for when stress shift inappropriately applied.

For clarity, I will refer to the potential trigger as the *prosodic disambiguating word* and the verbal phrase that follows as the *syntactic disambiguating phrase*.

2.4 Results

2.4.1 *Syntactic disambiguating phrase*
Table 1 shows that sentence had no significant effect on response times after the syntactic disambiguating phrase $F(7, 280) = 2.03$, $p = 0.052$, and a paired comparison shown in Table 2 reveals the only significant differences in response times were between sentence-pair (4) and sentence-pair (5) (see appendix for a list of those sentences).

There was a significant difference in response times between subjects $F(8, 279) = 8.03$, $p < 0.01$. Table 3 shows the results of an Analysis of Variance testing for subject effects. This was expected since some participants naturally react faster or slower than others.

There were no main effects for either factor TYPE $F(1, 8) = 1.53$, $p = 0.25$, NAT $F(1, 8) = 1.01$, $p = 0.34$, and there was no interaction TYPE*NAT $F(1, 8) = 0.42$, $p = 0.535$. Table 4 shows the descriptive statistics of each factor by level, and Table 5 shows the result of a repeated measures Analysis of Variance. Paired comparisons of each factor and level are shown in Table 6.

Table 1. Sentence type effects

	Sum of Squares	df	Mean Square	F	Sig.
Between Groups	723790.17	7	103398.60	2.03	0.052
Within Groups	14294961.78	280	51053.43		
Total	15018751.94	287			

Table 2. Paired comparisons of sentences

	2	3	4	5	6	7	8
1	0.974	0.998	0.496	0.903	0.997	1.000	1.000
2		1.000	0.978	0.298	0.692	1.000	0.998
3			0.893	0.515	0.879	1.000	1.000
4				0.024	0.132	0.833	0.718
5					0.999	0.609	0.741
6						0.927	0.972
7							1.000

See appendix for sentence pairs (1–8)

Table 3. Participant effects

	Sum of Squares	df	Mean Square	F	Sig.
Between Groups	2811672.26	8	351459.03	8.03	0.000
Within Groups	12207079.69	279	43752.97		
Total	15018751.94	287			

Table 4. Descriptives

	Stress shift	No stress shift	
M	514.43	537.83	Natural
SD	189.38	115.95	
M	465.76	512.92	Cross-spliced
SD	97.83	86.19	

Table 5. Multivariate tests

Effect	F	Hyp. df	Er. df	Sig.
TYPE	1.53	1	8	0.250
NAT	1.01	1	8	0.344
TYPE * NAT	0.42	1	8	0.535

TYPE = Stress shift factor (shift or no shift)
NAT = Sentence factor (natural or cross-spliced)

Prosodic disambiguating word

For response times following the prosodic disambiguating word, there was no effect from sentence-type $F(7, 280) = 0.59$, $p = 0.76$, but there was a participant effect $F(8, 279) = 5.75$, $p < 0.01$, as shown in Tables 7 and 8.

There were no main effects for either factor SS $F(1, 8) = 0.02$, $p = 0.90$, NAT $F(1, 8)2.15$, $p = 0.18$, and there was no significant interaction SS*NAT

Table 6. Paired comparisons

	t	df	Sig.
NAT_SS – NAT_NOSS	−0.59	8.00	0.57
NAT_SS – UN_SS	0.96	8.00	0.36
NAT_SS – UN_NOSS	0.02	8.00	0.98
NAT_NOSS – UN_SS	**4.27**	**8.00**	**0.00**
NAT_NOSS – UN_NOSS	0.88	8.00	0.40
UN_SS – UN_NOSS	−1.75	8.00	0.12

NAT_SS = Stress shift, naturally occurring
NAT_NOSS = No stress shift, naturally occurring
UN_SS = Stress shift, cross-spliced
UN_NOSS = No stress shift, cross-spliced

Table 7. Type effects

	Sum of Squares	df	Mean Square	F	Sig.
Between Groups	296918.94	7	42416.99	0.59	0.762
Within Groups	20067622.31	280	71670.08		
Total	20364541.25	287			

Table 8. Participant effects

	Sum of Squares	df	Mean Square	F	Sig.
Between Groups	2884163.72	8	360520.46	5.75	**0.000**
Within Groups	17480377.53	279	62653.68		
Total	20364541.25	287			

Table 9. Descriptives

	Stress shift	No stress shift	
M	490.81	451.06	Natural
SD	197.59	122.14	
M	385.57	439.08	Cross-spliced
SD	139.55	129.17	

$F(1, 8) = 3.49$, $p = 0.10$. A paired comparison of conditions revealed no significant differences, as shown in Table 11. Table 9 shows the descriptive statistics of response times following the prosodic disambiguating word for each factor by level, and Table 10 shows the result of a repeated measures Analysis of Variance.

Table 10. Multivariate tests

Effect	F	Hyp. df	Er. df	Sig.
TYPE	0.02	1	8	0.900
NAT	2.15	1	8	0.181
TYPE * NAT	3.49	1	8	0.099

TYPE = Stress shift factor (shift or no shift)
NAT = Sentence factor (natural or cross-spliced)

Table 11. Paired comparisons

Factor/level pair	t	df	Sig.
NAT_SS – NAT_NOSS	0.68	8	0.516
NAT_SS – UN_SS	2.01	8	0.079
NAT_SS – UN_NOSS	0.67	8	0.519
NAT_NOSS – UN_SS	1.22	8	0.257
NAT_NOSS – UN_NOSS	0.29	8	0.779
UN_SS – UN_NOSS	–0.92	8	0.386

NAT_SS = Stress shift, naturally occurring
NAT_NOSS = No stress shift, naturally occurring
UN_SS = Stress shift, cross-spliced
UN_NOSS = No stress shift, cross-spliced

2.5 Discussion

Results from Experiment 1 indicate that cues from stress shift are not useful. Alternatively, the design of the study may have failed to capture the effect that stress shift has on the parser. It was pointed out that the nature of the task prevented subjects from hearing a pause between intonational boundaries (Elizabeth Zsiga, personal communication, April 30, 2002). This was because subjects controlled the length between words by pressing the space bar to advance to the next word. The duration between words provided a means to measure the dependent variable, and thus was an important component of the study. However, the pause is a crucial cue for speakers to detect intonational boundaries, and its absence might have prevented subjects from confirming or reevaluating any predictions based on stress shift environments. For example, in cross-spliced sentences where stress shift inappropriately applied, I expected speakers to predict that the prosodic disambiguating word occurred within the same intonational phrase as the stress shift word. Without the pause, it is not clear how speakers would confirm their prediction. Thus, any effect of stress shift would be lost.

Even if the prosodic disambiguating word did not provide an appropriate cue to evaluate predictions based on stress shift, I would have expected that effects of stress shift would be revealed after the syntactic disambiguating phrase. After all, if speakers hear stress shift, they would assume the following word to be in the same intonational phrase since no intonational pause would provide a cue for them to think otherwise. In cross-spliced sentences of this type, however, speakers would have encountered an embedded clause with no subject. For example, sentence (16a) is a representation of a cross-spliced sentence where stress shift inappropriately occurred. When speakers would have encountered *are his* in (16a), there should have been a significant delay in response compared to *they're his* in its minimally paired natural sentence, represented in (16b).

(16)   a.   When my father watches TV soaps, <u>are his</u> favorite.
        b.   When my father watches TV soaps, <u>they're his</u> favorite.

This is not what happened, however. Results showed no significance between response times following the syntactic disambiguating phrase.

It might be argued that effects from the syntactic disambiguating phrase were not evident because the lengths of phrases with subjects are naturally longer than those without subjects. Therefore, the lengths of the phrases contributed to varying reaction times and erased any effect solely due to stress shift. However, a paired comparison of these lengths reveals no significant difference, $t(7) = 1.42$, $p = 0.20$, as shown in the descriptives in Table 12 and the result of a paired T-test in Table 13.

Even with these responses to possible confounds, design-error might still be what forced me to fail to reject the null hypothesis (that there was no effect). To ensure that effects were concealed by experimental design, a second experiment was conducted using methods known to show positive effects.

Table 12.   Descriptives

	M	SD
S+V	494.25	173.29
V	406.96	123.27

S+V = syntactic disambiguating phrase containing a subject
V = syntactic disambiguating phrase not containing a subject

Table 13.   Paired comparison

	M	SD	t	df	Sig.
V − S + V	87.29	173.42	1.42	7.00	0.20

S + V = syntactic disambiguating phrase containing a subject
V = syntactic disambiguating phrase not containing a subject

3.   Experiment 2

3.1 Participants

Eighteen (18) native speakers of English participated in this experiment. The participants were recruited from friends and colleagues of the researcher. In addition, several undergraduate psychology students took part in the study. None of the participants in this experiment took part in Experiment 1.

3.2 Procedure

The procedure followed closely to that of Nagel et al. (1996). A reader recorded the sentence materials (see appendix). The sentences were digitized and segmented into sound-files grouped by the initial and final material of the sentence. The rationale for segmenting the sentence in this way is because participants were asked to perform a task at the point of the cut, and the only way to make it salient for the experimental software being used (PsyScope) was to split each sentence into two, and have the software play both files one after another with no break in between. In slower computers, this would have caused a short pause between the first file being played and the second, but with a newer MAC used in this study, it was not a problem.

For sentences exhibiting stress shift, the initial material consisted of the string leading up to the point past the potential stress shift trigger; for example, *soaps* in (17a). The final material consisted of the string after the trigger (intonational boundary plus *they're his favorite*). For sentences not exhibiting stress shift, the initial material consisted of the string leading up to the point past the intonational boundary, and the final material consisted of the potential trigger plus the rest of the string, shown in (17b).

(17)   a.   [When my father watches TV soaps,] [they're his favorite.]
       b.   [When my father watches TV,] [soaps are his favorite.]

The crucial part to notice about this design is that the intonational break that was lost in Experiment 1 is preserved here.

For each sentence pair, the potential stress shift word from the shifted sentence was cross spliced with the potential stress shift word from the non-shift sentence, and vice versa. The result was 32 sentences separated into four sentence conditions: (a) stress shift within an intonational boundary, (b) non stress shift across an intonational boundary, (c) non stress shift within an intonational boundary, and (d) stress shift across an intonational boundary, just as in Experiment 1.

The sentences were grouped into four tests that exhibited a Latin-Square design. Participants heard only one sentence from each natural or unnatural pair, but were exposed to all four conditions. For any given test, participants heard eight of the 32 sentences.

Participants sat in front of a computer terminal, and were given one of the four tests. For each sentence they listened to, at the point immediately following the initial portion of the sentence, participants were asked to perform a lexical decision task, word or non-word.[3] A word appeared on the screen in Arial font, 18pt, for 800 ms. Participants used the keyboard as input device to respond with either "word" or "not a word." They were asked to make their decision as fast as they could. The word list consisted of words and non-words from four (4) to six (6) characters in length. The non-words were generated from the ARC Non-Word Database. Each of the non-words was set to have only orthographically existing rhymes and onsets, and only legal bigrams. There were 20 words and 20 non-words (see appendix for list). Response times following the presentation of the stimulus were measured. To ensure that participants were paying attention to the sentences, they were told that they would be given a short comprehension test at the end of the experiment. The experiment took about 20 minutes. The study was conducted during August and September, 2002.

3.3   Results

Table 14 shows a significant effect due to participant $F(17, 126) = 6.92$, $p < 0.01$, but this was expected since some participants naturally respond faster than others.

Likewise, Table 15 shows an effect due to which of the four tests the participants were given $F(3, 140) = 2.73$, $p < 0.05$. This follows naturally from participant effects because, for any effect due to participant response time, there is also a likely effect from any grouping of those participants.

Table 14.   Participant effects

	Sum of Squares	df	Mean Square	F	Sig.
Between Groups	7765763.28	17	456809.60	6.92	0.00
Within Groups	8312595.88	126	65972.98		
Total	16078359.16	143			

Table 15.   Latin square test effects

	Sum of Squares	df	Mean Square	F	Sig.
Between Groups	888155.77	3	296051.92	2.73	0.05
Within Groups	15190203.39	140	108501.45		
Total	16078359.16	143			

Table 16. Descriptives

	Shift	No shift	
M	878.11	808.61	Natural
SD	326.17	264.83	
M	798.81	849.31	Cross-spliced
SD	206.96	280.50	

Table 17. Multivariate tests

Effect	F	Hyp. df	Error df	Sig.
NAT	0.36	1	17	0.55
TYPE	0.05	1	17	0.82
NAT * TYPE	1.98	1	17	0.18

TYPE = Stress shift factor (shift or no shift)
NAT = Sentence factor (natural or cross=spliced)

Table 16 shows the descriptives by factor and type, and Table 17 shows the results from a repeated measure ANOVA. There was no effect due to factor TYPE $F(1, 17) = 0.05$, $p = .82$, NAT $F(1, 17) = 0.36$, $p = 0.55$, and there was no interaction TYPE*NAT $F(1, 17) = 1.98$, $p = 0.18$.

4.   Discussion

The results of both experiments together indicate that the parser is, at best, ambivalent toward stress shift. More precisely, if the parser has access to prosodic cues from stress shift, then it does not use them to make any parsing decisions.

Earlier, I argued that prosody is an excellent area for studying linguistic cues that might guide the parser to make decisions during online sentence processing. For one, linguists have been studying prosody for quite some time and have accumulated a substantial body of literature demonstrating that speakers are sensitive to a range of prosodic phenomena. Thus, it would seem possible that prosodic cues might facilitate parsing decisions in an otherwise ambiguous context. Also, compared to research in other areas (syntax and semantics, for example) studies of prosody and parsing are more or less rare. This is unfortunate because while myriad effects have been shown for these other areas, only a handful (by comparison) have been shown for prosody. The result is a gap in our understanding of which linguistic cues are important to the parser and which ones are ancillary.

In fact, an understanding of irrelevant linguistic cues to parsing might provide crucial insight into the nature of the parser. It has been a generally established observation that the parser and the grammar are separate modules (see Townsend & Bever 1999 Chpt. 4 for a general discussion). Evidence usually cited in support of this conclusion comes from sentences like (1b) repeated below which are grammatically productive but completely impossible to parse.

(1) c. The cat the dog the horse kicked chased ate the mouse.

The idea is that the parser has access to the grammar and uses that information to inform its decisions. There are also known discourse-level effects on parsing, which suggest the parser has access to a variety of linguistic modules other than the grammar alone (Townsend & Bever 1991, for one example). A natural question is whether the parser has equal access to the grammar and other components of language understanding. If the results of this study are any indication, some components of the linguistic system are more important to the parser than others.

Materials

Target sentences

1. a. When my father watches TV soaps, they're his favorite.
    b. When my father watches TV, soaps are his favorite.
2. a. Since they are academic questions, the debate will be interesting.
    b. Since they are academic, questions following the debate will be interesting.
3. a. Although Mary and Emma were OK players, they lost the match.
    b. Although Mary and Emma were OK, players from their team got sick.
4. a. When Britain refused to support the US officials, the operation was canceled.
    b. When Britain refused to support the US, officials canceled the operation.
5. a. Whenever he asks for first class tickets, they are not available.
    b. Whenever he asks for first class, tickets are not available.
6. a. Whenever NBC news contacts the UN envoys, they're out for lunch.
    b. Whenever NBC news contacts the UN, envoys are out for lunch.
7. a. When linguists discuss Japanese dialects, they never agree.
    b. When linguists discuss Japanese, dialects always come up.
8. a. Because scientists are worried about the North Pole controversy, they will go public with it.
    b. Because scientists are worried about the North Pole, controversy will likely result.

Filler sentences

1.   Even after their legs feel stiff, some runners don't stretch properly.
2.   Although some people don't believe it, most people think dinosaurs once ruled the earth.
3.   Even though John works for the government, he thinks there are too many federal workers.
4.   Although Mary enjoys tailgate parties, she'd rather just watch the game.
5.   Incredible as it may seem, many Americans believe in paranormal activity.
6.   Despite concern that the autoworkers would strike, executives made drastic pay cuts.
7.   Since evidence for the scandal was mostly hearsay, the newspaper did not run the story.
8.   Even though swimming after dark was popular, the summer camp director banned it.
9.   Because support for higher taxes was low, the board held off a vote.
10. After only two uses, the alarm clock Sarah bought broke.
11. At the end of the ceremony, the awardees were given their trophies.
12. Cathy will often eat steak rare, and sometimes John will too.
13. Before heading back to shore, Bill and John each caught six fish.
14. Instead of ordering the chili, Peter got the cheeseburger.
15. Usually quick to point out her dislike of public radio, Linda remained relatively silent.
16. Faced with overwhelming evidence, the thieves admitted their guilt.
17. The new school was made from stone that came from three quarries.
18. The windstorm toppled over 4000 acres of the old growth forest.
19. The airline company limited its service to just five cities.
20. The children that were lost in the woods were found by a group of hikers.
21. A tight budget forced the university president to cut athletic scholarships.
22. Jeff wanted to see the exhibit at the museum so he could impress his friends.
23. About half the farmers in the area adopted organic methods to meet consumer demand.
24. Heavy rainfall in the river valley caused disastrous flooding.
25. The restaurant refused service to the couple who were each wearing shorts and a tank top.
26. Mary likes her coffee strong and without cream or sugar, which is the way, she says, everyone should have it.
27. The pills the doctor gave Mark did not help his allergies.
28. The students who did not study forgot how to figure out the statistics without a calculator.
29. No one without a ticket was admitted to the concert.

30.   The cafeteria stopped serving liver because of too many complaints.
31.   The computer lab was closed for most of the summer.
32.   The canoeists paddled through the raids without any trouble.

Practice sentences

1.   Nearly every seat on the train to New York was taken.
2.   Not wanting to appear bored, Jenny pretended to be interested in the conversation.
3.   On weekends, the family usually heads north to the lake.
4.   Everyone in the office signed the card for the boos when she was sick.

Word list for lexical decision task

NON WORDS

yuth	thwafe	spox
skeuth	woused	gwucks
twuill	clorch	zird
slilns	brogs	splod
frief	pluth	spauge
soal	sibes	
gweats	brerd	

REAL WORDS

bath	seven	only
child	pants	tones
brain	after	busy
friend	lesson	catch
scrape	alive	dove
lend	queen	kelp
moon	thus	

Notes

* Thanks to Colin Phillips for providing insight for writing the experiment script using PsyScope software, to Jennifer Mittelstaedt for reading the sentence materials, and to Steven Weinberg for advice about converting sound files.

1. See Townsend & Bever (1999) Chpt. 6 Boxes 6.1–6.13 for a brief summary of several other tasks used to test linguistic effects on parsing.

2. Interestingly, Gibson & Schütze (1999) discovered that disambiguation preferences in certain nominal conjunctions did not significantly compare to corpus frequencies, as expected. Gibson & Schütze attribute the discrepancy to either a real difference, which would

indicate that category-frequency is not a straightforward way to account for why sentences such as *The old man the boat* is bad. Or, they suggest that the frequencies from the corpora they used do not match actual frequencies.

3. For the filler sentences, the word appeared on the screen at random times during the sentence.

References

ARC Non-Word Database. http://www.maccs.mq.edu.au/~nwdb/.

Beckman, M. (1996). The parsing of prosody. *Language and Cognitive Processes, 11* (1/2), 17–67.

Cutler, A. & Isard, S. (1980). The production of prosody. In B. Butterworth (Ed.), *Language Production: Vol. I Speech and talk* (pp. 245–269). New York: Academic.

Frazier, L. (1987). Sentence processing: A tutorial review. In M. Coltheart (Ed.), *Attention and Performance XII* (pp. 559–585). Hillsdale, New Jersey: Lawrence Erlbaum Associates.

Gibson, E. & Schütze, C. (1999). Disambiguation preferences in noun phrase conjunction do not mirror corpus frequencies. *Journal of Memory and Language, 40,* 1263–1279.

Grabe, E. & Warren, P. (1996). Stress shift: Do speakers do it or do listeners hear it? In B. Connel & A. Arvaniti (Eds.), *Papers in Laboratory Phonology IV: Phonology and Phonetic Evidence* (pp. 95–110). Cambridge: Cambridge University Press.

Jurafsky, D. (1996). Probabilistic model of lexical and syntactic access and disambiguation. *Cognitive Science, 20,* 137–194.

McAllister, J., Colrain I., & Gravatt, B. (1995). Prosodic cues in the interpretation of spoken garden path sentences: Evidence from event related brain potentials. MS: University of Auckland, New Zealand.

Nagel, H., Shapio L., Tuller, B., & Nawy, R. (1996). Prosodic influences on the resolution of temporary ambiguity during on-line sentence processing. *Journal of Psycholinguistic Research, 25,* 319–344.

Nicol, J. (1996). What can prosody tell a parser? *Journal of Psycholinguistic Research, 25* (2), 179–192.

Selkirk, E. (1984). *Phonology and Syntax.* Cambridge, Mass.: MIT Press.

Shattuck-Hufnagel, S., Ostendorf, M., & Ross, K. (1994). Stress shift and early pitch accent placement in lexical items in American English. *Journal of Phonetics, 22,* 357–388.

Taraban, R., & McClelland, J. (1988). Constituent attachment and thematic role assignment in sentence processing: Influences of content-based expectations. *Journal of Memory and Language, 27,* 597–632.

Townsend, D. & Bever, T. (1991). The use of higher-level constraints in monitoring for a change in speaker demonstrates functionally distinct levels of representation in discourse comprehension. *Language and Cognitive Processes, 6,* 49–77.

Townsend, D. & Bever, T. (1999). *Sentence Comprehension: The Integration of Habits and Rules.* Cambridge, Mass.: MIT Press.

Trueswell, J. & Kim, A. (1998). How to prune a garden path by nipping it in the bud: Fast priming of verb argument structure. *Journal of Memory and Language, 39,* 102–123.

Trueswell, J. & Tanenhaus, M. (1991). Tense, temporal context, and syntactic ambiguity resolution. *Language and Cognitive Processes, 6,* 303–338.

Trueswell, J., Sekerina, I., Hill, N., & Logrip, L. (1999). The kindergarten-path effect: Studying on-line sentence processing in young children. *Cognition, 73,* 89–134.

Vogel, I, Bunnel, T., & Haskins, S. (1994). The phonology and phonetics of the Rhythm Rule. In B. Connel & A. Arvaniti (Eds.), *Papers in Laboratory Phonology IV: Phonology and Phonetic Evidence* (pp. 111–127). Cambridge: Cambridge University Press.

Warren, P. (1996). Prosody and parsing: An introduction. *Language and Cognitive processes, 11,* 1–16.

Watt, S. & Murray, W. (1996). Prosodic form and parsing commitments. *Journal of Psycholinguistic Research, 25* (2), 291–318.

Computation

Morpho-syntax parsing[*]

Anna Maria Di Sciullo and Sandiway Fong
Université du Québec à Montréal / NEC Research Institute

This paper describes an implemented bottom-up parser for a theory of morphological selection proposed in Di Sciullo (1996a). Core lexical properties of derivational affixes, generally encoded in terms of subcategorization frames, are articulated in terms of asymmetrical relations. The selection of derivational affixes is couched in a uniform specifier-head-complement configuration, and predictions can be made with respect to composition and linking relation. Thus, the so-called lexical gaps fall out from the theory. Starting from a review of the underlying Asymmetry framework, the computational implications of three different implementations of this framework are discussed. In particular, the effect on bottom-up parsing from varying the specifier-head-complement order is discussed. Furthermore, computational motivation for the logical separation of overt and covert affixation is provided.

1. Introduction

We take morphological expressions to be asymmetrical [Specifier [Head Complement]] relations, where configurational selection (Di Sciullo 1996a, b) holds between the affix and the root,[1] and where the specifier, the head, and the complement can be overt or not. We show that the results of the implementation of configurational selection have consequences for the optimal recovery of the morpho-syntactic asymmetries.

The organization of this paper is the following. In the first section, we present the main features of configurational selection and show that the argument structure restrictions on morphological composition follow systematically. The second section considers different PAPPI (Fong 1991) implementations of the theory, and provides evidence to show that the positions of the Specifier and the Complement in morphological trees as well as the separation of overt and covert processing have an effect on tractability.

2.   Asymmetry

Asymmetry as a property of structural relations played a central role in syntax (Chomsky 1993, 1995, 2001; Kayne 1994; Moro 2000). The asymmetric property of morphological relations has been evidenced in Di Sciullo and Williams (1987), Di Sciullo (1996a, b, 1997, 1999b, 2005), Hale and Marantz (1993), Williams (1994), Roeper and Keyser (1995). Moreover it has been shown that asymmetry is also determinant in phonology (Raimy 2000, 2003). These converging results indicate that asymmetry is a salient property of the structural relations derived by the grammar. See also Di Sciullo (2003a, b).

2.1   Relations, operations, and conditions

Even though non-isomorphic,[2] morphological and syntactical expressions share a basic property: asymmetry.[3] More specifically, we take the representation in (1) or the equivalent tree structure in (2) including the asymmetric c-command relation, to be basic in the derivation of morphological expressions.[4]

(1)   [$_H$ specifier [$_H$ head complement]]

(2)

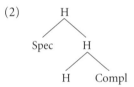

This is motivated as follows. First, a morphological expression includes a categorial head, as argued for in (Williams 1981) and (Di Sciullo & Williams 1987). Assuming, as in Chomsky (1995), that non-branching structures are excluded by minimalist assumptions and that each head has one complement, head-complement relations are part of morphological expressions. Second, assuming that a head-complement relation must be included in a specifier-head relation to be complete, a morphological expression is an asymmetric specifier-head-complement structure.[5] As derivational morphology affects not only the categorial features of a root but also the argument features of the root and given a configurational representation of argument structure (Hale & Keyser 1993, 2002), the [specifier [head complement]] configuration is part of the derivation of morphological expressions. Third, the asymmetric [specifier [head complement]] structure in morphology is motivated by the Universal Base Hypothesis (Kayne 1994), according to which the order of the base constituents is universally the following: the specifier precedes the head, and the head is followed by complement. Thus, there are theoretical justifications to the hypothesis that asymmetrical relations are part of the derivation of morphological expressions.

We assume that the grammar includes structure building and linking operations. The first operation derives complex categories on the basis of more elementary ones; the second operation relates features in derivations and representations. We also assume that the definition of the operations of the grammar is relativized to the sort of derivation.[6] Thus, for the derivation of morphological expressions, we have:

(3) Composition: An affix head projects an X-bar structure and combines with the full asymmetrical projection of a root by selecting an Argument feature of the Specifier or the complement of that projection. (Di Sciullo 1996a)

(4) Linking: Every non-argument feature (¬A) must be A-linked; Every argument features (A) may be A-Linked. (Di Sciullo 1996a)

The tree in (5), where H is an affixal head and R is a root is obtained from the first operation. The second operation relates non Argument (¬A) to Argument (A) feature positions distributed in the Spec and Compl positions.

(5)
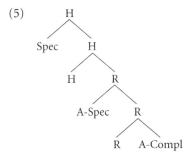

The next section brings empirical evidence from English and Romance languages for Configurational Morphology.

2.2 Coverage

Configuration Morphology makes more accurate predictions than other theories based on categorial selection or thematic-grids.

2.2.1 *Morphological selection*

A derivational affix combines with a projection according to its asymmetric A-structure properties. For example, the nominal suffix -*er* combines with unergative and transitive verbs, but not with unaccusative verbs. The nominal in (6a) is based on an unergative verb, that is, a verb that takes an external argument but no internal argument; the nomimal in (6b) is based on an unaccusative verb, that is, a verb that takes an internal argument but not an external argument.

(6) a.   He's a dreamer.
     b.   *Trains are arrivers.

Such restrictions do not follow from morphological theories based on categorial selection, as it is the case in Grimshaw (1990), Lieber (1992), Anderson (1992), Borer (1991), and Law (1997). In these theories, an affixal head selects on the basis of the categorial features of its sister-node.

The fact that the nominal suffix -*er* combines with intransitives, as in (6), as well as with transitives, as in (7), indicates that the restrictions on morphological composition are not thematic. The external argument of an unergative verb is not an Agent, whereas it can be in the case of a transitive verb.

(7) a.   the rider on the shore
     b.   the fighters in the ring

The restrictions on morphological composition are based on asymmetric relations. The fact that the affix may combine with unergatives, as depicted in (8), and transitives, but not with unaccusatives, constitutes evidence that the morphological composition is based on asymmetric relations.

(8)

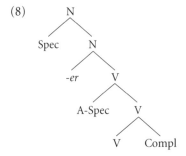

There are further restrictions to the composition of the nominal affix -*er* with a verbal projection. The examples in (9) illustrate the fact that the nominal affix may not combine with the obligatory ditransitive verb *put*, whereas it may do so with *send*, which is also ditransitive but does not require the obligatory presence of the prepositional complement.

(9) a.   *the putter of the letter in the mail
     b.   the sender of the letter

Morphological composition is thus restricted by specific asymmetrical relations, which prevent an affix, here the nominal affix -er, from combining with certain configurations, here with verbal projections including two obligatory internal arguments.

This situation is not restricted to nominal affixes, but obtains across the board for derivational affixes, irrespective of their categorial features. Thus, the configurational asymmetry with respect to morphological composition can be observed with adjectival, verbal, and nominal affixes, as we briefly illustrate below.

For example, the adjectival suffix -able combines with a transitive verbal projection, whether an agent is part of that projection or not, see (10a). However, it does not combine with an obligatory ditransitive verbal projection, see (10b). Furthermore, it may not combine with an unergative or an unaccusative projection, see (10c) and (10d).

(10)   a.   a desirable/buyable book
       b.   *a puttable book on this shelve
       c.   *a sittable chair
       d.   *a leaveable place

This property of -able is expressed in (11), where both the specifier and the complement of the verbal projection are argumental.

(11)

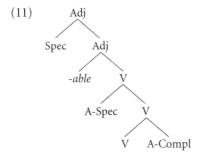

Verbal suffixes are not immune to restrictions with respect to morphological composition. Thus, the verbal suffixes -ify and -ize may combine with intransitive predicates, but not with transitive ones, as illustrated in (12). The restrictions are represented in (13), where the verbal affix combines with an adjectival or a nominal projection (Adj/N).

(12)   a.   a formalized theory
       b.   a computerized accounting system
       c.   *This equalizes the results.
       d.   *It's hard to friendize with him.

(13)

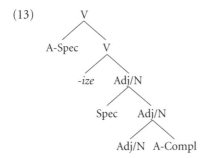

Given a configurational representation of argument structure, it is possible to account for the restrictions on the combination of affixes and roots which cannot be accounted for by morphological theories based on symmetrical categorial selection or thematic grids. In Configurational Morphology, an affix projects an asymmetric structure and selects an asymmetric structure. Affixes differ with respect to the specific argument structure requirement they impose on the configuration with which they combine, see (14) and (15):

(14)

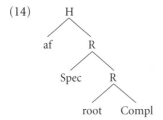

(15)   a.   (A-Spec): *-er*
       b.   (A-Compl): *-ize, -ify*
       c.   (A-Spec, A-compl): *-able,-ee ,-ive*

Morphological composition is restricted by the configurational asymmetries of the elements undergoing the operation. That asymmetric relations override categorial-selection and thematic grids in derivation is expected in our theory, which is based on the hypothesis that asymmetric relations are basic in grammar.

2.2.2   *Linking*
Argument features are part of asymmetric relations and are subject to morphological Linking. Morphological Linking determines what parts of the projection of a root is affected by an affix, and how the argument structure projected by the affix is used up.

For example, the causative affixes *-ize* and *-ify* project an A-Spec (external argument). Consequently, they may only combine with roots that lack an A-Spec, as there can be only one external argument per projection. Thus, in (16a) the verbal suffix -*ify* projects an A-spec and thus may combine with an adjective that lacks an A-spec. The example in (16b) shows that the verbal suffix cannot combine with an adjectival projection with an A-Spec.

(16)   a.   a simplified problem
       b.   *an enviousified neighbor

An adjectival suffix affects the argument structure of the verbal projection with which it combines. The A-Compl of the verbal projection is the specifier of the -*able* adjective, while the A-Spec of the verbal projection is the specifier of the -*ive* adjective. As such, the latter cannot combine with an unaccusative, and the former with an unergative.

(17)   a.   This puzzle is solvable (*of/by anybody).
       b.   *Rain is fallable.
       c.   Unicorns are impressive (*of/for people).
       d.   *Gentlemen are standable in trains.

A nominal suffix affects the argument structure of the verbal projection with which it combines. The complement of an -*er* nominal is the complement of the verbal base, whereas the complement of an -*ee* nominal is the specifier of the verbal base. The first affix cannot combine with verbs that do not project an A-Spec. The second affix cannot combine with verbs that do not project an A-Spec and an A-Compl.

(18)   a.   The adviser of Paul (*by John).
       b.   The advisee of John's (*of Paul).

(19)   a.   *This is the shiner and that is the shinee.
       b.   *Paul is the departer and Luc the departee.

Thus the asymmetric property of morphological relations, expressed in terms of the [specifier [head complement]] structure, plays a role in derivational morphology. It plays a role with respect to Composition and Linking. Moreover the notions of argument structure flexibility and argument structure shift proposed in Di Sciullo (2005) provides an account for the quasi-acceptable cases of derivation such as *easy-goer* and *early-departer*.

2.3 Prefixes

Asymmetric relations are also crucial in the derivation of prefixed forms. In the languages under consideration, contrary to a suffix, a prefix does not affect the argument structure of the projection with which it combines, see (20).

(20)   a.   John folded the map.
       b.   John unfolded the map.

    c.   His wise behavior was noticed by the board.

    d.   His unwise behavior was noticed by the board.

The combination of a prefix with a projection is independent of the argument structure properties of that projection, as illustrated in (21) and (22) with French, as verbal prefixation is more productive in that language than in English.

(21) a. *Jean est accouru.*   (*courir* 'to run' unergative)
           'John ran up.'

      b. *Paul a apporté la mallette.*   (*porter* 'to carry' transitive)
           'Paul brought the case.'

(22) a. *Luc est retombé du lit.*   (*tomber* 'to fall' ergative)
           'Luc fell from his bed.'

      b. *La bague a rebrillé.*   (*briller* 'to shine' unergative)
           'The ring shined again.'

      c. *Marie a relu la phrase.*   (*lire* 'to read' transititive)
           'Mary reread the sentence.'

      d. *Sophie a remis la tortue dans l'aquarium.* (*mettre* 'to put' ditransitive)
           'Sophie put the turtle back into the aquarium.'

In the example in (21a), the internal directional prefix *a-* combines with the unergative *courir* 'to run' and, in (21b), it combines with the transitive verb *porter* 'to carry'. The examples in (22) are cases of external prefixation. They illustrate the fact that the iterative prefix is not sensitive to the argument structure properties of the verbal projection with which it combines. It composes with an unaccusative in (22a), with an unergative in (22b), with a transitive in (22c), and with a di-transitive in (22d).

    A prefix selects a base verbal predicate on the basis of aspectual properties (Di Sciullo 1997, 1999a, b; Di Sciullo & Tenny 1997). Directional and Locational prefixes may add a terminus to the event denoted by the predicate to which they adjoin. Thus, they may only adjoin to predicates that are underspecified for a termi-nus. This is the case for a subset of predicates denoting activities, including *courir* 'to run' and *porter* 'to bring'.

(23) a. *Il a couru pendant cinq minutes.*
          'He ran for five minutes.'

      b. ???*Il est accouru pendant cinq minutes.*
          'He ran up for five minutes.'

(24) a. *Il a porté la malle pendant cinq minutes.*
          'He carried the trunk for five minutes.'

      b. ???*Il a apporté la malle pendant cinq minutes.*
          'He brought the trunk for five minutes.'

Thus, it appears that prefixes are different from suffixes with respect to Selection. Prefixes Select on the basis of aspectual features. They are also different with respect to Linking. While derivational suffixes generally determine the restrictions on argumental linking, prefixes generally determine the restrictions on aspectual linking. A prefix may restrict the aspectual features of the category to which it is associated either within the minimal argument structure projection of that category, or outside of this domain. The first situation arises with directional and locational prefixes, the second situation arises with iterative, inverse, and evaluative prefixes. The configurational difference between internal and external prefixes is expected within the theory, as the properties of a prefix follow from the domain of which it is part. We will be concerned here with the first sort of prefixes only, that is, with the internal ones, and we will not consider external prefixes.

2.4 Phonetically null positions

Covert specifier and complement are part of the morphological derivations. They have no phonetic features, however they do have argument features. Otherwise, it could be impossible to account for the configurational restrictions they impose on their complement.

For example, in (25a) the Spec of the base verb *break* in *breakable* is covert, whereas in (25c), it is the Compl of the base verb *impress* in *impressive* that is covert.

(25) a.   Murano jars are breakable.
      b.   Burano laces are sellable.
      c.   The guards are impressive.
      d.   This proposition is attractive.

Covert specifiers and complements in morphology are not equivalent to covert categories in syntax, such as copies and abstract pronouns, as the projection of covert Spec and Compl positions in morphology is determined exclusively by the argument features of the morphological head on which they are dependent.

Morphological expressions may also include covert heads. This can be seen by contrasting the English denominal verbs with no overt verbal head in (26) with the equivalent French forms in (27), as well as by comparing the English examples in (28), with no overt prepositional, with the equivalent French forms in (29):

(26) a.   Mary likes *to send* mail to her friends in the morning.
      b.   Paul prefers *to butter* bread with a spoon.
      c.   Luc suggests *to nail* R2V2 to the ship.

(27) a.   *Mary aime poster des lettres à ses amis le matin.*
           'Mary likes to send letters to her friends in the morning.'

    b.   *Paul préfère beurrer le pain avec une cuillère.*
        'Paul prefers to butter the bread with a spoon.'

    c.   *Luc suggère de clouer R2V2 au vaisseau.*
        'Luc suggests to nail R2V2 to the ship.'

(28) a.   John *stored* the books.

      b.   Lucy *bottled* the potion.

      c.   Marc *cashed* the check.

(29) a.   *John a enmagasiné les livres.*
        'John stored the books.'

      b.   *Lucy a embouteillé la potion.*
        'Lucy bottled the potion.'

      c.   *Marc a encaissé le chèque.*
        'Marc cashed the check.'

The examples in (26) and (27) show that English denominal and deadjectival verbs may include covert suffixes and prefixes, whereas they are overt in French. For example in (30a), the causative [CAU] verb is morphologically spelled out by the verbal suffix -*er*, the change of state/position inchoative [INC] verb is covert, the directional/locational prefix *en*- heading the resulting change of state/position constituent, the terminus of the event is overt. In (30b), the causative affix is null and the inchoative verb is spelled out by the suffix -*ir*. In both cases the prefix is overt, whereas in the equivalent English examples, the prefix is covert. (See Di Sciullo 1996a, 1997)

(30) a.

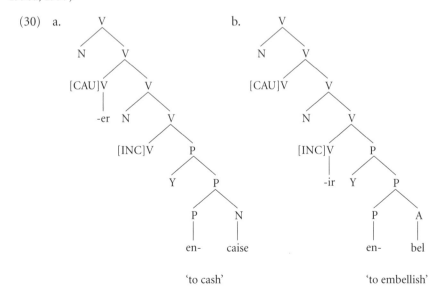

                  'to cash'   'to embellish'

While [Spec [Head Compl]] relations are required because of the asymmetric property of morphological relations, the overt or covert nature of the members of these relations is a consequence of language specific properties. The variation between languages reduces to a difference in the projection of a sub-feature of Aspect, as proposed in (Di Sciullo 1999a).

2.5 Summary

We brought further justifications to a theory that derives complex morphological expressions on the basis of the asymmetrical relations of their parts. The theory achieves greater descriptive and explanatory adequacy than theories based on categorial-selection and theta-grids. It also provides a systematic analysis of formal (categorial) and semantic (argument and aspect) features in derivational morphology.

3.   Three parsing models

Linguistic theory often provides enough freedom for a variety of different computational models to be tested. Whilst remaining faithful to the theory, from a computational perspective, we are also interested in improving the efficiency of parsing models. The contribution of particular elements of a theory to computational complexity can be determined through experimentation. In particular, we will discuss the effects of variation in specifier-head-complement order, and the contribution of empty heads and prefixes to the complexity of morphology within the framework of bottom-up shift-reduce parsing.

3.1 Background

In this section, we describe, in turn, the encoding of X′-structure, the lexical representation of morphemes and heads, and the implementation of the Linking constraint.

3.1.1   *X′ structure*
We assume heads uniformly project two-level X′ structure, as shown in (31), see Note 4.:

(31)

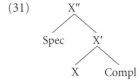

The corresponding context-free X′ grammar is shown in (32):

(32)   **rule** XP→ [X1,YP] **st** max(XP), bar(X1), proj(X1,XP), max(YP).
    rule X1→ [ZP,X] **st** bar(X1), head(X), proj(X,X1), max(ZP).
    rule xp→ [].

X, X1, and XP are logical variables ranging over category labels at the head, bar, and maximal projection levels respectively. Heads will be grounded in the lexicon. Maximal projections YP and ZP will be realized recursively as either X′-structures or as a special maximal projection xp introduced by the empty category rule shown above. The relevant categories and the projection relation are defined below:

(33)   head(n). head(v). head(a). head(p).
    bar(n1). bar(v1). bar(a1). bar(p1).
    max(np). max(vp). max(ap). max(pp). max(xp).
    proj(n,n1). proj(v,v1). proj(a,a1). proj(p,p1).
    proj(n1,np). proj(v1,vp). proj(a1,ap). proj(p1,pp).
    head(n1,n). head(v1,v). head(a1,a). head(p1,p).
    head(np,n). head(vp,v). head(ap,a). head(pp,p).

A LR(1) – based parser was adopted for analysis. LR(1)-parsing (Knuth 1965) is a well-known and highly-efficient method of shift-reduce (bottom-up) parsing that processes morphemes in a left-to-right manner using a single symbol of lookahead for local disambiguation.[7] The adopted algorithm relaxes the strict LR(1) requirement of zero conflict by allowing shift/reduce and reduce/reduce conflicts to exist in the table. Conflict resolution is handled by backtracking in the underlying Prolog system (Fong 1991).

3.1.2   The lexicon
The lexicon uses a default feature system for lexical entries. The following declaration expresses the lexical defaults for nouns, verbs, and adjectives:

(34)   default_features([n,v,a],[specR(f(a(-))),
                    selR(f(a(-)))]).

In (34), specR imposes restrictions on Specifier positions, and selR on Complement positions. f(a(−)) indicates that the referenced position should have feature a(−). By convention, A/A-bar-positions are encoded using a(±). Hence, by default, Specifiers and Complements are A-bar-positions (unless otherwise indicated).

    Consider the nouns in (35). By default, *computer* has two A-bar-positions. *Form* and *father*, on the other hand, have one and two A-positions, respectively.

(35)   lex(computer, n, []).
    lex(form,   n, [selR(f(a(+)))]).
    lex(father,   n, [specR(f(a(+))),selR(f(a(+)))]).

Affixes impose constraints on their Complement domain. For example, the nominal affix *-er*, e.g. as in *employer*, in (36), indicates that the specifier of its complement must be an A-position. Similarly, *-ee*, e.g. as in *employee*, restricts both the Specifier and Complement *within* its Complement to be A-positions.

(36) `lex(er,n,[link(spec), selR(spec(f(a(+))))]).`
      `lex(ee,n,[link(compl),selR([spec(f(a(+))),`
      `                            compl(f(a(+)))])]).`

Finally, the abstract causative morpheme, caus in (37), differs from the inchoative inc in terms of selection in that it has an A-Specifier as well as it restricts the specifier of its complement to be an A-bar-position.

(37) `lex(caus,v,[specR(f(a(+))), selR(spec(f(a(-)))), caus]).`
      `lex(inc, v,[link(compl), selR(spec(f(a(-)))), inc]).`

The *-er*, *-ee*, and inc morphemes have an additional feature link(Spec/Compl), which specifies the target of A-bar-Specifier Linking in a complement domain. We discuss the role of this feature in the next section.

3.1.3   *Linking*

There is a single free-standing principle that encodes the following rule:

(38) **Linking Rule**: All Affix A-bar-positions must be linked to A-positions in their complement domain (if one exists).

This is implemented by the universally-quantified (over tree structure) condition linkR shown in (39):

(39) `linkR` **`in_all_configuration`** `CF` **`where`**
      `        linkConfig(CF,XP,Type,Dom)`
      `    ` **`then`** ` findApos(YP,Type,Dom), coindex(XP,YP).`

      `linkConfig (CF,XP,Type,Dom) :-`
      `        maxProj(CF), CF has_feature link(Type),`[8]
      `        XP specifier_of CF, \+ XP has_feature a(+),`
      `        Dom complement_of CF.`

This definition looks for configurations meeting the requirements of `linkConfig`: i.e. CF must be a maximal projection with an A-bar-Specifier XP and a Complement Dom. For all satisfying configurations, `findApos` (definition not shown) will extract a phrase YP occupying an A-position of the appropriate sort indicated by `Type`. Here, `Type` refers to a lexical feature `link` and will be either `compl`, as in the case of *-er* in (36), or `spec`, as in the case of *-ee* and inc in (36) and (37), respectively. The resulting linking relation between XP and YP is indicated via coindexation.

All parses assigned an X′-structure will be filtered using this rule. If a linking configuration can be found, i.e. if some maximal projection with an A-bar-Specifier that needs to be linked exists, but `findApos` fails to report an A-position of the appropriate type, the parse will be rejected.

3.2 Specifier-head-complement asymmetry

In this section, we consider the computational consequences of varying the Specifier-Head linear order for the LR shift-reduce parsing framework, i.e. (40a) vs. (40b) below:[9]

(40) a. Specifier on the left   b. Specifier on the right

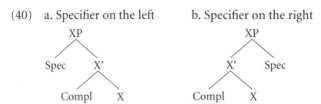

It turns out that there is a considerable difference both in terms of the number of LR actions performed and the stack depth required to process an example like *formalize*, analyzed as *form-al-i(z)-e* in (41) below:

(41) a. *Formalize* with left specifier   b. *Formalize* with right specifier

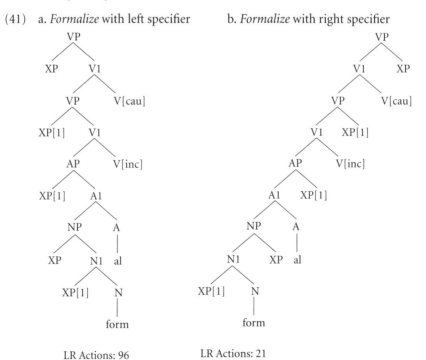

LR Actions: 96   LR Actions: 21

The simple explanation is that the LR machine has to be able to predict an arbitrary number of empty argument positions before it can shift or "read" the first item, namely *form*, in (41a).[10] Contrast this with the situation in (41b), where Specifiers are generated on the right side only. Here, the LR machine needs only to generate a single empty argument position before a shift can take place. Hence only 21 actions and a stack depth of 2 are required in this case, compared to 96 and a stack depth of 5 in (41b). The following table compares left and right Specifiers for a variety of examples:

(42)

Word	Items	LR actions	
		Left specifier	Right specifier
form	1	8	6
read-able	2	19	11
simpl(e)-i(f)-y	3	47	16
form-al-i(z)-e	4	96	21
form-al-i(z)-(e)-able	5	172	26

Finally, note that the right Specifier model is *nearly* optimal in terms of the minimum number of actions required to analyze each word.[11] In general, the minimum number is given by the formula $4i + 2$, i being the number of items in the analysis of the word.[12]

3.3   Empty heads and prefixes

In this section, we describe the implementation and discuss the computational consequences of introducing empty heads and prefixes into the system.

3.3.1   *Empty heads*

English has both zero and non-zero N→V conversion:

(43)   a.   John bottled the wine.
         b.   Mary computerized the accounting department.

In (43b), *computerize* is analyzed as the noun *computer* followed by the suffix *-ize*, which is, in turn, further decomposed into *-i(z)-e*, where the two constituents are merely instantiations of the (abstract) inchoative and causative morphemes, shown earlier in (37). As (44) indicates, we can analyze *bottle* along the same lines:

(44) a. Bottle   b. Computerize

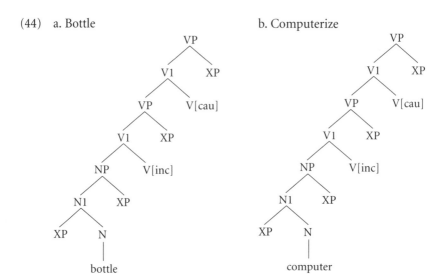

That is, the only difference with *bottle* as a verb is that the inchoative and causative morphemes are zero affixes. This is implemented by the following empty verb rule, defined to take on features from either abstract caus or inc:

(45) **rule** v **with** Fs → [] **st** emptyVFs(Fs).

```
emptyVFs(Fs) :- causative(Fs).
emptyVFs(Fs) :- inchoative(Fs).
```

Unlike the case of empty specifiers or complements, empty heads generally permit infinite recursion, and therefore, an endless number of parses for any word. We can address this in the case of inc and caus by appealing to semantic considerations: that is, they can occur at most once per singular event. This constraint is imposed by the following declarations:

(46) unique_feature_domain max.
      inc unique_feature_in max.
      caus unique_feature_in max.

      top(max). % *LR machine declaration*

The topmost (dummy) node returned by the LR machine, named max, is defined to be the domain for features inc and caus, which are declared as unique features, and therefore may be inserted at most once in max, thus guaranteeing parsing termination.[13]

3.3.2 *Empty prefixes*

There is reason to assume that a covert directional prefix is present in the structure for *bottle* as a verb:

(47) a. *embouteiller* (French)
　　　b. *imbottigliare* (Italian)
　　　c. (to) bottle

Here, *bottle* represents the final location of an object that is the target of the event. The directional prefix, call it *en-*, will identify or supply an A-position that is necessary for the proper linking of the A-bar-Specifier of inc. Similarly, *en-* is also required in the case of the verb *computerize*. The role of *en-* as a prefix is made explicit in the following parses:

(48) a. Bottle　　　　　　　　　　　b. Computerize

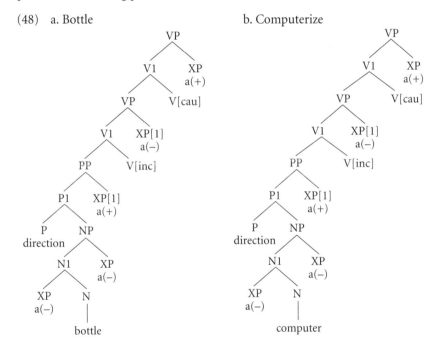

In (48a–b), the covert directional prefix selects for a phrase headed by *bottle* and *computerize*, respectively. This is implemented by adopting the following rule:

(49) **rule p with** Fs → [] **st** en(Fs).

The empty preposition defined in (49) references the lexical entry for *en-* in (50):

(50) lex(en, p, [direction,specR(f(a(+))),
　　　　　　　　selR([spec(f(a(-))),compl(f(a(-)))])]).

　　　direction unique_feature_in max.

This basically states that *en-* is a directional preposition that supplies an A-Specifier and selects for a (locative) Complement phrase containing no A-positions, as is the case with *bottle* and *computer*. As the indexation in (48a–b) indicates, the A-bar-position associated with inc links to the A-position provided by *en-*.

Finally, direction is declared as a unique feature for both semantic and termination reasons, as in the cases of inc and caus described earlier.

3.3.3   *A two-stage model*

The expansion of the LR(1) parsing engine to account for empty heads and prefixes actually resulted in a decrease in machine size from 117 to 71 states as shown in (51):

(51)

Machine	States	No conflict	Single conflict	Multiple Conflicts
Standard LR	117	371 63%	214 37%	0 0%
Plus empty heads/prefixes	71	145 41%	64 18%	146 41%

However, it is important to realize that a smaller machine does not necessarily mean a more efficient parser. The distribution of LR action conflicts provides a strong indication that the revised machine is computationally much less tractable. For instance, the number of state/lookahead pairs is split 2:1 in the case of the standard machine, with only one third of them registering a single conflict, i.e. there are two possible LR actions from which to choose. Contrast this with the revised machine which has a substantial proportion of multiple conflicts (40%), i.e. computational choice points with three (or more) possible LR actions. This is borne out empirically as (52) attests:

(52)

Example	LR Actions	
	Single-Stage	Two-Stage
form	53	7
bottle	80	7
readable	75	12
simplify	91	18
computerize	139	18
formalize	147	23
formalizable	157	27

Here we have two competing parsing engines: (A) a single-stage LR machine, containing both overt and non-overt heads and prefixes, and (B) a two-stage engine consisting of a simplified (overt only) LR machine, followed by a second, separate stage, responsible for adding back in any empty heads or prefixes.[14] By comparing the results of the two-stage engine against those shown earlier in (42), it should be clear that dividing up the computational burden up into two separate modules is a strategy that permits us to handle zero morphology in an efficient manner.

4.   Consequences and conclusions

This work has consequences for the properties of the grammar, the properties of the parser, and their interface. The results of the implementation bring evidence to the effect that the grammar and the parser are different systems. The grammar optimally derives asymmetrical relations in the [Spec [H Compl]] format. The parser optimally recovers asymmetrical relations where the basic relations are inverted. This cannot be otherwise as the grammar and the parser are two different systems. The grammar is a model of linguistic knowledge and the parser is a model of linguistic use. The systems may interface because of the asymmetrical properties of structural descriptions generated by the grammar.

We have provided further theoretical and empirical motivations for the projection of asymmetrical [Spec [H Compl]] structure in the derivation of words. This follows in a principled way from the theory. The implementations of this theory provided strong computational motivation for both specifier-right, complement-left pairing of morphological structure and for the separation of overt and non-overt affix heads into distinct modules.

Notes

1. This work is supported in part by funding from the Social Sciences and Humanities Research Council of Canada to the Asymmetry Project, grant number 214-97-0016, and by the NEC Research Institute. The asymmetric properties of morphological relations are discussed at length in Di Sciullo (2005).

2. See Di Sciullo & Williams 1987; Di Sciullo 1996a, b; Bach 1996; Williams 1994, among other works, for arguments motivating the non-isomorphy of morphological and syntactic derivations.

3. We assume that a relation is asymmetric in a set A if for each ordered pair (x, y) in A, there is no pair (y, x) in A. Asymmetric c-command is the typical relation that satisfies the property of an asymmetric relation in grammar. x asymmetrically c-commands y iff x and y are categories, and x excludes y, and every category that dominates x dominates y (Kayne 1994: 16). See also Epstein (1995), Robert & Vijay-Shanker (1995), Reuland (1997), and Chomsky (2001) for discussion of asymmetric c-command.

4. The configuration in (2) does not include bar levels, such as XP, X' and X, as in the standard X-bar notation. We will assume that maximal and minimal categories are identified configurationnally, as in Chomsky (1993), where a minimal category projects whereas a maximal category does not project anymore. However, we will assume bar-levels in the computational implementation of this paper, as they are part of PAPPI.

5. The [specifier [head complement]] configuration plays a crucial role in the derivation of the argument structure properties of morphological expressions, given a configurational representation of argument structure. (See Chomsky 1993, 1995, 1998; Di Sciullo 1996a, b; Hale & Keyser 1993, Pesetsky 1995, and related works.)

6. The architecture of our Model is defined in (Di Sciullo 1996a) and is based on the following hypotheses. According to the *Modularity of Computational Space* hypothesis, the computational space includes interacting types of derivations leading to optimal target types of configurations. The *Relativized Modularity* hypothesis, states that the principles of the grammar apply to types of derivations and interfaces according to their optimal target configurational properties. The differences between morphological and syntactic asymmetries follow in a principled way from the sort of grammatical derivations.

7. The small size of the grammar permits the adoption of full LR(1)-style parsing. The machines described here have of the order of about 100 states.

8. Features of the head such as link are also available at the maximal projection level.

9. By flipping the linear order of the head and complement, two other Specifier-Head-Complement configurations can be obtained. Here, we fix the head as being to the right of the complement for reasons of linearization.

10. This is a form of infinite looping. In the implementation, the amount of looping is controlled by a runtime adjustable limit on the number of consecutive empty categories that can be pushed onto the stack.

11. More precisely, the right Specifier model "garden-paths" for exactly one action at a particular shift/reduce conflict point for every affix. A more detailed analysis is beyond the scope of this paper.

12. A quick breakdown of the formula is in order here: to produce a two-bar-level structure, 2 reduce actions forming X' and X'' are required, plus another one for the xp specifier and a shift for the head. So the total is 4 per "phrase". The "plus 2" part of the formula comes from the accept and lowest complement xp reduce actions.

13. PAPPI implements it efficiently by checking for duplicates immediately at abstract affix insertion time.

14. The second stage actually consists of two smaller sub-modules, one responsible for *inc* and *caus* which runs in constant time, and the other for internal prefixes such as *en-*, running in time proportional to the depth of the parse.

References

Anderson, S. (1992). *A-Morphous Morphology*. Cambridge: Cambridge University Press.

Bach, E. (1996). On the grammar of complex words. In A. M. Di Sciullo (Ed.), *Configurations* (pp. 1–16). Summerville: Cascadilla Press.

Borer, H. (1991). The causative-inchoative alternation: A case study in parallel morphology. *The Linguistic Review, 8,* 119–158.

Chomsky, N. (1993). *Bare Phrase Structure*. Cambridge, Mass.: MIT Press.

Chomsky, N. (1995). *The Minimalist Program*. Cambridge, Mass.: MIT Press.

Chomsky, N. (1998). Minimalist inquiries. Ms. Cambridge, Mass.: MIT Press.

Chomsky, N. (2001). Derivation by phase. In M. Kenstowicz (Ed.), *Ken Hale: A Life in Language* (pp. 1–52). Cambridge, Mass: The MIT Press.

Di Sciullo, A. M. (1996a). X′ selection. In J. Roorick & L. Zaring (Eds.), *Phrase Structure and the Lexicon* (pp. 77–108). Dordrecht/Boston/London: Kluwer.

Di Sciullo, A. M. (1996b). Modularity and x^0/xp asymmetries. *Linguistic Analysis, 26,* 1–26.

Di Sciullo, A. M. (1997). Prefixed verbs and adjunct identification. In A.-M. Di Sciullo (Ed.), *Projections and Interface Conditions* (pp. 52–73). New York: Oxford University Press.

Di Sciullo, A. M. (1999a). Verbal structure and variation. In E. Trevino & J. Lema (Eds.), *Semantic Issues in Romance Syntax* (pp. 39–57). Amsterdam/Philadelphia: John Benjamins.

Di Sciullo, A. M. (1999b). The Local Asymmetry Connection. In L. Pylkkänen, A. van Hout, & H. Harley (Eds.), *Papers from the UPenn/MIT Roundtable on the Lexicon. MIT Working Papers in Linguistics* (pp. 26–45). Cambridge, Mass.

Di Sciullo, A. M. (Ed.). (2003a). *Asymmetry in Grammar. Vol. l: Syntax and Semantics.* Amsterdam: John Benjamins.

Di Sciullo, A. M. (Ed.). (2003b). *Asymmetry in Grammar. Vol. 2: Morphology, Phonology Acquisition.* Amsterdam: John Benjamins.

Di Sciullo, A. M. (2005). *Asymmetry in Morphology*. In press. Cambridge, Mass.: The MIT Press.

Di Sciullo, A. M. & Tenny C. (1997). Modification, event structure and the word/phrase asymmetry. In Kusumoto, K. (Ed.), *Proceedings of NELS 28* (pp. 375–389). GLSA: University of Massachusetts at Amherst.

Di Sciullo, A. M. & Williams, E. (1987). *On the Definition of Word*. Cambridge, Mass.: MIT Press.

Epstein, S. (1995). The derivation of syntactic relations. Ms. Harvard University.

Fong, S. (1991). Computational properties of principle-based grammatical theories. Ph.D. Dissertation. Artificial Intelligence Laboratory. MIT.

Grimshaw, J. (1990). *Argument Structure*. Cambridge, Mass.: MIT Press.

Hale, K. & Keyser, S. J. (1993). On argument structure and the lexical expression of syntactic relations. In K. Hale & S. J. Keyser (Eds.), *The View from Building 20* (pp. 53–109). Cambridge, Mass.: MIT Press.

Hale, K. & Keyser, S. J. (2002). *Prolegomena to a Theory of Argument Structure*. Cambridge, Mass.: MIT Press

Hale, K. & Marantz, A. (1993). Distributed morphology and the pieces of inflection. In K. Hale & S. J. Keyser (Eds.), *The View from Building* 20 (pp. 111–176). Cambridge, Mass.: MIT Press.

Kayne, R. (1994). *The Antisymmetry of Syntax*. Cambridge, Mass.: MIT Press.

Knuth, D. E. (1965). On the translation of languages from left to right. *Information and Control, 8* (6), 607–639.

Law, P. (1997). Modularity in nominalizations. In A.-M. Di Sciullo (Eds.), *Projections and Interface Conditions*. Oxford University Press.

Lieber, R. (1992). *Deconstructing Morphology*. University of Chicago Press.

Moro, A. (2000). *Dynamic Antisymmetry*. Cambridge, Mass.: MIT Press.

Pesetky, D. M. (1995). *Zero Syntax: Experiencers and Cascades*. Cambridge, Mass.: MIT Press.

Raimy, E. (2000). Remarks on backcopying. *Linguistic Inquiry, 31*, 541–552.

Raimy, E. (2003). Asymmetry and linearization in phonology. In A.M. Di Sciullo (Ed.), *Asymmetry in Grammar, Vol 2: Morphology, Phonology, Acquisition* (pp. 129–146). Amsterdam: John Benjamins.

Reuland, E. (1997). Deriving c-command in binding. In *NELS, 18*.

Roeper, T. & Keyser, J. (1995). Asymmetry and leftward movement in morphology. Ms, University of Massachusetts and MIT.

Robert, F. & Vijay-Shanker, K. (1995). C-command and grammatical primitives. In *GLOW Newsletter* (pp. 24–25).

Williams, E. (1981). Argument structure and morphology. *Linguistic Review, 1*, 81–114.

Williams, E. (1994). *Thematic Structure in Syntax*. Cambridge, Mass.: MIT Press.

A Minimalist implementation of Hale-Keyser incorporation theory

Sourabh Niyogi and Robert C. Berwick
Massachusetts Institute of Technology

At least since the classic work of Fillmore, traditional verb subcategorization models have required either numerous syntactic rules to cover alternative constructions and cross-language variation, or else complex linking rules mapping semantic event thematic roles to syntactic forms. Here we exhibit a third approach: an implemented parser and lexicon grounded on the incorporation theory of Hale & Keyser (1993, 1998). This model systematically covers most patterns in Levin's English Verb Classes and Alternations (Levin 1993), typically using only 1 or 2 lexical entries per verb. We replace the notion of "thematic roles" with precise structural configurations. The parser uses the Merge and Move operations formalized by Stabler (1997) in the minimalist framework of Chomsky (2001). As a side benefit, we extend the minimalist recognizer of Harkema (2000) to a full parsing implementation. We summarize the current compactness and coverage of our account and provide this minimalist lexicon and parser online at http://web.mit.edu/niyogi/www/minimal.htm

1. The problem of verb subcategorization

Why do certain verbs undergo particular certain alternations and not others? On some accounts for example, Levin (1993), referred to hereafter as EVCA, alternations provide insight into verb subcategorization and hence hooks to parsing, cross-language variation, machine translation, and class-based verb learning. However, fully implemented accounts of the phenomena remains an open problem, with at least three alternative models, displayed in Figure 1.

Accounts may be solely descriptive – for example, classifying verbs as having an intransitive, transitive, and/or ditransitive form, as is familiar. Traditional computational accounts (see Figure 1, Part 1) map these forms into individual grammar rules, (perhaps by macro expansion-like techniques) adding as many rules as nec-

---

0. Verb Subcategorization Phenomena

*Bob put.	Butter was put on the bread.
*Bob put butter.	What was put on the bread?
Bob put butter on the bread.	Where was the butter put?

1. Traditional

$VP \Rightarrow V0\ NP\ PP_{loc}$ $V0 \Rightarrow put$

$VP \Rightarrow was\ VPass$ $VPass \Rightarrow V0\ PP_{loc}$

$VP/NP \Rightarrow V0\ NP/NP\ PP_{loc}$ $VP/NP \Rightarrow V0\ NP\ PP_{loc}/NP$

$PP_{loc} \Rightarrow P_{loc}\ NP$ $P_{loc} \Rightarrow on \mid in \mid ...$

$PP_{loc}/NP \Rightarrow P_{loc}\ NP/NP$

Properties: Exhaustive modelling with a *considerable* number of grammatical rules. Semantics separate, otherwise unspecified.

2. Lexical Semantics

[put V NP_j PP_k CAUSE([BOB]$_i$, GO([BUTTER]$_j$, TO([BREAD]$_k$))))]
Properties: Syntax handled by numerous argument-fusing "linking rules", typically difficult to formalize. Semantic templates mirror alternation patterns, but are ad-hoc.

3. Hale-Keyser Incorporation

/put/ $=p_{loc:1,fg:1} =d\ v_1$ $(\lambda(=p_{loc:1,fg:1})\ (\lambda(=d)\ (=p_{loc:1,fg:1} =d)))$

/on/ $=d +k\ p_{loc:1,fg:1}$ $(\lambda(=d)\ (\lambda(x)\ ((go\ x)\ (path\ self =d))))$

// $>v_1 +k =d\ voice$ $(\lambda(>v_1)\ (\lambda(=d)\ ((cause\ >v_1) =d)))$

/-ed/ $>voice ++k\ t$ $(\lambda(>voice)\ (tense\ >voice\ 'past))$

Properties: *Small* number of lexical entries handle all syntactic phenomena.
Semantics *directly encoded* in lexical entry.
Entries structurally governed by small number of rules, specifying how N/A/P are related.

Figure 1. Three different accounts of verb subcategorization

essary to account for 'naturally' occurring constructions (wh-movement, passive forms, etc.) For each grammatical rule, a separate semantic decomposition is required, typically labeling component phrases with one of several "thematic roles." A richer account provided by lexical semantics (Figure 1, Part 2), exemplified in Jackendoff (1983, 1990) and Rappaport-Hovav & Levin (1998), is one that hypothesizes semantic templates, but this requires linking rules associating syntactic frames with semantic templates governed by a particular verb. Often these semantic templates are constructed in an ad hoc manner, and the corresponding linking rules are consequently a collection of difficult-to-implement heuristics. In this chapter we implement a rather different formalism (Hale & Keyser's Incorporation theory, Figure 1, Part 3), where fewer lexical entries govern syntactic and semantic behavior, with no appeal to thematic roles or complex linking rules.

Incorporation theory

At the heart of our new model of verb subcategorization is the marriage of Hale & Keyser's (1993, 1998) argument structure theory with Stabler's (1997) 'minimalist' structure building rules. In the Hale-Keyser theory, a particular head (labeled X), may or may not take a complement, 'C', and may or may not project a specifier, S, resulting in 4 possible structural configurations:

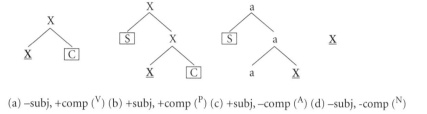

(a) −subj, +comp (V) (b) +subj, +comp (P) (c) +subj, −comp (A) (d) −subj, -comp (N)

Figure 2. Four fundamental primitives in Hale and Keyser's incorporation theory

The combinatorial possibilities of incorporation with X=V, P, A, N heads, plus "head movement," is designed to yield the space of possible syntactic argument structure configurations, presumably across all languages. Thematic role notions of agent, patient, instrument, theme, goal, etc. are not 'primitives', but are *derived* from positions in structural configurations. In English (but not necessarily in all languages), (a) the category V takes a complement but projects no specifier; (b) the category P takes both a complement and projects a specifier; (c) the category A takes no complement but projects a specifier; (d) the category N takes neither.

The combinatorial possibilities of incorporation with X=V, P, A, N heads, plus "head movement," are designed to yield the space of possible syntactic argument structure configurations, presumably across all languages. Thematic role notions of agent, patient, instrument, theme, goal, etc. are not 'primitives', but are *derived* from positions in structural configurations. In English (but not necessarily in all languages), (a) the category V takes a complement but projects no specifier; (b) the category P takes both a complement and projects a specifier; (c) the category A takes no complement but projects a specifier; (d) the category N takes neither complement nor specifier. A particular verbal entry, being of category V, may incorporate one or more of these structures as its complement, as in Figure 3.

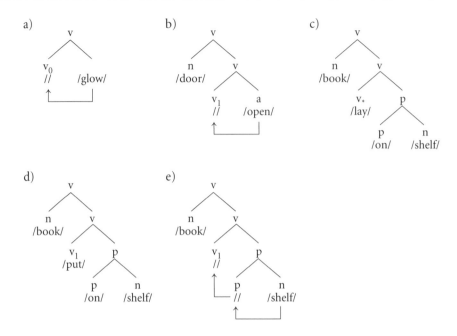

Figure 3. Examples of Structure Building in Hale and Keyser's Incorporation Theory

- Nouns incorporated directly into a verbal entry yield structures such as (a): no subject is projected by the N. The phonetic material of the noun head *incorporates* (undergoes *head movement*) into the phonetic material of the verb head, which itself may undergo further movement. Verbs such as these are intransitive by nature, generating, e.g., /The light glow -ed/ but */Bob glow -ed the light/. This argument structure typifies purely internally caused processes.

- Adjectives incorporated into a verbal entry yields structures such as (b): a subject is *projected* by the A (e.g. /the door/). The phonetic material of the adjective head *incorporates* into the verb head, which again, may undergo further movement. Verbs such as these are transitive by nature, resulting in /The door open -ed/ and /Bob open -ed the door/. This argument structure typifies externally causable state changes.

- Incorporated prepositions yield fundamentally transitive verbs such as (c), thus both /The book lay -ed on the shelf/ and /Bob lay -ed the book on the shelf/ is grammatical.

- To account for why /The book lay -ed on the shelf/ is grammatical but */Bob put -ed on the shelf/ is not, it is hypothesized that either the manner of the external argument (as in /put/) or the internal argument (as in /lay/) is indexed in the verbal entry, as shown in (d).

–   Multiple incorporations are possible, such as in (e), where a preposition is incorporated into a verbal entry, and the preposition itself has a noun incorporated into it (e.g. /shelf/) – the preposition *projects* a subject (e.g. /book/) through the verbal structure it is incorporated into. This kind of argument structure is common for figure-incorporation, ground-incorporation, and instrument-incorporation.

Minimalist operations

We can now show how one can implement Hale and Keyser's incorporation theory in the framework of the Minimalist Program (Chomsky 2000). In this framework, there are at least 2 fundamental structure-building operations, *Merge* and *Move*. Stabler (1997, 2000) has formalized these into 4 specific structure-building operations for *Merge* and 2 for *Move*. In this model, a lexical entry (a *simple* structure) has the following form:

/phonetic-content/ feature-list λ-expression

where phonetic-content (possibly null, denoted //) is what is actually pronounced, and feature-list is an ordered list of features chosen from a set of licensors (e.g. >a, <a, =a, marking theta role assignment), licensees (e.g. a, intuitively, marking an argument needing a theta-role), movement triggers (e.g. ++k, +k, intuitively, case assigners), and movement requirements (e.g. –k, intuitively, marking that an argument needs to be assigned case).

Structures can be *simple*, as in the above case, or *complex*, where the operation of *Merge* on two structures A and B (simple or complex) creates a new complex structure (A, B, <, λ-expression) or (B, A, >, λ-expression):

–   [A] the head of a Merge operation, whose feature-list is headed by a licensor and whose λ-expression is of the form (λ(=a) exp), whose body exp returns a semantic structure using semantic primitives and the argument =a
–   [B] the argument of Merge, whose feature-list is headed by a matching licensee and whose λ-expression is of any form val.

Here the > and < symbols denote which piece of the complex structure was the head prior to *Merge*. In this new complex structure, the resulting new internal A and B structures have the licensor-licensee feature pairs deleted, phonetic material may be rearranged, and the λ-expression of the licensor is applied to that of the licensee.

Move, operating on just one structure A, also cancels features (the movement triggers/requirements), but is semantically vacuous: the semantic result of the new

OPERATION	Example
Simple Merge	
/h/ =a $\delta(\lambda(=a)$ exp)	/the/ =n d –k $(\lambda(=n)$ =n)
/c/ a γ val	/book/ n self
=> (/h/ δ, /c/ γ, <, (($\lambda(=a)$ exp) val))	=> (/the/ d –k, /book/, <, ...)
Complex Merge	
(/h/ =a δ, ..., ..., ($\lambda(=a)$ exp))	(/put/ =d v_1, (/on/, (/the/, /shelf/, <), <),<, ...)
/s/ a γ... val	/what/ d –k –wh (unknown self)
=> (/s/ γ... (/h/ δ, ...), >, (($\lambda(=a)$ exp)	(/what/ –k –wh, (/put/ v_1, (/on/, (/the/, /shelf/,
val)) =>	<), <), <), >, ...)
Left Incorporate	
/h/ <a δ... ($\lambda(<a)$ exp)	/de-/ <$n_{fg:1,ter:0}$ =d v_1
/c/ a γ val	/bone/ $n_{fg:1,ter:0}$ self
=> (/h c/ δ, // γ, <, (($\lambda(<a)$ exp) val))	=> (/de- bone/ =d v_1, //, <, ...)
Right Incorporate	
/h/ >a δ... ($\lambda(>a)$ exp)	/–s/ >n d –k $(\lambda(>n)$ (plural >n))
/c/ a γ val	/book/ n self
=> (/c h/ δ, // γ, <, (($\lambda(>a)$ exp) val))	=> (/book -s/ d –k, //, <, (plural (book)))
Covert Move	
(... (/h/ +k δ, ...(/c/ –k γ, ...), ...)	(/open/ +k =d voice, (((/the/ –k, /door/, <),
=> (... (/h/ δ, ... (/c/ γ, ...), ...)	(//, //, <), >, ...)
	=> (/open/ =d voice, (((/the/, /door/, <),
	(//, //, <), >, ...)
Overt Move	
(... (/h/ ++k δ, ... (/c/ –k γ, ...), ...)	(/open -ed/ ++k t, (// voice, (((/the/ –k,
=> (/c/ γ, (... (/h/ δ, ... (*, ...), ...), >)	/door/, <), (//, //, <), >), <)
	=> (((/the/, /door/, <), (/open -ed/ t,
	(// voice, (*, (//, //, <), >), <), >, ...)

Figure 4. Minimalist structure-building rules: *Merge* and *Move*

complex has the same value as the old complex. To generate a derivation, structures undergo repeated Merge and Move operations, canceling pairs of features from the feature lists until no features remain except a single goal feature c, which specifies that a complete derivation has been constructed. We omit here the clear comparison to categorial grammar and its relatives; see Stabler (1997) and Berwick & Epstein (1995) for additional details. The *Merge* and *Move* rules, summarized from Stabler (1997), are exhibited in Figure 4.

We illustrate the use of the above structure-building rules with the following lexicon, deriving /Bob put -ed the book on the shelf/:

1. Simple Merge: /the/ =n d –k (λ(=n) =n) and /shelf/ n self => (/the/ d –k, /shelf/, <, (shelf))

2. Simple Merge: /on/ =d +k $p_{loc:1,fg:1}$ (λ(=d) (λ(x) ((go x) (path self =d)))) and (1) => (/on/ +k $p_{loc:1,fg:1}$, (/the/ –k, /shelf/, <), <, (λ(x) ((go x) (path (on) (shelf)))))

3. Covert Move: (2) => (/on/ $p_{loc:1,fg:1}$, (/the/, /shelf/, <), <, (...))

4. Simple Merge: /put/ =$p_{loc:1,fg:1}$ =d v_1 (λ(=$p_{loc:1,fg:1}$) (λ(=d) (=$p_{loc:1,fg:1}$=d))) and (3) => (/put/ =d v_1, (/on/, (/the/, /shelf/, <), <), <, (λ(=d) ((λ(x) ((go x) (path (on) (shelf)))) =d)))

5. Simple Merge: /the/ =n d –k (λ(=n) =n) and /book/ n self => (/the/ d –k, /book/, <, (book))

6. Complex Merge: (4) and (5) => ((/the/ –k, /book/, <), (/put/ v_1, (/on/, (/the/, /shelf/, <), <), <), >, ((go (book)) (path (on) (shelf))))

7. Right Incorporate: // >v_1 +k =d voice (λ(>v_1) (λ(=d) ((cause > v_1) =d))) and (6) => (/put/ +k =d voice, ((/the/ –k, /book/, <), (//, (/on/, (/the/, /shelf/, <), <), <), >), <, (λ(=d) ((cause ((go (book)) (path (on) (shelf)))) =d)))

8. Covert Move: (7) => (/put/ =d voice,(((/the/, /book/, <), (//, (/on/, (/the/, /shelf/, <), <), <), >), <, (...))

9. Complex Merge: /Bob/ d –k self and (7) => (/Bob/ –k, (/put/ voice, (((/the/, /book/, <), (//, (/on/, (/the/, /shelf/,<),<),<),>),<),>, ((cause ((go (book)) (path (on) (shelf)))) (Bob)))

10. Right Incorporate: /-ed/ >voice ++k t (λ(>voice) (tense >voice 'past)) and (9) => (/put -ed/ ++k t,(/Bob/ –k, (//, (((/the/, /book/,<),(//, (/on/, (/the/, /shelf/, <), <), <), >), <), >), <, (tense ((cause ((go (book)) (path (on) (shelf)))) (Bob)) 'past)

11. Overt Move: (10) => (/Bob/, (/put -ed/ t, (*, (//, (((/the/, /book/, <), (//, (/on/, (/the/, /shelf/, <),<),<),>),<),>),<),>, (...))

12. Simple Merge: // =t c (λ(=t) =t) and (11) => (// c, (/Bob/, (/put -ed/, (*, (//, (((/the/, /book/, <), (//, (/on/, (/the/, /shelf/, <),<),<),>),<),>),<),>),<, (tense ((cause ((go (book)) (path (on) (shelf)))) (Bob)) 'past))

Using semantic-structure building primitives such as:

unknown	(λ(x) '(? ,x))
query	(λ(event) '(query :event ,event)))
cause	(λ(event) (λ(agent) '(cause :agent ,agent :effect ,event)))
go	(λ(theme) (λ(path) '(go :theme ,theme :path ,path)))
path	(λ(dir ground) '(path :oper ,dir :terminal+ ,ground))
tense	(λ(event val) (append event (list ':tense val)))
become	(λ(a) (λ(thing) '(become :theme ,thing :goal ,a)))

we can reformat the result in any style desired, for example, as in Jackendoff (1983):

(cause :agent (bob) :effect
        (go :theme (book) :path (path :oper (onto) :terminal+ (shelf)))
:tense past)

Using a small number of additional entries:

/did/ =voice +k t	(λ(=voice) (query (tense =voice 'past)))
/where/ $p_{loc:1,fg:1}$ –wh	(λ(x) ((go x) (path () (unknown self))))
// =t ++wh c	(λ(=t) =t)
/what/ d –k –wh	(unknown self)
/who/ d –k –wh	(unknown self)

we can derive /what did Bob put on the shelf/:

4. See above =>
    (/put/ =d v_1, (/on/, (/the/, /shelf/, <), <), <, (λ(x) ((go x) (path (on) (shelf)))))

5. Complex Merge: /what/ d –k –wh (unknown self) and (4) =>
    (/what/ –k –wh, (/put/ v_1, (/on/, (/the/, /shelf/, <), <), <), >, ((go (unknown self)) (path (on) (shelf))))

6. Right Incorporate: // >v_1 +k =d voice (λ(>v_1) (λ(=d) ((cause >v_1) =d))) and (5) => (/put/ +k =d voice, (/what/ –k –wh, (//, (/on/, (/the/, /shelf/, <), <), <), >), <, (λ(=d) ((cause ((go (unknown self)) (path (on) (shelf)))) =d)))

7. Covert Move: (6) =>(/put/ =d voice, (/what/ –wh, (//, (/on/, (/the/, /shelf/,<), <),<),>),<, (λ(=d) ((cause ((go (unknown self)) (path (on) (shelf)))) =d)))

8. Complex Merge: /Bob/ d –k self and (7) => (/Bob/ –k, (/put/ voice, (/what/ –wh, (//, (/on/, (/the/, /shelf/, <), <), <), >), <), >, ((cause ((go (unknown self)) (path (on) (shelf)))) (Bob)))

9. Simple Merge: /did/ =voice +k t (λ(=voice) (query (tense =voice 'past))) and (8) => (/did/ +k t, (/Bob/ –k, (/put/, (/what/ –wh, (//, (/on/, (/the/, /shelf/, <), <), <), >), <), >), <, (query (tense ((cause ((go (unknown self)) (path (on) (shelf)))) (Bob)) 'past))))

10. Covert Move: (9) => (/did/ t, (/Bob/, (/put/, (/what/ –wh, (//, (/on/, (/the/, /shelf/,<), <), <), >), <), >), <,(...))))

11. Simple Merge: // =t ++wh c (λ(=t) =t) and (10) => (// ++wh c, (/did/, (/Bob/, (/put/, (/what/ –wh, (//, (/on/, (/the/, /shelf/, <), <),<),>),<),>),<), <, (...))))

12. Overt Move: (11) => (/what/, (// c, (/did/, (/Bob/, (/put/, (*, (//, (/on/, (/the/, /shelf/, <), <), <), >), <), >), <), <), >, (query (tense ((cause ((go (unknown self)) (path (on) (shelf)))) (Bob)) 'past)))) => (query :event (cause :agent (bob) :effect (go :theme (? (what)) :path (path :oper (on) :terminal+ (shelf))) :tense past))

It is straightforward to show that we can derive simple wh-movement variations on the above in a comparable number of steps:

/What did Bob put the book on/
=> (query : event (cause :agent (bob) :
          effect (go :theme (book) :path (path :oper (on) :terminal+
(? (what)))) :tense past))

/Where did Bob put the book/
=> (query : event (cause :agent (bob)
          :effect (go :theme (book) :path (path :oper () :terminal+
(? (where)))):tense past))

Likewise, we derive passive forms with 3 new entries:

/was/ <voice$_p$ ++k t (λ(<voice$_p$) (tense <voice$_p$ 'past))
/-ed/ >v$_1$ =p$_p$? voice$_p$ (λ(>v$_1$) (λ(=p$_p$) (=p$_p$ >v$_1$)))
/by/ =d +k =p$_p$ (λ(=d) (λ(event) ((cause event) =d)))

Note how =p$_p$ is encoded as an optional licensor feature, marked with a ? in the entry for /-ed/. This is *Optional Merge*, where the licensor feature can be cancelled without a corresponding licensee feature. However, the semantic value of the missing licensee is taken from a database of λ-expression applications, one per licensee possibility, generated through an application of what would ordinarily be expected in such a position. For example, for the licensor =p$_p$, the semantic value for the missing licensee is ((λ(=d) (λ(event) ((cause event) =d))) 'somebody), i.e. the same merge as /by/ /somebody/. Illustrating the course of the derivation of /the book was put -ed on the shelf/:

6. See above => (((/the/ –k,/book/,<),(/put/ v$_1$, (/on/, (/the/, /shelf/, <), <), <), >, ((go (book)) (path (on) (shelf)))

7. Simple Merge: /-ed/ >v$_1$ =p$_p$? voice$_p$ (λ(>v$_1$) (λ(=p$_p$) (=p$_p$ >v$_1$))) and (6) => (/put -ed/ =p$_p$? voice$_p$, (((/the/ –k, /book/, <), (//, (/on/, (/the/, /shelf/, <), <), <), >), <, (λ(=p$_p$) (=p$_p$ ((go (book)) (path (on) (shelf)))))

8. Optional Merge: (7) with ((λ(=d) (λ(event) ((cause event) =d))) 'somebody) => (/put -ed/ =p$_p$? voice$_p$, (((/the/ –k, /book/, <), (//, (/on/, (/the/, /shelf/, <), <), <), <), >), <, ((cause ((go (book)) (path (on) (shelf)))) 'somebody))

9. Left Incorporate: /was/ <voice$_p$ ++k t (λ(<voice$_p$) (tense <voice$_p$ 'past)) and (8) => (/was put -ed/ ++k t, (//,(((/the/ –k,/book/,<), (//, (/on/, (/the/, /shelf/, <), <), <), >), <), <, (tense ((cause ((go (book)) (path (on) (shelf))))) 'somebody) 'past))

10. Overt Movement: (9) => (((/the/, /book/, <), (/was put -ed/ t,(//, (*, (//, (/on/, (/the/, /shelf/, <), <), <), >), <), <), >, (...))

11. Simple Merge: // =t c and (10) => (// c,(((/the/, /book/, <), (/was put -ed/, (//,(*,
//, (/on/, (/the/, /shelf/, <), <), <), >), <), <), >), <, (tense ((cause ((go (book))
(path (on) (shelf))))) 'somebody) 'past)) => (cause :agent (somebody) :effect
(go :theme (book) :path (path :oper (on) :terminal+ (shelf))))

Using the above rules, we have thus extended the work of Harkema (2000) from
a recognizer to a parser: it is straightforward to design a bottom-up chart-based
parser that recovers the derivation steps and semantic structure from a given input
sentence. See Appendix A for the basic algorithm.

Incorporation

We now show how Hale and Keyser's Incorporation theory can be implemented
with the above minimalist framework, recognizing that other grammatical frameworks, such as lexicalized Tree Adjoining Grammars (e.g. Vijay-Shanker & Weir
1999) or categorial grammars (e.g. Steedman 2000), are likely to be capable of
implementing the same theory. Using Incorporation theory, we will show how A-
incorporation, P-incorporation, and N-incorporation compact grammars to a very
small number of entries (1 or 2) per verb.

A-Incorporation

Adding just 5 new entries to the grammar we have built so far:

/open/[(45.4)] a	self
// >a =d v*	$(\lambda(>a) (\lambda(=d) ((become >a) =d)))$
// >v* +k =d voice	$(\lambda(>v*) (\lambda(=d) ((cause >v*) =d)))$
// >v* voice	$(\lambda(>v*) >v*)$
/-ed/ >v* =p_p? voice_p	$(\lambda(>v*) (\lambda(=p_p) (=p_p >v*)))$

derives /The door open -ed/:

1. Simple Merge: /the/ =n d –k $(\lambda(=n) =n)$ and /door/ n self => (/the/ d –k,
   /door/, <, (door))
2. Right Merge: // >a =d v* $(\lambda(>a) (\lambda(=d) ((become >a) =d)))$ and /open/ a self
   => (/open/ =d v*, //, <, $(\lambda(=d) ((become (open)) =d)))$
3. Complex Merge: (1) and (2) => (((/the/ –k, /door/, <), (/open/ v*, //, <), >,
   ((become (open)) (door)))
4. Right Merge: // >v* voice $(\lambda(>v*) >v*)$ and (3) => (/open/ voice, (((/the/ –k,
   /door/, <), (//, //, <), >, (...))

5. Simple Merge: /-ed/ >voice ++k t and (4) => (/open -ed/ ++k t, (//, (((/the/ –k, /door/, <), (//, //, <), >), <, (tense ((become (open)) (door))) 'past))

6. Overt Move: (5) => (((/the/, /door/,<), (/open -ed/ t, (//, (*, (//, //, <), >), <), >, (...))

7. Simple Merge: // =t c (λ(=t) =t) and (5) => (// c, (((/the/, /door/, <), (/open -ed/, (//, (*, (//, //, <), >), <), >), <,(...))

=> (become :theme (door) :goal (open) :tense past)

Likewise, the derivation of /Bob open -ed the door/ proceeds from step (3) above as follows:

4. Right Merge: // >v⋆ +k =d voice (λ(>v⋆) (λ(=d) ((cause > v⋆) =d))) and (3) => (/open/ +k =d voice,(((/the/ –k,/door/,<), (//, //, <),>, (λ(=d) ((cause ((become (open)) (door))) =d)))

5. Covert Move: (4) => (/open/ =d voice, (((/the/, /door/, <), (//, //, <), >, (...))

6. Simple Merge: (5) and /Bob/ d –k self => (/Bob/ –k, (/open/ voice, (((/the/, /door/, <), (//, //, <), >), >, ((cause ((become (open)) (door))) (Bob)))

7. Simple Merge: /-ed/ >voice ++k t (λ(>voice) (tense >voice 'past)) and (6) => (/open -ed/ ++k t, (/Bob/ –k, (//, (((/the/, /door/, <), (//, //, <), >), >, (tense ((cause ((become (open)) (door))) (Bob)) 'past))

8. Overt Move: (7) => (/Bob/, (/open -ed/ t, (*, (// voice, (((/the/, /door/, <), (//, //, <), >), >), >, (...))

9. Simple Merge: // =t c (λ(=t) =t) and (8) => (// c, (/Bob/, (/open -ed/, (*, (// voice, (((/the/, /door/, <), (//, //, <), >), >), >), <, (...)))

=> (cause :agent (bob) :effect (become :theme (door) :goal (open)) :tense past)

We derive passives and questions using the lexical entries above as well:

/the door was open -ed/
=> (cause :agent (somebody) :effect (become :theme (door) :goal (open)) :tense past)
/who open -ed the door/
=> (cause :agent (? (who)) :effect (become :theme (door) :goal (open)) :tense past)
/what open -ed/
=> (become :theme (? (what)) :goal (open)) :tense past)
/what was open -ed/
=> (cause :agent (somebody) :effect (become :theme (? (what)) :goal (open)) :tense past)
/did bob open the door/
=> (query :event (cause :agent (bob) :effect (become :theme (door) :goal

(open)) :tense past))
/Was Bob open -ed the door/
/Who open the door/
/What was open (by Bob)/
/What did open -ed (by Bob)/

P-Incorporation

We have already seen how verbal entries incorporate prepositional entries: /put/ selects $p_{loc:1,fg:1}$, and "locative" prepositions such as /onto/, /on/, /in/, /into/, /below/, etc., have entries of the same form:

/onto/ =d +k $p_{loc:1,fg:1,ter:1}$ (λ(=d) (λ(x) ((go x) (path self =d))))

For a verbal entry like /lay/, on the other hand, we require a separate entry:

/lay/ =$p_{loc:1,fg:1,ter:-}$ =d v* (λ(=$p_{loc:1,fg:1,ter:-}$) (λ(=d) (=$p_{loc:1,fg:1,ter:-}$ =d)))

where "stative locative" prepositions /on/ but not /onto/, /in/ but not /into/, etc. have $p_{loc:1,fg:1,ter:-}$ entries:

/on/ =d +k $p_{loc:1,fg:1,ter:-}$ (λ(=d) (λ(x) ((be-location x) (place self =d))))

which are differentiated by the ter feature.

This derives, as desired:

/Book -s lay -ed on/*onto the shelf/
=> (be-location : patient (plural (book))
                     : location (place :oper (on) :location (shelf)) :tense past)
/Bob lay -ed book -s on/*onto the shelf/
=> (cause : agent (bob)
            : effect (be-location : patient (plural (book)))
                     : location (place :oper (on) (shelf)) :tense
past)

As another illustration of preposition incorporation, consider the dative alternation (/Bob give -ed water to Sue/ /Bob give -ed Sue water/). In this case, we have 2 entries for /give/ (cf. Pinker (1989)), one for the *to*-form and another for the "double object" form, and have similar entries for other "spaces" of location, identity, and information, shown in Figure 5.

The /to/ preposition codes the + terminal of a path, and the "space" is marked to differentiate between verbs of transfer. Otherwise the derivation of /Bob give -ed water to Sue/ is similar to /Bob put -ed the book on the shelf/. The dative form

Space	/to/ =d +k $p_{b:1,ter:1}$ $(\lambda(=d)\ (\lambda(x)$ $((go\ x)\ (path+\ =d))))$	// =d =d p_{have} $(\lambda(=d)\ (\lambda(=d2)$ $((have\ =d)\ =d2)))$
Possession	/give/$^{(13.1)}$ =$p_{b:1,ter:1}$ =d v_1 $(\lambda(=p_{b:1,ter:1})\ (\lambda(=d)$ $(space\ 'poss\ (=p_{b:1,ter:1}\ =d))))$ /Bob give -ed water to Sue/	/give/$^{(13.1)}$ =p_{have}? +k ++k v_2 $(\lambda(=p_{have})$ $(space\ 'poss\ =p_{have}))$ /Bob give -ed Sue water/
Location	/send/$^{(11.1)}$ =$p_{b:1,ter:1}$? =d v_1 $(\lambda(=p_{b:1,ter:1})\ (\lambda(=d)$ $(space\ 'loc\ (=p_{b:1,ter:1}\ =d))))$ /Bob send -ed a letter to Sue/	/send/$^{(11.1)}$ =p_{have}? +k ++k v_2 $(\lambda(=p_{have})\ (space\ 'loc\ =p_{have}))$ /Bob send -ed Sue a letter/
Identity	/turn/$^{(26.6)}$ =$p_{b:1,ter:1}$ =$p_{b:1,ter:0}$? = d v_* $(\lambda(=p_{b:1,ter:1})\ (\lambda(=p_{b:1,ter:0})\ (\lambda(=d)$ $(space\ 'ident\ (combine\text{-}paths$ $(=p_{b:1,ter:1}\ =d)\ (=p_{b:1,ter:0}\ =d))))))$ /Bob turn -ed (from a prince) into a frog/	/appoint/$^{(26.1)}$ =p_{have}? +k ++k v_2 $(\lambda(=p_{have})\ (space\ 'ident\ =p_{have}))$ /Sue appoint -ed Bob sheriff/
Information	/read/$^{(37.1)}$ =$p_{b:1,ter:1}$? =d v_1 $(\lambda(=p_{b:1,ter:1})\ (\lambda(=d)$ $(space\ 'info\ (=p_{b:1,ter:1}\ =d))))$ /Bob read -ed a story to Sue/	/read/$^{(37.1)}$ =p_{have}? +k ++k v_2 $(\lambda(=p_{have})\ (space\ 'info\ =p_{have}))$ /Bob read -ed Sue a story/

Figure 5. Different spaces with P-incorporation

is different, and results in a different semantic gloss. Following Baker (1997) and Harley (2000), the double object form derivation is:

1. Simple Merge: // =d =d p_{have} $(\lambda(=d)\ (\lambda(=d2)\ ((have\ =d)\ =d2)))$ and /Sue/ d –k self = (// =d p_{have}, /Sue/ –k, <, $(\lambda(=d2)\ ((have\ (Sue))\ =d2)))$

2. Complex Merge: (1) and /water/ d –k self => (/water/ –k, (// phave, /Sue/ –k, <), >, ((have (Sue)) (water)))

3. Simple Merge: (2) and /give/ =p_{have} +k ++k v_2 $(\lambda(=p_{have})\ (space\ 'poss\ =p_{have}))$ => (/give/ +k ++k v_2, (/water/ –k, (//, /Sue/ –k, <), >), <, (space 'poss ((have (Sue))(water))))

4. Covert Move: (3) => (/give/ ++k v_2, (/water/, (//, /Sue/ –k, <), >), <, (...))

5. Overt Move: (4) => (/Sue/, (/give/ v_2, (/water/, (//, *, <), >), <), >, (...))

6. Right Incorporate: (5) and // >v_2 =d voice $(\lambda(>v_*)\ (\lambda(=d)\ ((cause\ >v_*)\ =d)))$ => (/give/ =d voice, (/Sue/, (//, (/water/, (//, *, <), >), <), >), <, $(\lambda(=d)\ ((cause$ (space 'poss ((have (Sue)) (water)))) =d))))

7. Complex Merge: (6) and /Bob/ d –k self => (/Bob/ –k, (/give/ voice, (/Sue/, (//, (/water/, (//, *, <), >), <), >), <), >, ((cause (space 'poss ((have (Sue)) (water))) (Bob)))

8. Right Incorporate: (7) and /-ed/ >voice ++k t (λ(>voice) (tense >voice 'past))
   => (/give -ed/ ++k t, (/Bob/ −k, (//, (/Sue/, (//, (/water/, (//, *, <), >), <), >),
   <), >), >, (tense ((cause (space 'poss ((have (Sue)) (water))) (Bob)) 'past))
9. Overt Move: (8) => (/Bob/, (/give -ed/ t, (*,(//, (/Sue/, (//, (/water/, (//,*,<),>),
   <), >), <), >), >), >, (...))
10. Simple Merge: (9) and // =t c => (// c, (/Bob/, (/give -ed/, (*, (//, (/Sue/, (//,
    (/water/, (//, *, <), >), <), >), <), >), >), >), >, (tense ((cause (space 'poss
    ((have (Sue)) (water))) (Bob)) 'past))

=> (cause :agent (bob) :effect (have :possessor (Sue) :theme (water) :space 'poss)
:tense past)

N-Incorporation

Nouns incorporate trivially into verbs, as with verbs like /glow/, or into prepositions, which can be incorporated into verbs in turn, as with verbs like /butter/
(figure), /shelf/ (ground), and /shovel/ (instruments); see Figure 6. Considering
the derivation of /Bob shelf -ed the book/ vs. /Bob butter -ed the bread/, the core
distinction is in how the arguments /the book/ and /the bread/ are applied to the
two primitives $p_{loc:1,fg:1}$ and $p_{loc:1,fg:0}$ that have different orders of selecting "figure"
and "ground".

$p_{loc:1,fg:1}$ (λ(figure) (λ(ground) ((go figure) (path () ground))))
$p_{loc:1,fg:0}$ (λ(ground) (λ(figure) ((go figure) (path () ground))))

The two derivations proceed identically in form, but result in a different semantic structure as a result of the above figure-ground reversal:

/Bob butter -ed the bread/
=> (cause :agent (bob)
        :effect (go :theme (butter) :path (path :oper (bread) :terminal+
())) :tense past)
/Bob shelf -ed the book/
=> (cause :agent (bob)
        :effect (go :theme (book) :path (path :oper (shelf) :terminal+
())) :tense past)

The same alternation patterns seen in /butter/, /shelf/, and /shovel/ can be observed in a variety of other "spaces" in addition to the "location" space – removal,
possession, impression, identity, emotion, information, body possession, material
possession, and perceptual space as can be seen in Figure 6.

Root/Nominal Entry	Verbal Entry	EVCA Sections
Processes/Activities		
$/\text{glow}/^{(40.2)}$ n_{emission} Ex: /a glow/	$// >n_{\text{emission}}\ v_0$ $(\lambda(>n_{\text{emission}})\ (\text{do} >n_{\text{emission}}))$ Ex: /The light glow -ed/	
Figures		
$/\text{butter}/^{(9.9)}$ $n_{\text{fg:1,loc:1,d:1}}$ Ex: /the butter/, /butter/	$// >n_{\text{fg:1,loc:1}} =d\ v_1$ $(\lambda(>n_{\text{fg:1,loc:1}})\ (\lambda(=d)$ $((p_{\text{loc:1,fg:1}} =d) >n_{\text{fg:1,loc:1}})))$ Ex: /Bob butter -ed the bread/	$/\text{pit}/^{(10.7)}$, $/\text{whale}/^{(13.7)}$, $/\text{cut}/^{(21.1)}$, $/\text{dye}/^{(24)}$, $/\text{autograph}/^{(25.3)}$, $/\text{calf}/^{(28)}$, $/\text{knight}/^{(29.8)}$, $/\text{love}/^{(31.2)}$, $/\text{whisper}/^{(37.3)}$, $/\text{vomit}/^{(40.1.2)}$, $/\text{braid}/^{(41.2.2)}$, $/\text{smell}/^{(43.3)}$, $/\text{fracture}/^{(54.2)}$
Grounds		
$/\text{shelf}/^{(9.10)}$ $n_{\text{fg:0,loc:1}}$ Ex: /a shelf/	$// >n_{\text{fg:0,loc:1}} =d\ v_1$ $(\lambda(>n_{\text{fg:0,loc:1}})\ (\lambda(=d)$ $((p_{\text{loc:1,fg:0}} =d) >n_{\text{fg:0,loc:1}})))$ Ex: /Bob shelf -ed the book/	$/\text{mine}/^{(10.9)}$, $/\text{videotape}/^{(25.4)}$, $/\text{tutor}/^{(29.8)}$
Instruments		
$/\text{shovel}/^{(9.3)}$ $n_{\text{inst:1,loc:1}}$ Ex: /the shovel/	$// >n_{\text{inst:1,loc:1}} =p_{\text{loc:1,fg:1}}? =d\ v_1$ $(\lambda(>n_{\text{inst:1,loc:1}})\quad (\lambda(=p_{\text{loc:1,fg:1}})$ $(\lambda(=d)$ $((\text{using} >n_{\text{inst:1,loc:1}})\ (=p_{\text{loc:1,fg:1}}$ $=d)))))$ Ex: /Bob shovel -ed the dirt (onto the truck)/	$/\text{mop}/^{(10.4.2)}$, $/\text{whip}/^{(8.3)}$, $/\text{clamp}/^{(2.4)}$, $/\text{pencil}/^{(25.2)}$, $/\text{email}/^{(37.4)}$, $/\text{ferry}/^{(11.5)}$, $/\text{cycle}/^{(51.4.1)}$, $/\text{paddle}/^{(51.4.2)}$

Figure 6. Different kinds of N-incorporation

Implementation Analysis

We have modeled all of the verb classes in Levin (1993) through combinations of N-incorporation, A-incorporation, and P-incorporation in verbal entries. Our current lexicon contains a total of 347 entries, where:

- 199 are verbal entries. Frequently, one entry covers more than 1 EVCA verb class.
- 51 are pure root entries (e.g. /glow/ n_{emission}), 37 are nominalizing entries (e.g. $// >n_{\text{emission}}$ n)
- 20 are preposition entries (e.g. /on/ $=d +k\ p_{\text{loc:1,fg:1}}$). One entry often covers more than one preposition (e.g. /on/, /in/)
- 81 are "other" entries (e.g. $// =t$ c), including noun entries.

INTRANSITIVES : Not Externally Causable	/The light glow -ed/ */Bob glow -ed the light/
$// >v_0$ voice $\quad\quad (\lambda(>v_0)\,(>v_0 =d))$	$/glow/^{(40.2)}\; n_{emission}$ self $// >n_{emission}\; v_0 \quad\quad (\lambda(>v_0)$ $(do >n_{emission}))$
INTRANSITIVE/TRANSITIVES: Externally Causable	/The door open -ed/ /Bob open -ed the door/
$// >v_* +k =d$ voice $(\lambda(>v_*)\,((cause >v_*) =d))$ $// >v_*$ voice $\quad\quad\quad (\lambda(>v_*)\,>v_*)$ $/-ed/ >v_* =p_p?$ voice$_p \quad (\lambda(=p_p)\,(=p_p >v_*))$	$/open/^{(45.4)}$ a $\quad\quad$ self $// >a\; v_*\; (\lambda(>a)\,(\lambda(=d)\,((become >a)$ $=d)))$
TRANSITIVES : Externally Caused	/Bob put -ed the book on the shelf/
$// >v_1 +k =d$ voice $(\lambda(>v_1)\,((cause >v_1) =d))$ $/-ed/ >v_1 =p_p?$ voice$_p \quad (\lambda(=p_p)\,(=p_p >v_1))$	$/put/ \quad\quad =p_{loc:1,fg:1} =d\; v_1$ $(\lambda(=p_{loc:1,fg:1})\,(\lambda(=d)\,(=p_{loc:1,fg:1} =d)))$
DITRANSITIVES : Externally Caused	/Bob give -ed Sue the book/
$// >v_2 =d$ voice $\quad (\lambda(>v_2)\,((cause >v_2)=d))$ $/-ed/ >v_2 =p_p?$ voice$_p \quad (\lambda(=p_p)\,(=p_p >v_2))$	$/give/ =p_{have} +k ++k\; v_2(\lambda(=p_{have})$ $=p_{have})$

Figure 7. Broad verb classes in our implementation

Of the 199 verbal entries (marked with v_0, v_*, v_1, etc.), 142 contain 1 or more instances of P-incorporation, 60 contain N-incorporation, and 4 contain A-incorporation. To the extent that the core meaning of the verbs is reflected in the types of structures that are incorporated, this illustrates how prevalent incorporation is. At present, these verbal entries fall into traditional broad classes.

However, the *reason* a particular verb is in a particular verb class requires appealing to notions of whether an event is not externally causable (/glow/ vs. /open/), or whether it must be externally caused (/lay/ vs. /put/). Verbs such as /open/ (A-incorporation) or /lay/ (P-incorporation) are of the v_* class, and need only one entry to generate 2 alternation patterns, as discussed earlier. Verbs such as /put/, on the other hand, require only one entry because they have only one canonical surface realization, and *must* be externally caused. In some cases, verbs such as /give/ require two entries for each of their canonical surface realizations. A very small number of entries (3) generate all the passive forms for the v_*, v_1, v_2 broad classes: one for each class.

For the 183 verb classes of EVCA, a distributional analysis of entries per class reveals that 141 sections have exactly 1 entry in our lexicon (e.g. the /put/ class, the /lay/ class, the /open/ class), 32 sections have exactly 2 entries in our lexicon (e.g. the /give/ class), and only 10 sections have 3 or more entries in our lexicon (e.g. the /email/ class). Using incorporation theory, we have reduced the vast majority of EVCA sections (77%) to just 1 entry. Only a minority (42/183, 23%) need more than 1 entry, and we suspect that some of these may reduce to 1 entry with further analysis. We should simultaneously stress, however, that at present not all alternations described in Levin (1993) can be currently modeled fully, requiring new operations (selection, adjunction, agreement, reflexives, particles, aspect, etc.) We summarize our present coverage in Figure 8.

ALTERNATIONS MODELED	ALTERNATIONS NOT MODELED
Modeled, does not need 2 entries:	Requires selection/adjunction:
1.1.2 Causative	2.5 Reciprocal Alternations
2.4.3/2.4.4 Total Transformation	2.13 Possessor-Attribute Factoring Alterna-
5.1 Verbal Passive	tions
5.2 Prepositional Passive	3.1 Time Subject Alternation
	3.2 Natural Force Subject Alternation
Currently requires 2 or more entries	3.3 Instrument Subject Alternation
but probably can be reduced to 1:	3.4 Abstract Cause Subject Alternation
1.1.1 Middle (+effect)	3.5 Locatum Subject Alternation
1.3 Conative (+motion, +contact)	3.6 Location Subject Alternation
2.12 Body-Part Possessor Ascension Alter-	3.7 Container Subject Alternation
nation	3.8 Raw Material Subject
7.1 Cognate Object Construction	3.9 Sum of Money Subject Alternation
7.2 Cognate Prepositional Phrase Con-	3.10 Source Subject Alternation
struction	7.3 Reaction Object Construction
Modeled, currently needs 2 entries when 2	7.4 X's Way Construction
alternations possible:	7.5 Resultative Construction
1.1.3 Substance / Source Alternation	7.8 Direction Phrases with Nondirected
1.2 Unexpressed Object Alternation	Motion
1.4. Preposition Drop Alternation	8.5 Obligatory Adverb
2.1 Dative (give)	8.6 Obligatory Negative Polarity Element
2.2 Benefactive (carve)	Requires binding/reflexive operations:
2.3 Locative Alternation	4.1 Virtual Reflexive Alternation
2.4.1/2.4.2 Material/Product Alternation	4.2 Reflexive of Appearance
2.6 Fulfilling Alternation	5.3/5.4 Adjectival Passive
2.7 Image Impression Alternation	6.1 There-insertion
2.8 With/Against Alternation	7.6 Unintentional Interpretation of Object
2.9 Through/With Alternation	7.7 Bound Nonreflexive Anaphor as Prepo-
2.10 Blame Alternation	sitional Object
2.11 Search Alternation	8.1 Obligatory Passive
2.14 As Alternation	8.2 Obligatory Reflexive Object
	8.3 Inalienably Possessed Body-Part
	8.4 Expletive It Object

Figure 8. Coverage of the current implementation

Our reduction to one or two entries per verb class is in stark contrast to a typical CFG, which would contain many more entries. Whereas /lay/ =d =$p_{loc:1,fg:1,ter:-}$ is represented with 1 entry in our implementation, we would expect at least seven grammar rules to handle basic constructions in a typical CFG:

VP => V0 NP PP$_{loc}$	/He lay -ed the book on the shelf/
VP => V0 PP$_{loc}$	/The book lay -ed on the shelf/
VPass => V0 PP$_{loc}$	/The book was lay -ed on the shelf/
VP/NP => V0 PP$_{loc}$/NP	/What did the book lay on/
VP/NP => V0 NP/NP PP$_{loc}$	/What was lay -ed on the shelf/
VP/PP => V0 PP$_{loc}$/PP	/Where did the book lay/
VP/NP => V0 NP PP$_{loc}$ /NP	/Where was the book lay -ed/

We do not claim that the minimalist implementation presented here is the only account that can reduce the majority of EVCA verb classes to just one entry per verb. It is likely that other frameworks such as lexicalized TAGs or categorial grammars (e.g. Vijay-Shankar & Weir 1999; Steedman 2000) that also compactly handle movement, passivization, and the like can also simulate Hale and Keyser incorporation operations present in our implementation, resulting in a more compact grammar/lexicon. The key lesson to be learned is that by implementing Hale and Keyser's incorporation theory in *some* framework, there is enormous compaction, resulting in a grammar that is more easily engineered or learned.

Our parser and lexicon (written in MIT Scheme), and an extensive array of sample derivations and resulting semantic structures is freely available at http://web.mit.edu/niyogi/www/minimal.htm

Acknowledgements

We thank Kenneth Hale and Jay Keyser for valuable discussions. This work was supported in part by a Provost's grant to Joel Moses and supported in part by the National Science Foundation under grant NSF-KDI #ECS-9873451.

References

Baker, M. (1997). Thematic roles and syntactic structure. In L. Haegeman (Eds.), *Elements of Grammar: Handbook of Generative Syntax* (pp. 73–137). Dordrecht: Kluwer.

Berwick, R. C. & Epstein, S. (1995). Computational minimalism: The convergence of the minimalist syntactic program and categorial grammar. AMILP '95 Workshop.

Chomsky, N. (2000). Minimalist inquiries. In R. Martin, D. Michaels, & J. Uriagereka (Eds.), *Step by Step: Essays on Minimalist Syntax in Honor of Howard Lasnik*. (pp. 89–155). Cambridge, Mass.: MIT Press.

Chomsky, N. (2001). Derivation by phase. In M. Kenstowicz (Ed.), *Ken Hale: A Life in Language* (pp. 1–52). Cambridge, Mass.: MIT Press.

Harley, H. (2000). Possession and the double object construction. Ms., University of Arizona.

Hale, K. & Keyser, S. J. (1993). On argument structure and lexical expression of syntactic relations. In K. Hale & S. J. Keyser (Eds), *The View from Building 20* (pp. 53–109). Cambridge, Mass.: MIT Press.

Hale, K. & Keyser, S. J. (1998). The basic elements of argument structure. In H. Harley (Ed.), *Papers from the UPenn/MIT Roundtable on Argument Structure and Aspect* (pp. 73–118). *MIT Working Papers in Linguistics, 32*. Cambridge, Mass.

Harkema, H. (2000). A recognizer for minimalist grammars. In the Sixth International Workshop on Parsing Technologies (IWPT).

Jackendoff, R. S. (1983). *Semantics and Cognition*. Cambridge, Mass.: MIT Press.

Jackendoff, R. S. (1990). *Semantic Structures*. Cambridge, Mass.: MIT Press.

Levin, B. (1993). *English Verb Classes and Alternations: A Preliminary Investigation*. Chicago, Illinois: University of Chicago Press.

Pinker, S. (1989). *Learnability and Cognition*. Cambridge, Mass.: MIT Press.

Rappaport Hovav, M. & Levin, B. (1998). Building verb meanings. In M. Butt & W. Geuder (Eds.), *The Projection of Arguments: Lexical and Compositional Factors* (pp. 97–134). Stanford, CA: CSLI Publications.

Stabler, E. (1997). Derivational minimalism. In Retore (Ed.), *Logical Aspects of Computational Linguistics* (pp. 68–95). Springer.

Stabler, E. (2000). Minimalist grammars and recognition. Manuscript for the SFB340 workshop at Bad Teinach.

Steedman, M. (2000). *The Syntactic Process*. Cambridge, Mass.: MIT Press.

Vijay-Shanker, K. & Weir, D. (1999). Exploring the underspecified world of lexicalized tree adjoining grammars. In *Proceedings of 6th Mathematics of Language Conference*, Orlando, USA.

Appendix A

Below is a definition of an agenda-driven, chart-based parser for minimalist grammars. For a given grammar and input string, there is a set of items, call them axioms, that are taken to represent true grammatical claims. Given these axioms, and the structure-building rules that allow us to make new true grammatical claims, we can design a parser, which, given an input string, determines the truth of the input string. If a structure has a particular set of goal features (i.e. c) and phonetic features that match the input, then the input string is in the language defined by our grammar. Our procedure to find all items that are true for a given grammar and input string works as follows:

1. Initialize the chart and the agenda (both modeled as an indexable stack) to be an empty set of items – an item has the form (S, f, i_A, i_B) where the first element S is a simple or complex structure, the second element f is a symbol representing the source of the structure (Merge, Move, Optional-Merge, or Axiom), and i_A and i_B are indices into elements in chart which created S. The axioms are pushed onto the agenda, with f=Axiom, $i_A=i_B=0$, and S being a underived simple structure of the form /phonetic/ feature-list λ-expression. In our case, the axioms are the union of (1) all phonetically null lexical items and (2) the lexical entry(ies) for each word in the input.

2. Repeat the following until the agenda is empty:

   a. Pop an item off the agenda, call it the trigger.

   b. Push the trigger onto the chart, if the trigger has not already been placed on the chart.

   c. If the trigger item was added to the chart in (b), then:

      – generate all items that can be derived from *Merge* of the trigger item and any items of the chart, pushing each new item onto the agenda with f=Merge, and i_A being the index to the licensor item and i_B being the index to the licensee item (one of i_A or i_B being the trigger's index)

      – generate all items that can be derived from the trigger item solely (via *Move*, or *Optional Merge*), pushing each new item onto the agenda with f=Move or f=Optional-Merge, i_A being the index of the trigger item, $i_B=0$.

3. When the agenda is empty, scan all items in the chart for structures that contain solely the goal features (a c feature). If such a structure exists, then its phonetic content is "spelled-out" – if the phonetic content matches the input string, then we print the derivation recovery and computed semantic structure:

   a. To print the derivation of an item (S, f, i_A, i_B), we can print the derivations of item i_A and i_B (if non-zero), and then print the resulting structure S.

   b. To compute the semantics of an item (S, f, i_A, i_B), we condition the result on f:

      – if f=Merge, then return the result of applying the semantics of item i_A to that of item i_B

      – if f=Move, then return the semantics of item i_A

      – if f=Optional-Merge, then return the result of applying the semantics of item i_A to a precomputed λ-expression based on the optional feature skipped.

      – if f=Axiom, then return the λ-expression of the axiom S, guaranteed to be a simple structure.

Minimalist languages and the correct prefix property

Henk Harkema
University of Sheffield

This paper describes a top-down recognition method for languages generated by Minimalist Grammars. Minimalist Grammars are formal grammars that incorporate certain aspects of current transformational linguistic theories: phrases are derived by applying structure building functions to lexical items and intermediate structures, and the applicability of these functions is determined by the syntactic features of the structures involved. The recognition method presented in this paper reduces phrase structures to simple expressions that encode the behavior of these structures with regard to the structure building functions. The recognizer has the correct prefix property: for an ungrammatical sentence, it will halt at the first word of the sentence that does not fit into a grammatical structure.

1. Introduction

In this paper, we will describe a method for top-down recognition of languages generated by Minimalist Grammars (Stabler 1997). Minimalist Grammars are a rigorous formalization of the kind of grammars proposed in the linguistic framework of Chomsky's Minimalist Program (Chomsky 1995). The grammar formalism will be introduced in Section 2.

Harkema (2000) presents a chart-based, bottom-up recognizer for Minimalist Grammars. A bottom-up parser has no predictive power. Hence, the chart will contain numerous items that are not involved in the derivation of the sentence to be parsed. In particular, in order to be complete, a bottom-up parser has to assume that any phonetically empty category can intervene between any two adjacent words in a sentence. A top-down parser, however, has the ability to predict the presence of phonetically empty categories in a sentence based on the structure built so far. Phonetically empty functional projections are ubiquitous in present-day transformational theories of language, so this issue is an important motivation for the formulation of a top-down recognizer for Minimalist Grammars. The design of the top-down recognizer will be discussed in Sections 3 and 4.

Another motivation for the current project is the specification of a parser for Minimalist Grammars which has the correct prefix property. A parser has the correct prefix property if it goes through the input sentence from left to right and, in case of an ungrammatical input sentence, will halt at the first word of the sentence that does not fit into a grammatical structure, i.e., the parser will not parse a prefix that cannot be extended to a grammatical sentence in the language (e.g. Sippu & Soisalon-Soininen 1988). A parser with the correct prefix property is computationally advantageous, because it will not spend any effort on trying to complete a parse for a sentence once it is known that the sentence is ungrammatical.[1] Because of its lack of predictive power, the bottom-up recognizer in Harkema (2000) does not have the correct prefix property. Section 5 will show how the top-down recognizer outlined in Section 4 can be turned into a recognizer that has the correct prefix property.

Michaelis (1998) has demonstrated that the set of languages generated by Minimalist Grammars as defined in Stabler (1997) falls within the set of languages generated by Multiple Context-Free Grammars (Seki et al. 1991). Harkema (2001a) and Michaelis (2001) present proofs showing the reverse. Hence, Minimalist Grammars are equivalent to Multiple Context-Free Grammars, which, in turn, are known to be equivalent to Linear Context-Free Rewriting Systems (Vijay-Shanker et al. 1987), Multi-Component Tree-Adjoining Grammars (Weir 1988), and Simple Positive Range Concatenation Grammars (Boullier 1998). To my knowledge, at the time of writing this paper, no recognizer with the correct prefix property has been published for the class of languages defined by these grammars.

2.   Minimalist Grammars

In this section, we will present the Minimalist Grammar formalism, following Stabler (1997). A Minimalist Grammar defines a set of trees. These trees are derived by closing the lexicon, which is a set of trees itself, under two structure building functions, *merge* and *move*. Consider for example Minimalist Grammar G_1 with a lexicon containing the following (6) elements:

(1)   d –k *Lavinia*

(2)   d –k *Titus*

(3)   =d vt –v *praise*

(4)   =pred +v +k i *s*

(5)   =i c ε

(6)   =vt +k =d pred ε

Each lexical item is a 1-node tree labeled with syntactic features of various kinds and a phonetic form.[2] The last two lexical items in the list above are phonetically empty. The features determine how the structure building functions will apply to the lexical items and the trees derived from these. Two trees, one of which has a feature =x and the other of which has a feature x, will trigger an application of the structure building function *merge*. For example, the lexical items =d vt −v *praise* and d −k *Lavinia* will merge to form the tree below:

(7)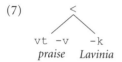

The resulting tree includes the original expressions =d vt −v *praise* and d −k *Lavinia*, minus the pair of features =d and d that triggered the function *merge*. These features have been checked and deleted. The '<' points to the head of the tree. For *merge*, the head of the tree that has the feature =x (before this feature is deleted by *merge*) will be the head of the resulting tree. The features of the head of the tree determine what other structure building functions will apply. The order of the features matters: the application of the structure building functions is triggered by the left-most features of the sequences of features of the expressions involved. Thus, *merge* does not apply to the lexical items =vt +k =d pred ε and =d vt −v *praise*, because the feature vt is not left-most in the lexical item =d vt −v *praise*.

  A tree that consists of more than one node, such as the tree in (7), is called a complex tree. Lexical items are simple trees, as they consist of just one node. We will use the following notation for complex trees: $[_<τ, υ]$ denotes a complex tree with immediate subtrees τ and υ, τ preceding υ, whose head is the head of τ; similarly, $[_>τ, υ]$ denotes a complex tree with immediate subtrees τ and υ, τ preceding υ, whose head is the head of υ. For example, in this notation the tree in (7) is written as $[_<vt −v$ *praise*, −k *Lavinia*]. The head of a simple tree is the single node making up the simple tree.

  The structure building function *merge* is defined in the following way. A pair of trees τ, υ is in the domain of *merge* if the left-most feature of the head of τ is =x and the left-most feature of the head of υ is x. Then $merge(τ, υ) = [_<τ', υ']$ if τ is simple, and $merge(τ, υ) = [_>υ', τ']$ if τ is complex, where τ' is like τ except that feature =x is deleted, and υ' is like υ except that feature x is deleted. So simple trees take sisters to their right, and complex trees take sisters to their left.

  The derivation will continue with merging the lexical item =vt +k =d pred ε and the tree in (7). The result is given in (8).

(8)

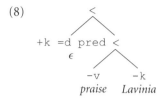

The left-most feature of the head of the tree in (8) is +k. The tree also contains a node whose left-most feature is −k. In this situation, the structure building function *move* will apply. It will move the maximal subtree whose head has the feature −k to the specifier position of the original tree, as in (9) below. A subtree φ is maximal if any subtree τ properly containing φ has a head other than φ. In this case, the subtree that moves is the tree consisting of the single node −k *Lavinia*. As in the case of *merge*, the features triggering the application of *move* are checked and deleted.

(9)

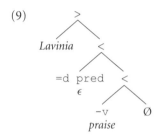

Formally, the structure building function *move* is defined as follows. A tree τ is in the domain of *move* if the left-most feature of the head of τ is +f and τ has exactly one maximal subtree τ_0 the left-most feature of the head of which is −f. Then $move(\tau) = [_{>}\tau_0', \tau']$, where τ_0' is like τ_0 except that feature −f is deleted, and τ′ is like τ except that feature +f is deleted and subtree τ_0 is replaced by a single node without features. A node without features will be labeled ∅.[3]

All derivations in a Minimalist Grammar are subject to the Shortest Movement Constraint, which is built in into the definition of the domain of the structure building function *move*: this function does not apply to a tree if the left-most feature of the head of the tree is +f and the tree contains more than one subtree whose head begins with the feature −f. In this case, all subtrees want to move to the same position, but moving any one subtree will deprive the other subtrees of their "shortest move", as they will now have to move to the specifier of some higher head which has the feature +f.[4]

The left-most feature of its head being =d, the tree in (9) can merge with the lexical item d −k *Titus*. Because the tree in (9) is a complex tree, the second clause of the definition of *merge* will apply. The result is the tree in (10).

(10)

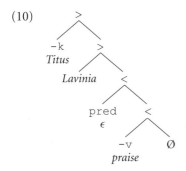

The head of the tree in (10) is labeled `pred`. The tree will be merged with the lexical item `=pred +v +k i` *s*. This will produce the tree in (11).

(11)

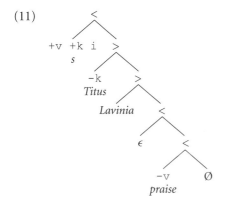

The next step of the derivation is another *move*, triggered by the feature +v on the head of the tree in (11) and the feature −v on the head of one of its subtrees. This is an instance of remnant movement: the object of the verb phrase that moves is no longer inside the verb phrase. The tree in (12) is the result.

(12)

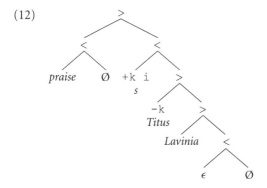

The pair of features +k and −k in the tree in (12) will trigger another application of *move*, which will yield the tree in (13).

(13)

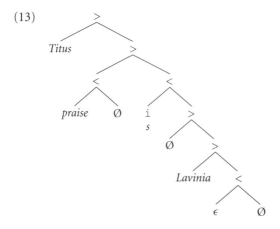

Finally, the tree in (13), whose head has the feature i, will be selected by the lexical item =i c ε. The result of this final *merge* is the tree in (14). This tree contains only one unchecked syntactic feature, namely c, and this feature labels the head of the tree. We have thus established that the yield of the tree in (14), ε *Titus praise s Lavinia* ε, i.e., *Titus praises Lavinia*, is a string of category c, using an analysis along the lines of Mahajan (2000) for deriving simple SVO sentences without head movement.[5]

(14)

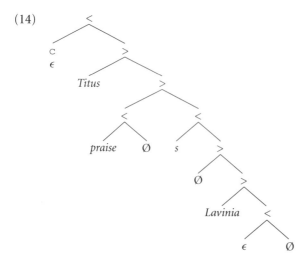

The total number of features occurring in the lexical items involved in the derivation of the sentence *Titus praises Lavinia* is 17. Therefore, the derivation of the tree in (14) takes exactly 8 steps, for each application of *merge* and *move* removes 2 features and the tree in (14) has one single feature left.

Formally, the language derivable by a Minimalist Grammar G consists of the yields of the complete trees in the closure of the lexicon under the structure building functions *merge* and *move*, where a complete tree is a tree without syntactic features, except for the distinguished feature c, which must label the head of the tree. The yield of a tree is the concatenation of the phonetic forms appearing at the leaves of the tree, ordered as in the tree.

(15)   (14)

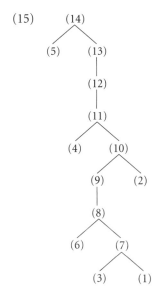

The derivation of the sentence *Titus praises Lavinia* is summarized in the derivation tree given in (15). In this tree, the numbered nodes stand for the trees given above, including the lexical items. A derivation tree indicates how a sentence is derived from a set of lexical items via the structure building functions *merge* and *move*. The leaves of a derivation tree are lexical items, which are simple trees. Each internal node is a complex tree that is derived from its immediate daughters by one application of the structure building functions *merge* or *move*. The root of a derivation tree is a complete tree for the sentence being derived. A derivation tree is thus a tree whose nodes are trees themselves.

3.   Context-Free Derivations

Michaelis (1998) has shown that the class of languages defined by Minimalist Grammars is included in the class of languages defined by Multiple Context-

Free Grammars (Seki et al. 1991) by demonstrating how to construct a Multiple Context-Free Grammar G′ which defines the same language as a given Minimalist Grammar G. For every tree τ generated by grammar G, there will be a non-terminal symbol A in grammar G′ which encodes the purely syntactic properties of τ, that is, its behavior with regard to the structure building functions *merge* and *move*. These properties are completely determined by the syntactic features appearing in the tree and whether the tree is simple or complex. The phonetic forms appearing in a tree are not relevant for the applicability of *merge* and *move*, nor does the geometry of the tree matter, except for the fact that the syntactic features of the head of the tree should be distinguished from any syntactic features appearing at other nodes in the tree. Hence, for syntactic purposes, a tree may be collapsed into a sequence of sequences of syntactic features. These are the non-terminal symbols of the Multiple Context-Free Grammar G′, which will be referred to as categories.

Formally, a category is a sequence of the form $[\gamma_0 \cdot \delta_0, \ldots, \gamma_n \cdot \delta_n]_t$, with γ_j, $\delta_j \in \mathrm{Cat}^*$, $0 \leq j \leq n$, $t \in \{c, s, l\}$, and Cat the set of syntactic features of Minimalist Grammar G. A category A represents a set of trees $T_c(A)$. A tree τ is in $T_c([\gamma_0 \cdot \delta_0, \ldots, \gamma_n \cdot \delta_n]_t)$ if, and only if, the following four conditions are met:

1. If $t = s$, τ is a simple tree; if $t = c$, τ is a complex tree; and if $t = l$, τ is a lexical tree.[6]
2. For every i, $0 \leq i \leq n$, there is a leaf l_i in τ such that:

   (a) The syntactic features of l_i are δ_i.
   (b) The maximal subtree headed by l_i is a projection of a lexical item with features $\gamma_i \delta_i$.[7]

3. Leaf l_0 is the head of τ.
4. Besides the leaves $l_0, \ldots, l_n$, there are no other leaves with syntactic features in τ.

For example, the tree in (4) is an element of $T_c([\cdot=\texttt{pred} +\texttt{v} +\texttt{k i}]_s)$, the tree in (10) is an element of $T_c([=\texttt{vt} +\texttt{k} =\texttt{d}\cdot\texttt{pred}, \texttt{d}\cdot\texttt{-k}, =\texttt{d vt}\cdot\texttt{-v}]_c)$, and the tree in (11) is an element of $T_c([=\texttt{pred}\cdot+\texttt{v} +\texttt{k i}, \texttt{d}\cdot\texttt{-k}, =\texttt{d vt}\cdot\texttt{-v}]_c)$.

One can think of a category as an abbreviation of a possibly infinite set of trees. We will only be interested in relevant categories, that is, categories A for which $T_c(A)$ includes a tree generated by grammar G which does not violate the Shortest Movement Constraint. Any tree τ that violates the Shortest Movement Constraint is useless in that it is not a complete tree by itself and cannot participate in the derivation of a complete tree. The structure building function *move* does not apply to such a tree τ, wherefore its outstanding $-\texttt{f}$ features cannot be deleted. The crucial observation in Michaelis (1998) is that the set of relevant categories for Minimalist Grammar G is finite. This is essential for grammar G′ to be definable at all, since a Multiple Context-Free Grammar cannot have an infinite number of non-terminal symbols or categories.

With regard to the phonetic forms of the trees generated by G, any category A in G′ will be associated with a tuple of strings, rather than with just one string, as in plain Context-Free Grammars. For a category A corresponding to a tree τ generated by G, this tuple of strings includes all and only the phonetic forms appearing in τ. Phonetic forms that will move independently from one another will be kept separate. In order to formalize this notion, let the narrow yield Y_n of a tree be defined as follows. The narrow yield of a simple tree φ is its yield as defined in the previous section. If φ is a complex tree, then, in case $\varphi = [_>\tau, \upsilon]$, $Y_n(\varphi) = Y_n(\tau)^\frown Y_n(\upsilon)$ if the left-most feature of the head of τ is not of the kind $-f$, and $Y_n(\varphi) = Y_n(\upsilon)$ otherwise.[8] If $\varphi = [_<\tau, \upsilon]$, then $Y_n(\varphi) = Y_n(\tau)^\frown Y_n(\upsilon)$ if the left-most feature of the head of υ is not of the kind $-f$, and $Y_n(\varphi) = Y_n(\tau)$ otherwise. Then, a category $A = [\gamma_0 \cdot \delta_0, \dots, \gamma_n \cdot \delta_n]_t$ as defined above will be associated with a tuple of strings $(s_0, \dots, s_n)$ if, and only if, there is a tree $\tau \in T_c(A)$ for which the narrow yield of the maximal projection of leaf l_i in τ labeled with syntactic features δ_i is s_i, $0 \leq i \leq n$.

For example, for the tree given in (10), the narrow yield of the maximal projection of the leaf labeled *pred*, i.e. the narrow yield of the tree itself, is *Lavinia* $\varepsilon = $ *Lavinia*; for the leaf labeled $-k$ it is *Titus*; and for the leaf labeled $-v$ it is *praise*. Hence, the category $[=\text{vt} +k =d \cdot \text{pred}, d \cdot -k, =d \text{ vt} \cdot -v]_c$ to which tree (10) belongs will be associated with the triple (*Lavinia, Titus, praise*). Similarly, the category $[\cdot =\text{pred} +v +k \text{ i}]_s$ of tree (4) will be associated with the 1-tuple (s), and the category $[=\text{pred} \cdot +v +k \text{ i}, d \cdot -k, =d \text{ vt} \cdot -v]_c$ of tree (11) will be associated with the triple (*s Lavinia, Titus, praise*). We can conveniently combine a category and its associated tuple of phonetic forms and write $[\textit{Lavinia}:=\text{vt} +k =d \cdot \text{pred}, \textit{Titus}:d \cdot -k, \textit{praise}:=d \text{ vt} \cdot -v]_c$ for the tree in (10), for example.

In order to derive the categories and their associated tuples of strings, Multiple Context-Free Grammar G′ contains a set of context-free rewrite rules which mirror the effects of the structure building operations *merge* and *move* in Minimalist Grammar G. Since the set of relevant categories is finite, a finite set of rewrite rules suffices to describe all derivations. Thus the Multiple Context-Free Grammar G′ for Minimalist Grammar G_1 contains the context-free rewrite rule $[p^\frown q:=\text{pred} \cdot +v +k \text{ i}, r:d \cdot -k, t:=d \text{ vt} \cdot -v] \rightarrow [p:=\text{pred} +v +k \text{ i}] [q:=\text{vt} +k =d \cdot \text{pred}, r:d \cdot -k, t:=d \text{ vt} \cdot -v]$. This rule mirrors the step in the derivation in which the tree in (11) is derived from the tree in (4) and the tree in (10). The rule will derive the category with phonetic forms $[s \textit{ Lavinia}:=\text{pred} \cdot +v +k \text{ i}, \textit{Titus}:d \cdot -k, \textit{praise}:=d \text{ vt} \cdot -v]_c$ from $[s:=\text{pred} +v +k \text{ i}]_s$ and $[\textit{Lavinia}:=\text{vt} +k =d \cdot \text{pred}, \textit{Titus}:d \cdot -k, \textit{praise}:=d \text{ vt} \cdot -v]_c$.

Using categories to abbreviate trees, the derivation tree in (15), whose nodes are trees generated by grammar G_1, can be represented as the tree in (16).

(16) $[\textit{Titus praise s Lavinia}:=\text{i}\cdot\text{c}]_c$

$[\epsilon:=\text{i}\ \ \text{c}]_s$ $[\textit{Titus praise s Lavinia}:=\text{pred} +\text{v} +\text{k}\cdot\text{i}]_c$

$[\textit{praise s Lavinia}:=\text{pred} +\text{v}\cdot+\text{k}\ \ \text{i}, \textit{Titus}:\text{d}\cdot-\text{k}]_c$

$[\textit{s Lavinia}:=\text{pred}\cdot+\text{v} +\text{k}\ \ \text{i}, \textit{Titus}:\text{d}\cdot-\text{k}, \textit{praise}:=\text{d}\ \ \text{vt}\cdot-\text{v}]_c$

$[\textit{s}:=\text{pred} +\text{v} +\text{k}\cdot\text{i}]_s$ $[\textit{Lavinia}:=\text{vt} +\text{k} =\text{d}\cdot\text{pred}, \textit{Titus}:\text{d}\cdot-\text{k}, \textit{praise}:=\text{d}\ \ \text{vt}\cdot-\text{v}]_c$

$[\textit{Lavinia}:=\text{vt} +\text{k}\cdot =\text{d}\ \ \text{pred}, \textit{praise}:=\text{d}\ \ \text{vt}\cdot-\text{v}]_c$ $[\textit{Titus}:\text{d}\ \ -\text{k}]_s$

$[\epsilon:=\text{vt}\cdot+\text{k} =\text{d}\ \ \text{pred}, \textit{praise}:=\text{d}\ \ \text{vt}\cdot-\text{v}, \textit{Lavinia}:\text{d}\cdot-\text{k}]_c$

$[\epsilon:=\text{vt} +\text{k} =\text{d}\ \ \text{pred}]_s$ $[\textit{praise}:=\text{d}\cdot\text{vt}\ \ -\text{v}, \textit{Lavinia}:\text{d}\cdot-\text{k}]_c$

$[\textit{praise}:=\text{d}\ \ \text{vt}\ \ -\text{v}]_s$ $[\textit{Lavinia}:\text{d}\ \ -\text{k}]_s$

The translation of a Minimalist Grammar G into an equivalent Multiple Context-Free Grammar G′ reveals that the derivation trees of Minimalist Grammars are context-free, even though the languages defined by Minimalist Grammars are beyond the power of Context-Free Grammars. The next section will show how this insight can be used to obtain a transparent top-down recognizer for languages generated by Minimalist Grammars.

4.   Top-down recognition

Like its bottom-up counterpart in Harkema (2000), the top-down recognizer for Minimalist Grammars that is presented in this section is based on the principle of parsing as deduction as described in Shieber et al. (1995). The recognizer uses a chart to store items, which embody predictions about the syntactic structure of the sentence to be recognized. Initially, the chart is filled with a set of axioms. These axioms are then closed under a set of rules of inference. If the closure contains a distinguished goal item, the sentence is in the language defined by the grammar, otherwise it is not.

4.1 Items and invariant

An item is a sequence $\Delta_1 + \ldots + \Delta_m$, where each subitem Δ_i, $1 \leq i \leq m$, is a prediction regarding the syntactic features and narrow yields of a tree involved in the derivation of the input sentence. A subitem is a category with position vectors and is of the general form $[(x_0, y_0):\gamma_0 \cdot \delta_0, \dots, (x_n, y_n):\gamma_n \cdot \delta_n]_t$, with γ_j, δ_j, and t as in the previous section, and x_j, $y_j \in \mathbb{N}$, $0 \le j \le n$. A subitem Δ abbreviates a set of trees $T_s(\Delta)$. For an input string $w = w_1 \dots w_k$ and a subitem $\Delta = [(x_0, y_0):\gamma_0 \cdot \delta_0, \dots, (x_n, y_n):\gamma_n \cdot \delta_n]_t$, tree a τ is in $T_s(\Delta)$ if, and only if, the following holds:

1. $\tau \in T_c([\gamma_0 \cdot \delta_0, \dots, \gamma_n \cdot \delta_n]_t)$.
2. The narrow yield of the maximal projection of leaf l_i in τ labeled δ_i is $w_{x_i+1} \dots w_{y_i}$, $0 \le i \le n$.

On the assumption that sentences are strings of the distinguished category c, the items generated by the recognizer will be interpreted under the following invariant: given an item $\Delta_1 + \dots + \Delta_m$, the sequence of trees $\tau_1, \dots, \tau_m$, for arbitrary $\tau_i \in T_s(\Delta_i)$, $0 \le i \le m$, is a cut of a (partial) derivation tree whose root is a complete tree ρ of category c with yield w.[9],[10] Recall that the nodes of a derivation tree are trees generated by a Minimalist Grammar (cf. the derivation tree in (15)).

4.2 Axioms

If c is the distinguished feature of grammar G and k is the length of the input string w, then for any lexical item with the single syntactic feature c there will be an axiom $[(0, k)::c]_s$, and for any lexical item with syntactic features γc, there will be an axiom $[(0, k):\gamma \cdot c]_c$, $\gamma \in Cat^+$.

As is easily checked, any $\tau \in T_s([(0, k)::c]_s)$ or $\tau \in T_s([(0, k):\gamma \cdot c]_c)$ constitutes a cut through the root of a partial derivation tree whose root is a complete tree of category c with yield w; the root is τ.

4.3 Rules of inference

The rules of inference encode the context-free rewrite rules of the Multiple Context-Free Grammar G′ that is equivalent to Minimalist Grammar G. Grammar G′ contains a rewrite rule for every single application of the structure building functions *merge* and *move*, but the definitions of these functions allow us to condense these rewrite rules into five rules of inference: three Unmerge rules and two Unmove rules. Given a particular subitem Δ_i appearing in some item $\Delta_1 + \dots + \Delta_m$, the rules of inference will predict how the trees in $T_s(\Delta_i)$ can be 'unmerged' and 'unmoved' into smaller trees by specifying the particular subitems that these smaller trees belong to. In addition to the Unmerge and Unmove rules, there is also a Scan rule for reading the input string.

Unmerge-1:   given an item $\Delta_1 + \ldots + \Delta_m$ such that $\Delta_i = [(p, q){:=}x{\cdot}\gamma, S]_c$, $1 \leq i \leq m$, then, for any lexical item with syntactic features βx, add the items $\Delta_1 + \ldots + \Delta_{i-1} + [(p, v){:}{\cdot}{=}x\gamma]_s + [(v, q){:}\beta{\cdot}x, S]_t + \Delta_{i+1} + \ldots + \Delta_m$ to the chart, for all possible values of v such that $p \leq v \leq q$; for all possible values of t such that $t = s$ if $\beta = \emptyset$, $t = c$ if $\beta \neq \emptyset$, and if $t = s$ then $S = \emptyset$.

Unmerge-2:   given an item $\Delta_1 + \ldots + \Delta_m$ such that $\Delta_i = [(p, q){:}\alpha{=}x{\cdot}\gamma, S]_c$, $1 \leq i \leq m$, $\alpha \neq \emptyset$, then, for any lexical item with syntactic features βx, add the items $\Delta_1 + \ldots + \Delta_{i-1} + [(v, q){:}\alpha{\cdot}{=}x\gamma, U]_c + [(p, v){:}\beta{\cdot}x, V]_t + \Delta_{i+1} + \ldots + \Delta_m$ to the chart, for all possible values of v such that $p \leq v \leq q$; for all possible values of U, V such that $U \cup V = S$; for all possible values of t such that $t = s$ if $\beta = \emptyset$, $t = c$ if $\beta \neq \emptyset$, and if $t = s$ then $V = \emptyset$.

Unmerge-3:   given an item $\Delta_1 + \ldots + \Delta_m$, such that $\Delta_i = [(p, q){:}\alpha{=}x{\cdot}\gamma, S, (v, w){:}\beta x{\cdot}\delta, T]_c$, $1 \leq i \leq m$, then add the items $\Delta_1 + \ldots + \Delta_{i-1} + [(p, q){:}\alpha{\cdot}{=}x\gamma, U]_{t_1} + [(v, w){:}\beta{\cdot}x\delta, V]_{t_2} + \Delta_{i+1} + \ldots + \Delta_m$ to the chart, for all possible values of U, V such that $U \cup V = S \cup T$; for all possible values of t_1 such that $t_1 = s$ if $\alpha = \emptyset$, $t_1 = c$ if $\alpha \neq \emptyset$, and if $t_1 = s$ then $U = \emptyset$; for all possible values of t_2 such that $t_2 = s$ if $\beta = \emptyset$, $t_2 = c$ if $\beta \neq \emptyset$, and if $t_2 = s$ then $V = \emptyset$.

Unmove-1:   given an item $\Delta_1 + \ldots + \Delta_m$, such that $\Delta_i = [(p, q){:}\alpha{+}y{\cdot}\gamma, S]_c$, $1 \leq i \leq n$, $\alpha \neq \emptyset$, then, for any lexical item with syntactic features $\beta{-}y$, $\beta \neq \emptyset$, add the items $\Delta_1 + \ldots + \Delta_{i-1} + [(v, q){:}\alpha{+}y\gamma, (p, v){:}\beta{\cdot}{-}y, S]_c + \Delta_{i+1} + \ldots + \Delta_m$ to the chart, for all possible values of v such that $p \leq v \leq q$.

Unmove-2:   given an item $\Delta_1 + \ldots + \Delta_m$, such that $\Delta_i = [(p, q){:}\alpha{+}y{\cdot}\gamma, S, (v, w){:}\beta{-}y{\cdot}\delta, T]_c$, $1 \leq i \leq m$, $\alpha \neq \emptyset$, $\beta \neq \emptyset$, add the item $\Delta_1 + \ldots + \Delta_{i-1} + [(p, q){:}\alpha{\cdot}{+}y\gamma, S, (v, w){:}\beta{\cdot}{-}y\delta, T]_c + \Delta_{i+1} + \ldots + \Delta_m$ to the chart.

Scan: given an item $\Delta_1 + \ldots + \Delta_m$, such that $\Delta_i = [(p, q){:}{\cdot}\gamma]_s$, $1 \leq i \leq m$, then, if there is a lexical item ℓ with syntactic features γ and phonetic features covering $w_{p+1} \ldots w_q$ of the input string, i.e. $\ell \in T_s(\Delta_i)$, add the following item to the chart: $\Delta_1 + \ldots + \Delta_{i-1} + [(p, q){:}{\cdot}\gamma]_l + \Delta_{i+1} + \ldots + \Delta_m$.

The rules of inference Unmove-1 and Unmove-2 come with the restriction that no items violating the Shortest Movement Constraint should be added to the chart. An item violates the Shortest Movement Constraint if it contains a subitem $[(x_0, y_0){:}\gamma_0 \cdot \delta_0, \ldots, (x_n, y_n){:}\gamma_n \cdot \delta_n]_t$ such that there are δ_i, δ_j whose left-most features are the same feature $-f$, $1 \leq i < j \leq n$.

4.4 Goal items

Any item of the form $[(x_0, y_0):\cdot\gamma_0]_l + \ldots + [(x_m, y_m):\cdot\gamma_m]_l$ is a goal item. It follows from the definition of the Scan rule that there are lexical items $\ell_i \in T_s([(x_i, y_i):\cdot\gamma_i]_l)$, $0 \leq i \leq m$. According to the invariant, the sequence $\ell_1, \ldots, \ell_m$ is a cut of a partial derivation tree whose root is a complete tree ρ of category c with yield w. Since all $\ell_i, 0 \leq i \leq m$, are lexical items, the derivation tree is in fact a 'complete' derivation tree, which means that w is in the language defined by G.

4.5 Example

The recognition of the example sentence $w = {}_0Titus_1praise_2s_3Lavinia_4$ according to grammar G_1 given in Section 2 will start with the assertion of the single axiom $[(0, 4):=\texttt{i}\cdot\texttt{c}]_c$. This item represents a cut through the root of the derivation tree in (15). Of course, for each cut of the tree in (15), there is a corresponding cut of the derivation tree in (16).

Rule Unmerge-1 will apply to the axiom, as there is a lexical item with features $=\texttt{pred}\ +\texttt{v}\ +\texttt{k}\ \texttt{i}$. One of the items produced is $[(0, 0):=\texttt{i}\ \texttt{c}]_s + [(0, 4):=\texttt{pred}\ +\texttt{v}\ +\texttt{k}\cdot\texttt{i}]_c$. This item corresponds to a cut through the nodes labeled (5) and (13) in derivation tree in (15). Rule Unmerge-1 also produces four other items: $[(0, p):\cdot=\texttt{i}\ \texttt{c}]_s + [(p, 4):=\texttt{pred}\ +\texttt{v}\ +\texttt{k}\cdot\texttt{i}]_c, 1 \leq p \leq 4$. These four additional items also obey the invariant defined in Section 4.1, but they do not correspond to a cut of the particular derivation tree in (15).

The item $[(0, 0):\cdot=\texttt{i}\ \texttt{c}]_s + [(0, 4):=\texttt{pred}\ +\texttt{v}\ +\texttt{k}\cdot\texttt{i}]_c$ can be rewritten in two ways. Either the Scan rule will apply to produce the item $[(0, 0):\cdot=\texttt{i}\ \texttt{c}]_l + [(0, 4):=\texttt{pred}\ +\texttt{v}\ +\texttt{k}\cdot\texttt{i}]_c$, or rule Unmove-1 will apply to produce the item $[(0, 0):\cdot=\texttt{i}\ \texttt{c}]_s + [(1, 4):=\texttt{pred}\ +\texttt{v}\cdot+\texttt{k}\ \texttt{i}, (0, 1):\texttt{d}\cdot-\texttt{k}]_c$ (plus another four items $[(0, 0):\cdot=\texttt{i}\ \texttt{c}]_s + [(p', 4):=\texttt{pred}\ +\texttt{v}\cdot+\texttt{k}\ \texttt{i}, (0, p'):\texttt{d}\cdot-\texttt{k}]_c, p' = 0$ or $2 \leq p' \leq 4$). Item $[(0, 0):\cdot=\texttt{i}\ \texttt{c}]_s + [(0, 4):=\texttt{pred}\ +\texttt{v}\cdot+\texttt{k}\ \texttt{i}\ (0, 0):\texttt{d}\cdot-\texttt{k}]_c$ corresponds to a cut through the nodes labeled (5) and (12) of the tree in (15). Rule Unmove-1 will also apply to the other four items produced in the previous step $(1 \leq p \leq 4)$, but Scan will not.

Eventually, the item $[(0, 0):\cdot=\texttt{i}\ \texttt{c}]_l + [(2, 3):\cdot=\texttt{pred}\ +\texttt{v}\ +\texttt{k}\ \texttt{i}]_l + [(4, 4):\cdot=\texttt{vt}\ +\texttt{k}\ =\texttt{d}\ \texttt{pred}]_l + [(1, 2):\cdot=\texttt{d}\ \texttt{vt}\ -\texttt{v}]_l + [(3, 4):\cdot\texttt{d}\ -\texttt{k}]_l + [(0, 1):\cdot\texttt{d}\ -\texttt{k}]_l$ will be deduced. This is a goal item, corresponding to a cut through the leaves of the derivation tree in (15).

4.6 Correctness and complexity

The recognizer presented above is sound and complete: every deducible item respects the invariant given in Section 4.1, and for every string that is in the language defined by the grammar, there is a deduction of a goal item from the axioms. The correctness proofs are provided in Harkema (2001b). There it is also shown that the time complexity of the recognizer is polynomial in the length of the input sentence (considering the shortest deduction of a goal item for a sentence).

Unfortunately, since items produced by the recognizer correspond to cuts of derivation trees, the recognizer will fail to halt if the grammar is recursive. A Minimalist Grammar is recursive if there is a complete tree τ which is derived from a tree υ_1 via *merge* and *move*, and tree υ_1, in turn, is derived from a tree υ_2 such that υ_1 and υ_1 belong to the same category, i.e., there is a category A such that $\upsilon_1 \in T_c(A)$ and $\upsilon_2 \in T_c(A)$.[11]

5.   Correct prefix property

For the recognizer to possess the correct prefix property, it must read the words of the input sentence from left to right, and it must not predict items with subitems whose categories represent trees that cannot be derived from lexical trees in the grammar. These two restrictions will be discussed in the following two sections.

5.1 Left to right

Obviously, the recognizer described in the preceding sections does not scan the input sentence from left to right, because the rules of inference can rewrite any subitem of an item as long as it matches the antecedent of a rule. To ensure a left-to-right sweep through the sentence, the items are extended to include a pointer π, which points to the next word of the sentence to be read. The rules of inference are restricted to rewrite only subitems whose trees are predicted to dominate the word the pointer π is pointing to. The pointer will be incremented when all the words at a particular position in the sentence have been scanned successfully.

For a proper implementation of the pointer mechanism, it is important to realize that phonetically empty words at position x in a sentence come before a phonetically non-empty word at position x. If the recognizer does not scan the words at position x in this order, a violation of the correct prefix property may result, as illustrated by the following example. Consider a grammar G_2 which is like grammar G_1 of Section 2, except that the phonetically empty lexical item =i c ε has been replaced with the phonetically non-empty lexical item =i c *that*. Thus, all the sentences generated by grammar G_2 will start with the overt complementizer *that*. In the process of trying to recognize the ungrammatical sentence *Titus praise s Lavinia*, the recognizer described in the previous section will derive the item [(0, 0):·=i c]$_s$ + [(2, 3):·=pred +v +k i]$_s$ + [(3, 4):=vt +k·=d pred, (1, 2):=d vt·-v]$_c$ + [(0, 1):·d -k]$_s$ (for grammar G_1 this item would correspond to the cut

5-4-9-2 in the derivation tree in (15)). The first subitem of this item amounts to the prediction of a phonologically empty complementizer at position 0, i.e., at the left edge of the sentence. The last subitem predicts the word *Titus* to occur at the left edge of the sentence. Scanning the non-empty word *Titus* before the predicted empty complementizer leads to a violation of the correct prefix property, because no sentence generated by G_2 starts with the word *Titus*. The recognizer should halt after failing to scan the empty complementizer and before scanning anything else – a phonetically empty complementizer is a prefix of no sentence in G_2.

The example above shows that we have to distinguish between the situation in which the recognizer is looking for a phonetically empty word at position x and the situation in which the recognizer is looking for a phonetically non-empty word at position x. Therefore, pointer π will have two parts. If $\pi = (x, \varepsilon)$, the recognizer finds itself in the former situation, if $\pi = (x, \not\varepsilon)$, in the latter. The values that π will run through are ordered in such a way that (x, ε) comes immediately before $(x, \not\varepsilon)$, and $(x, \not\varepsilon)$ comes immediately before $(x + 1, \varepsilon)$. The first value of π is $(0, \varepsilon)$; the last value is (n, ε), where n is the length of the input sentence.

In order to determine what subitems should be rewritten given some value of π, we define a containment relation between position vectors of items and values of π. The containment relation is used to determine what positions in a sentence are potentially covered by trees for subitems with particular position vectors. Position vector (q, q) in a simple subitem contains the following position: (q, ε). The yield of any tree $\tau \in T_s([(q, q):\gamma \cdot \delta]_s)$ can only be a phonetically empty word at position q. Position vector (q, r), $q < r$, in a simple subitem contains the following positions: $(q, \not\varepsilon), \ldots, (r - 1, \not\varepsilon)$. Positions (q, ε) and (r, ε) are not included, because the yield of any simple tree τ in $T_s([(q, r):\gamma \cdot \delta]_s)$ is the string $s = w_{q+1} \ldots w_r$. Since $q < r$, string s is not a phonologically empty word at position q, nor a phonologically empty word at position r. However, if the position vector (q, r), $q < r$, appears in a complex subitem, these positions are included in the set of positions contained in position vector (q, r), because the derivation of a tree whose yield includes the string $s = w_{q+1} \ldots w_r$ may very well involve trees whose yields are phonologically empty words at positions q or r. Hence, position vector (q, r), $q \leq r$, in a complex subitem includes the following positions: $(q, \varepsilon), \ldots, (r, \varepsilon)$. A rule of inference can only apply to some item if its triggering subitem Δ_i contains the current value of π. For example, the rule of inference Unmerge-1 now reads:

Unmerge-1: given an item $(\Delta_1 + \ldots + \Delta_m, \pi)$ such that $\Delta_i = [(p, q):=x\cdot\gamma, S]_c$, $1 \leq i \leq m$, and one of the position vectors of Δ_i contains π, then, for any lexical item with syntactic features βx, add the items $(\Delta_1 + \ldots + \Delta_{i-1} + [(p, v):\cdot=x\gamma]_s + [(v, q):\beta\cdot x, S]_t + \Delta_{i+1} + \ldots + \Delta_m, \pi)$ to the chart, for all possible values of v such that $p \leq v \leq q$; for all possible values of t such that $t = s$ if $\beta = \emptyset$, $t = c$ if $\beta \neq \emptyset$, and if $t = s$ then $S = \emptyset$.

The other rules of inference are updated in the same way, except for Scan, which will be discussed shortly.

Returning to our example grammar G_2, when recognition of the ungrammatical sentence *Titus praise s Lavinia* has reached the item $([(0, 0):\cdot=\text{i c}]_s + [(2, 3):\cdot=\text{pred} +\text{v} +\text{k i}]_s + [(3, 4):=\text{vt} +\text{k}\cdot=\text{d pred}, (1, 2):=\text{d vt}\cdot-\text{v}]_c + [(0, 1):\cdot\text{d} -\text{k}]_s, (0, \varepsilon))$, only subitem $[(0, 0):\cdot=\text{i c}]_s$ can be scanned, because its position vector contains $(0, \varepsilon)$, whereas the position vector of subitem $[(0, 1):\cdot\text{d} -\text{k}]_s$ does not. Thus, the correct prefix property is safe.

The position vector $(0, n)$ of any axiom is split in such a way that every item generated by the recognizer has exactly one position vector that contains the value $(x, \not\varepsilon)$, $0 \leq x \leq n - 1$. This, of course, reflects the obvious truth that there is exactly one phonetically non-empty word at any position x in a sentence of length n. Therefore, after having scanned the one and only non-empty word at position x, the recognizer can increment the value of the pointer π from $(x, \not\varepsilon)$ to $(x + 1, \varepsilon)$, assuming that the phonetic content of a phonetically non-empty lexical item amounts to one word. In contrast, there can be more than one phonetically empty word at some position x in a sentence. Consider for example grammar G_3, which has empty pronouns. The lexicon of G_3 includes the lexicon of grammar G_1 and the additional lexical item $\text{d} -\text{k } \varepsilon$. One of the sentences generated by this grammar is $\varepsilon \ \varepsilon$ *praise s Lavinia*, in which one of the empty elements is an empty complementizer and the other is an empty determiner phrase.[12] In order to recognize this sentence both empty elements have to be scanned. Thus, after having scanned one of them, the recognizer can not increment the value of the pointer π from $(0, \varepsilon)$ to $(0, \not\varepsilon)$, because then it would miss the other empty element. If the current value of the pointer is (x, ε), it can only be incremented if the item under consideration does not have any subitems left whose position vectors contain (x, ε), except for subitems with subscript l, that is: when all predicted empty elements at position x have been scanned successfully. So the rule of inference Scan is split into two rules, covering 'empty' and 'non-empty' scans, and a rule of inference for updating π without scanning any word is added. This last rule will apply when the recognizer is supposed to be looking for an empty word at some position x, but none is predicted to occur at that position or all have been scanned successfully.

Scan-ε: given an item $(\Delta_1 + \ldots + \Delta_m, (p, \varepsilon))$ such that $\Delta_i = [(p, p):\cdot\gamma]_s, 1 \leq i \leq m$, then, if there is a lexical item with syntactic features γ and phonetic features ε, add the following item to the chart: $(\Delta_1 + \ldots + \Delta_{i-1} + [(p, p):\cdot\gamma]_l + \Delta_{i+1} + \ldots + \Delta_m, (p, \varepsilon))$.

Scan-$\not\varepsilon$:   given an item $(\Delta_1 + \ldots + \Delta_m, (p, \not\varepsilon))$ such that $\Delta_i = [(p, q):\cdot\gamma]_s, p < q, 1 \leq i \leq m$, then, if there is a lexical item with syntactic features γ and phonetic features covering $w_{p+1} \ldots w_q$ of the input string, add the following item to the chart: $(\Delta_1 + \ldots + \Delta_{i-1} + [(p, q):\cdot\gamma]_l + \Delta_{i+1} + \ldots + \Delta_m, (q, \varepsilon))$.

Update-π: given an item $(\Delta_1 + \ldots + \Delta_m, (p, \varepsilon))$ such that none of the Δ_i, $1 \leq i \leq m$, includes a simple or complex subitem whose position vectors contain (p, ε), then add the following item to the chart: $(\Delta_1 + \ldots + \Delta_m, (p, \not\varepsilon))$.

For grammar G_3 and the grammatical sentence *praise s Lavinia*, the recognizer will generate the item $([(0,0):\cdot=\text{i c}]_s + [(1, 2):\cdot=\text{pred +v +k i}]_s + [(2, 3):=\text{vt +k}\cdot=\text{d pred}, (0, 1):=\text{d vt}\cdot-\text{v}]_c + [(0, 0):\cdot\text{d -k}]_s, (0, \varepsilon))$. At this point, the rule Scan-ε can apply twice, but after these applications, rule Update-π cannot apply, because $(0, \varepsilon)$ is contained in the position vector $(0, 1)$ occurring in a complex subitem – a tree represented by this subitem may be derived from a tree with an empty element at position 0, which should be scanned before π is incremented. We will only know for sure that there are no further empty elements at position 0 other than the empty complementizer and determiner phrase when the recognizer has generated the item $([(0, 0):\cdot=\text{i c}]_l + [(1, 2):\cdot=\text{pred +v +k i}]_s + [(3, 3):\cdot=\text{vt +k =d pred}]_s + [(0, 1):\cdot=\text{d vt -v}]_s + [(0, 0):\cdot\text{d -k}]_l, (0, \varepsilon))$. (For grammar G_1, this item represents the cut 5-4-6-3-1-2 of the derivation tree in (15).) The rule Update-π will apply to this item, incrementing the value of π to $(0, \not\varepsilon)$. Next, three applications of Scan-$\not\varepsilon$, each followed by an application of Update-π, will produce a goal item, which now are items of the form $([(x_0, y_0):\cdot\gamma_0]_l + \ldots + [(x_m, y_m):\cdot\gamma_m]_l, (n, \not\varepsilon))$, where n is the length of the input sentence.

The need for a pointer to enforce a left-to-right scan of the input sentence reflects a crucial difference between Minimalist Grammars and Context-Free Grammars. As the derivation tree in (15) and (16) illustrates, a depth-first, left-to-right traversal of a derivation tree for some sentence w generated by a Minimalist Grammar will in general not visit the lexical expressions at the leaves of the tree in the order in which their phonetic forms appear in w. For a Context-Free Grammar, however, the words at the leaves of a (derivation) tree, ordered according to the precedence relation of the tree, always constitute a grammatical sentence.

5.2 Useless categories

To illustrate the second aspect of the correct prefix property, that the recognizer must not generate items with subitems whose categories represent trees that cannot be derived from lexical trees in the grammar, consider grammar G_4, which is grammar G_1 with two additional lexical items: =p pred ε and p −k *Rufus*. Assume the input sentence is *Rufus praise s Lavinia*, which is not a sentence of the language generated by G_4, since neither lexical item =p pred ε nor lexical item p −k *Rufus* can be part of a derivation of a complete tree. At a certain point, the recognizer

operating as described before will have produced the item $([(0, 0):\cdot\text{-}=\texttt{i c}]_s + [(2,$
$3):\cdot\text{-}=\texttt{pred +v +k i}]_s + [(3, 4):=\texttt{p}\cdot\texttt{pred}, (0, 1):\texttt{p}\cdot\text{-k}, (1, 2):=\texttt{d vt}\cdot\text{-}\texttt{-v}]_c, (0, \varepsilon))$,
from which the item $([(0, 0):\cdot\text{-}=\texttt{i c}]_s + [(2, 3):\cdot\text{-}=\texttt{pred +v +k i}]_s + [(3, 4):\cdot\text{-}=\texttt{p}$
$\texttt{pred}, (1, 2):=\texttt{d vt}\cdot\text{-}\texttt{-v}]_c, + [(0, 1):\cdot\texttt{p -k}]_s, (0, \varepsilon))$ will be deduced by an application of the rule Unmerge-1. Next, the empty complementizer will be scanned, after
which π will be updated, producing the item $([(0, 0):\cdot\text{-}=\texttt{i c}]_l + [(2, 3):\cdot\text{-}=\texttt{pred +v}$
$+\texttt{k i}]_s + [(3, 4):\cdot\text{-}=\texttt{p pred}, (1, 2):=\texttt{d vt}\cdot\text{-}\texttt{-v}]_c, + [(0, 1):\cdot\texttt{p -k}]_s, (0, \cancel{\varnothing}))$. In the next
step, the first non-empty word of the input sentence will be scanned, in violation
of the correct prefix property, because *Rufus* is not a prefix of any sentence in the
language generated by G_3.

   This example shows that the predictions of the recognizer have to be limited
to items that do not contain any useless subitems. A subitem $\Delta = [(x_0, y_0):\gamma_0 \cdot \delta_0,$
$\ldots, (x_n, y_n):\gamma_n \cdot \delta_n]_t$ is useless if its category $A = [\gamma_0 \cdot \delta_0, \ldots, \gamma_n \cdot \delta_n]_t$ is useless,
that is, if there are no trees in $T_c(A)$ that participate in the derivation of a complete
tree, cf. the notion 'useless non-terminal symbol' for Context-Free Grammars, e.g.
Sippu and Soisalon-Soininen (1988). It follows from the invariant in Section 4.1
that for a subitem Δ occurring in some item, any tree $\tau \in T_c(A)$, where A is the category corresponding to Δ, is part of a partial derivation of a complete tree. Hence,
we still have to make sure that category A is such that set $T_c(A)$ contains a tree
that is derivable from the lexical items of the grammar. We can compute the set
of categories with this property in the following way. For each lexical item of the
grammar labeled with syntactic features $\gamma \in Cat^+$, the initial set of categories contains the category $[\cdot\gamma]_s$. This initial set will then be closed under the following five
rules:

Merge-1: $[\cdot=x\gamma]_s, [\beta\cdot x, S]_t \rightarrow [=x\cdot\gamma, S]_c$[13]

Merge-2: $[\beta\cdot=x\gamma, S]_c, [\mu\cdot x, T]_t \rightarrow [\beta=x\cdot\gamma, S, T]_c$

Merge-3: $[\beta\cdot=x\gamma, S]_t, [\mu\cdot x\delta, T]_t \rightarrow [\beta=x\cdot\gamma, S, \mu x\cdot\delta, T]_c \ (\delta \neq \varnothing)$

Move-1: $[\beta\cdot+y\gamma, S, \mu\cdot-y, T]_c \rightarrow [\beta+y\cdot\gamma, S, T]_c$

Move-2: $[\beta\cdot+y\gamma, S, \mu\cdot-y\delta, T]_c \rightarrow [\beta+y\cdot\gamma, S, \mu-y\cdot\delta, T]_c, (\delta \neq \varnothing)$

In all rules of inference, $t \in \{s, c\}$. The rules Move-1 and Move-2 are constrained
so as not to apply to categories of the form $[\gamma_0 \cdot \delta_0, \ldots, \gamma_i\cdot-f\delta_i, \ldots, \gamma_j\cdot-f\delta_j,$
$\ldots, \gamma_n \cdot \delta_n]_c$, which violate the Shortest Movement Constraint. The rules Merge-
1, $\ldots$, Move-2 are in fact the rules of inference of the bottom-up recognizer in
Harkema (2000), but without position vectors. It is easy to see that for any Minimalist Grammar the closure of the initial set under the rules Merge-1, $\ldots$, Move-2
is finite.

Let $U^\uparrow$ denote the closure of the initial set of categories under the rules Merge-1, …, Move-2. Then, whenever the recognizer is about to add a new item to the chart according to the rules of inference in Section 4.3, it will check whether the categories of all its subitems are in the set $U^\uparrow$, and only add the item to the chart if this is so. Together with reading the sentence from left to right, this will ensure that the recognizer has the correct prefix property. In our example grammar G_4, category $[\text{=p·pred, p·-k, =d vt·-v}]_c$ is not an element of $U^\uparrow$, whence the prediction that led to the violation of the correct prefix property will no longer be generated.

It is also possible to compute the set $U^\downarrow$ in advance, where $U^\downarrow$ contains all categories A such that set $T_c(A)$ consists of trees that participate in a partial derivation of a complete tree. For each lexical item of the grammar with syntactic features γc, the initial set of categories will contain a category $[\gamma \cdot c]_t$, $t = s$ if $\gamma = \emptyset$, $t = c$ if $\gamma \in$ Cat$^+$ (cf. the axioms of the top-down recognizer in Section 4.2). The initial set is then closed under the rules Unmerge-1 …, Unmove-2 from Section 4.3, ignoring the position vectors. Now the set of useful categories U, which is the complement of the set of useless categories, is the set $U^\uparrow \cap U^\downarrow$. This set – or rather: $U^\downarrow$, because all lexical items are in $U^\uparrow$ – can be used to prune from a Minimalist Grammar G those lexical items which are not involved in any derivation of a complete tree. A recognizer using a grammar reduced in this way is expected to have the correct prefix property, although this claim still awaits confirmation by formal proof. The critical issue is that a top-down recognizer using a reduced grammar does not necessarily generate items containing subitems whose categories are in $U^\uparrow$. For example, not all the ways in which the contents of set S in the antecedent of the rule of inference Unmerge-2 in Section 4.3 can be divided over the sets U and V in the consequent of that rule will correspond to subitems whose categories are in $U^\uparrow$. However, at this point it is not clear whether items containing these spurious subitems will ever give rise to predictions of lexical items that cause violations of the correct prefix property.

6.   Conclusion

In this paper, we have motivated the usefulness of a top-down approach to recognizing languages defined by Minimalist Grammars. We described the design of a pure top-down recognizer and added a pointer mechanism to obtain a recognizer with the correct prefix property. The recognizer can be turned into a parser by extending items with a field for recording their immediate ancestors, and using this field to retrieve trees or forests from the chart of items produced by the algorithm.

Because of its complexity and potential non-termination, the recognizer *per se* is of limited practical value. However, the top-down perspective on Minimalist

Grammars that is explored in this paper provides an understanding of the grammar formalism that is very useful for formulating an Earley-style recognizer for Minimalist Grammars which will terminate for all grammar and sentence pairs (Harkema 2001b).

The techniques outlined in this paper can also be used to design a recognizer for Asymmetry Grammars (e.g. Di Sciullo 1999). The structure building functions of these grammars are sensitive to certain configurational properties of the trees they apply to, so these properties have to be encoded in the categories that represent trees. Since the rules of inference of the recognizer are very closely related to the structure building functions of the grammar, this will show in what ways the asymmetry inherent in Asymmetry Grammars is computationally advantageous.

Notes

1. The parser of the human sentence processor also seems to have the correct prefix property: the ungrammaticality of a sentence is detected at the first word that makes the sentence ungrammatical, and for garden path sentences the human parser will generally hesitate at the first word that does not fit into the structure that is hypothesized for the sentence.

2. Lexical items also have semantic features, but we will not discuss these features in this paper.

3. The structure building function *move* defined here implements overt phrasal movement. The Minimalist Grammars specified in Stabler (1997) also include mechanisms for head movement and covert phrasal movement. We will not discuss these kinds of movement in this paper. However, the recognizer formulated in this paper can be extended to deal with Minimalist Grammars that allow head movement and covert movement; see Stabler (2001), Harkema (2001b).

4. The Shortest Movement Constraint formulated in Stabler (1997) is a rather strong condition. If the head of the tree has more than one $+f$ feature, the subtrees whose heads begin with the feature $-f$ could all move to become specifiers of the same head, which would make these moves equally short from a linguistic point of view. However, under the current version of the Shortest Movement Constraint a tree with more than one exposed $-f$ feature is not in the domain of the function *move*, so no movements will take place.

5. In traditional notation, the tree in (14) would be presented as in (14b).

(14b)

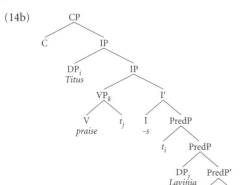

6. All lexical trees are assumed to be simple trees, but not all simple trees are lexical trees. For example, the tree d −k ɛ is a simple tree, but it is not a lexical tree in grammar G_1 discussed in Section 2.

7. Any lexical item ℓ is a projection of itself. If τ is a projection of ℓ and τ, υ are in the domain of *merge*, then $\varphi = merge(\tau, \upsilon)$ is a projection of ℓ. If τ is a projection of ℓ and τ is in the domain of *move*, then $\varphi = move(\tau)$ is a projection of ℓ.

8. For two strings p and q, $p\frown q$ denotes their concatenation in the obvious order.

9. A partial derivation tree is a derivation tree whose root is a complete tree, but whose leaves are not necessarily lexical items.

10. A sequence of nodes C of a tree T is a cut of T if (1) none of the nodes in C dominates another node in C, (2) every node in T and not in C either dominates or is dominated by a node in C, and (3) the nodes in C are ordered according to the precedence relation of T.

11. If the recognizer is made to scan the words of the sentence from left-to-right as in Section 5.1, the recognizer will fail to halt if the grammar is left-recursive, analogously to top-down recognizers for Context-Free Grammars. A Minimalist Grammar is left-recursive if it is recursive, i.e., there are trees τ, υ_1, and υ_2 with the properties mentioned in the text, and moreover the phonetic material of υ_2 contains a string that in the sentence w specified by τ is to the left of all the phonetic forms of υ_2. For example, the Minimalist Grammar whose lexicon consists of the three lexical items $[a{:}b -f]_s$, $[b{:}=b +f\ b -f]_s$, $[\varepsilon{:}=b +f\ c]_s$ is left-recursive – see Harkema (2001b) for more discussion.

12. According to the derivation tree of the sentence, the empty complement precedes the empty determiner phrase, but for the recognizer the order between multiple empty elements at the same position in a sentence is immaterial.

13. This notation should be understood as follows: if the set contains the categories $[\cdot{=}x\gamma]_s$ and $[\beta{\cdot}x, S]_t$, then add the category $[{=}x{\cdot}\gamma, S]_c$ to the set.

References

Boullier, P. (1998). *Proposal for a Natural Language Processing Syntactic Backbone* [Research Report 3342]. Rocquencourt, France: INRIA-Rocquencourt.

Chomsky, N. (1995). *The Minimalist Program.* Cambridge, MA: MIT Press.

Di Sciullo, A. M. (1999). "The local asymmetry connection". In *MIT Working Papers in Linguistics, 35,* 25–47.

Harkema, H. (2000). "A recognizer for minimalist grammars". In *Proceedings of the 6th International Workshop on Parsing Technologies* (pp. 111–122). Trento, Italy: ITC-IRST.

Harkema, H. (2001a). "A characterization of minimalist grammars". In P. de Groote, G. F. Morrill, & C. Retoré (Eds.), *Logical Aspects of Computational Linguistics* [Lecture Notes in Artificial Intelligence 2099] (pp. 193–211). Berlin, Germany: Springer.

Harkema, H. (2001b). *Parsing Minimalist Languages.* PhD thesis. Los Angeles, CA: UCLA.

Mahajan, A. (2000). "Word order and remnant movement: Eliminating head movement". In *GLOW Newsletter, 44,* 44–45. Tilburg, the Netherlands: Tilburg University.

Michaelis, J. (1998). "Derivational minimalism is mildly context-sensitive". In M. Moortgat (Ed.), *Logical Aspects of Computational Linguistics* [Lecture Notes in Artificial Intelligence 2014] (pp. 179–198). Berlin, Germany: Springer.

Michaelis, J. (2001). "Transforming linear context-free rewriting systems into minimalist grammars". In P. de Groote, G. F. Morrill & C. Retoré (Eds.), *Logical Aspects of Computational Linguistics* [Lecture Notes in Artificial Intelligence 2099] (pp. 228–244). Berlin, Germany: Springer.

Seki, H., Matsumura, T., Fujii, M., & Kasami, T. (1991). "On multiple context-free grammars". *Theoretical Computer Science, 88,* 191–229.

Shieber, S. M., Schabes, Y., & Pereira, F. C. N. (1995). "Principles and implementation of deductive parsing". *Journal of Logic Programming, 24* (1, 2), 3–36.

Sippu, S. & Soisalon-Soininen, E. (1988). *Parsing Theory; Vol. I: Languages and Parsing.* Berlin, Germany: Springer.

Stabler, E. P. (1997). "Derivational minimalism". In C. Retoré (Ed.), *Logical Aspects of Computational Linguistics* [Lecture Notes in Artificial Intelligence 1328] (pp. 68–95). Berlin, Germany: Springer.

Stabler, E. P. (2001). "Recognizing head movement". In P. de Groote, G. F. Morrill, & C. Retoré (Eds.), *Logical Aspects of Computational Linguistics* [Lecture Notes in Artificial Intelligence 2099] (pp. 228–244). Berlin, Germany: Springer.

Vijay-Shanker, K., Weir, D. J., & Joshi, A. K. (1987). "Characterizing descriptions produced by various grammatical formalisms". In *Proceedings of the 25th Annual Meeting of the Association for Computational Linguistics* (pp. 104–111). Stanford, CA: Stanford University.

Weir, D. J. (1988). *Characterizing Mildly Context-Sensitive Grammar Formalisms.* PhD thesis. Philadelphia, PA: University of Pennsylvania.

Computation with probes and goals
A parsing perspective

Sandiway Fong
University of Arizona

This paper examines issues in parsing architecture for a left-to-right implementation of the probe-goal Case agreement model, a theory in the Minimalist Program (MP). Computation from a parsing perspective imposes special constraints. For example, in left-to-right parsing, the assembly of phrase structure must proceed through elementary tree composition, rather than using the generative operations MERGE and MOVE directly. On-line processing also poses challenges for the incremental computation of probe/goal relations. We describe an implemented parser that computes these relations and assembles phrase structure, whilst respecting the incremental and left-to-right nature of parsing. The model employs two novel mechanisms, a Move box and a Probe box, to implement efficient parsing, without "lookback" or unnecessary search of the derivational history.

1. Introduction

Recently, there has been a shift in the structure of linguistic theories of narrow syntax from abstract systems of declarative rules and principles, e.g. Chomsky (1981), to systems where design specifications call for efficient computation within the human language faculty. In particular, recent work in the Minimalist Program, e.g. Chomsky (1998, 1999), has highlighted the role of locally deterministic computation in the construction of syntactic representation.

Instead of a system involving Spec-Head agreement, Chomsky re-analyzes the Case-agreement system in terms of a system of *probes*, e.g. functional heads like T and v*, that target and agree with *goals*, e.g. referential and expletive Ns, within their c-command domain. Within this system, probe-goal agreement can be long-distance and need not trigger movement, e.g. as in the case of *there*-expletive constructions and Quirky Case agreement in Icelandic.[1] The implemented parser described in this paper represents a first implementation of the probe-goal account.

The logical separation of agreement and movement distinguishes this system from those based on the Minimalist Grammar (MG) formalism (Stabler 1997). In the MG formalism, formal feature-checking always precipitates movement.

Efficient assembly, i.e. locally deterministic computation, from a generative perspective with respect to (bottom-up) MERGE does not guarantee that parsing with probes and goals will also be similarly efficient. By *locally deterministic computation*, we mean that the choice of operation to apply to properly continue the derivation is clear and apparent at each step of the computation. In the case where it is not possible to decide between actions, we have a *choice point*. A theory that efficiently assembles phrase structure starting from a primitive lexical array (LA) may not have a correspondingly efficient procedure for the left-to-right recovery of that phrase structure since the LA is not available prior to parsing. A simpler example can be used to illustrate the point. There is a well-known, efficient procedure for forming the product r of two prime numbers, p and q. On the other hand, decomposing r into p and q requires a relatively computationally expensive procedure, necessitating guesswork or search.

This paper describes a implemented system that handles a range of examples discussed in Chomsky (1998, 1999). In particular, it explores the computational and empirical properties of the probe-goal system from a left-to-right, incremental parsing perspective.

Instead of MERGE and MOVE as the primitive combinatory operations for the assembly of phrase structure, we describe a system driven by elementary tree composition with respect to a range of heads in the extended verb projection (v^*, V, c and T). Elementary tree composition is an operation that is a basic component of Tree-Adjoining Grammars (TAG), (Joshi & Schabes 1997), and Asymmetry Theory (Di Sciullo 2002, 2005).

The system described here is *on-line* in the sense that once an input element has fulfilled its function, it is discarded, i.e. no longer referenced. To minimize search, there is not only no lookahead, but there can also be no *lookback* in the sense of being able to examine or search the derivational history. Instead, we make use of two novel devices with well-defined properties: a Move Box that encodes the residual properties of CHAINs and theta theory, and a single or current Probe Box to encode structural Case assignment and to approximate the notion of (strong) Phase boundaries. In particular, the restriction to a single Probe Box means that probes cannot "see" past another probe; thereby emulating the Phase Impenetrability Condition (PIC). Limiting the Move Box to operate as a stack will allow nesting but not overlapping movement. A consequence of this is that extraction through the edge of a strong Phase is not longer possible. Examples of parses will be used to illustrate the empirical properties of these computational elements. The system is also *incremental* in the sense that a partial parse is available at all stages of processing. In particular, it extends the derivation to the right in a manner reminiscent of Phillips (1995).[2]

The basic questions explored in this paper are as follows: (1) what are the situations where left-to-right computation pose problems for deterministic computation, (2) what computational elements are necessary to implement the on-line assembly of phrase structure in an efficient manner, and (3) what are the consequences of eliminating computational choice points introduced by the extra machinery.

2. The lexicon

We begin with the definition of a lexicon: the heart of the implemented system. Following directly from Chomsky (1998, 1999), we assume the parser operates with a system of functional and lexical categories with properties and features, interpretable and uninterpretable, of the form shown in Figure 1 below. The property of selection and uninterpretable feature matching will drive the parsing process. In the course of computation, unintepretable features belonging to analyzed constituents will be eliminated through probe-goal agreement in a manner to be described in detail in Section 6. A (valid) parse is a phrase structure that obeys the selectional properties of the individual lexical items, covers the entire input, and has all uninterpretable features properly valued.

There are five basic types of heads listed in the table:

(1) C

Two types of complementizer are represented here; declarative c and c(wh) for *Wh*-questions.

(2) T

Two types of tense; T for tensed clauses, and φ-incomplete or defective T, represented by $T_{\bar{\varphi}}$, for infinitivals.

Small v comes in three basic flavors: transitive v*, for verbs like *hit*, unergative v#, for verbs like *swim* and unaccusative v, for verbs like *arrive*. Past participles are also analyzed as instances of v.

(3) V

In conjunction with the variety of small *v*s, two basic types of V with respect to complement-taking are listed. Transitive and unaccusative V select for a complement, but not unergative V.

(4) N

Lexical Item (LI)	Properties	Uninterpretable Features		Interpretable
		φ-features	Other	Features
v* (transitive)	select(V) spec(select(N)) value(case(acc))	per(P) num(N) gen(G)	(epp)	
v (unaccusative)	select(V)			
v# (unergative)	select(V) spect(select(N))			
PRT (passive participle)	select(V)	per(P) num(N)	case(_)	
V (transitive) (unaccusative)	select(N)			
V (unergative)				
V (raising)	select(T_{\bar{\varphi}})			
T	select(v) value(case(nom))	per(P) num(N) gen(G)	epp	
T_{\bar{\varphi}}	select(v)	per(P)	epp	
c	select(T)			
c (wh)	select(T)		epp	wh
N (referential)			case(_)	per(P) num(N) gen(G)
N (wh)		wh	case(_)	per(P) num(N) gen(G)
N (expletive)		per(P)		

Figure 1. A sample lexicon

We restrict our attention to simple nominals, excluding from discussion complex nominals that select for complements or take adjuncts.

The heads c(wh), T, $T_{\bar{\varphi}}$, v* and v are *probes* with uninterpretable features, and participate in the fundamental Agree operation, to be discussed in Section 6.

The elements, properties and features, of this table are rendered in pseudo-PROLOG notation and are grouped as follows:

(5)   select:

For example, select(V) is a property of v*; that is, v* selects for a (complement) phrase headed by V. v* also has the property spec(select(N)); this notation is used to indicate that v* pre-selects for a phrase headed by N in its specifier position.[3]

(6)   φ-Features:

The structures per(_), num(_) and gen(_) are used to represent the φ-features person, number and gender, respectively, with the anonymous logic variable (_) representing the uninstantiated slot for the value of each feature. In the case of the probe v*, these features are uninterpretable (and come unvalued). For nominals, these features are interpretable (and come valued). Probe-goal agreement will value the uninterpretable features, i.e. fill the slots indicated by the anonymous logic variable.

(7)   value:

For example, T has property value(case(nom)); that is, T as a probe values nominative Case for an appropriate goal. Similarly, in this system, (transitive) v* values accusative Case.

Defective T, indicated by $T_{\bar{\varphi}}$, differs from T in that it has an incomplete set of φ-features (just person per(_)), and cannot value Case (no value(case(_)) property). Selectionally, they are the same, i.e. they both select for phrases headed by v.

(8)   case:

Nominals will have the uninterpretable feature case(_) (with an open slot for a value). Through the Agree relation, probes with the property value(case(V)), where logic variable V is nom or acc will instantiate an appropriate slot in a nominal goal, thus eliminating the uninterpretable feature for the goal.

(9)   epp:

The EPP is an uninterpretable feature with a special property. Elements that possess this feature (epp) may trigger MOVE, defined in (13). epp licenses a specifier position as the landing site for movement. If the MOVE operation succeeds, unintepretable epp is eliminated. Unique among the features introduced here, the EPP feature (or property) can also be satisfied by MERGE. For example, T has feature EPP. It can be eliminated either by raising, say, the internal subject of v* to specifier-T or by direct merge of an expletive like *there* as in *there is a man in the room*.

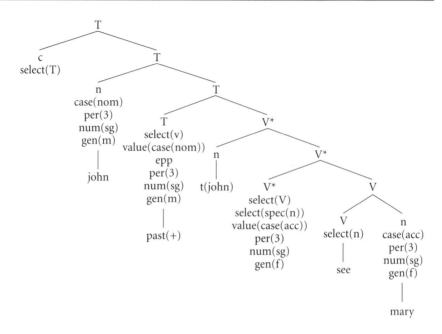

Figure 2. Example parser for *John saw Mary*

(10)   Q and wh:

We assume that the *Wh*-word fronting system works in a parallel fashion to the Case agreement system. Q, or c(wh) here, has interpretable feature wh, which cancels with uninterpretable feature wh for *Wh*-nominals under Agree.

The lexical definitions given above, along with an appropriate encoding of Agree and Move, suffice to determine basic phrase structure. For example, the parse generated by the system for the simple sentence *John saw Mary* is shown in Figure 2. In this case, the displayed features show that *John* is subject to MOVE (to be elaborated on in Section 4), receiving nominative Case from T. In return, T's φ-features are valued. There is a similar exchange in the case of v* and *Mary* with respect to accusative Case.

3.   Elementary trees

The basic operations MOVE and MERGE, defined in (11) and (12) respectively, are fundamentally bottom-up operations for the assembly of phrase structure. An online, left-to-right parser cannot make use of these operations directly. In this section, we describe an alternative mechanism based on the composition of (possibly underspecified) elementary trees.

(11)   Merge(α,β) = {α,β} = γ, LB(γ) = LB(α) or LB(β)

α, β and γ are syntactic objects. Syntactic objects are either primitive lexical items (LI) or the products of Merge. LB is the label function.

Agree (defined later in Section 6) in the presence of EPP triggers Move.

(12)   Move(p, g) holds if:

    a.   Agree(p, g) holds, and

    b. p has an EPP-feature.

         Then:

    c.   Identify some PP(g) (pied-piping), and

    d.   Merge PP(g) to some specifier-p leaving a trace, and

    e.   EPP-p is deleted

Probe p and goal g are syntactic objects. g is in the c-command domain of p.

Elementary trees form the base component of Tree-Adjoining Grammars (TAG) [Joshi & Schabes 1997]. We will assume parsing proceeds (in part) through composition of elementary trees that contain open positions. The range of elementary trees is determined by lexical properties. Given the lexicon of Figure 1, we define the 9 *ground* elementary trees shown in Figure 3 below. By *ground*, we mean that all the sub-components of the tree are defined or specified. (We return to discuss examples of *non-ground* or underspecified trees shortly.)

Elementary trees are basically projections of functional and lexical heads with open complement and specifier positions pre-determined by lexical entries. For example, the lexicon in Figure 1 defines three versions of v. Both transitive v^* and unergative $v^\#$ have selectional properties select(V) and spec(select(N)) represented by elementary trees with two open positions, as shown in (e) and (g) in Figure 3. Unaccusative v has selectional property select(V) only, so it has just one open position (for its complement). In the case of T and $T_{\bar{\varphi}}$, the epp feature translates into an open specifier position, as shown in (c).

With these basic building blocks, it is a straightforward matter to "paste together" or perform elementary tree composition to form a parse tree for a complete sentence such as *John saw Mary* in Figure 2, filling in the open positions on the edge of the tree from the input in a linear, left-to-right fashion. The basic procedure is given in (13) and the sequence of steps to assemble Figure 2 beginning with the complementizer (c) is given in Figure 4.[4]

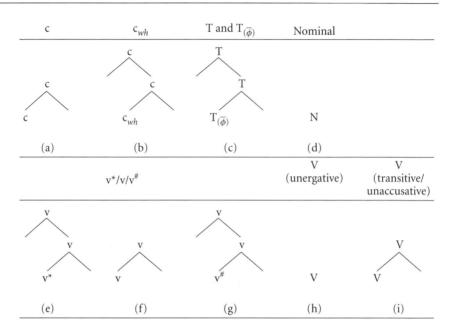

Figure 3. Elementary trees

Step	Phrase Structure	Input
(i)	$[_c c \_]$	John saw Mary
(ii)	$[_c c [_T T \_ [_T T \_]]]$	John saw Mary
(iii)	$[_c c [_T John [_T T \_]]]$	saw Mary
(iv)	$[_c c [_T John [_T [_T past(+)] \_]]]$	see Mary
(v)	$[_c c [_T John [_T [_T past(+)] [_v \_ [_v [_v v^* \_]]]]]]$	see Mary
(vi)	$[_c c [_T John [_T [_T past(+)] [_v t(John) [_v [_v v^* \_]]]]]]$	see Mary
(vii)	$[_c c [_T John [_T [_T past(+)] [_v t(John) [_v [_v v^* [_v V \_]]]]]]]$	see Mary
(viii)	$[_c c [_T John [_T [_T past(+)] [_v t(John) [_v [_v v^* [_v [_v see] \_]]]]]]]$	Mary
(ix)	$[_c c [_T John [_T [_T past(+)] [_v t(John) [_v [_v v^* [_v [_v see] Mary]]]]]]]$	*(empty)*

Notes:

(i)	c:select(T)
(ii)	fill specifier-T
(iii)	fill head-T
(iv)	Assume *saw* $\longrightarrow$ past(+) *see*.
(v)	T:select(v)
(vi)	Insertion of t(John). See Section 4.
(vii)	v:select(V)
(viii)	fill head-V
(ix)	fill complement-V

Figure 4. Assembly of *John saw Mary*

(13)   Parse:
   a.   Given a category c, pick an elementary tree headed by c.
   b.   From the input:
      i.   Fill in the specifier (if one exists)
      ii.   Fill in the head
      iii.   Fill in the complement by recursively calling parse with c' where c has lexical property select(c)

Less straightforward is the matter of picking out the right elementary tree each time around the parse procedure. In Chomsky's generative model, assembly begins with a one-time selection from the lexicon that produces a lexical array (LA). In other words, the correct components for assembly are laid out in a separate step ahead of assembly time. In the case of on-line parsing, no pre-determined LA is available. Lexical items associated with the input can only be discovered in the course of assembly. Not knowing the LA forces the introduction of a choice point at elementary tree selection time, e.g. the selection of v^* (over v and $v^\#$) in (v) and transitive/unaccusative V (over unergative V) in (vii) in Figure 4.

We can limit choice point formation in some cases by underspecifying or keeping non-ground parts of the elementary tree. More abstractly, an elementary tree can be *linearly underspecified* with respect to whether it has a complement, e.g. V, and its lexical properties, e.g. $T/T_{\bar\phi}$. An abstract elementary tree can be substituted in these cases and the final shape of the elementary tree determined when the head is inserted (modulo lexical polysemy). In cases where underspecification of the specifier is required, as with v^* versus $v^\#$/v, this strategy will not result in choice point elimination since the (potential) specifier position must be filled before the head in strict left-to-right order.

Summarizing with respect to Figure 3, limited elementary tree underspecification in the implementation permits cases (e) and (g) to be conflated; also cases (h) and (i). With respect to the sequence of steps in Figure 4, underspecification allows (local) determinism to be maintained for steps (ii), selection of T, and (vii), selection of V; but not for steps (i), selection of c, and (v), selection of v, where the option of the specifier position cannot be resolved without the benefit of lookahead.

The fact that v and V are largely decoupled here, in the sense that different variants of v may co-occur with a given V, permits the system to flexibly handle examples of causative/unaccusative alternations such as (14a–b) at the cost of introducing non-determinism.[5]

(14)   a. $[_T$ The sun $[_T$ T $[_v$ t(sun) $[_v$ v^* $[_V$ melted the ice $]]]]]$
      b. $[_T$ The ice $[_T$ T $[_v$ v $[_V$ melted t(ice) $]]]]$
      c.   *$[_T$ The sun $[_T$ T $[_v$ v $[_V$ melted the ice $]]]]$

Note that parser cannot detect that (14c), cf. (14b), is illicit until it reaches the verb object position. That is, local determinism in the choice of v cannot be maintained.[6]

4.   The Move Box

The Move Box is used by the parser to encode phrasal movement.[7] The Move Box represents a "holding cell" or a piece of short-term memory that is used to hold constituents that undergo MOVE. Open positions in the parse tree may be filled by the contents of the Move Box. This component of the parser is reminiscent of the *ad hoc* HOLD register used for filler-gap dependencies in Augmented Transition Networks (ATN) Woods (1970). However, the Move Box defined here is simply an embodiment of, and strictly respects, theta theory. In other words, box manipulation is strictly constrained by a small set of operations that encode theta theory as it applies to traditional Chains, encoding the history or derivation of movement.

Initially, let us assume the simplest case of a single Move Box. The introduction of this data structure immediately presents a problem for deterministic computation. We have introduced a choice point; namely, the option of filling an open position from the Move Box instead of the input. Let us eliminate this choice point immediately with the following preference rule:

(15)   Move Box Preference Rule
       When filling open positions, always prefer the Move Box over the input.

In particular, (15) asserts that, provided the Move Box is non-empty, we must always select from the Move Box, irrespectively of the contents of the input. There is no choice involved. In other words, (15) removes the choice point in step (b) of the (revised) parse procedure, as shown below in (16). (We will return to consider the empirical consequences of this strategy later.)

(16)   Parse:
       a.   Given a category c, pick an elementary tree headed by c.
       b.   From the Move Box *or* input:
            i.   Fill in the specifier (if one exists)
            ii.   Fill in the head
            iii. Fill in the complement by recursively calling parse with c' where c has lexical property select(c')

We now turn to the operating conditions of the Move Box, i.e. the conditions under which the box may be initialized, filled and emptied. At the start of the parse, the Move Box contains nothing:

(17)   Move Box: *Initial Contents*
       Empty.

Hence, initially, elementary tree open positions are filled from the input. However, whenever an open position is filled from the input, we will make a copy and place it in the Move Box:

(18)   Move Box: *Fill Condition*
       When filling from input, copy to Move Box.

As mentioned earlier, the Move Box respects theta theory. In particular, once we arrive at a selected position that needs to be filled, we have essentially determined the original MERGE position of the moved phrase, and the parser's (re-)construction of the "chain" of movement is complete. As the contents of the Move Box are no longer required by computation, it is deleted:

(19)   Move Box: *Empty Condition*
       At a selected position, empty it.

(In this model, the selected positions are the theta positions spec(select(N)) and select(N) for v^* and V in Figure 1, respectively.)

   Note also that conditions (18) and (19) logically combine to fill and immediately empty the Move Box in the case of *in situ* elements.

   We are now in a position to illustrate the operation of the Move Box. Consider again the sequence of operations shown in Figure 4 for the simple sentence *John saw Mary*. The corresponding manipulations for the Move Box are documented in Figure 5 below.

Step	Phrase Structure	Input
(i)	$[_c \, c \, \_ \,]$	John saw Mary
(iii)	$[_c \, c \, [_T \, \text{John} \, [_T \, T \, \_ \,]]]$	saw Mary
(vi)	$[_c \, c \, [_T \, \text{John} \, [_T \, [_T \, \text{past}(+)] \, [_v \, t(\text{John}) \, [_v \, [_v \, v^* \, \_ \,]]]]]]]$	see Mary
(ix)	$[_c \, c \, [_T \, \text{John} \, [_T \, [_T \, \text{past}(+)] \, [_v \, t(\text{John}) \, [_v \, [_v \, v^* \, [_v \, [_v \, \text{see}] \, \text{Mary} \,]]]]]]]]$	(*empty*)

Move Box notes:

Step	Move Box	
(i)	(*empty*)	Initial condition.
(iii)	John	Fill specifier-T from input, copy *John* to Move Box
(vi)	(*empty*)	Fill from Move Box, t(*John*). Empty Move Box. (Specifier-v^* is a selected position.)
(ix)	(*empty*)	Move Box is emty. Fill from input (*Mary*).

Figure 5. Move Box computation for *John saw Mary*

Note that the Move Box must be empty at the start of step (ix) in Figure 5, given the Move Box preference rule. However, it is also important that the lifespan of the box be carefully controlled and not, for example, be emptied prematurely. Consider example (20a) and the corresponding parse in (20b). Here, the Move Box containing *prizes* must be available for successive cyclic movement.

(20)   a.   Several prizes are likely to be awarded
         b.   [$_c$ c [$_T$ several prizes [$_T$ [$_T$ past(-) [$_v$ [$_v$ be][$_A$ [$_A$ likely][$_T$ t(prizes) [$_T$ T$_{\bar{\phi}}$[$_v$ [$_v$ PRT][$_v$ award t(prizes)]]]]]]]]]

There is one further complication that needs to be addressed. To accommodate expletive movement, i.e. the movement of an expletive from one non-selected position to another (possibly iterated), we need to refine condition (20) as follows:

(21)   Move Box: Empty Condition for Expletives
        Fill from Move Box at a non-selected position: if box contains an expletive, *optionally* empty it.

Note that we have introduced an (unavoidable) choice point in (21). Emptying is made an option to accommodate the possibility of recursion, as illustrated in (22). With recursion, it is not possible to locally determine whether a given non-selected position is the last or original (MERGE) position of the expletive.

(22)   a.   There are prizes awarded[8]
         b.   There are likely *t*(there) to be prizes awarded
         c.   There are supposed *t*(there) to be likely *t*(there) to be prizes awarded

Making (21) deterministic by not emptying the Move Box in the case of an expletive will also produce incorrect results. For example, in (22b), the Move Box must be emptied otherwise the parser will not be able to pick up *prizes* from the input.

The Move Box preference rule (15) also has certain desirable consequences. Consider again (14c), the case of (incorrectly) selecting unaccusative v over transitive v*, repeated here as (23):

(23)   *[$_T$ The sun [$_T$ T [$_v$ v [$_v$ melted the ice]]]]

(24) summarizes the state of the computation at the point where the parser is poised to complete the verb object position. The parser has not encountered any selected positions, so it must fill from the non-empty Move Box, thereby orphaning or stranding the contents of the input (*the ice*). Hence, (23) is ungrammatical.

(24)   a.   [$_c$ c [$_T$ The sun [$_T$ [$_T$ past(+)] [$_v$ v [$_v$ melt _]]]]]
         b.   the ice (Input)
         c.   the sun (Move Box)

A Move Box preference also blocks illicit passivization of a indirect object, as in (25):

(25) *Mary was given a book to t(Mary)

Assuming a small clause-style analysis of the double object construction, e.g. along the lines of Pesetsky (1995), the parser must select *Mary* from the Move Box (over *a book*) to fill the specifier-P open position in (26).

(26)   a. $[_c$ c $[_T$ Mary $[_T$ $[_T$ past(+)$]$$[_v$ PRT $[_v$ $[_v$ give$]$$[_P$ _ $[_P$ $[_P$ to$]$ _ $]]]]]]]$
       b.   a book (Input)
       c.   Mary (Move Box)

5.   Limitations of the Move Box

The single Move Box system has some design limitations. In some cases, as will be discussed in this section, it will become necessary to invent additional boxes. However, for example, with two or more boxes, we will have the problem of choosing which one to fill from. Hence, multiple boxes are to be avoided if possible, or at least constrained in a manner that does not promote non-determinism in the system. Organizing boxes into a non-flat data structure such as a stack, i.e. nesting, is an example of a strategy that does not promote non-determinism. The access rules for the stack data structure are clear, i.e. we can only pick or have access to the (current) top box. No choice is involved.

5.1 Nesting

Consider the two cases of *wh*-object extraction in (27a–b):

(27)   a.   Who did Bill see?
       b.   Who was a book given to?

(27a–b) contain examples of *nested* movement, as shown in (28a–b), respectively. For both cases, *who* occupies the Move Box when the parser reaches the specifier-T (or subject) position. The subject, *Bill* in (27a) and *a book* in (27b), also needs to occupy the Move Box, since it is also part of a (non-trivial) chain, originating in specifier-v and specifier-P, respectively.

(28)   a.   Who did $[_T$ Bill $[_v$ t(Bill) $[_v$ v* $[_v$ see t(who) $]]]]$
       b.   Who was $[_T$ a book $[_T$ $[_T$ past(+)$]$$[_v$ PRT $[_v$ give $[_P$ t(book)
            $[_P$ to t(who) $]]]]]]$

In both cases, the problem can be solved by allowing Move Boxes to be nested by recency, i.e. in stack fashion. The following three rules govern the creation and deletion of multiple boxes:

(29)   Move Box: *Nesting*
       (When filling non-selected open positions) allow filling from the input
       (*creating a new Move Box*).

(30)   Move Box Preference Rule
       Operations may only reference the most recently created Move Box

(31)   Move Box: *Deletion*
       When a Move Box is emptied, it is deleted.

For example, (29) allows *Bill* in (non-selected) specifier-T in (28a) to begin a new Move Box. This second box is the new top-of-stack. By the second preference rule (30), all box operations must now reference this box, thereby eliminating a potential choice point. Proceeding normally, this second box is emptied when t(*Bill*) is inserted in specifier-v (a selected position). At this point, the second box can be discarded, following rule (31), as it has fulfilled its theta duties in the sense that the movement chain is now complete, and the original Move Box containing *who* can be reactivated. Parsing proceeds normally, and this box is subsequently emptied at the verb object position. A similar sequence of actions apply in (28b), with the second box containing *a book* emptied and eliminated at specifier-P.

Finally, note that the parser will still (correctly) reject (25). In state (26), the open position is *not* a non-selected position, and thus a new box cannot be created.

5.2 Overlap

We distinguish nesting from *overlap* with respect to chains. In this paper, we consider all cases of overlap to be undesirable, as it requires more powerful parsing machinery. Consider example (27a) again, repeated below as (32a). In Chomsky's model, heads such as c and v* constitute (largely impenetrable) strong Phases. The Phase Impenetrability Condition (PIC) limits the scope of probes for feature matching. For example, in order for *who* to be visible to the *wh*-probe c(wh), it has to be first extracted to the Object Shift position, an "escape hatch" at the edge of the phase. As can be seen in (32b), this results in movement chain overlap that cannot be accommodated by the machinery described earlier for nesting.

(32)   a.   Who did Bill see?
       b.   [$_c$ Who [$_c$ [$_c$ c(wh)] did [$_T$ Bill [$_v$ t(who) [$_v$ t(Bill)
            [$_v$ v* [$_v$ see t(who)]]]]]]]]

Both overlap and nesting require multiple boxes. However, in (32b), we require access to two boxes, or the ability to choose between them, thereby compromising determinism. Put another way, overlap requires more powerful machinery (than nesting) in the sense that it introduces an extra choice point. For parsing, as will be described in the next section, on-line, left-to-right processing implies that Agree between *who* and c(wh) can be obtained without going beyond strong Phase boundaries. In particular, there is no need for movement to the edge for such cases, and we will obtain much of the force of the Phase model through the architectural limit of a single Probe Box, without having to expand beyond the nesting mechanism.

6. Probes and goals

In this section, we introduce the notion of a Probe Box. Agree is the central relation computed by the parser. The operation that implements Agree will always involve the participation of a current probe, stored in the Probe Box, with a freshly introduced element of the input. In other words, Agree is performed as early as possible in an on-line fashion.

6.1 Agree and value

Formally, Agree is defined in (33) in terms of matching features (φ-features or *wh*) between active probes and goals. Syntactic objects are *active* if they have one or more (undeleted) uninterpretable features.

(33) Agree(p, g) if
   a. Match(p, g) holds. Then:
   b. Value(p, g) for matching features, and
   c. Value(p, g) for property value(f)

Probe p and goal g are syntactic objects. f is a feature.
   Following Chomsky's definitions, if Match(p, g) holds, the goal g may value uninterpretable features in the probe p, indicated by Value(g, p):

(34) Value(α, β) holds if:
   a. (Unify) Unify matching φ-feature values of α and β.
   b. (Assign) If α has property value(f), f for β receives its value from α.
   α and β are syntactic objects or features of syntactic objects.

For example, as the parse in Figure 2 indicates, v*'s (unintepretable) φ-features are valued by matching φ-features of *Mary*. Proceeding in the opposite direction, a probe p may value uninterpretable features of a goal g if p has the property of valuing some feature f. For example, T and v^* in Figure 2 have property value(case(nom)) and value(case(acc)), valuing the (uninterpretable) structural Case feature of *John* and *Mary*, respectively. (Note that the φ-incomplete probe $T_{\bar{\varphi}}$ does not have this property and thus cannot value uninterpretable features.)

The model here deviates from Chomsky's basic account in that logical unification is used in (34a) in order to maintain the single Probe Box story in the context of φ-incomplete probes, as will be explained below.

6.2 The Probe Box

For parsing, the probe p in (33) will always refer to the current contents of the Probe Box. At the start of the computation, the Probe Box is empty:

(35)   Probe Box: *Initial Contents*
      Empty.

We modify the parse procedure to call Agree and update or maintain the contents of the Probe Box in an on-line fashion, as shown in (36). The basic strategy is to run Agree on items as soon as they are inserted into phrase structure. With this strategy, no new choice points need be introduced.

(36)   Parse:
    a.   Given a category c, pick an elementary tree headed by c.
    b.   From the Move Box *or* input:
        i.   Fill in the specifier (if one exists)
        ii.   Run Agree(p, s) if p and s are non-empty
        iii.   Fill in the head h
        iv.   Run Agree(p, h) for goal h or φ-incomplete h
        v.   Copy h to Probe Box p if h is a probe
        vi.   Fill in the complement by recursively calling parse with c' where c has lexical property select(c)

Assuming the current elementary tree contains a specifier s, step (36b–ii) runs Agree(p, s) as soon as the specifier position is filled. Next, as the head of the elementary tree is filled, if it is a probe, it is copied to the Probe Box by step (36b–v), possibly overwriting a pre-existing probe. Only a single probe is permitted. Note step (36b–iv) also stipulates that Agree is also run on heads that are φ-incomplete probes. (We return to discuss this operation in the next section.)

We are now in a position to illustrate the operation of the Probe Box for a simple sentence. Consider again the sequence of operations shown in Figure 4 for *John*

Step	Phrase Structure	Input
(i)	$[_c$ c _]	John saw Mary
(iv)	$[_c$ c $[_T$ John $[_T$ $[_T$ past (+)] _]]]	see Mary
(vi)	$[_c$ c $[_T$ John $[_T$ $[_T$ past(+)] $[_v$ t(John) $[_v$ $[_v$ v* _]]]]]]	see Mary
(ix)	$[_c$ c $[_T$ John $[_T$ $[_T$ past(+)] $[_v$ t(John) $[_v$ $[_v$ v* $[_v$ $[_v$ see] Mary]]]]]]]	(*empty*)

Probe Box notes:

Step	Probe Box	
(i)	(*empty*)	Initial condition.
(iv)	$[_T$ past (+)]	Fill head of T from input,
		$[_T$ past (+)] is a probe, copy $[_T$ past (+)] to Probe Box
(vi)	$[_T$ past (+)]	Fill specifier-v from Move Box
		Apply (37b-ii), run Agree($[_T$ past (+)], *John*).
		value(φ-*John*, φ-T), value(T, Case-*John*).
(vi)	v*	New head v* is a probe, copy v* to Probe Box
		($[_T$ past (+)] is displaced.)
(ix)	v*	Fill complement-V from input,
		Apply (37b-iv), run Agree(v*, *Mary*).
		value(φ-*Mary*, φ-v*), value(v*, Case-*Mary*).

Figure 6. Probe Box computation for *John saw Mary*

saw Mary. The corresponding manipulations for the Probe Box are documented in Figure 6.

The Probe Box is filled by $[_T$ past(+)] in step (iv). In step (vi), Agree is carried out on specifier-v *John*. The φ-features of *John* value the φ-features of the current probe T, and T values the Case feature of *John*. The single Probe Box strategy implies that the new probe v* displaces T as the current probe. In step (ix), Agree is carried out on complement-V. The φ-features of *Mary* value the φ-features of v*, and v* values the Case feature of *Mary*.

The single Probe Box model incorporates and preserves much of the property of Phases with respect to locality. A probe cannot penetrate into the domain of a lower probe since it will be displaced as soon as the parser encounters the second probe.

6.3 φ-Incomplete probes

So far, the current probe has been determined by left-to-right parse order. Let us now turn to situations of the kind considered by Chomsky involving intervening φ-incomplete probes such as infinitival $T_{\bar{\phi}}$ and PRT, shown here in (37)–(39).

(37) a. We expect there to arrive a man
      b. We T expect [$_T$ there $T_{\bar{\phi}}$ arrive a man]

(38) a. There are likely to be awarded several prizes
      b. There T are likely [$_T$ t(there) $T_{\bar{\phi}}$[$_V$ PRT [$_V$ award several prizes]]]

(39) a. There are expected to arrive a man
      b. There T [$_V$ PRT [$_V$ expect [$_T$ t(there) $T_{\bar{\phi}}$ arrive a man]]]

There are two problems to be addressed in examples (37)–(39). (1) the presence of φ-incomplete probes blocking matrix T from agreeing with the object of the embedded clause, and (2) the valuation of the unintepretable features belonging to φ-incomplete probes.

Matrix T must value the Case feature of the embedded object and its φ-features must be valued by the embedded object. Under the single probe model, matrix T must not be displaced by $T_{\bar{\phi}}$. or PRT, since the contents of the Probe Box must be preserved until the parser reaches the embedded object position and can run Agree. This is encoded in (40):

(40) **Probe Box:** φ-*Incomplete Probes*
      φ-incomplete probes may not occupy the Probe Box.

However, (40) by itself is insufficient since φ-incomplete probes also have uninterpretable features that must be valued for the computation to succeed. With respect to the lexicon defined earlier in Figure 1, $T_{\bar{\phi}}$ has a single uninterpretable φ-feature person(_), and the participle PRT has uninterpretable features {person(_),number(_)}. Assuming feature unification, the solution to this problem is given in parsing step (36b–iv). When a head h that is also a φ-incomplete probe is analyzed, Agree(p, h) is applied. For example (37), Agree(T, $T_{\bar{\phi}}$.) will unify the (still) unvalued features of T and $T_{\bar{\phi}}$. In particular, T-person(_) is unified with $T_{\bar{\phi}}$.-person(_). More precisely, the feature value slots, denoted by "_", are unified and will share values once instantiated. T stays in the Probe Box and goes on to complete Agree(T,*man*). The unintepretable φ-features of T are valued. Furthermore, $T_{\bar{\phi}}$. person(_) is also valued by association from the earlier unification. Similar considerations apply for $T_{\bar{\phi}}$. and PRT for (38) and (39). In the case of PRT, in addition to its φ-features, it also has an uninterpretable Case feature, which is valued by Agree(T,PRT). Hence, the single Probe Box can be maintained and no additional choice points need be created.[9]

6.4 Probe inactivation

In the account so far, the Probe Box is only superceded when a new (φ-complete) probe comes along to fill the box. In particular, a probe may remain in the Probe Box even after its uninterpretable φ-features have been valued. In other words, the Probe Box may hold an inactive probe. In this section, we give evidence that this strategy is essentially correct. Consider example (20a) again, repeated below as

(41a). (b) encodes the state in computation where the embedded specifier-T has just been filled with *prizes* from the Move Box:

(41)   a.   Several prizes are likely to be awarded
   b. $[_c$ c $[_T$ several prizes $[_T$ $[_T$ past(-) $[_v$ $[_v$ be $][_A$ $[_A$ likely $][_T$ t(prizes) $[_T$
      $T_{\bar{\phi}_-}$]]]]]]]
   c.   prizes (Move Box)
   d.   T (Probe Box)

In accordance with applying Agree as soon as possible, Agree(T,*prizes*) at step (41b) will value T's φ-features (and the Case feature of *prizes*). Without outstanding uninterpretable features, T is rendered inactive. However, as (42) indicates, it is necessary to allow T to remain in the Probe Box as there are still φ-incomplete probes, namely $T_{\bar{\phi}}$ and PRT, that need to have unintepretable features valued through Agree with T.

(42) $[_c$ c $[_T$ several prizes $[_T$ $[_T$ past(-) $[_v$ $[_v$ be $][_A$ $[_A$ likely $][_T$ t(prizes) $[_T$ $T_{\bar{\phi}}$ $[_v$
      $[_v$ PRT $][_v$ award t(prizes)]]]]]]]]]]

7.   A preliminary comparison

In this section, we compare the number of computational steps taken by the probe-goal parser to that taken by a corresponding parser, PAPPI Fong (1991), in the Government-and-Binding (GB) framework Chomsky (1981), for the analysis of examples (43a–b):

(43)   a.   There are likely to be awarded several prizes
   b.   Several prizes are likely to be awarded

We should point out that the results reported in Figures 7 and 8 are preliminary. The parses given in Figures 7 and 8 are for example (43b) for the GB-based and probe-goal parsers, respectively. Although the parses recovered are similar to one another, the linguistic coverage of the two parsers are quite different. Currently, the GB-based parser has much wider coverage, and carries more overhead in terms of computational machinery, thereby affecting the results to some degree. However, even with this caveat in mind, the difference in computational efficiency between the probe-goal parser and the GB-based parser is noteworthy. This is reflected both in terms of the amount of structure built and the number of movement operations during parsing. In the former case, the GB-based parser constructs approximately an order of magnitude more syntactic objects than its probe-goal counterpart. (The reported results are normalized in terms of *elementary trees units* (eT).[10]) With

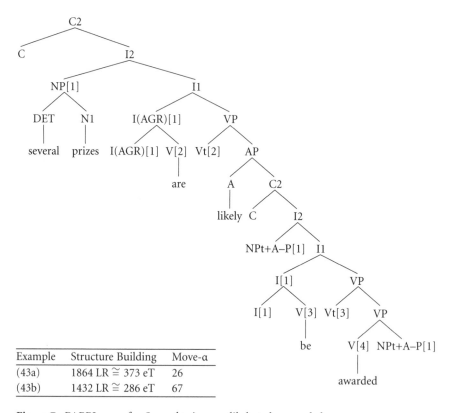

Example	Structure Building	Move-α
(43a)	1864 LR ≅ 373 eT	26
(43b)	1432 LR ≅ 286 eT	67

Figure 7. PAPPI parse for *Several prizes are likely to be awarded*

respect to movement, there is a similar order of magnitude difference. One reason for this striking difference is that the GB-based parser is designed around a
generate-and-test model of computation, where declarative principles interact and
freely combine both to provide for (and limit) the range of possible parses without regard for linear order. By contrast, the probe-goal parser has been designed
around a more constrained model where linguistic constraints strictly follow the
order imposed by left-to-right, on-line computation.

8.   Conclusions

This paper has outlined a parsing-centric view of computation with probes and
goals. The use of elementary tree fragments instead of MERGE and MOVE follows
from left-to-right parsing constraints.

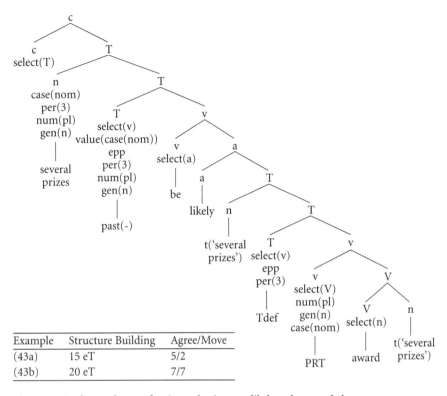

Example	Structure Building	Agree/Move
(43a)	15 eT	5/2
(43b)	20 eT	7/7

Figure 8. Probe-goal parse for *Several prizes are likely to be awarded*

Two data structures, the Move and Probe boxes, have been introduced to encode theta-theory and probe-goal locality, respectively. At any given point, the two boxes carry forward deeper into computation syntactic objects that must still interact with other objects not yet parsed. The short-term or "cache" memory represented by the boxes obviate the need to perform *lookback*, i.e. search back into the computational history for appropriate matching elements. No lookback is a constraint imposed by the commitment to on-line processing. To avoid unnecessary search whilst allowing movement sequences to nest, the Move Box follows a stack organization. The Probe Box is able to hold onto tighter bounds; it maintains its singularity through probe-goal unification in the case of φ-incomplete intermediate probes.

Finally, preliminary investigations suggest that following through on these design elements may result in more efficient computational systems, as compared to earlier theories. Further work is required to determine whether this can be maintained as the linguistic coverage of the probe-goal system expands.

Acknowledgements

This work has been supported in part by NEC Laboratories America. The author is indebted to Roger Martin for his help in getting started on this project. Parts of this paper have also been presented at the CUNY Psycholinguistics Supper Club. The author is also grateful for comments received there.

Notes

1. In this system, probe-goal agreement may trigger concomitant movement by the principle of Maximize Matching Effects, Chomsky (1999).

2. The term "reminiscent" is used here because Phillips (1995) pre-dates the probe-goal Case agreement framework discussed here.

3. As will be explained below, select(V) plays only a role in elementary tree composition. In particular, it is not a participant in the central operations Agree or Move.

4. In Figure 4, the underscore character (_) is used to denote (unfilled) open positions.

5. Lexico-semantic constraints external to the system described here will be needed to rule out cases like *John arrived Mary.

6. In Chomsky's bottom-up generative framework, (15c) cannot be assembled. Agree(T,ice) will force the raising of the object according to the principle of maximizingmatching effects, i.e. Agree will trigger move if possible. For the parsing model, as will be explained later, assembly will fail at the verb object position due to constraint (16), i.e. the preference for the Move Box over the input.

7. We do not consider the computation of affixes and head movement in this paper. The computation of these elements may fall outside the purview of narrow syntax.

8. For the examples in (22), Chomsky assumes an English-particular rule of Thematization/Extraction (TH/EX) at PF will front *prizes* ahead of the verb *award*. This rule is currently unimplemented in the parser described here.

9. Actually, we also need to add that the parser runs Agree(c(wh),*wh*-N locally, i.e. when the *wh*-N is first filled at specifier-c, to maintain the single Probe Box story for *wh*-movement.

10. The GB-based parser builds structures by composing individual phrases rather than in elementary tree-sized chunks. The exchange rate is roughly 5-to-1 since each fully populated elementary tree contains 5 syntactic objects.

References

Chomsky, N. A. (1981). *Lecture on Government and Binding.* Dordrecht: Foris.
Chomsky, N. A. (1998). *Minimalist Inquiries: The Framework*, MITWPL.
Chomsky, N. A. (1999). *Derivation by Phase.* MITWPL.

Di Sciullo, A. M. (2002). Asymmetry, antisymmetry and tractability. Paper presented at the *Second Conference of the Federation on Natural Language Processing: Language, Brain, and Computation*, University of Venice, Italy.

Di Sciullo, A. M. (2005). *Asymmetry in Morphology*. In press. Cambridge, Mass.: The MIT Press.

Fong, S. (1991). Computational properties of principle-based grammatical theories. Ph.D. Dissrtation. Artificial Intelligence Laboratory. MIT.

Joshi, A. & Schabes, Y. (1997). Tree-adjoining grammars. In G. Rosenberg & A. Saloma (Eds.), *Handbook of Formal Languages, Vol. 3* (pp. 69–123). Springer-Verlag.

Pesetsky, D. M. (1995). *Zero Syntax: Experiencers and Cascades*. Cambridge, Mass.: MIT Press.

Phillips, C. (1995). Order and structure. Ph.D. Dissertation. MIT.

Stabler, E. P. Jr. (1997). Derivational Minimalism. In C. Retoré (Ed.), *Logical Aspects of Computational Linguistics* (pp. 68–95). Springer.

Woods, W. A. (1970). Transition network grammars for natural language analysis. *Communications of the Association for Computing Machinery, 13* (10), 591–606.

Deep & shallow linguistically based parsing

Parameterizing ambiguity in a hybrid parser

Rodolfo Delmonte

Università "Ca Foscari"

In this paper we will present an approach to natural language processing which we define as "hybrid", in which symbolic and statistical approaches are reconciled, i.e. the analysis of natural language sentences is at the same time a deterministic and a probabilistic process. In the paper we will criticize current holistic statistical approaches for being inherently ill-founded. We purport the view that the implementation of sound parsing algorithms must go hand in hand with sound grammar construction. A number of parsing strategies and graceful recovery procedures are then proposed which follow a strictly parameterized approach to their definition and implementation.

1. Introduction

In this paper we will present an approach to natural language processing which we define as "hybrid", in which symbolic and statistical approaches are reconciled. In fact, we claim that the analysis of natural language sentences (and texts) is at the same time a deterministic and a probabilistic process. In particular, the search space for syntactic analysis is inherently deterministic, in that it is severely limited by the grammar of the specific language, which in turn is constituted by a set of peripheral rules to be applied in concomitance with the more general rules of core grammar. Variations on these rules are only determined by genre, which can thus contribute a new set of peripheral rules, or sometimes just a set of partially overlapping rules with the ones already accepted by a given linguistic community.

Probabilistic processes come into play whenever lexical information is tapped to introduce knowledge into the parsing process. The determination of meaning at propositional level is the product of the meaning of its internal component, the process being compositional in nature. At a semantic level, meaning variations at word and at phrase level come into play to contribute uncertainty to the overall process. Word sense disambiguation procedures coupled with constituent attachment disambiguation should be used to take decisions as to the most probable clause level analysis to assign to a given input sentence.

In this paper we will criticize current holistic statistical approaches for being inherently ill-founded. People working in the empirical framework have tried to credit the point of view that what happened to the speech research paradigm was also applicable to the NLP paradigm as a whole. People like Ken Church have paved the way to the NLP scientific community by presenting the task of NLP as being parallel with what the speech community did, in the Introduction to the Special Issue on Using Large Corpora published by Computational Linguistics in Armstrong-Warwick (1993). In this seminal but partially misleading article, the author claimed that what happened to the speech community in the last 20 years or so, that is a slow transformation of their approach to natural language understanding from a knowledge-based approach to an empirical statistically-based approach, could also be applied to NLP. Given that both communities were apparently dealing with the same basic materials, linguistic units of some kind, the transition to the empirical approach was simply to be treated as a truism by people of the NLP community. The only true part of the argument was on the contrary constituted by the need felt by most computational linguists to move away from the analysis of hand-made list of sentences and start tackling 'real texts', that is, the need to move away from what theoretical linguists would still regard as a sufficiently representative sample of the language under analysis – usually a list of 3–4000 simplex sentences, in order to start using large corpora. However, it is just the fact that the linguistic units being addressed as their main object were totally different, that the comparison does not hold and is badly misleading. In the section below, we will discuss in detail the reason why in our opinion the empirical statistical approach to NLP in its current experimental and empirical design should not be pursued, and in fact this would be the same reason why the speech community has come to the same conclusions already some time ago with respect to the need to address higher level linguistic units in the speech waveform usually referred to as prosodic units (Delmonte 2000). In particular, both the speech synthesis community and the speech recognition community have implicitly admitted to the fact that the choice of the linguistic units to be addressed, i.e. a segmental unit, constitutes nowadays the bottleneck for further improvements in the field (see R. Sproat & J. van Santen 1998).

On a strictly intuitive basis, the segmental unit approach is wrong for the simple reason that one would need to model information coming from all linguistic levels into one single segment – be it a phone, a phoneme, a diphone unit or a triphone unit from the n-gram approach advocated by the speech community and transferred by the new empiricists onto the part-of-speech tagging task. This position is both untenable and implausible. It is untenable for reasons related to tagset size and linguistic coverage, i.e. how big a training corpus should be in order to cope with the well-known problem of data sparseness or sparsity. For instance in the LinGO framework, the tagset being used amounts to over 8,000 different single tags, which makes it very hard even with a database of 10,000 utterance to make up a representative and statistical useful training corpus, as their authors comment in the entry webpage of the project at http://lingo.stanford.edu under the title "Why Another (Type of) Treebank?" which we report here below:

> For the past decade or more, symbolic, linguistically oriented methods like those pursued within the HPSG framework and statistical or machine learning approaches to NLP have typically been perceived as incompatible or even competing paradigms; the former, more traditional approaches are often referred to as 'deep' NLP, in contrast to the comparatively recent branch of language technology focussing on 'shallow' (text) processing methods. Shallow processing techniques have produced useful results in many classes of applications, but they have not met the full range of needs for NLP, particularly where precise interpretation is important, or where the variety of linguistic expressions is large relative to the amount of training data available. On the other hand, deep approaches to NLP have only recently been able to achieve broad enough grammatical coverage and sufficient processing efficiency to allow the use of HPSG-type systems in certain types of real-world applications.
>
> Fully-automated, deep grammatical analysis of unrestricted text remains an unresolved challenge. In particular, realistic applications of analytical grammars for natural language parsing or generation require the use of sophisticated statistical techniques for resolving ambiguities. We observe general consensus on the necessity for bridging activities, combining symbolic and stochastic approaches to NLP...
>
> An important recent advance in this area has been the application of log-linear models (Agresti 1990) to modeling linguistic systems. These models can deal with the many interacting dependencies and the structural complexity found in constraint-based or unification-based theories of syntax. The availability of even a medium-size treebank would allow us to begin exploring the use of these models for probabilistic disambiguation of HPSG grammars.

Further on, the webpage includes details of the implementation, which we report here below:

> The key innovative aspect of the Redwoods approach to treebanking is the anchoring of all linguistic data captured in the treebank to the HPSG framework and a generally-available broad-coverage grammar of English, viz. the LinGO English Resource Grammar. Unlike existing treebanks, there will be no need to define a (new) form of grammatical representation specific to the treebank (and, consequently, less dissemination effort in establishing this representation). Instead, the treebank will record complete syntacto-semantic analyses as defined by the LinGO ERG and provide tools to extract many different

types of linguistic information at greatly varying granularity. Depth of Representation and Transformation of Information Internally, the [incr tsdb()] database records analyses in three different formats, viz. (i) as a derivation tree composed of identifiers of lexical items and constructions used to construct the analysis, (ii) as a traditional phrase structure tree labeled with an inventory of some fifty atomic labels (of the type S, NP, VP et al.), and (iii) as an underspecified MRS meaning representation... While (ii) will in many cases be similar to the representation found in the Penn Treebank, (iii) subsumes the functor-argument (or tectogrammatical) structure as it is advocated in the Prague Dependency Treebank or the German TiGer corpus. Most importantly, however, representation (i) provides all the information required to replay the full HPSG analysis...

Even though the overall tone of the researchers involved in the LinGO consortium is enthusiastic, the actual coverage of the PET parser in real texts is as usual limited by grammar and vocabulary coverage. However, we find the approach in line with ours even though the underlying technical framework is totally different.

1.1   Shallow and partial parsing and statistical processing

In their Chapter – Language Analysis and Understanding (Karlsson & Karttunen 1995) in the section dedicated to Shallow Parsing (ibid.: 113–114), they use the term shallow syntax as a generic term for analyses that are less complete than the output from a conventional parser. The output from a shallow analysis is not a phrase-structure tree. A shallow analyzer may identify some phrasal constituents, such as noun phrases, without indicating their internal structure and their function in the sentence. Another type of shallow analysis identifies the functional role of some of the words, such as the main verb, and its direct arguments. Systems for shallow parsing normally work on top of morphological analysis and disambiguation. The basic purpose is to infer as much syntactic structure as possible from the lemmata, morphological information, and word order configuration at hand. Typically shallow parsing aims at detecting phrases and basic head/modifier relations. A shared concern of many shallow parsers is the application to large text corpora. Frequently partial analyses are allowed if the parser is not potent enough to resolve all problems.

Abney (1996) comments on statistical methods applied to the problem of Part-of-Speech Tagging as being quite a success story. People engaging in this kind of pioneering research effort at the beginning of the '90s showed that it was possible to "carve part-of-speech disambiguation out of the apparently monolithic problem of natural language understanding, and solve it with impressive accuracy" (Abney 1996: 1). What the people (Church (1988), DeRose (1988), Garside (1987)) involved in that approach were actually interested in showing was that even if the exact solution to the NLU problem is far beyond reach, a reasonable approximate solution is quite feasible.

In Abney (1996) the author discusses the feasibility of another important aspect of the NLU problem: that of syntactic analysis, by proposing as a solution what he defines "Partial Parsing". This is regarded as a cover term for a range of different techniques for recovering some but not all of the information contained in a traditional syntactic analysis. As he comments "Partial parsing techniques, like tagging techniques, aim for reliability and robustness in the face of the vagaries of natural text, by sacrificing completeness of analysis and accepting a low but non-zero error rate."(Abney 1996:3)

Further on in the same paper, we are told that a 5% error rate is certainly a remarkable achievement in terms of accuracy, and can be achieved in a very short term indeed – one month work of a computational linguist. However, if we consider the sentence as the relevant unit onto which to gauge the goodness of such an accuracy figure, we come up with a completely different figure: assuming an average of 20-word sentences and 4% per-word error rate we end up with a 56% per-sentence error rate. To get a 4% per-sentence error rate, we require accuracy figures which range beyond 99%, actually 99.98%. This is clearly unfeasible for any statistically or even rule-based tagger presented in the literature.

Partial parsing tries to offer a solution to the problem posed by unrestricted texts to traditional parsers which, due to the incompleteness of both lexicon and grammar, are subject to failures and errors. Errors are also a subproduct of the length of sentences and the inherent ambiguity of grammars. What partial parsers do is recovering the nonrecursive core of constituent structure by factoring out the parse into those pieces of structure that can be reliably recovered with a small amount of syntactic information. This is usually done without using lexical information, as would typically do all unification based parsers. Chunks and simplex clauses can then safely be used for bootstrapping lexical association information which is used to take decisions related to attachment of arguments and adjuncts. The output of any such chunkers can be regarded as a useful intermediate representation to be used for any further computation. In terms of efficiency, as Abney (1996: 10) reports, the fastest parsers are all deterministic rule-based partial parsers.

We have developed our partial parser as a finite-state cascaded machine that produces a final parse by cycling on the input and passing the output of each parse to the following FSA. The parser was originally a recursive transition network, and has been built expressedly to eliminate recursion from the parsing process. However, even if the partial parser is good at recognizing constituent chunks or to do phrase-spotting, without having to analyze the entire sentence, when it comes to clauses the error rate increases a lot up to statistically valid threshold of 5–6%. As Church, Gale, Hanks, & Hindle, (1989) have shown, a partial parser can be put to use in a variety of ways, in particular in extracting subject-verb and verb-object pairs in order to provide a crude model of selectional restrictions.

1.2 Issues related to the use of partial and shallow approaches

In his Chapter on Sentence Modeling and Parsing, Fernando Pereira (1995), defines what are in his opinion the main issues in applying linguistic theory to the development of computational grammars: coverage, predictive power and computational requirements. However, this is done in order to promote the use of statistically based approaches to parsing and thus the issues are highlighted as shortcomings.

As far as Coverage is concerned his comment is that linguistic structures of real texts are not only limited to "the relationships between active and passive sentences, the constraints on use of anaphoric elements, or the possible scopes of quantifying elements such as determiners and adverbs" and "involves a wide range of other phenomena and constructions, such as idioms, coordination, ellipsis, apposition and extraposition, which may not be germane to the issues addressed by a particular linguistic theory or which may offer unresolved challenges to the theory." What he calls "a practical grammar" will have to go far beyond the proposals of any given theory to cover a substantial proportion of observed language. Even then, coverage gaps are relatively frequent and difficult to fill, as they involve laborious design of new grammar rules and representations. In other words, there is a lack of Predictive Power of linguistic grammars, which in his opinion "... being oriented towards the description of linguistic competence, are not intended to model distributional regularities arising from pragmatics, discourse and conventional use that manifest themselves in word and construction choice. Yet those are the regularities that appear to contribute most to the estimation of relative likelihoods of sentences or analyses." (Pereira 1995: 137).

As far as Computational Requirements are concerned, recent implementations seem to have made progress in the direction towards tractable grammatical formalisms which are reported to constitute polynomial-time and space parsing algorithms: however, he then asserts that, "... even polynomial-time algorithms may not be sufficiently fast for practical applications, given effect of grammar size on parsing time." (ibid.: 138).

Eventually in his "Future Directions" paragraph, Pereira comments on the current challenge which we also endorse fully:

> The issue that dominates current work in parsing and language modeling is to design parsers and evaluation functions with high coverage and precision with respect to naturally occurring linguistic material (for example, news stories, spontaneous speech interactions). Simple high-coverage methods such as n-gram models miss the higher-order regularities required for better predic-

tion and for reliable identification of meaningful relationships, while complex hand-built grammars often lack coverage of the tail of individually rare but collectively frequent sentence structures (cf. Zipf's law). Automated methods for grammar and evaluation function acquisition appear to be the only practical way to create accurate parsers with much better coverage. The challenge is to discover how to use linguistic knowledge to constrain that acquisition process. (ibid.: 140)

So, even though this conclusion has been written some seven years ago, it is still very much applicable to the current situation. On the same overall tone is the Chapter on Robust Parsing by Ted Briscoe (1995), where he comments on the question of disambiguation, a question that we'll also discuss further on in this paper. Here is his comment:

Despite over three decades of research effort, no practical domain-independent parser of unrestricted text has been developed. Such a parser should return the correct or a useful close analysis for 90% or more of input sentences. It would need to solve at least the following three problems, which create severe difficulties for conventional parsers utilizing standard parsing algorithms with a generative grammar:

1. chunking, that is, appropriate segmentation of text into syntactically parsable units;
2. disambiguation, that is, selecting the unique semantically and pragmatically correct analysis from the potentially large number of syntactically legitimate ones returned; and
3. undergeneration, or dealing with cases of input outside the systems' lexical or syntactic coverage.

Conventional parsers typically fail to return any useful information when faced with problems of undergeneration or chunking and rely on domain-specific detailed semantic information for disambiguation.

... Disambiguation using knowledge-based techniques requires the specification of too much detailed semantic information to yield a robust domain-independent parser. Yet analysis of the Susanne Corpus with a crude parser suggests that over 80% of sentences are structurally ambiguous... (statistically based) systems have yielded results of around 75% accuracy in assigning analyses to (unseen) test sentences from the same source as the unambiguous training material. The barrier to improvement of such results currently lies in the need to use more discriminating models of context, requiring more annotated training material to adequately estimate the parameters of such models. This approach may yield a robust automatic method for disambiguation of acceptable accuracy, but the grammars utilized still suffer from undergeneration, and are labour-intensive to develop. (Briscoe 1995: 142)

He then comments on the use of rule relaxation strategies, which in his opinion is an approach which is "... similar to the canonical parse approach to ambiguity, is labour-intensive and suffers from the difficulty of predicting the types of error or extragrammaticality liable to occur." (ibid.: 142)

In his Chapter on Statistical Parsing, John A.Carroll (2000) gives a rather pessimistic view of current and future possibilities for statistical approaches in NLP. This even though he is among the people working within the HPSG constrain unification framework quoted above in the LinGO project, who seem convinced of the contrary and are actually working with optimistic plans as the presentation of the Redwoods Treebank effort and subsequent parser creation and testing demonstrates. Carroll (2000: 525) states what in his opinion, are the major problems that parsing of natural language should address, namely:

a. how to resolve the (lexical, structural, or other) ambiguities that are inherent in real-world natural language text;
b. how to constrain the form of analyses assigned to sentences, while still being able to return "reasonable" analyses for as wide a range of sentences as possible.

He then criticizes NLP approaches wrought within the generative linguistic tradition because in his opinion they have a number of major drawbacks that disqualify them as adequate and successful candidates for the analysis of real texts. These parsing systems – like ours – use hand-built grammars in conjunction with parsing algorithms which either;

c. return all possible syntactic analyses, which would then be passed on to detailed, domain-dependent semantic and pragmatic processing subsystems for disambiguation;
d. use special purpose, heuristic parsing algorithms that are tuned to the grammar;
e. invoke hand-coded linguistic or domain-specific heuristics to perform disambiguation;
f. invoke grammar relaxation techniques to cope with extragrammatical input

a position which I find totally in line with our approach except for c, being deterministic and as such using all possible semantic knowledge as soon as possible and in any case before any major constituent is being licensed.

However, Carroll (2000: 526) finds that such an approach cannot be good because it has the following dramatic drawbacks;

g. computing the full set of analyses for a sentence of even moderate length with a wide-coverage grammar is often intractable (we also agree with this point);

h.   if this is possible, there is still the problem of how to apply semantic processing and disambiguation efficiently to a representation of a (possibly very) large set of competing syntactic analyses (same as above);

i.   although linguistic theories are often used as devices for explaining interesting facts about a language, actual text in nontrivial domains contains a wide range of poorly understood and idiosyncratic phenomena, forcing any grammar to be used in a practical system to go beyond established results and requiring much effort in filling gaps in coverage;

j.   hand-coding of heuristics is a labour-intensive task that is prone to mistakes and omissions, and makes system maintenance and enhancement more complicated and expensive;

k.   using domain-specific hand-coded knowledge hinders the porting of a system to other domains or sublanguages.

As to i.-k., since j.-k. are given as a logical/natural consequence to the widely acceptable and shared assertion contained in i. it needs looking into the quite obvious fact that neither hand-crafted grammars nor statistical ones are exempt from being inherently language-dependent abstract representations of the linguistic structure of a specific language in a specific genre and domain. Statistically built parsers will do that by tuning their grammar to a given training corpus with a certain number of caveats that we will discuss in detail below. Contrary to what is being assumed by Carroll, rule-based symbolic systems can take advantage of the generality of core grammars which, as we will discuss further on in the paper, offer core rules to be applied over an enormous gamut/range of natural languages, something which empirically built systems cannot take advantage of.

So it would seem that a lot of the current debate over the uselessness, inefficiency, inherent inability of rule-based symbolic systems is due to a fundamental choice in the type of parsing strategy and parsing algorithm, which as I understand reflects Carroll's choice of constraint-based and unification-based formalisms. These formalisms supplanted ATNs and RTNs in the '80s and slowly came to fore of the linguistic audience supported by a number of linguistic theories. One of these theories, LFG, is also at the heart of the system I will be presenting in this paper.

It seems to me that there hasn't been enough nerve in taking decisions which could counter the pervading feeling of the time when people working with mathematically sound and clean constraint-based unification-based parsers discovered their inefficiency, and simply denounce that. The effort devoted to the construction of hand-built lexica and rules are useful nonetheless to the theoretical linguistic community and certainly to students. These algorithms are unfit for the parsing of real texts required by systems for Information Retrieval and the more ambitious Natural Language Understanding community.

In addition to this, HMMs based statistical parsers also suffer from another drawback, pointed out by Klein and Manning (2002), who they take into account parameter estimation vs the use of conditional model structures:

> This paper separates conditional parameter estimation, which consistently raises test set accuracy on statistical NLP tasks, from conditional model structures, such as the conditional Markov model used for maximum-entropy tagging, which tend to lower accuracy. Error analysis on part-of-speech tagging shows that the actual tagging errors made by the conditionally structured model derive not only from label bias, but also from other ways in which the independence assumptions of the conditional model structure are unsuited to linguistic sequences...
>
> The claim is that the independence assumptions embodied by the conditionally structured model were the primary root of the lower accuracy for this model. Label bias and observation bias are both explaining-away phenomena, and are both consequences of these assumptions. Explaining-away effects will be found quite generally in conditionally structured models, and should be carefully considered before such models are adopted.
>
> (Klein & Manning 2002:9)

In other words, the independence hypothesis which is at the heart of the use of Markov models imported from the speech community into the empirical statistical approaches to NLP does not seem to be well suited to the task at hand simply because the linguistic units under consideration – the word, the single tag or both – are insufficient to assure enough contextual information, given language model building techniques based on word-tags with tagsets containing only lexical and part-of-speech information. It is precisely because of the independence hypothesis that people within the LinGO project have tried to map onto the tagset all layers of linguistic information, from morphological up to syntactic, semantic and possibly pragmatic information. However, this move will make it very hard for a corpus to have statistical significance, considering that the number of occurrences required to cover most cases useful to serve any n-gram model will certainly be over tens of millions of words.

2.   Linguistically-based parsing and linguistic strategies

Shallow parsing is currently considered as the only viable solution to the problem of unlimited vocabulary text understanding, in general. This is usually accomplished by a sequence of cascaded partial syntactic analyzers, or chunkers, which are specialized to take care of particular linguistic structures – say, NPs, APs and PPs. The remaining part of the input text is either left unparsed or is passed on to another processor, and this is repeated in a cascade until clause level is reached.

Ambiguity is one of the main problems faced by large-scale computational grammars. Ambiguities can arise basically from Part Of Speech (POS) tagging associated to any given word of the input sentence. Natural languages, with narrow tagset of say 100 tags, will come up with an average ambiguity ratio of 1.7/1.8 per word: i.e. each input word can be assigned in average to two different tags. This base level ambiguity has to be multiplied by rule interactions, via alternative subcategorization frames related to governing lexical entries, or simply from linguistically motivated syntactic ambiguities. As opposed to human speakers, computational grammars are not yet able to always (100%) determine the contextually correct or intended syntactic analysis from a set of alternative analyses. Thus, a computational grammar based on unification and constraint based formalisms, and covering a realistic fragment of natural language will, for a given sentence, come up with a large number of possible analyses, most of which are not perceived by humans or are considered inappropriate in the given context. In order to reduce the number of possible analyses, local tag disambiguation is carried out on the basis of statistical and syntactic algorithms. For a sentence like,

(1)   John wanted to leave.

there should only be one analysis available due to local linguistic and statistically derived restrictions that prevent the word "to" from being interpreted as a preposition after the word "wanted" (a verb and not a noun) and be assigned to the category of complementizers or verb particles. So, even though on the basis of a bottom up analysis, a word like "leave" could be analyzed both as a noun and as a base verb, by means of disambiguation carried out in a topdown fashion, the word "to" will trigger the appropriate interpretation of the word "leave" as base verb and not as noun. This is not always ensured, particularly in case a chart parser with a bottom up policy is chosen and all possible linguistic analyses are generated in a parallel fashion.

Disambiguation should be carried out on a separate module, and not be conflated with parsing in case one wants to simulate Garden Paths while at the same time avoiding crashes or freezing of the parser. This allows the topdown depth-first parser to backtrack and try the other analysis. However, backtracking should be allowed only whenever real Garden Path are in order. This kind of information is not hidden but can be derived from linguistic information.

In this paper we will discuss our proposal to solve ambiguity by means of linguistically related lexical and structural information which is used efficiently in a number of disambiguation strategies. Since the parser we will present is a multilingual parser, strategies will be also related to UG parameters in order to take advantage of the same Core Grammar and use Peripheral Rules for that task.

2.1   Shallow and deep parsing

The shallow parsing approach is very efficient and usually prevents failures. However, the tradeoff with deep parsing is a certain percentage of text not being fully parsed due to local failures, especially at clause level. This may also result as a wrong choice of tag disambiguation, which carries on to constituent level. Another important shortcoming is the inherent inability of this approach to ensure a semantically consistent mapping of all resulting constituent structures. This is partly due to the fact that clause level analysis is only approximated and not always fully realized. In addition, all attachments are also approximated in lack of a stable clause level analysis. Finally, subcategorization frames cannot be used consistently either, but only tentatively matched with the available information.

As a counterpart to this situation, shallow parsers can easily be ported to other languages and so satisfy an important requirement, that of reusability. In theoretical linguistic terms, this concept is easily understood as a subdivision of tasks between the parameters and principles components vs the rule component which being universal, relies on X-bar based constituency.

Though X-bar based parsing may be inefficient, one way to improve it would be that of encoding lexical ambiguity, both at word level and at the ensuing structural level. We would like to assume that specialization in language dependent ambiguity resolution is one of the components of the language acquisition process. We assume that, be it shallow or deep, parsing needs to be internally parameterized in oder to account for ambiguities generated both at structural and at semantic level.

The parser we present has been built to simulate the cognitive processes underlying the grammar of a language in use by a speaker, taking into account the psychological nuances related to the wellknown problem of ambiguity, which is a pervading problem in real text/life situation, and it is regarded an inseparable benchmark of any serious parser of any language to cope with.

In order for a parser to achieve psychological reality, it should satisfy three different types of requirements: psycholinguistic plausibility, computational efficiency in implementation, coverage of grammatical principles and constraints. Principles underlying the parser architecture should not conform exclusively to one or the other area, disregarding issues which might explain the behaviour of the human processor. In accordance with this criterion, we assume that the implementation should closely mimick phenomena such as Garden Path effects, or an increase in computational time in presence of semantically vs. syntactically biased ambiguous structures. We also assume that a failure should ensue from strong Garden Path effects and that this should be justified at a psycholinguistic interpretation level.

In other words, looking at parsing from a performance-based perspective, to justify speakers' psycholinguistic behaviour and its simulation in a running parser, we think it should be organized as a topdown depth-first symbolic rule compiler ordered according to efficiency criteria and using Lookahead and a Well-Formed Substring Table (WFST) not to duplicate effort.

This is just the opposite of a Unification Grammar which uses Chart parsing in a bottom up breadth-first manner which is norm in Constraint-Based formalisms like HPSG or LFG. However, what's more important, the parser should know what kind of ambiguities could cause unwanted Garden-Paths and Crashes, to refrain from unwanted failures in order to mimick human processing. Constraint unification is in our opinion unable to satisfy the efficiency requirements and prevent unwanted failures: we assume that it is insufficient to simply have a list of lexical items with their features, and a grammar with a list of rules which obey to a certain number of principles and constraints. A "sound" parser needs to be told which ambiguous structures are expected in which language.

In general terms, ambiguity is generated by homophonous words in understanding activities and by homographs in reading activities. In both cases Garden Paths or Crashes may only result in a given language in presence of additional conditions which are strictly dependent on the structure of the lexicon and the grammar. But some UG related parameters, like the "OMISSIBILITY OF THE COMPLEMENTIZER" in English may cause the parser to crash or freeze. Generally speaking, all types of ambiguity affecting parsing at a clause level will cause the parser to go into a Garden Path. The typical example quoted in psycholinguistic literature is the reduced relative case, determined by the lexical ambiguity of English verbs being at the same time interpretable as Past Participle – Past Tense. Shown below is the well-known example of a Reduced Relative Clause:

(2) The horse raced past the barn fell.

The English speaker will attempt treating the verb "raced" as the main tensed verb, but on discovery of sentence final verb "fell" which can only be interpreted as past tense, the whole sentential level analysis crashes and a Garden Path ensues causing a complete restart of the mental parser.

We assume that from a psycholinguistic point of view, parsing requires setting up a number of disambiguating strategies, basically to tell arguments apart from adjuncts and reduce the effects of backtracking.

The system is based on LFG theoretical framework (see Bresnan 2001, 1982) and has a highly interconnected modular structure. It is a top-down depth-first DCG-based parser written in Prolog which uses a strong deterministic policy by means of a lookahead mechanism with a WFST to help recovery when failure is unavoidable due to strong attachment ambiguity.

It is divided up into a pipeline of sequential but independent modules which realize the subdivision of a parsing scheme as proposed in LFG theory, where a c-structure is built before the f-structure can be projected by unification into a

DAG. In this sense we try to apply in a given sequence phrase-structure rules as they are ordered in the grammar: whenever a syntactic constituent is successfully built, it is checked for semantic consistency, both internally for head-spec agreement, and externally, as in the case in which a non-substantial head – like a preposition – dominates the lower NP constituent; other important local semantic consistency checks are performed with modifiers like attributive and predicative adjuncts. In case the governing predicate expects obligatory arguments to be lexically realized they will be searched and checked for uniqueness and coherence as LFG grammaticality principles require.

Whenever a given predicate has expectancies for a given argument to be realized either optionally or obligatorily, this information will be passed below to the recursive portion of the parsing: this operation allows us to implement parsing strategies like Minimal Attachment, Functional Preference and others (see Delmonte 2002).

As to multilinguality, the basic tenet of the parser is based on a UG-like perspective, i.e. the fact that all languages share a common core grammar and may vary at the periphery: internal differences are predicted by parameters. The DCG grammar allows the specification of linguistic rules in a highly declarative mode: it works topdown and by making a heavy use of linguistic knowledge, it may achieve an almost complete deterministic policy. Parameterized rules are scattered throughout the grammar so that they can be made operative as soon as a given rule is entered by the parser.

In particular, a rule may belong either to a set of languages, e.g. Romance or Germanic, or to a subset thereof, like English or Italian, thus becoming a peripheral rule. Rules are activated at startup and whenever a switch is being operated by the user, by means of logical flags appropriately inserted in the right hand side of the rule. No flags are required for rules belonging to the common core grammar.

Some such rules include the following ones: for languages like Italian and Spanish, a Subject NP may be an empty category, either a referential little pro or an expletive pronoun; Subject NPs may be freely inverted in postverbal position, i.e. preverbal NP is an empty category in these cases. For languages like Italian and French, PP or adverbial adjuncts may intervene between Verb and Object NP; adjectival modifiers may be taken to the right of their head Noun. For languages like English and German, tense and mood may be computed in CP internal position, when taking the auxiliary or the modal verb. English allows an empty Complementizer for finite complement and relative clauses, and negation requires do-support. Italian only allows for a highly genre marked (literary style) untensed auxiliary in Comp position.

Syntactic and semantic information is accessed and used as soon as possible: in particular, both categorial and subcategorization information attached to predicates in the lexicon is extracted as soon as the main predicate is processed, be it adjective, noun or verb, and is used to subsequently restrict the number of possible structures to be built. Adjuncts are computed by semantic compatibility tests on the basis of selectional restrictions of main predicates and adjuncts heads.

Syntactic rules are built using CP-IP functional maximal projections. Thus, we build and process syntactic phenomena like wh- movement before building f-structure representations, where quantifier raising and anaphoric binding for pronominals takes place. In particular, all levels of Control mechanisms which allow coindexing at different levels of parsing give us a powerful insight into the way in which the parser should be organized.

Yet the grammar formalism implemented in our system is not fully compliant with the one suggested by LFG theory, in the sense that we do not use a specific Feature-Based Unification algorithm but a DCG-based parsing scheme. In order to follow LFG theory more closely, unification should have been implemented. On the other hand, DCGs being based on Prolog language, give full control of a declarative rule-based system, where information is clearly spelled out and passed on and out to higher/lower levels of computation. In addition, we find that topdown parsing policies are better suited to implement parsing strategies that are essential in order to cope with attachment ambiguities (but see below). We use XGs (extraposition grammars) introduced by Martin (1980), Pereira (1981, 1983). Prolog provides naturally for backtracking when allowed, i.e. no cut is present to prevent it. Furthermore, the instantiation of variables is a simple way for implementing the mechanism for feature percolation and/or for the creation of chains by means of index inheritance between a controller and a controllee, and in more complex cases, for instance in case of constituent ellipsis or deletion. Apart from that, the grammar implemented is a surface grammar of the chosen languages. Also functional Control mechanisms – both structural and lexical – have been implemented as close as possible to the original formulation, i.e. by binding an empty operator in the subject position of a propositional like open complement/predicative function, whose predicate is constituted by the lexical head.

Being a DCG, the parser is strictly a top-down, depth-first, one-stage parser with backtracking: differently from most principle-based parsers presented in Berwick et al. (1991), which are two-stage parsers, our parser computes its representations in one pass. This makes it psychologically more realistic. The final output of the parsing process is an f-structure which serves as input to the binding module and logical form: in other words, it constitutes the input to the semantic component for computation of logical relations. In turn the binding module may add information as to pronominal elements present in the structure by assigning a controller/binder in case it is available, or else the pronominal expression will be available for discourse level anaphora resolution. As to the most important features of DCGs, we shall quote from Pereira & Warren (1980), in a comparison with ATNs:

Considered as practical tools for implementing language analysers, DCGs are in a real sense more powerful than ATNs, since, in a DCG, the structure returned from the analysis of a phrase may depend on items which have not yet been encountered in the course of parsing a sentence. ... Also on the practical side, the greater clarity and modularity of DCGs is a vital aid in the actual development of systems of the size and complexity necessary for real natural language analysis. Because the DCG consists of small independent rules with a declarative reading, it is much easier to extend the system with new linguistic constructions, or to modify the kind of structures which are built. ... Finally, on the philosophical side, DCGs are significant because they potentially provide a common formalism for theoretical work and for writing efficient natural language systems. (ibid.: 278).

2.2 Disambiguating constituency with functional mapping

As shown in Figure 1 below, the parser is made up of separate modules:

1. The Grammar, based on DCGs, incorporates Extraposition to process Long Distance Dependencies, which works on annotated c-structures: these constitute the output to the Interpretation Module;
2. The Interpretation Module checks whether f-structures may be associated to the input partially annotated c-structure by computing Functional Uniqueness, Coherence and Completeness. Semantic roles are associated to the input grammatical function labels at this level, after semantic selectional restrictions are checked for membership;
3. The Mapping scheme translates trees into graphs, i.e. maps c-structures onto f-structures. The parser builds an annotated c-structure, where the words of the input sentence are assigned syntactic constituency and functional annotations. This is then mapped onto the f-structure, i.e. constituent information is dropped and DAGs are built in order to produce an f-structure configuration.

Mapping onto f-structure is a one-to-many operation: each major constituent may be associated with different functional values: this is why we activate grammatical function calls whenever possible in order to take into account the position of constituents to be built by the parser. This is particularly true for NPs, but can also be applied to other constituents as can be seen from the following discussion on constituent-grammatical function mapping:

a. NP → SUBJect, both in preverbal and postverbal position – VP internally, VP adjoined and IP adjoined (see Delmonte 1987) – with any kind of verbal category; OBJect, usually in VP internal position, but also in preverbal position at Spec CP in case of reversed transitive structures; NCOMP predicative function – if not proper noun – occurring with copulative, and ECM verbs like "consider, believe"; closed ADJunct with [temporal] value, as the corresponding English example "this morning", which however in Italian can be freely inserted in sentence structure;

b.   AP → Modifier of an NP head, occurring as attribute in prenominal and as predication in postnominal position; ACOMP predicative function occurring with copulative, and ECM verbs; open XADJunct occurring freely at sentence level. Other examples of open adjuncts are: floating quantifiers, which however may only occur VP internally; doubling emphatic pronoun "lui" himself which also occurs VP internally and is computed as open adjunct;

c.   AdvP → Open or closed Adjuncts according to their selectional properties, occurring anywhere in the sentence according to their semantic nature;

d.   P → OBLiques, when selected by a given predicate; PCOMP predicative function, when selected by a given predicate – both of these two types of argument usually occur VP internally but may be fronted; open XADJunct or closed ADJunct according to semantic compatibility checks;

e.   VP' → VCOMP infinitivals, when selected by a given predicate; SUBJect propositional clauses; closed ADJuncts with semantic markers like "for"; VP' gerundive and participial, which are always computed respectively as closed ADJuncts and as open ADJuncts;

f.   S' → or CP as main clauses, or subordinate clauses, as well as sentential complements and SUBJect propositional clauses;

g.   Clitics and Pronominal elements are also computed as NPs or PPs, because they are assigned grammatical functions when not associated to NP dislocation in preverbal position: in that case, the clitic is simply erased and TOPic function is associated with the binder NP.

2.3   Tracing c-structure rules

The parser looks for syntactic constituents adjoined at CP level: in case of failure, it calls for IP level constituents, including the SUBJect which may either be a clause or an NP. This is repeated until it reaches the Verbal Phrase: from that moment onward, the syntactic category associated to the main verb – transitive, unergative, unaccusative, impersonal, atmospheric, raising, psych, copulative – and the lexical form of the predicate, are both used as topdown guidelines for the surface realization of its arguments. Italian is a language which allows for empty or morphologically unexpressed Subjects, so that no restriction may be projected from the lexicon onto c-structure: in case it is empty, a little pro is built in subject position, and features are left as empty variables until the tensed verb is processed.

The grammar is equipped with a lexicon containing a list of fully specified inflected word forms where each entry is followed by its lemma and a list of morphological features, organized in the form of attribute-value pairs. However, morphological analyzers for Italian and English are also available with big root dictionaries (90,000 for Italian, 25,000 for English), which only provide for syntactic subcategorization. The fully specified lexicon has been developed for Italian, English and German and contains approximately 5,000 entries for each language. In addition to that, there are all the lexical forms provided by a fully revised version of COMLEX; and in order to take into account phrasal and adverbial verbal compound forms, we also use lexical entries made available by UPenn and TAG encoding. Their grammatical verbal syntactic codes have then been adapted to our formalism and are used to generate an approximate subcategorization scheme with an approximate aspectual and semantic class associated to it. Semantic inherent features for Out of Vocabulary Words, be they nouns, verbs, adjectives or adverbs, are provided by a fully revised version of WordNet in which we used labels similar to those provided by CoreLex.

Once the word has been recognized, lemmata are recovered by the parser in order to render available the lexical form associated to each predicate. Predicates are provided for all lexical categories, noun, verb, adjective and adverb and their description is a lexical form in the sense of LFG. It is composed of both functional and semantic specifications for each argument of the predicate: semantic selection is operated by means of both thematic role and inherent semantic features or selectional restrictions. Moreover, in order to select adjuncts appropriately at each level of constituency, semantic classes are added to more traditional syntactic ones like transitive, unaccusative, reflexive and so on. Semantic classes are of two kinds: the first class is related to extensionality vs intensionality, and is used mainly to build discourse relations; the second class is meant to capture aspectual restrictions which decide the appropriateness and adequacy of adjuncts, so that inappropriate ones are attached at a higher level (see Delmonte 1995).

Grammatical functions are used to build f-structures and the processing of pronominals. They are crucial in defining lexical control: as in Bresnan (1982), all predicative or open functions are assigned a controller, lexically or structurally. Lexical control is directly encoded in each predicate-argument structure, and in case shallow parsing does not make that information available it will be impossible for the parser to bind the empty subject of all predicative open functions built in all predicative structures (or small clauses) to the approriate syntactic controller (or binder).

As said above, we believe it is highly important to organize c-structure rules for sentence level representation by means of the introduction of functional major constituents at the following basic levels:

CP → Spec, C'
C' → C, IP
IP → Spec=NP(subject), I'
I' → Inflected Tensed Verb Form, VP.

According to this configuration, adjuncts and constituents like wh- words for questions and topicalized NPs, adjoined at sentence level, will be computed at first in

Table 1. Some higher level rules of the parser

utterance	→ assertion_direct
utterance	→ standard_utterance
standard_utterance	→ wh_question
standard_utterance	→ yes_no_question
standard_utterance	→ assert_cp
assert_cp→	aux_to_comp
	adjunct_cp
	i_double_bar
assert_cp→	object
	adjunct_cp
	(pro=SI
	verb_phrase_impersonal
	;
	negat
	pro=CLI, {Case=acc}
	verb_phrase_focalized)
assert_cp→	object
	subject
	i_double_bar
i_double_bar→	subject
	negat
	adjs_preverbal
	parenthetical
	i_one_bar
i_one_bar→ verb_phrase_pass_canonic	
i_one_bar→ clitics,	
	{ germanic_aux,
	clitics,
	adjs_post_aux,
	germanic_vp ;
	all_languages_vp }
verb_phrase_copulative→	adv_phrase
	check_clitic_object
	xcomp
	prepositional_phrases

a CP constituent and then passed down to the lower level of analysis. This organization of constituency allows for complementizers, i.e. the head of CP, to be kept separate in C' level so that a nice interaction may be possible, if needed.

Below, we list some of the higher rules of the grammar with one of the interpretation rules for copulative constructions in Table 1.

Notice that i_one_bar rewrites as passive VP and, in case of failure, as active VP: again this is required by the need to activate the appropriate interpretation rule for transitive verbs which in most languages is morphologically determined by the presence of the appropriate auxiliary/ies and the past participle of the main verb.

2.4 Elliptical structures

In a framework like this, all elliptical structures are left over at the end of grammar traversal, simply because they cannot possibly be computed as any of the grammatically complete sentence level analyses, either as main clauses, as complement clauses or as subordinate or coordinate clauses. Just consider a simple case like (3), taken from a test text for NLUnderstanding distributed by Mitre:

(3)   The nights must be cold and the days warm

In order to compute the vp-ellipsis the rest of the previous computation constituted by the string [and, the, days, warm] must be evaluated in relation to the overall input sentence which is available from the lookahead stack. This is done in order to check for some parallel pattern at the level of tag assignment. Another reason may be the need to certify failures due to some form of agrammaticality present in the input sentence. When the parallelism has been ascertained, the main clause is used in order to duplicate the governing elliptical verbal predicate and the rest of the sentence is parsed in its component constituents. This is done by accessing an iterative call which is being used by all complements whenever a transitive verb has been detected or simply whenever there is not enough information to decide on verb subcategorization frame. The resulting list of constituents is then interpreted as in any normal non elliptical sentence by adding all verb related syntactic and semantic information which is lacking in elliptical sentences. The output will be a coordinate sentential structure which has the same verb information as the main preceding clause.

The call to recover from failures with elliptical structures is also used in case of ungrammatical structures with a feedback message being generated on the basis of the words still to be processed. In one case we manage to recover from failure due to ambiguously computed constituents which however do not motivate any preliminary choice either from the tag disambiguation procedure or from parsing strategy. These are cases of adjunct PP or similar constructions which do not depend on lexical information for their interpretation. One example is a case of parasitic gap constructions like the following,

(4)   This is the kind of food that must be cooked before Mary eats.

In this example, "before Mary" will be computed as a PP which will then be appropriately interpreted as adjunct to the main verb "cook". So the ending word "eats" will be left over to be filtered by the rule for elliptical constructions. This will be the trigger to recover the wrong analysis.

The shallow parser which runs in parallel with the deep parser is built as shown in Figure 2 below, with standard components like a statistical/syntactic tagger and a cascaded shallow parser which in a final run turns syntactic constituents into functionally labelled arguments/adjuncts. Subcategorization information is derived from COMLEX as well as from the subcategorized lexicon made available by UPenn. Semantic information is encoded in the 200,000 entries semantic lexicon built on the basis of EuroWordnet with a number of additions coming from computer, economics, and advertising semantic fields. Semantic class encoding has followed CoreLex close semantic set labeling with 60 semantic labels. We use the information derived from this parser only as a last resort, i.e. in case both complete and partial parsing do not come out with a successful result.

2.5 Parameters and strategies

Here below is a short list of parameterized ambiguities: some of them are to be solved by parsing preferences which according to J.Fodor's latest work (2002), are typological in nature. It appears that speakers of English prefer to adopt a Minimal Attachment strategy while this is not so for speakers of Romance languages. In particular, in the case of Relative Clause Attachment, this might be related to the influence of Latin on Romance language: Italian allows relative clauses as independent sentences to be attached in the discourse, just like Latin does.

A. Omissibility of Complementizer
o NP vs S complement
o S complement vs relative clause

B. Different levels of attachment for Adjuncts
o VP vs NP attachment of PP
o Low vs high attachment of relative clause

C. Alternation of Lexical Forms
o NP complement vs main clause subject

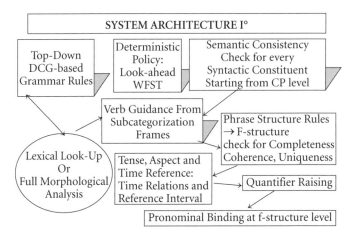

Figure 1. GETARUN Parser Architecture

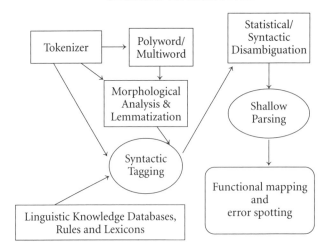

Figure 2. Shallow GETARUNS Architecture

D. Ambiguity at the level of lexical category

o Main clause vs reduced relative clause

o NP vs S conjunction

E. Ambiguities due to language specific structural properties

o Preposition stranding

o Double Object

o Prenominal Modifiers

o Demonstrative-Complementizer Ambiguity

o Personal vs Possessive Pronoun

F. Clitic Pronouns

G. Aux-to-Comp

2.5.1   *Linguistically-plausible relaxation techniques*

With the grammar listed above and with the parameters, we are now able to establish apriori positions in the parser where there could be recovery out of loop with ungrammatical structures with the possibility to indicate which portion of the input sentence is responsible for the failure. At the same time, parsing strategies could be devised in such a way to ensure recovery from local failure. We will start by commenting on Parsing Strategies and their implementation in our grammar.

As said above, we assume that the implementation should closely mimick phenomena such as Garden Path effects, or an increase in computational time in presence of semantically vs. syntactically biased ambiguous structures. We also assume that a failure should ensue from strong Garden Path effects and that this should be justified at a psycholinguistic interpretation level (see Pritchett 1992).

Differently from what is asserted by global or full paths approaches (Schubert 1984), we believe that decisions on structural ambiguity should be reached as soon as possible rather than deferred to a later level of representation. In particular, Schubert assumes "...a full paths approach in which not only complete phrases but also all incomplete phrases are fully integrated into (overlaid) parse trees dominating all of the text seen so far. Thus features and partial logical translations can be propagated and checked for consistency as early as possible, and alternatives chosen or discarded on the basis of all of the available information" (ibid., 249). And further on in the same paper, he proposes a system of numerical 'potentials' as a way of implementing preference trade-offs. "These potentials (or levels of activation) are assigned to nodes as a function of their syntactic/semantic/pragmatic structure and the preferred structures are those which lead to a globally high potential. Among contemporary syntactic parsing theories, the garden-path theory of sentence comprehension proposed by Clifton & Ferreira (1989), Frazier (1987a, 1987b), among others, is the one that most closely represents our point of view. It works on the basis of a serial syntactic analyzer, which is top-down, depth-first, i.e. it works on a single hypothesis, as opposed to other theories which take all possible syntactic analysis in parallel and feed them to the semantic processor. From our perspective, it would seem that parsing strategies should be differentiated according to whether there are argument requirements or simply semantic compatibility evaluation for adjuncts. As soon as the main predicate or head is parsed, it makes available all lexical information in order to predict – if possible – the complement structure, or to guide the following analysis accordingly. As an additional remark, note that not all possible syntactic structures can lead to ambiguous interpretations: in other words, we need to consider only cases which are factually relevant also from the point of view of language dependent ambiguities.

3.   Treebank derived structurals relations

As noted above in the Introduction, an important contribution to the analysis of PP attachment ambiguity resolution procedures is constituted by the data made available in syntactic Treebanks. Work still underway on our Venice Italian Corpus of 1million occurrences (Delmonte 2004a) revealed a distribution of syntactic-semantic relations which is very similar to the one reported by Hindle & Roth in their recent paper and shown in Table 2.

As the data reported above clearly show, most of the prepositional phrases are constituted by arguments of Noun, rather than of Verb. As to the remaining data, adjuncts are represented approximately by the same amount of cases, 11% of the sample text.

At first we collected all information on prepositions as a whole and then we searched into our Treebank looking for their relations as encoded in syntactic constituent structure. Here below we report data related to prepositions for the whole corpus: notice that in Italian as in English, preposition "of"/di would be used mainly as a Noun argument/modifier PP.

In contrast to English, however, nominal pre-nominal modifiers do not exist in Italian, and the corresponding Italian Noun-Noun modification or argument

Table 2. Shallow Parsing & Statistical Approaches (Data from D. Hindle & M. Roth 1993)

Structural Types	Nos. Preps.	% Preps.	Tot. Preps.
Argument noun	378	39.5	
Argument verb	104	11.8	
Light verb	19	2.1	
Small clause	13	1.5	
Idiom	19	2.1	57%
Adjunct noun	91	10.3	
Adjunct verb	101	11.5	
Locative indeterminacy	42	4.8	
Systematic indeterminacy	35	4	
Other	78	8.8	39.4%
TOTAL	880	100	

Table 3. Shallow Parsing & Statistical Approaches

Venice Italian Corpus
1 million tokens
All prepositions – 54 different types or wordforms:
170,000 occurrences
Argument-like prepositions 71.1%

DI/of and its amalgams	78,077 → 46%
A/to and its amalgams	29,191 → 17.2%
DA/by-from and its amalgams 13,354 → 7.9%	

Adjunct-like prepositions 23.2%

IN and its amalgams –	21,408 → 12.6%
PER and its amagalms –	12,140 → 7.1%
CON and its amalgams –	5,958 → 3.5%

Table 4. Quantitative Syntactic and Semantic Distribution of PPs in VIC

All PPs & Types of Adjs. Vs. Args.	Tot. Preps.	Tot. Types	% Types	% Preps
PPs not headed by DA or DI	3977			51%
Argument of verb		944	23.7%	
Argument of Noun		1300	32.7%	
Adjunct of Noun or Verb		1733	43.6%	
PPs headed by DA	504			6.5%
Argument of Verb		164	32.5%	
Argument of Noun		114	22.6%	
Adjunct of Noun or Verb		226	44.9%	
PPs headed by DI	3314			42.5%
Argument of Verb		72	2.17%	
Argument of Noun		2733	82.5%	
Adjunct of Noun or Verb		509	15.4%	
TOTAL	7795			100%
Arguments of Verb		1180	15%	
Arguments of Noun		4147	53%	
Ambiguous PPs		2468	32%	

relation without preposition would be postnominal. Such cases are not very frequent and constitute less than 1% of Noun-Noun head relations.We then selected 2000 sentences and looked at all prepositional phrases in order to highlight their syntactic and semantic properties, and we found out the following:

– The number of prepositional phrases in Italian texts is four times bigger than the one reported for English Texts, and this might be due to the poor use of nominal modifiers which in Italian can only be post-nominal modifiers, attested from an analysis of the sample text;

- PPs Arguments of Nouns are 53% in Italian and 39% in English, i.e. 14% more in Italian;
- PPs Arguments of Verbs are 15% in Italian and 17% in English – if we sum all argument types and idioms together –, i.e. 2% more in English;
- Adjuncts of Nouns and Verbs are 31% in English and 32% in Italian.

Thus, the only real big difference between the two languages can be traced back in the behaviour of PP noun arguments, which in turn can be traced back to a language specific typological difference: the existence of prenominal modifiers in English and not in Italian – or at least, not yet substituted by the use of postnominal modification.

3.1   Two mechanisms at work

We implemented two simple enough mechanisms in order to cope with the problem of nondeterminism and backtracking. At bootstrapping we have a preparsing phase where lexical lookup applies and morphological information is searched for: at this level of analysis of all input tokenized words, we create the lookahead stack, which is a stack of pairs input wordform – set of preterminal categories, where preterminal categories are a proper subset of all lexical categories which are actually contained in our lexicon. The idea is simply to prevent attempting the construction of a major constituent unless the first entry symbol is well qualified. The following list of preterminal 14 symbols is used, see Table 5.

Table 5. Preterminal symbols used for lookahead

1. v=verb-auxiliary-modal-clitic-cliticized verb
2. n=noun – common, proper;
3. c=complementizer
4. s=subordinator;
5. e=conjunction
6. p=preposition-particle
7. a=adjective;
8. q=participle/gerund
9. i=interjection
10. g=negation
11. d=article-quantifier-number-intensifier-focalizer
12. r=pronoun
13. b=adverb
14. x=punctuation

As has been reported in the literature (see Tapanainen & Voutilainen 1994; Brants & Samuelsson 1995), English is a language with a high level of homography: readings per word are around 2 (i.e. each word can be assigned on average two different tags). Lookahead in our system copes with most cases of ambiguity: however, we also had to introduce some disambiguating tool before the input string could be safely passed to the parser. Disambiguation is applied to the lookahead stack and is operated by means of Finite State Automata. The reason why we use FSA is simply that for some important categories, English has unambiguous tags which can be used as anchoring in the input string, to reduce ambiguity. We are now referring to the class of determiners which is used to tell apart words belonging to the ambiguity class [verb,noun], the most frequent in occurrence in English.

In order to cope with the problem of recoverability of already built parses we built a more subtle mechanism that relies on Kay's basic ideas when conceiving his Chart (see Martin 1980; Stock 1989). Differently from Kay, however, we are only interested in a highly restricted topdown depthfirst parser which is optimized so as to incorporate all linguistically motivated predictable moves. Any already parsed NP/PP is deposited in a table lookup accessible from higher levels of analysis and consumed if needed. To implement this mechanism in our DCG parser, we assert the contents of the structure in a table lookup storage which is then accessed whenever there is an attempt on the part of the parser to build up a similar constituent. In order to match the input string with the content of the stored phrase, we implemented a WellFormed Substring Table(WFST) as suggested by Woods (1973).

Now consider the way in which a WFST copes with the problem of parsing ambiguous structure. It builds up a table of well-formed substrings or terms which are partial constituents indexed by a locus, a number corresponding to their starting position in the sentence and a length, which corresponds to the number of terminal symbols represented in the term. For our purposes, two terms are equivalent in case they have the same locus and the same length.

In this way, the parser would consume each word in the input string against the stored term, rather than against a newly built constituent. In fact, this would fit and suit completely the requirement of the parsing process which rather than looking for lexical information associated to each word in the input string, only needs to consume the input words against a preparsed well-formed syntactic constituent.

Lookahead is used in a number of different ways: it may impose a wait-and-see policy on the topdown strategy or it may prevent following a certain rule path in case the stack does not support the first or even second match:

a. to prevent expanding a certain rule
b. to prevent backtracking from taking place until there is a high degree of confidence in the analysis of the current input string.

It can be used to gather positive or negative evidence about the presence of a certain symbol ahead: symbols to be tested against the input string may be more than one, and also the input word may be ambiguous among a number of symbols. Since in some cases we extend the lookahead mechanism to include two symbols and in one case even three symbols, possibilities become quite numerous.

Consider now failure and backtracking which ensues. Technically speaking, by means of lookahead we prevent local failures in that we do not allow the parser to access the lexicon where the input symbol would be matched against. It is also important to say that almost all our rules satisfy the efficiency requirement to have a preterminal in first position in their right-hand side. This is usually related to the property belonging to the class of Regular Languages. There are in fact some well-known exceptions: simple declarative sentence rules, yes-no questions in Italian. Noun phrase main constituents have a multiple symbol lookahead, adjectival phrase has a double symbol lookahead, adverbial phrase has some special cases which require the match with a certain word/words like "time/times" for instance. Prepositional phrase requires a single symbol lookahead; relative clauses, interrogative clauses, complement clauses are all started by one or more symbols. Cases like complementizerless sentential complements are allowed to be analyzed whenever a certain switch is activated.

Suppose we may now delimit failure to the general case that may be described as follows: a constituent has been fully built and interpreted but it is not appropriate for that level of attachment; failure would thus be caused only by semantic compatibility tests required for modifiers and adjuncts or lack of satisfaction of argument requirements for a given predicate.

Technically speaking we have two main possibilities:

A.   the built constituent is displaced on a higher level after closing the one in which it was momentarily embedded.

This is the case represented by the adjunct PP "in the night" in the example below:

(5)   The thieves stole the painting in the night.

The PP is at first analyzed while building the NP "the painting in the night" which however is rejected after the PP semantic features are matched against the features of the governing head "painting". The PP is subsequently stored on the constituent storage (the WFST) and recovered at the VP level where it is taken as an adjunct.

B.   the constituent built is needed on a lower level and there is no information on the attachment site.

In this case a lot of input string has already been consumed before failure takes place and the parser needs to backtrack a lot before constituents may be safely built and interpreted.

To give a simple example, suppose we have taken the PP "in the night" within the NP headed by the noun "painting". At this point, the lookahead stack would be set to the position in the input string that follows the last word "night". As a side-effect of failure in semantic compatibility evaluation within the NP, the PP "in the night" would be deposited in the backtrack WFST storage. The input string would be restored to the word "in", and analysis would be restarted at the VP level. In case no PP rule is met, the parser would continue with the input string trying to terminate its process successfully. However, as soon as a PP constituent is tried, the storage is accessed first, and in case of non emptiness its content recovered. No structure building would take place, and semantic compatibility would take place later on at sentence level. The parser would only execute the following actions:

- match the first input word with the (preposition) head of the stored term;
- accept new input words as long as the length of the stored term allows it by matching its length with the one computed on the basis of the input words.

As said above, the lookahead procedure is used both in presence and in absence of certain local requirements for preterminals, but always to confirm the current choice and to prevent backtracking from taking place. As a general rule, one symbol is sufficient to take the right decision; however in some cases, more than one symbol is needed. In particular when building a NP, the head noun is taken at first by nominal premodifiers, which might precede the actual head noun of the NP. The procedure checks for the presence of a sequence of at least two nouns before consuming the current input token. In other cases the number of preterminals to be checked is three, and there is no way to apply a wait-and-see policy.

Reanalysis of a clause results in a Garden Path(GP) in our parser, because nothing is available to recover a failure that encompasses clause level reconstruction: we assume that GP obliges the human processor to dummify all naturally available parsing mechanisms, for instance lookahead, and to proceed by a process of trial-and-error to reconstruct the previously built structure in order not to fall into the same mistake. The same applies to our case which involves interaction between two separate modules of the grammar.

As an example, consider processing time 3.8 secs with strategies and all mechanisms described above activated, as compared to the same parse when the same are disactivated – 6.5 secs, in relation to the following highly ambiguous example taken from a legal text:

(6) Producer means the manufacturer of a finished product, the producer of any raw material or the manufacturer of a component part and any person who by putting his name, trade mark or other distinguishing feature on the product presents himself as its producer.

Computation time is calculated on a Macintosh G4.

In more detail, suppose we have to use the information that "put" is a verb which requires an oblique PP to be present lexically in the structure, as a result from a check in its lexical form. We take the verb in I position and then open the VP complement structure, which at first builds a NP in coincidence with "the book". However, while still in the NP structure rules, after the head has been taken, a PP is an option freely available as adjunct.

We have implemented two lookahead based mechanisms which are used in the PP building rule and are always triggered, be it from a position where we have a noun as head and we have already built part of the corresponding constituent structure, or from a position where we have a verb as head and we want to decide whether our PP will be adequate as argument rather than as adjunct – in the latter case it will become part of the Adjunct Set.

The first one is called, *Cross Compatibility Check (CCC)*. This mechanism requires the head semantic features or inherent features to be checked against the preposition, which in turn activates a number of possible semantic roles for which it constitutes an adequate semantic marker. For instance, in the example below,

(6.1)   Mary put the book on the table.

the preposition "on" is an adequate semantic marker for "locative" semantic role, this will cause the compatibility check to require the presence, in the governing heading, of inherent or semantic features that allow for location. A predicate like "dress" is computed as an object which can be assigned a spatial location, while a predicate like "want" is computed as a subjective intensional predicate which does not require a spatial location. However, in order to take the right decision, the CCC must be equipped with the second mechanism we implemented.

The second one is called, *Argument Precedence (AP)*. This mechanism allows the parser to satisfy the subcategorization requirements in any NP constituent it finds itself at a given moment in the parsing process. Suppose that after taking "put" as the main verb, this mechanism is activated, by simply copying the requirements on PP oblique locative present in the lexical form associated with the predicate "put" in the lexicon, in the AP. As soon as the NP "the book" is opened, after taking "book" as N at the head position, the parser will meet the word "on", which allows for a PP adjunct. While in the P head position, the parser will fire the CCC mechanism first to see whether the preposition is semantically compatible, and in case it is, the second AP mechanism will be fired. This will cause the system to do the following steps:

i.   check whether the requirements are empty or not;
ii. and in case it is instantiated, control the semantic role associated with it;
iii. verify whether the P head is a possible semantic marker for that semantic role:
     in our case, "on" is a possible semantic marker for "locative" semantic role;

iv. finally cause the parser to fail on P as head of a PP adjunct of the head noun;
v.   produce a closure of NP which obeys Minimal Attachment principle.

3.2 Some examples

In the texts reported below we give empirical evidence for the need to use lexical information in order to reduce parsing loads resulting from backtracking procedures: we mark decision points with a bar.

(7)   Council directive | **of** july 1985 | **on** the approximation | **of** the laws, | regulations and | administrative provisions | **of** the Member States | concerning liability | **for** defective products.

At the first boundary we have "of" which is non semantically marked and no prediction is available, so that the default decision is to apply Late Closure, which turns out to be the correct one. When the second preposition is found we are in the NP of the PP headed by "of", and we have taken the date "1985": this will cause the CCC to prevent the acceptance of the preposition "on" as a semantically compatible marker thus preventing the construction of the NP headed by "approximation".

Notice that in case that would be allowed, the NP would encompass all the following PPs thus building a very heavy NP: "the approximation of the laws, regulations and administrative provisions of the Member States concerning liability for defective products". In case the parser had a structure monitoring strategy all this work would have to be undone and backtracking would have to be performed. Remember that the system does not know where and how to end backtracking unless it tries all possible available combinations along the path. In our case, the presence of a coordinate structure would render the overall process of structure recoverability absolutely untenable.

Another important decision has to be taken at the boundary constituted by the participial head "concerning": in this case the CCC will take the inherent features of the head "States" and check them with the selectional restrictions associated in the lexical form for the verb "concern". Failure in this match will cause the NP "the Member States" to be closed and will allow the adjunct to be attached higher up with the coordinated head "laws, regulations and administrative provisions". In this case, all the inherent features are collected in a set that subsumes them all and can be used to fire CCC.

Notice that the preposition "for" is lexically restricted in our representation of the noun "liability", and the corresponding PP that "for" heads is interpreted as a complement rather than as an adjunct. We include here below the relevant portion of each utterance in which the two mechanisms we proposed can be usefully seen at work. We marked with a slash the place in the input text in which, usually when the current constituent is a NP, a decision must be taken as to whether causing the parser to close (MA) or to accept more text (LC) is actually dependent upon the presence of some local trigger. This trigger is mostly a preposition; however, there are cases in which, see Oepen, Flickinger, Manning, Toutanova (webpage of the project), Karlsson & Karttunen (1995), Briscoe (1995), Agresti (1990), the trigger is a conjunction or a participle introducing a reduced relative clause. Coordinate NPs are a big source of indecision and are very hard to be detected if based solely on syntactic, lexical and semantic information. For instance, (12) can be thus disambiguated, but (15) requires a matching of prepositions. In the case represented by Agresti (1990) we put a boundary just before a comma: in case the following NP "the Member State" is computed as a coordination – which is both semantically, syntactically and lexically possible – the following sentence will be deprived of its lexical SUBJect NP. As a result, the grammar activates a monitoring procedure independently so that backtracking will ensue, the coordinate NP destroyed and the comma computed as part of the embedded parenthetical (which is in turn an hypothetical within a subordinate clause!!). Notice also that a decision must be taken in relation to the absolutes headed by a past participle which can be intended as an active or a passive past participle: in the second case the head noun would have to be computed as an OBJect and not as a SUBJect. The following examples are small fragments from bigger sentences which are used to enforce our point:

(8)   a differing degree of protection of the consumer | **against** damage caused by a defective product | **to** his health or property

(9)   in all member states | **by** adequate special rules, it has been possible to exclude damage of this type | **from** the scope of this directive

(10)   to claim full compensation for the damage | **from** any one of them

(11)   the manufacturer of a finished product, the producer of any raw material or the manufacturer of a component part | **and** any person

(12)   the liability of the producer | **arising** from this directive

(13)   any person who imports into the community a product | **for** sale, hire or any form of distribution | **in** the course of his business

(14)   both by a defect in the product | **and** by the fault of the injured person

(15)   However, if... the commission does not advise the Member State | concerned that it intends submitting such a proposal | to the council | , the Member State

This is where disambiguation processes could be in need of deeper insights, whenever local and higher attachment sites are in competition and are both licensed by lexical information as semantically appropriate. Subcategorization frames can only afford local information depending on the governing head and we may establish preferences for conflicting cases such as the one related to the well-known example,

(16)   John saw the man in the park with the telescope

To tell apart competing hypothesis, knowledge stored in an ontology (Delmonte 2004b) may be needed: lexical information might lead to a preferred reading where SEE has as a viable option the presence of a secondary predication which in this case is represented by the PP "with the telescope". However this might be in conflict with knowledge provided by the context where "the telescope" is part of the "park", or is being carried by the "man". Such ambiguous cases are common in any communicative exchange and may simply cause the speakers to update their semantic model, but they should be avoided to avoid for a smooth understanding in text reading. Here below we formulate our grammatically motivated model for parsing preferences:

3.3 Principles of sound parsing

- Principle One: Do not perform any unnecessary action that may overload the parsing process: follow the Strategy of Minimal Attachment;
- Principle Two: Consume input string in accordance with look-ahead suggestions and analyze incoming material obeying the Strategy Argument Preference;
- Principle Three: Before constructing a new constituent, check the storage of WellFormed Substring Table (WFST). Store constituents as soon as they are parsed on a stack organized as a WFST;
- Principle Four: Interpret each main constituent satisfying closer ties first – predicate-argument relations – and looser ties next – open/closed adjuncts as soon as possible, according to the Strategy of Functional Preference;
- Principle Five: Erase short-memory stack as soon as possible, i.e. whenever clausal constituents receive Full Interpretation.
- Strategy Functional Preference: whenever possible try to satisfy requirements posed by predicate-argument structure of the main governing predicate as embodied in the above Principles; then perform semantic compatibility checks for adjunct acceptability.
- Strategy Minimal Attachment: whenever Functional Preference allows it apply a Minimal Attachment Strategy.

The results derived from the application of Principle Four are strictly linked to the grammatical theory we adopt, but they are also the most natural ones: it appears very reasonable to assume that arguments must be interpreted before adjuncts can be, and that in order to interpret major constituents as arguments of some predicate we need to have completed clause level structure. In turn adjuncts need to be interpreted in relation both to clause level properties like negation, tense, aspect, mood, possible subordinators, and to arguments of the governing predicate in case they are to be interpreted as open adjuncts.

As a straightforward consequence, owing to Principle Five we have that re-analysis of a clause results in a Garden Path(GP) simply because nothing is avail-able to recover a failure that encompasses clause level reconstruction: we take that GP obliges the human processor to dummify all naturally available parsing mechanisms, like for instance look-ahead, and to proceed by a process of trial-and-error to reconstruct the previously built structure in order not to fall into the same mistake.

3.4 Graceful recovery actions

As discussed above, recovery from garden-path requires a trial and error procedure, i.e. the parser at first has to fail in order to simulate the garden-path effect and then the recovery will take place at certain conditions.

Now consider the well-known case of Reduced Relatives which have always been treated as a tough case (but see Stevenson & Merlo 1997). From an empiri-cal point of view we should at first distinguish cases of subject attachment reduced relatives from all other cases, because it is only with subject attachement that a garden-path will actually ensue. This is easily controllable in our parser given the fact that NPs are computed by means of functional calls. In this way the infor-mation as to where the NP is situated in the current sentence analysis is simply a variable that is filled with one of the following labels: subj, obj, obj2, obl, adj, ncomp, where the last label stands for predicative open complements. Again from a purely empirical point of view, we also visited the WSJ corpus in order to detect cases of subject attachment vs all other cases for reduced relatives and we came up with the following figures:

SUBJECT–ATTACHEMENT 530
OTHERS 2982
TOTAL 3512

From the total number we must subtract present participle cases of reduced rela-tives which do not constitute ambiguous words: the total number is lowered down to 340. Subject-attachments thus constitute the 9.68% of all cases, certainly a negli-gible percentage. In addition, 214 of all subject-attachments are passive participles and lend themselves to easy computation being followed by the preposition "by". So there will reasonably be only 116 possible candidates for ambiguous reduced rel-atives. The final percentage comes down 3.3% which is very low in general, and in

Table 6. List of 27 verb-types used in WSJ in subject-attached reduced relatives

accused	afforded	based	boosted
bought	canceled	caught	caused
completed	contacted	derived	designed
filed	honed	involved	led
listed	made	managed	owned
paid	purchased	related	represented
requested	*sold*	unsettled	

Table 7. List of 36 verb-types used in SUSANNE in subject-attached reduced relatives

altered	become	*bent*	*burned*
charged	clouded	compared	*cooled*
cut	deserted	distilled	*dominated*
estimated	fed	figured	filmed
focused	frozen	internalized	intertwined
known	left	made	*opened*
posted	proposed	puckered	put
removed	reported	seen	shown
shut	soiled	studied	torn

particular when computed over the whole 1 million occurences, it comes down to a non classifiable 0.0116%. The same results can be obtained from an investigation of the Susanne Corpus, where we found 38 overall cases of reduced relatives with ambiguous past participles, 0.031% which is comparable to the 0.035% of the WSJ.

If we closely look into matter, then we come up with another fairly sensible and easily intuitive notion for reduced relatives disambiguation: whenever the governing Noun is not an agentive, nor a proto-agent in any sense of the definition (see (Agresti 1990; Filip 1998), no ambiguity may arise simply because non agentive nominal governors may end up with an ambiguous interpretation only when the verb is used as ergative. However, not all transitive verbs can be made ergatives and in particular none of the verbs used in WSJ in subject-attachment for reduced relatives can be ergativized, apart from "sell". We report here above verb-types, i.e. verb wordforms taken only once. As it can be easily seen, none of the verbs are unergative nor unaccusatives.

If we look at the list of 36 verb-types used in the Susanne Corpus, we come up with a slightly different and much richer picture:

The number of ergativizable verbs increases and also the number of verb types which is strangely enough much higher than the one present in WSJ. We also underlined verbs that can be intransitivized, thus contributing some additional ambiguity. In some cases, the past participle is non ambiguous, though, see "frozen, seen, shown and torn". In some other cases, the verb has different meanings with different subcategorization frames: this is case of "left".

In any case, the parser will procede by activating any possible disambiguation procedure, then it will consider the inherent semantic features associated to the prospective subject: in order to be consistent with a semantic classification as proto-agent, one of the following semantic classes will have to be present: "animate, human, institution, (natural) event, social role, collective entity".

In the affirmative case, and after having checked for the subject position/functional assignment, the analysis will proceed at NP internal adjunct modifier position. If this is successful, the adjunct participial clause will be interpreted locally. Then the parser will continue its traversal of the grammar at i_double_bar position, searching for the finite verb.

In case no finite verb is available, there will be an ensuing failure which will recover gracefully by a recovery call for the same main constituent expected by the grammar in that position. The following actions will take place:

- the current input word will be checked and has to be a nonfinite verb;
- the already parsed portion of the input sentence must contain a possibly ambiguous finite verb;
- this token word should correspond to the predicate lemma heading the modifier adjunct clause computed inside the NP which is scanned to search for the appropriate structural portion.

The first two actions are carried out on the lookahead stack, while the third action is carried out on the NP structure already parsed and fully interpreted by the parser.

3.5 General rule relaxation techniques

As noted above, people working in the statistical framework assume that deep parsers would not easily come to terms with the need to relax rules and constraints both because it would be a too cumbersome task to be appropriately instantiated in a grammar and because it would be too labour-intensive to cover all needed structural occurrences as observed in real texts.

There are two conditions, on the contrary, that play in favour of fulfilling such an achievement in rule-based parsers: the first one being the overall organization into a sequence of well-controllable rules; the other being related to relaxing semantic constraints, which are the necessary requirement for lexical information to be treated as both predictive and imperative as far as predicate-argument relations and adjuncts' attachment is concerned. In any rule-based parser, adding one default case as the "anywhere else" solution is fairly straightforward to apply. There are at least two general cases in which such an addition would be welcome:

the first one is constituted by the lack of lexical information to apply selectional restrictions for the assignment of grammatical function and semantic roles to successfully parsed constitutents. The default reasoning would licence verbs with a shallow syntactic classification as the one provided by CELEX corpus or the UPenn lexicon as belonging either to transitive and intransitive to constitute a case of intransitivization – which is the optional omission of the object NP – as opposed to the ergativization where the object would be raised to subject and carry the semantic role of Patient of Affected Theme. However, there are cases in which both Intransitivization and Ergativization are allowed and the only way to take the adequate solution is left to semantic information associated to the parser constituent in the inherent features of its head noun. Semantic class information is in our case coming from CoreLex and WordNet, in our revised version. In case no information is made available from these two lexical sources a default decision must be taken.

A simple default case must then be included for all those cases in which semantic information provided by the lexicon does not apply to the current input. This can be due basically to two cases:

– subcategorization frames do not contain the parsed structural configuration;
– selectional restrictions do not allow the licensing of the parsed constituents' heads.

The first case can be circumvented by building on the fly and asserting into memory a new subcategorization frame for the current verb/noun/adjective, which contains the current structural configuration and the semantic features associated to the heads as selectional restrictions. The same would happen with totally unknown lexical predicates which will be associated on the fly with appropriate subcategorization information. With respect to the second case, semantic features associated to the head/heads of already parser constituents must be inspected in order to allow for the most plausible lexical representation.

From a structural point of view, constituents are usually taken within a given complement structure rule cluster which may be ordered differently from the one expected within the more general case of transitive verbs. In case a failure takes place the input sentence will be passed to a generic rule sequence applicable for any lexically motivated governor. This call duplicates the rule for VP complements and adjuncts and thus allows the parser to take advantage of the already parsed portion of text.

A more structurally motivated case is the computation of parenthetical adjuncts which in many cases constitutes a problem for rule-based parsers owing to the fact that they may occur in positions which have not been previously foreseen and thus will not be expected to occur. In case a failure ensues which encompasses a much bigger portion of the input sentence than the one already parsed – and this may take place at different escape points in the grammar – a search is performed for parentheticals, i.e. a portion of input text delimited by a same punctuation sign. This is erased from the sentence and the new sentence is reparsed tentatively with a newly asserted lookahead stack.

Whenever all previously attempted techniques fail, the parser has access to the rules for the treatment of elliptical sentences which also have a last resort rule. At first we attempt to achieve a bottom-up sentence construction on the basis of the roughly formulated criterion: try to parse any non sentence-level constituent you can, then in case of failure look for a verb or a semantic marker for complement, subordinate or coordinate clause and then start the process again.

In case this fails again, we try a sort of island-based approach by searching the most probable clause level markers as defined above, before starting any parsing. Then we cut a portion of the input sentence and proceed until we can parse as much as possible of the input sentence.

The counterproof to these recovery procedures is constituted by the quite natural case of a word being tagged with the wrong tag or not being tagged at all and being simply assigned the default "noun" tag reserved for all OutOfVocabulary words which do not receive any analysis from the morphological decomposition. Other cases are constituted by patent ungrammatical portions of text or the introduction of uncouth and unforseeable punctuation marks. For all these cases, there will be no recovery from failure and the parser will have to use the output of the shallow parser.

4. Parser evaluation

An evaluation carried out lately on the Susan Corpus related GREVAL testsuite made of 500 sentences has been reported (Delmonte 2004) to have achieved 90% F-measure over all major grammatical relations. We achieved similar results with the partial cascaded parser, limited though to only SUBJect and OBJect relations. The partial parser has also been tested on the Xerox LFG 700 treebank, containing 700 sentences from the WSJ, where it achieved 85% recall again on SUBJ and OBJ grammatical relations.

References

Abney, S. (1996). Part-of-speech tagging and partial parsing. In K. Church, S. Young, & G. Bloothooft (Eds.), *Corpus-Based Methods in Language and Speech* (pp. 118–136). Dordrecht: Kluwer Academic Publishers.

Agresti, A. (1990). *Categorical Data Analysis*. New York: John Wiley & Sons.

Armstrong-Warwick, S. (1993). Preface. *Computational Linguistics, 19* (1), Special Issue on Using Large Corpora: I, iii–iv.

Berwick, R., Abney S. & Tenny, C. (1991*). Principle-Based Parsing.* Dordrecht: Kluwer.

Brants, T. & Samuelsson, C. (1995). Tagging the Teleman Corpus. In *Proceedings 10th Nordic Conference of Computational Linguistics* (pp. 1–12). Helsinki.

Bresnan, J. (1982), *The Mental Representation of Grammatical Relations*, Cambridge Mass.: MIT Press.

Bresnan, J. (2001). *Lexical-Functional Syntax.* Blackwells.

Briscoe, T. (1995). Robust parsing. In G.B. Varile & A. Zampolli (Eds.), *Survey of the State of the Art in Human Language Technology, Language Analysis and Understanding* (pp. 113–114). Cambridge, England; New York: Cambridge University.

Carroll, J. A. (2000). Statistical parsing. In R. Dale, H. Moisl, H. Somers (Eds.), *Handbook of Natural Language Processing* (pp. 525–543). New York: Marcel Dekker.

Church, K. (1988). A stochastic parts program and noun phrase parser for unrestricted texts. *Proceedings of the 2nd Conference on Applied Natural Language Processing* (pp. 136–143). Austin, Texas.

Church, K., Gale, W., Hanks, P. & Hindle, D. (1989). Parsing, word associations and typical predicate-argument relations. *IWTP* (pp. 389–398).

Clifton, C., & Ferreira, F. (1989). Ambiguity in Context. *Language and Cognitive Processes, 4,* 77–103.

Delmonte R. (1987). Grammatica e ambiguità in Italiano. *Annali di Ca' Foscari, XXVI* (1–2), 257–333.

Delmonte R. (1995). Lexical Representations: Syntax-Semantics interface and World Knowledge. In *Notiziario AIIA* (Associazione Italiana di Intelligenza Artificiale) (pp. 11–16). Roma.

Delmonte, R. (2000). SLIM prosodic automatic tools for self-learning instruction. *Speech Communication, 30,* 145–166.

Delmonte R. (2002). GETARUN PARSER – A parser equipped with Quantifier Raising and Anaphoric Binding based on LFG. *Proc. LFG 2002 Conference, Athens* (pp. 130–153). http://cslipublications.stanford.edu/hand/miscpubsonline.html.

Delmonte R. (2004). Evaluating GETARUNS Parser with GREVAL Test Suite, Proc. *ROMAND – 20th International Conference on Computational Linguistics – COLING* (pp. 32–41). University of Geneva.

Delmonte R. (2004a). Strutture sintattiche dall'analisi computazionale di corpora di italiano. In A. Cardinaletti & F. Frasnedi (Eds.), *Intorno all'Italiano Contemporaneo, Franco Angeli* (pp. 187–220). Bologna.

Delrnonte R. (2004b). Text Understanding with GETARUNS for Q/A and Summarization. *Proc. ACL 2004 2nd Workshop on Text Meaning & Interpretation* (pp. 97–104). Barcelona, Columbia University.

DeRose, S.(1988). Grammatical category disambiguation by statistical optimization. *Computational Linguistics, 14* (1), 31–39.

Filip, H. (1998). Reduced relatives: Lexical constraint-based analysis. *Proceedings of the Twenty- Fourth Meeting of the Berkeley Linguistic Society* (pp. 1–15).

Fodor, J. D. (2002). Psycholinguistics cannot escape prosody. In *Proceedings of the Speech Prosody 2002 Conference* (pp. 83–88). Aix-en-Provence.

Frazier, L. (1987a). Sentence processing. In M. Coltheart (Ed.), *Attention and Performance* (pp. 559–586). Hillsdale, N.J.: Lawrence Elbaum.

Frazier, L. (1987b). Theories of sentence processing. In J. Garfield (Ed.), *Modularity in Knowledge Representation and Natural Language Understanding* (pp. 291–308). Cambridge, Mass.: MIT Press.

Garside, R.(1987). The CLAWS word-tagging system. In R. Garside, F. Leech & G. Sampson (Eds.), *The Computational Analysis of English* (pp. 30–41). Longman.

Hindle, D. & Roth, M. (1993). Structural ambiguity and lexical relations. *Computational Linguistics, 19* (1), 103–120.

Karlsson, F., & Karttunen, L. (1995). Shallow parsing. In G.B. Varile & A. Zampolli (Eds.), *Survey of the State of the Art in Human Language Technology, Language analysis and understanding* (pp. 113–114). Cambridge, England; New York: Cambridge University Press.

Klein, D. & Manning, C. D. (2002). Conditional structure versus conditional estimation in NLP models. *2002 Conference on Empirical Methods in Natural Language Processing (EMNLP 2002)* (pp. 9–16).

Martin, K. (1980). Algorithm schemata and data structures in syntactic processing. *CSL-80-12*, Xerox Corporation, Palo Alto Research Center.

Oepen, S., Flickinger, D., Manning, C. Toutanova, K. The LinGO Redwoods – A rich and dynamic treebank for HPSG. Webpage of the project.

Pereira, F. (1981). Extraposition grammars. *American Journal of Computational Linguistics, 7* (4), 243–256.

Pereira, F. (1983). Logic for natural language analysis. *Technical Note, 275.* Artificial Intelligence Center, SRI International.

Pereira, F. (1995). Sentence modeling and parsing, In G.B. Varile & A. Zampolli (Eds.), *Survey of the State of the Art in Human Language Technology, Language Analysis and Understanding* (pp. 113–114). Cambridge, England; New York: Cambridge University Press.

Pereira, F. &. Warren, D. (1980). Definite clause grammar for language analysis – a survey of the formalism and a comparison with ATN. *Artificial Intelligence, 13*, 231–278.

Pritchett, B. L. (1992). *Grammatical Competence and Parsing Performance.* Chicago: The University of Chicago Press.

Schubert, L. K. (1984). On parsing preferences. *Proceedings of COLING* (pp. 247–250), Stanford.

Sproat, R. & van Santen, J. (1998). Automatic ambiguity detection. *ICSLP 98.*

Stevenson, S. & Merlo, P. (1997). Lexical structure and parsing complexity. In M. C. MacDonald (Ed.), *Lexical Representations and Sentence Processing* (pp. 349–399). Psychology Press.

Stock, O. (1989). Head-Driven Bidirectional Parsing. In *Proceedings of the Workshop on Parsing Technologies.* Pittsburgh.

Tapanainen, P. & Voutilainen, A. (1994). Tagging accurately – don't guess if you know. *Proceedings of ANLP '94* (pp. 47–52). Stuttgart, Germany.

Woods, W. A. (1973). An experimental parsing system for transition network grammars. In Rustin, R., editor, *Natural language processing.* Algorithmics Press, New York.

Towards a quantitative theory of variability

Philippe Blache

LPL-CNRS, Université de Provence

We present in this paper a general framework making it possible to describe and explain relations between different components of linguistic analysis (e.g. prosody, syntax, semantics, etc.). We propose more specifically a stability principle specified for a given object by means of weights defined for each component plus an equilibrium threshold to be reached. The basic mechanism consists in summing up the different weights, the result being the quantity to be compared with the threshold. Such an approach explains some variability phenomena: the possibility of choosing between different realizations for an object at a given domain depends on whether the stability threshold is reached my means of the weights of other domains. This kind of information, on top of its linguistic interest, constitutes a first element of answer for an account of variability in some natural language processing applications.

1. Introduction

Relations between different components of linguistic analysis, such as prosody, morphology, syntax, semantics, discourse, etc. remains a problem for a systematic description (see Blache 2003). However, this is a main challenge not only from a theoretical point of view, but also for natural language processing, especially in human/machine communication systems or speech processing (e.g. synthesis). Several phenomena highlighting such relations has been described. This is typically the case for relations existing between prosody and syntax (see Selkirk 1984; Di Cristo 1985; or Bear & Price 1990). However, explanations are often empirical and exceptionally given in the perspective of an actual theory of language. It is for example possible to specify some relations existing between topicalization and syllable duration (cf. Doetjes, Delais-Roussarie, & Sleeman 2002) or between prosodic architecture and discourse organization after focus (cf. Di Cristo & Jankowski 1999). However, the modularity perspective, which relies on the independence of linguistic components, remains the rule in this kind of description and doesn't support a global vision of the problem.

One of the difficulties in the elaboration of a general account of this problem comes from the fact that there are only few cases of superposition between structures of the different components. It is for example difficult to precise some congruence possibilities between syntax and prosody (see Hirst & Di Cristo 1998; Mertens, Goldman, Wehrli, & Gaudinat 2001). In the same way, and these aspects are related, the problem of variability is not taken into account in a systematic way for example in the framework of a theory. Indeed, we observe situations in which prosody can be realized in a very variable way whereas in some other cases, strong constraints have to be considered.

We think that this question of the interaction between the different linguistic components is usually addressed in the wrong (or incomplete) way. It is impossible to explain relations by means of a bijection superposing structures (for example stipulating direct relations between a syntactic tree and a prosodic hierarchy). One of the problems comes from the fact that the linguistic objects are not the same for syntax and prosody: a word can be formed with several syllables, but a syllable can in turn be formed with different words (cf. Hirst & Di Cristo 1998).

More generally, the problem comes from the conception of linguistic information organization. It is difficult (and probably not useful) to try to represent each analysis component (1) in an homogeneous and hierarchized way by means of a total relation and (2) independently from other components. In other words, we think that each component of linguistic analysis is not necessarily fully structured: it is often difficult, or even impossible, to specify a relation between two elements of the same domain. It is for example the case of the utterance (1) in which two parts are not connected with a precise syntactic relation but with an implicit subordination relation.

(1)   *il pleut tu es mouillé* (*it rains you are wet*)

The same observation can be done for other components of linguistic analysis. There are for example some prosodic phenomena that are typical and recurrent in this domain (we use in this paper a simplified prosodic description limited to the notion of contour presented in Rossi (1999)), but it is not necessary to represent them into a hierarchized structure covering the entire input. Generally speaking, each component participates in a partial manner to the elaboration of the informational content of an utterance. We are then far away from the classical modular conception of analysis consisting in describing this process as sequential and relying on a complete and sequential analysis of each domain (organized in level analysis, from phonetics to pragmatic). We think that the interpretation of an utterance is done thanks to pieces of information coming from any component, eventually in a redundant way. There is redundancy when congruence between components exists. But this is not the general case in which part of information can come from prosody, another one from syntax, and another from pragmatic, for example.

We propose in this paper an approach taking advantage of this conception of linguistic analysis and making it possible to describe relations between different components, not at the structure level, but directly between objects belonging to different components involved in the relation. It becomes then possible to describe relations with a variable granularity linking objects that can be at a different level from one component to the other. We can for example describe a relation between an interrogative morpheme and an intonative contour or between a phrase and some prosodic stress.

Such relations constitute a basis for describing and explaining variability. This phenomenon cannot be interpreted by means of descriptions coming from a unique domain. We propose an account of variability bringing together information coming from different components and stipulating an equilibrium relation between these components. The idea consists in indicating that as soon as a certain quantity of information (an information threshold) is reached thanks to some linguistic components, then variability can appear in other components. We will see for example that in the case where syntax contains information enough by itself, then prosody becomes variable.

We propose to start from some examples illustrating some variability phenomena in the prosodic realization. We can then provide first some constraint specifying this variability. We define finally a principle providing a general framework for describing variability.

2. Some examples

We present in this section some examples together with a stylized intonative contour. This kind of representation doesn't allow to represent the set of prosodic phenomena that should be taken into account for a precise study. It allows however a first approximation in the perspective of the question addressed in this paper. We use for this some of the notion proposed in Rossi (1999), in particular the notion of conclusive, parenthetic and continuative contours.

(2) il pleut tu es mouillé
     it rains you are wet

This utterance is formed by two distinct parts, not linked with any explicit syntactic relation. Intonation gives a correlative interpretation indicating *"it rains, because you are wet".*

(3)　il　pleut　tu　es　mouillé
　　　it　rains　you　are　wet

The same utterance, with a different intonation, receives a causative interpretation indicating "*if it rains, then you are wet*".

(4)　Marie　la　robe　elle　lui　va　bien
　　　Marie　the　dress　it to　her　fits　well

Example of a dislocation of two NPs with an anaphoric relation with two clitics. The intonation follows the same rising schema for each dislocated NP.

(5)　Marie　la　robe　elle　lui　va　bien
　　　Marie　the　dress　it to　her　fits　well

The same example can be realized with a different intonative contour. In both cases, the interpretation of a double NP dislocation is favored, without many ambiguity ("*the dress fits Mary well*").

(6)　Marie　la　garce　elle　lui　donne　rien
　　　Marie　the　bitch　she to　her　gives　nothing

The syntactic structure is identical to the one of the previous example. However, the preferred interpretation is that of an apposition more than a multiple dislocation. This interpretation is reinforced by a different intonative contour between the NPs, the second one being parenthetic.

(7)　*Marie　la　garce　elle　lui　donne　rien
　　　Marie　the　bitch　she to　her　gives　nothing

The same example seems difficult to realize with an intonative contour typical to a double dislocation.

(8)　Marie　elle　devrait　faire　attention
　　　Marie　she　should　pay　attention

The syntactic structure corresponds to a simple dislocation. The rising contour of the NP constitutes a strong prosodic mark.

(9) Marie elle devrait faire attention
Marie she should pay attention

The form of this example is the same as in the previous example. However, the interpretation is rather a vocative one, more than a dislocated. This interpretation is then driven by the intonation, not by the syntactic structure.

(10) c'est la personne qui m'intéresse
it is the person that me interests

The syntactic structure is that of a cleft. In this realization, the intonation of the cleft NP is marked with a fall. The interpretation is something like*"it is the person that interests me (not the clothes)"*.

(11) c'est la personne qui m'intéresse
it is the person that me interests

In this example, the interpretation is that of a relative more than a cleft (of the kind *"this is her, effectively "*). It is driven by the intonation that presents a continuative contour rather than a conclusive one.

(12) *c'est un truc qu'on préfère
it is a trick that we prefer

The interpretation of this example is that of a relative. Such interpretation is natural, without taking into account prosody (it is difficult to associate a cleft interpretation to this element which has a poor semantic content). A typical cleft intonation (with a conclusive contour) cannot be easily realized in this case.

(13) les vieux c'est la nuit qu'on est malades
the old it is the night that we are sick

In this example, the cleft interpretation is given by the syntactic structure (with a dislocated). This effect is reinforced by a conclusive intonative contour on the cleft NP.

(14) *la techno c'est la musique qu'on préfère
the techno this is the music that we prefer

Contrarily to the previous example, the preferred interpretation is that of a relative. Such interpretation is given by the semantic level, the general form being identical with that of the previous example. The intonation reinforces this interpretation.

(15)   la techno   c'est   la musique   qu'on préfère
       the techno   this is   the music   that we prefer

A conclusive intonation, rather typical of a cleft, cannot be easily realized in this example.

3.   Basic constraints

The classical description of prosody/syntax relation is generally done by means of constraints representing either the necessity of a specific realization or its impossibility. In the perspective of a constraint-based approach, this kind of information is represented directly by means of properties of the objects. This is the case for example of Property Grammars, described in Blache (2001), that rely on different kinds of constraints (e.g. requirement, exclusion, linear precedence, etc.).

At this stage, it is possible to stipulate a first set of constraints that will constitute a preliminary step in the description of the relations.

3.1   Describing an object with several components

A same linguistic object is described by means of information coming from different components. This characteristics is illustrated by several examples of the previous section. Let's focus more precisely on examples (7)–(8). This case is apparently simple and regular. Indeed, if the data are verified, each interpretation (being vocative or not) is associated to a specific intonative contour without possibility of variation. We obtain then the several constraints that make it possible to precise some principles.

> [p1] *SN[detached]* ∧ *Contour[conclusive]* ⇒ *[−vocative]*
> [p2] *SN[detached]* ∧ *Contour[continuative]* ⇒ *[+vocative]*

Constraint [p1] stipulates that a dislocated phrase, when coming with a marked intonation (typically a conclusive contour), takes a vocative interpretation. We are then in the case of a classical dislocation coming together with an anaphoric relation between the dislocated NP and the clitic. The vocative interpretation described in [p2] implies a detached NP plus an intonational fall. In these constraints, the objects belong to three different components: syntax, semantics and prosody. It is necessary to precise these domains. Moreover, it is also necessary to precise their respective positions. The solution making it possible to build a representation independently from any theoretical presupposition consists in indicating the position of the object in the acoustic signal (cf. Bird & Liberman 1999). This kind of indication is direct for prosodic information, but difficult to specify for other domains such as syntax, semantics or pragmatics. We propose (see Blache 2003) a general indexation mechanism specifying a different kind of localization for any objects. We propose then to use an anchor containing a different kind of indexation: localization in the signal, in the string or in the context. A complex feature represents such anchor as follows:

$$anchor \rightarrow \begin{bmatrix} \text{TEMPORAL}\langle i, j \rangle \\ \text{POSITION}\langle k, l \rangle \\ \text{CONTEXT } c \end{bmatrix}$$

The temporal index is represented by two values (beginning and end). The position is also a couple of indexes (corresponding to nodes in a chart interpretation) localizing an object in the input. The CONTEXT feature implements the notion of *universe* (i.e. a set of discourse referents) as in DRT. An object can then be specified by means of three kinds of information: its *domain*, its *anchor* and its *characterization* (the set of corresponding properties). The following example describes an object from the syntactic domain, with a precise localization both on the temporal and the linear axis:

$$obj \rightarrow \begin{bmatrix} \text{DOMAIN } synt \\ \text{ANCHOR} \begin{bmatrix} \text{TEMP}\langle 880, 1000 \rangle \\ \text{POSITION}\langle 2, 3 \rangle \end{bmatrix} \\ \text{CHARAC} \begin{bmatrix} \text{CAT } Det \end{bmatrix} \end{bmatrix}$$

As detailed above, constraints [p1] and [p2] are expressed in terms of implication. However, the kind of relation represented there consists more precisely in a co-variation of the different values. It is moreover necessary, in particular for the representation of information at a finer level than that of the atomic object, to express an element under the form of a set of features, each one being an attribute/value pair. This is the case for example of a phoneme that can be characterized by a set of segments or a syntactic category that corresponds to a set of morphological, syntactic and semantic features. The relation [p2] concerns in fact different features of a same object characterizing a subpart of the utterance. This object is represented as follows:

$$
p2 \rightarrow \left[
\begin{array}{l}
\text{SYNT} \left[
\begin{array}{l}
\text{CAT} \left[\text{NP}_{detached}\right] \\
\text{POS}\langle i, j\rangle
\end{array}
\right] \\[1em]
\text{SEM} \left[
\begin{array}{l}
\text{TYPE } +vocative \\
\text{POS}\langle i, j\rangle
\end{array}
\right] \\[1em]
\text{PROS} \left[
\begin{array}{l}
\text{CONTOUR } continuative \\
\text{POS}\langle i, j\rangle
\end{array}
\right]
\end{array}
\right]
$$

Such a feature structure makes it possible to represent at the same time information coming from different components and participating to the description of a same object or, more generally, a same linguistic phenomenon. Each characteristic is associated with position in the signal represented by the complex feature ANCHOR. The different information is still represented separately, the feature structure being a way for describing an object containing features connected with some relations.

The covariation relation specified above is expressed by the specification of a simultaneous variation of the value of some features in a structure. There are several ways to represent this kind of relation, one of them being the use of "named disjunctions" (cf. Kasper 1994; or Blache 1998). The mechanism consists in enumerating the set of possible values for each feature and indicating the values that are in a mutual dependency. All values belonging to the same part of the disjunction covary: when a value is instantiated, then all other values of the same rank in the named disjunction are also instantiated.

$$
detached/dislocated \rightarrow \left[
\begin{array}{l}
\text{SYNT} \left[
\begin{array}{l}
\text{CAT} \left\{\left[\text{NP}_{detached}\right] \vee_1 \left[\text{NP}_{dislocated}\right]\right\} \\
\text{ANCH}\langle i, j\rangle
\end{array}
\right] \\[1em]
\text{SEM} \left[
\begin{array}{l}
\text{TYPE} \left\{+\text{VOCATIVE } \vee_1 -\text{VOCATIVE}\right\} \\
\text{ANCH}\langle i, j\rangle
\end{array}
\right] \\[1em]
\text{PROS} \left[
\begin{array}{l}
\text{CONTOUR} \left\{\text{CONTINUATIVE } \vee_1 \text{ CONCLUSIVE}\right\} \\
\text{ANCH}\langle i, j\rangle
\end{array}
\right]
\end{array}
\right]
$$

In this example, the named disjunction is represented by $\vee_1$. The values $NP_{detached}$, $+vocative$ and $continuative$ are then dependent (first part of the disjunction), as well as the values $NP_{dislocated}$, $-vocative$ and $conclusive$. The previous structure works then as a constraint on the concerned objects. As soon as an utterance description needs a set of features specified in this structure, their values have to satisfy the constraint.

3.2 Information on different parts of a same object

A quick study of examples (9)–(14), describing cases of clefts and relatives, exhibits a first property constraining the relative. This one is incompatible with a conclusive contour as in the case of a cleft. This restriction is represented by the following constraint stipulating that a set of categories constituting a NP with a relative cannot be realized with an intonative stress on the name, which corresponds to a parenthetic contour.

$$
relative \rightarrow
\begin{bmatrix}
\text{SYNT} \begin{bmatrix}
\left\langle \begin{bmatrix} \text{CAT Det} \\ \text{ANCH}\langle i, j\rangle \end{bmatrix}, \begin{bmatrix} \text{CAT N} \\ \text{ANCH}\langle k, l\rangle \end{bmatrix}, \begin{bmatrix} \text{CAT Rel} \\ \text{ANCH}\langle m, n\rangle \end{bmatrix} \right\rangle \\
\text{ANCH}\langle i, n\rangle
\end{bmatrix} \\
\text{SEM} \begin{bmatrix} \text{TYPE } \textit{-focus} \\ \text{ANCH}\langle i, l\rangle \end{bmatrix} \\
\text{PROS} \begin{bmatrix} \text{CONTOUR } \textit{parenthetic} \\ \text{POS}\langle i, l\rangle \end{bmatrix}
\end{bmatrix}
$$

In this example, we can remark on top of the constraint on the relative, the possibility for a same object to represent information on different parts. Syntactic information concerns then the entire structure whereas semantic and prosodic information only concerns a subset. The feature ANCH implements this aspect.

4. Variability

The kind of constraints presented above can represent many different relations between components of linguistic analysis. However, it is impossible to provide general descriptions that cannot be captured by covariation. In particular, it is difficult, or even impossible, using such an approach to explain why prosodic realization seems less constrained under certain circumstances. In the case of the distinction between clefts and relatives, a constraint can characterize the general realization of the relative, but nothing can be said as for the cleft: we can remark a great variability for this construction. Different corpus studies show that it seems possible to realize clefts without any specific prosodic mark or with many different marks. The same phenomenon appears when a semantic feature reinforces a syntactic turn. This is the case of the examples (3)–(6) that present some cases of simple or multiple dislocations. In the case of multiple dislocation (example (3)), two clitics are in an anaphoric relation with the detached NP. In this case, we have a morpho-syntactic criterion (two clitics agreeing with the NPs) plus a semantic index (the anaphoric relation). We can then consider that, whatever the prosody, the interpretation is constrained enough by information coming from syntax and semantics. On the contrary, when the anaphoric relation doesn't exist, as in the examples (5) and (6), prosody is strongly constrained and plays an important role in the interpretation. For example, the second realization that would consider the two NPs at the same level (favoring a double dislocation interpretation) is impossible.

Generally speaking, we can consider that, when an utterance cannot be disambiguated with a morpho-syntactic mark, then the prosody would play this role. In the examples (1)–(2), intonation in itself makes it possible to distinguish between causative and correlative interpretations. More clearly, in the case of the examples (9)–(11), intonation drives the interpretation as relative or cleft. A salient turn cannot be assigned to a relative, a cleft interpretation is then favored in this case. Cleft variability would then come from the fact that this turn is strongly marked from a morpho-syntactic point of view (more than the relative). In the same way as for double dislocation, morpho-syntactic and semantic constraints are strong enough and the interpretation doesn't need more information, for example a prosodic one. This characteristic is also clear in the examples (12)–(14). One can observe in the same way a syntactic variability allowed by prosody. For example, a rising intonative contour is classically associated with interrogative turns. We consider in this case that the intonative schema is not very ambiguous, it can be associated with an heavy *weight* for prosody (in the same way as clefts have an heavy weight for syntax). Such a characteristic allows variability of the syntactic form. In a general way, and for any component of linguistic analysis, the weight value is proportional to the ambiguity degree of the form. For example, a conclusive contour, specific to certain constructions, or a major break are associated to heavy weights for prosody. In the same way, marked syntactic constructions with strong morpho-syntactic elements (such as clefts) correspond to heavy syntactic weights.

There exists then a relation between syntax, semantics and prosody that cannot be represented classically in terms of correspondences between the respective structures. More precisely, the only constraints that can be proposed in this perspective are those of cooccurency restrictions, but without providing an account of variability.

5.   Equilibrium principle

We propose here a general framework explaining relations between the different linguistic components and their variability. It is important to remind first some points. We think that it is not necessary to try to describe directly relations between components. Only some constructions or some phenomenon can be explained in this way. In the case in which no explicit relation exists between the domains, the realization of each component can be done independently from the others. Moreover, such a relation can concern the entire component or one of its subpart.

We consider that each phenomenon bears a specific weight encoding in some way its importance in the component. We have seen in the previous section some examples of heavy weights: cleft for syntax, conclusive contours for prosody, anaphoric relations for semantics, etc. But such information taken separately for each component doesn't explain in itself variability or insistence phenomena.

The hypothesis relies on a principle stipulating that an equilibrium between the different components has to be reached. In other words, a certain amount of information has to be given before allowing variability. This information can come from the different domains or components. Concretely, the sum of the weights of each component has to reach a certain threshold. In this perspective, variability becomes possible within a component if the sum of the weights is greater than this threshold. For example, if for some construction, the threshold is reached only by means of a the weights coming from syntax and semantics, then the weight of the prosody is not constrained and can take any value. Concretely, this means that intonation is not anymore constrained and can be realized in a variable way (following however the intrinsic constraints related to the utterance). On the contrary, when the syntactic and the semantic weights are not heavy enough, then the weight of the prosody becomes necessary to reach the threshold and the intonation is less variable. Obviously, as it is shown in the previous section, the threshold can be reached by means of the sum of the weights of any components (including a single one). We can reach for example the threshold by means of prosodic and semantic weights, the syntax becoming variable.

The insistence effects are explained in the same manner: the threshold only needs to be reached in order to observe eventually such phenomenon. For example, if the syntactic and semantic weights are heavy enough to reach the threshold, then the realization of a marked intonation (associated to an heavy prosodic weight) is not necessary. If it occurs, it is interpreted then as an insistence effect whereas the same contour in the configuration of a light syntactic weight (not sufficient to reach the threshold with the semantic one) would not receive the same interpretation.

The equilibrium principle explaining this weight repartition can be described by the following constraint indicating that the weight of a structure is the sum of the syntactic, semantic and prosodic weights and that this value has to reach a given threshold t:

$$\textit{Equilibrium Principle} \rightarrow \begin{bmatrix} \text{SYNT} \begin{bmatrix} \text{WEIGHT } a \end{bmatrix} \\ \text{SEM} \begin{bmatrix} \text{WEIGHT } b \end{bmatrix} \\ \text{PROS} \begin{bmatrix} \text{WEIGHT } c \end{bmatrix} \\ \text{THRESHOLD } (a+b+c) \geq t \end{bmatrix}$$

In the examples presented in the first section, we have seen that some constructions such as relatives don't have much possibility of variability. This is explained by the fact that each component contributes necessarily to the equilibrium of the structure. This is described by a constraint on the respective weights of the components describing the relative:

$$\textit{Relative} \rightarrow \begin{bmatrix} \text{SYNT} \begin{bmatrix} \text{WEIGHT } 1 \end{bmatrix} \\ \text{SEM} \begin{bmatrix} \text{WEIGHT } 1 \end{bmatrix} \\ \text{PROS} \begin{bmatrix} \text{WEIGHT } 1 \end{bmatrix} \\ \text{THRESHOLD } 3 \end{bmatrix}$$

In this constraint, the threshold is set (arbitrarily) to 3. It is reached minimally by the sum of the weights of each component. None of them can then vary. They are all considered as light. On the contrary, the situation is different in the case in which a component has a heavy weight, such as clefts which have a heavy syntactic weight. The weight values of each component are described in this case in terms of local constraints specifying the variability. The syntax bears a weight set to 2. The semantic has a weight at least equal to 1. If the threshold is set to 3, then the prosodic weight can have any value, including 0, for a realization prosodically unmarked.

$$\textit{Cleft} \rightarrow \begin{bmatrix} \text{SYNT} \begin{bmatrix} \text{WEIGHT } 2 \end{bmatrix} \\ \text{SEM} \begin{bmatrix} \text{WEIGHT } b>0 \end{bmatrix} \\ \text{PROS} \begin{bmatrix} \text{WEIGHT } c \end{bmatrix} \\ \text{THRESHOLD } 3 \end{bmatrix}$$

Such a constraint describes then a certain variability for semantic and a free variability for prosody.

6. Conclusion

The description of the relations between the different linguistic components relies on two propositions presented in this paper: the possibility of representing several kinds of information on a same object and the specification of an equilibrium principle between these components. Such a principle relies on the possibility of assigning a weight to each component plus an equilibrium threshold to be reached for any specific construction.

Several aspects of this proposition still remain to be precised. First, the notion of weight relies essentially on the ambiguity level of the concerned domain. However, several other parameters could be used such as structure frequency, its morphological specificity, etc. In another way, the different objects or constructions also have to be specified. In the same way as the notion of weight is new in linguistics, the use of a description unit common to several linguistic domains comes to propose the idea of a more general object, composed with several linguistic components. Such an object also constitutes a new description tool that remains to be defined, but already provides some elements of analysis for phenomena such as variability. Concretely, the principle proposed here provides a precise framework making it possible to implement variability in some applications such as natural language generation or speech synthesis.

References

Bear, J. & Price P. (1990). Prosody, syntax and parsing. In *Proceedings of the ACL-90*.

Bird, S. & Liberman, M. (1999). A formal framework for linguistic annotation. Technical Report MS-CIS-99-01. Dept of Computer and Information Science, University of Pennsylvania.

Blache, P. (1998). Parsing ambiguous structures using controlled disjunctions and unary quasi-trees. In *Proceedings of COLING-ACL'98*.

Blache, P. (2001). *Les Grammaires de Propriétés : Des contraintes pour le traitement automatique des langues naturelles*. Hermhs.

Blache, P. (2003). Representing interaction between linguistic. Submitted.

Di Cristo, A. (1985). *De la microprosodie à l'intonosyntaxe*. Publications Université de Provence.

Di Cristo, A. & Jankowski, L. (1999). Prosodic organisation and phrasing after focus in French. In *Proceedings of ICPhS-99*.

Doetjes, J., Delais-Roussarie, E., & Sleeman, P. (2002). The prosody of left detached constituent in French. In *Proceedings of Speech Prosody 2002*.

Hirst, D. & Di Cristo, A. (1998). *Intonation Systems*. Cambridge Universtity Press.

Kasper, R. (1994). Adjuncts in the Mittelfeld. In J. Nerbonne, K. Netter & C. Pollard (Eds.), *German in Head-Driven Phrase Structure Grammar*, Stanford: CSLI Lecture Notes Series 46 (pp. 36–69). University of Chicago Press.

Mertens, P., Goldman, J.-P., Wehrli, E. & Gaudinat, A. (2001). La synthèse de l'intonation à partir de structures syntaxiques riches. *Revue TAL, 42* (1).

Pollard, C. & Sag, I. (1994). *Head-driven Phrase Structure Grammars*. CSLI, Chicago University Press.

Rossi, M. (1999). *L'intonation, le système du français: description et modélisation*. Ophrys.

Sag, I. & Wasow, T. (1999). *Syntactic Theory. A Formal Introduction*. CSLI.

Selkirk, E. (1984). *Phonology and Syntax: The Relation between Sound and Structure*. MIT Press.

Index

In the series *Linguistik Aktuell/Linguistics Today* the following titles have been published thus far or are scheduled for publication:

A complete list of titles in this series can be found on the publishers website, **www.benjamins.com**